THE
LOST
LOGO

Stephen Brown and Dan Brown are similar in several significant respects: middle-aged, failed musicians, educators by profession, afflicted by alliterative affectations. They even share the same DNA (debatable narrative ability). One is famous for *The Da Vinci Code, Angels and Demons* and *The Lost Symbol*, the other has written *The Marketing Code, Agents and Dealers* and *The Lost Logo*. A coincidence? A conspiracy? A counterpart? Who can tell.

THE
LOST
LOGO

Stephen Brown

John,

It's sluggish to start, but
if you can stick with it, the
story picks up rapidly after
chapter 12, or so.

Kind regards

mc Marshall Cavendish
Business

First published in 2009 by

Marshall Cavendish Limited
Fifth Floor
32–38 Saffron Hill
London EC1N 8FH
United Kingdom
T: +44 (0)20 7421 8120
F: +44 (0)20 7421 8121
sales@marshallcavendish.co.uk
www.marshallcavendish.co.uk

Marshall Cavendish is a trademark of Times Publishing Limited

Other Marshall Cavendish offices:
Marshall Cavendish International (Asia) Private Limited, 1 New Industrial Road,
Singapore 536196 • Marshall Cavendish Corporation. 99 White Plains Road,
Tarrytown NY 10591–9001, USA • Marshall Cavendish International (Thailand) Co
Ltd. 253 Asoke, 12th Floor, Sukhumvit 21 Road, Klongtoey Nua, Wattana, Bangkok
10110, Thailand • Marshall Cavendish (Malaysia) Sdn Bhd, Times Subang, Lot 46,
Subang Hi-Tech Industrial Park, Batu Tiga, 40000 Shah Alam, Selangor Darul Ehsan,
Malaysia

A CIP record for this book is available from the British Library

ISBN 978-0-462-09917-0

Printed and bound in the UK by
CPI William Clowes Beccles NR34 7TL

Timeline

The events described in *The Lost Logo* take place between Chapters Fifty and Fifty-One of *The Marketing Code*.

Fact

It is six long years since the publication of Dan Brown's blockbusting bestseller, *The Da Vinci Code*, which catapulted the author from comparative obscurity to mind-boggling levels of popularity and notoriety. In that time, many commentators have speculated on Brown's failure to publish a follow-up novel and the reasons for the delay. Some allege that the author is blocked, unable to deliver the goods now that customer expectations are enormous. Others contend that the religious controversy triggered by *Da Vinci* has taken its psychic toll, as have the (unfounded) accusations of plagiarism. Yet others have seized upon the market established by Brown and written copycat conspiracy thrillers of their own. More than one hundred *Da Vinci Code* imitations have been published since March 2003, many with identikit covers. Numerous debunking books have also appeared, each detailing where Brown went badly wrong. There are even authoritative guidebooks to the author's alleged work in progress, *The Solomon Key*.

This novel describes what *really* happened. It exposes the heinous conspiracy behind the hold-up, albeit with tongue firmly in cheek. A sequel to *The Marketing Code* and *Agents and Dealers, The Lost Logo* is a parody of a thriller that doesn't exist (or didn't at the time of writing). Although several of its characters are "real people", it must be stressed that these creations are entirely fictitious. They bear no resemblance whatsoever to "actual" individuals who share the same name. They are parodies, rather, of the public personae of the people concerned. The same is true of all the places, products, brands and marketing strategies recounted within.

Apart from that, it's gospel.

Prologue

A Season in Hell

Zut alors.

Francine Lafarge cursed beneath her breath as she reversed Fifi, a bright red Renault Espace, into the narrow parking bay. It had been a long day, much more stressful than she'd anticipated. One of her group had wandered off in the early afternoon, then turned up chewing a *canelé*. The rest of the group was raging. Not because they were inconvenienced, though that was a contributory factor. But because the pastry looked delicious and they hadn't got one themselves! It smelled delicious too, lingering for a long time in the people carrier, compounding the agony for everyone else. She could have stopped at a *pâtisserie* to let the group assuage their gastric urges. However, that would have made a mess of Fifi, her *cherie voiture*. Tourists were such uncouth eaters. Americans especially. Much as she relied on their generosity, there were limits to her hospitality.

"Okay everyone," Francine said over her right shoulder, while applying the handbrake with a Francophone flourish. Fifi shrugged in concert. "This is our last stop. The highlight of the tour. We'll walk *La Grande Galerie* where Jacques Saunière was brutally murdered. We'll spend some time in the *Salle des Etats*, where Sophie Neveu and Robert Langdon discovered the first cryptic message, So Dark the Con of Man. And after all that, we'll see *La Pyramide Inversée*, where the climax of Brown's book unfolds. Is it the final resting place of Mary Magdalene, wife of Jesus Christ, mother of his son and begetter of the Merovingian line that is protected by the shadowy Priory of Sion and, indeed, carries His genes to this very day?"

"Arrgh, you've just spoiled the ending," a voice interrupted from the back of the van. Everyone laughed. The pastry incident was forgotten in the mounting excitement of the moment. Thank heaven for small mercies ... and little girls. *Mais oui*?

As she steered her flock through the underground garage and into the elevators – where she made her usual joke about Robert Langdon's claustrophobia – Francine Lafarge counted her Dan Brown blessings. A mousey, middle-aged, mild-mannered Monoprix-wearer, she'd been running Da Vinci Code Tours for more than four years, and the fans kept coming. Numbers waxed and waned with the seasons and the weather and of course movie releases and DVDs and internet rumours of a new novel by the famously reclusive author. But even in the depths of winter, when the book had long since disappeared from the bestseller lists, there were hardy Americans keen to see the settings, stroll the streets, follow the action, spot the art or debate the finer points of Brown's blockbuster with fellow fanatics and thriller seekers.

The long trudge through the connecting passageways commenced. Uninviting though the dimly lit corridors were, they always seemed to heighten the anticipation of her tour parties. Francine took the opportunity to trot out a potted history of the Louvre – its twelfth-century start, its role as a royal residence, its conversion to a museum in 1793, the construction of I. M. Pei's controversial glass pyramid in 1989 – then segued into a bunch of believe-it-or-not factlets. "Shaped like an enormous horseshoe, the Louvre is the largest building in Europe. It stretches further than three Eiffel towers laid end to end. Walking the perimeter is a 4.8 kilometre journey. There are 65,300 pieces of art on display in the building and it is estimated that five full days are needed to see it all. We have one hour!"

Surprisingly few of Francine's groups recognized the source of her data. They were taken directly from *The Da Vinci Code* and, like most of the book's supposedly "true" facts, they were incorrect. There were only 24,000 art works on display in the museum but, even if you only allowed one minute's viewing per piece, it would still take eight weeks to "appreciate" them all. Four years ago, when she first started the tours, she'd taken great pleasure in pointing out the gaping plot-holes in Brown's novel. But Dan's fans, she'd found, didn't like having their illusions shattered by pernickety Parisians, much less pedantic art historians.

So she told them what they wanted to hear. Her tips-take soared accordingly.

"And this," Francine said dramatically, as they emerged into Napoleon Hall, an enormous atrium filled with bright refracted sunlight, "is the Pyramid." The great glass edifice soared above them. Like it or loathe it, Pei's pyramid certainly impressed the paying public, especially those who emerged, blinking, from the bowels of underground parking garage.

Francine was about to go into her potted patter on the Pyramid's 666 panes of glass – the number of the Antichrist, insisted upon by President Mitterrand – when a pushy passerby started speaking. "Built fifty-seven feet beneath ground level," he announced to the assembled group, "the Louvre's newly constructed 70,000-square-foot lobby spread out like an endless grotto. Constructed in warm ochre marble to be compatible with the honey-coloured stone of the Louvre façade above, the subterranean hall was usually vibrant with sunlight and tourists. Tonight, however, the lobby was barren and dark, giving the entire space a cold and crypt-like atmosphere."

The speaker paused for dramatic effect. "That's from page twenty-two of the airport edition!" They all laughed. "Have a nice one, guys," he added, before disappearing off down a corridor in the general direction of *La Pyramide Inversée*. The tour party applauded. "Way to go, bro," the porcine pastry purchaser shouted after their bespectacled, backpack-wearing informant. He raised his baseball cap and waved over his shoulder, without turning round.

Ordinarily, Francine Lafarge would have welcomed the erudite contribution. It was a pleasant surprise that bonded the group. And a bonded group meant bigger tips. But there was something vaguely disturbing about the softly spoken American stranger. She'd seen him before, somewhere. A previous tour party? On the Champs-Elysées? At Saint Sulpice, where she usually sat outside having a cigarette and watching the world go by while the party pottered and poked and, occasionally, prayed within?

Francine couldn't remember. She wasn't as young as she used to be. It would come to her.

Unsettled now, the interruption disturbed Francine's flow,

her time-grooved spiel. She ploughed on regardless. Group tickets bought and distributed, she led the way to the Denon wing. As per the "Louvre Lite" tour in Brown's book, she paused to point out *Winged Victory*, steered the group around *Venus de Milo* – wryly adding that authentic replicas of her nail varnish, hand cream, fingerless gloves and charity wristbands were on sale in the museum shop – and finally emerged into the resplendent *Grande Galerie*. With its famous parquet floor, unbroken line of Renaissance masterpieces and non-existent security gates that dropped down to trap intruders (wrong again, Dan!), it was far and away the highlight of the day, the moment when the *Mona Lisa* made her imperious entrance. The *Salle des Etats* was the holy of holies, the sanctum sanctorum, the room with a view – a very distant view – of Leonardo's greatest hit.

It was only during her recitation on the history of *La Joconde* – tour groups, she'd found, much preferred to hear about the 1911 theft than debunking Dan Brown's daft symbology – that a curious thought hit Francine. Maybe it was the author himself who'd delivered the word-perfect peroration. Surely not. She'd have heard if Dan were back in town. Wouldn't she? The other tour guides would've talked. Wouldn't they? Maybe not, it's a dog-eat-dog business, where juicy titbits of information were hoarded rather than shared.

Dismissing such unproductive thoughts, Francine reassembled her group. She reminded them that they were free to roam around the galleries when the tour ended and herded them towards the bank of elevators at the mid-point of *La Grande Galerie*. Talking excitedly, the tight-packed party descended to the lower levels, where they went one way to see *La Pyramide Inversée* and she went the other to the underground car park. Some would wander back up to the peerless galleries, others would make do with the subterranean shopping precinct, where every other store stocked *Da Vinci Code* souvenirs. It was hard to believe that the Louvre's bureaucrats once dismissed Dan's book as a cretinous cultural travesty or that the crusty clergymen at Saint Sulpice initially refused entry to *Da Vinci Code* enthusiasts. Money talks the world over, but in the City of Light the tourist euro shouts loudest of all.

Time to say Francine's fond farewell. She usually concluded with a dash of Dan's doggerel, a word-for-word recap of the final lines of Brown's book, the ones that pointed to *La Pyramide Inversée*. But Brown had been recited once already that afternoon. *L'étranger* had stolen her thunder. So she settled for "*merci, merci, merci*," shaking hands with each individual in turn. Naturally, she started with the ones most likely to give a gratuity – they were easy to spot, since they'd fiddled in their pockets and purses on the way down – because once one started, the rest inevitably followed suit, regardless of their reluctance. No one likes to appear cheap, not on holiday anyway. Actually, much as she disliked Americans in the round (and many of them were very round indeed), this particular cheese-eating surrender monkey recognized that Freedom Fries-lovers were very big tippers. "Enjoy the rest of your stay in Paris. *Au revoir.*"

"*Au revoir,*" they called out, as each went their separate ways.

"Another day, another Danfan," Francine sighed. She'd done well, despite the unsettling interruption and the pastry incident earlier. Fantasizing about the hot bath to come and maybe a revivifying glass or two of Pouilly-Fumé, she walked quickly along the long corridor that led to the car parks. Passing Starbucks, she glanced haughtily at the god-forsaken American pissoir. Call that coffee? *Merde*, maybe.

Then she saw him. There he was. That's where she'd seen him before! At the table by the window. Watching, watching, watching. Always watching. Every day this week. Francine accidently caught his eye, then looked away quickly. She hurried to the elevator, descended three levels and looked around for Fifi. Where was she? Which bay? Wrong level? She wandered, lost, around the crypt-like car corral. "Ah, there you are, you cheeky scamp."

With a smile of relief, Francine squeezed her key fob. Fifi's sidelights flashed flirtatiously. The locks released with a resounding thunk.

"*Pardonnez-moi*, Madame Lafarge." The voice was American. Masculine. Menacing.

Panic-stricken, Francine whirled round wildly, eyes agape, mouth open.

Her interlocutor laughed. "Sorry to frighten you, Francine.

I forgot my scarf." It was Mr Pastry. Panic over. Phew. Punters were always leaving something behind in the van. Gloves, hats, perfume, passports. You name it, they forgot it. She opened the sliding side door and let him sidle in. The Burberry scarf lay curled in the back seat, like a plaid python. Obviously embarrassed by the scare he'd given her, Mr Pastry started chatting about his holiday plans. Eiffel Tower ascent. Day trip to Versailles. Notre Dame. Sacré Coeur. Blah, blah, blah. Out of politeness, Francine walked him back to the bank of elevators then said her final fond farewell. Yes, she'd definitely drop in when passing through Peoria, Illinois. *Mon dieu*!

Fifi burst into life, eager to escape the lowest Louvre level. Francine slipped her pride and joy into first, prepared to release the handbrake and automatically eyed the rear-view, even though there was only a blank wall behind.

There was a face as well. His face. She tried to scream, but a hand covered her mouth. She stood on the accelerator but the handbrake held firm. She made a grab for her assailant, but he snapped her head back sharply. She so wanted to live but that wasn't going to happen. She felt the knife slit her throat and saw bright-red arterial blood spurting everywhere. All over Fifi, her precious! This isn't happening. This can't be happening. This isn't a trashy Dan Brown thriller, where a minor character gets brutally murdered in the very first chapter. Or, even worse, the prologue…

Chapter One

Everything's Coming My Way

"Oh what a beautiful morning," Abby Maguire bellowed, while towelling off after a bracing cold shower. "Oh what a beautiful day," her rich contralto boomed, compensating in volume what it lacked in control. "I've got a wonderful feeling," the raven-haired twenty-five-year-old with a pretty face and a figure to match, continued sonorously...

Everything didn't quite come Abby's way, however. Because the music-loathing biddy in the apartment above started banging on her floor with a broom handle. As neighbourliness is next but one to godliness, Abby made the ultimate ablutionary sacrifice by stopping mid-show tune. "Good morning, Letitia," she shouted at the ornate ceiling, only to receive a staccato response in pidgin Morse Code. Abby chuckled to herself, knowing full well that it was the *other* old biddy who was doing the banging and who *hated* being mistaken for Letitia. "Sorry," Abby shouted. "Good morning to you too, Bernice." A grumpy thump descended by way of reply.

Despite her neighbours' inability to appreciate good music, Abby wouldn't swap Letitia Trelawney and Bernice Brannigan for anything. Nosy, argumentative and interfering though they were, the old biddies knew everybody's business, were full of chat about what was what, told ribald stories about their seriously misspent youths and were as protective as she-lions towards the single woman beneath their feet. Abby assumed they'd heard about the horrid events in Carrickfergus, where she was viciously attacked by a pair of psychotic paramilitary thugs. But they never mentioned the sensitive subject, nor gave any indication that they were party to Abby's private life. They simply encouraged her to keep up the self-defence classes, as well as the rough, tough rowing sessions on the nearby River Lagan.

Looking at her toned body in the mirror, Abby was glad she'd decided to get fit and get real. She'd never felt so full of energy or looked as good as she did. Most of the weight she'd gained at university had been burned off in the busy, busy, busy world of business, though not as much as she'd have liked. Especially now that she was a television star and had to take care of her appearance. Well, okay, Abby wasn't exactly a star, more a regular on the local news bulletins. She supplied snappy soundbites when the BBC needed comments on business affairs, High Street happenings and entrepreneurial activities generally. She was the "face of business" in Belfast – big, bold, bright, beautiful. Her own business may have failed spectacularly, but Abby's reputation as a self-starting, give-it-a-go, don't-stop-me-now entrepreneur remained miraculously undimmed. If anything, ironically, it was enhanced by her company's controversial collapse, since she had parlayed the commercial disaster into a David-versus-Goliath epic and made her media reputation into the bargain. The fact that she turned out to be a natural on television was as welcome as it was unexpected. Things got better and better as she shed the pounds, smartened herself up, attended the media training courses, pre-prepared her off-the-cuff comments and did all the unnatural things that TV people do to appear natural on screen.

Just as well, then, that Abby was taking evening classes in psychology. Guerrilla Psychology, to be exact. She never did complete her Retail Marketing degree and, although formal qualifications made very little difference in the day-to-day, make-a-buck world of cut-and-thrust commerce, the fact that she'd failed to finish what she'd started nagged at her incessantly. Granted, it often stopped nagging on wet and windy nights, when it was time for class, Häagen-Dazs was in the fridge and a Bridget Jones-clone rom-com was on the box. But the threat of an imminent TV appearance, where the extra kilos always showed, plus the sheer pleasure of the part-time degree course, kept her backsliding in check and personal development on track.

Still, this was the first day of the rest of her life, as the old saying said. It *was* a beautiful morning, what's more. Wasn't it? Abby peeked through the heavy silk curtains of her big bay window, just to check that the dawn was following instructions.

A thick mist enveloped the boughs of the horse chestnuts opposite, like a clichéd CGI effect in a creepy Hollywood movie. The dawn was obviously having a lie-in, the lazybones.

No matter what the weather, Abby loved the humungous horse chestnuts across the street and the beautiful rose garden just beyond and the brassy Victorian bandstand beyond that, to say nothing of the boisterous rhododendron bushes and the aromatic hyacinths when in season and the curvilinear cast-iron Palm House and the oak, spruce and sycamore-studded greensward of Belfast's Botanic Gardens, which were sprinkled during the summer with lovestruck couples, lazy students, energetic Frisbee throwers and buzzing swarms of uniformed schoolchildren. Come autumn, the season of mists and mellow fruitfulness, the deciduous parkland shed most of its visitors, leaving only evergreen dog-walkers and the cold-blooded senior citizens who flourished in the heat of its Tropical Ravine. Autumn was Abby's favourite time of year and kicking up plumes of fallen leaves was Abby's favourite pastime. Pity she didn't have a partner to kick with, or even a boyfriend. But after Dr Dave Kelley dropped out of her life in such a dramatic fashion, she'd no real desire to get involved with another heartbreaker. She'd had her business to run, which was a 24/7 operation. She'd had the emotional trauma of seeing her Web 2.0 dreams turn into an RL nightmare. She'd had the TV and the media and the evening classes and the weekly rowing with Ladies Who Launch and the daily struggle to look better than her best. There was little time left over for a significant other. Men were more trouble than they were worth. Who needs them? I mean, really.

Full-length mirrors never lie – except those slightly convex ones that sneaky retailers fit in ladies changing rooms – and Abby's was saying "lookin' good". She checked out her bottom and, while it wasn't exactly pert, it was an awful lot perter than before. She was tempted to give it an encouraging slap, but feared instigating some kind of subcutaneous avalanche that'd leave her with chronic, possibly terminal, cellulite and enormously swollen ankles that'd not only make buying boots a bitch but slap together like bell-bottoms as she walked. Indeed, if sufficient flab plummeted southwards she'd turn into one of those lead-weighted, self-righting children's toys that can't be knocked over no matter how hard they're pushed. She'd roll backwards and forwards and backwards again, forever and a day. Might be handy on a hen night, though.

Running late, Abby scampered into her walk-in wardrobe, a bijou spare bedroom that had inexplicably filled itself with clothes racks and shoe boxes and handbag hooks and bulging chests of drawers. She struggled into her trusty magic knickers – a girl's gotta do what a girl's gotta do, no matter how buff the butt – slipped on a plain white Dolce & Gabbana blouse and, after tugging the coat-hanger chorus-line back and forth and back again for what must have been a record number of curtain calls, finally settled on a classic Chanel two-piece suit in navy blue, with white twill trim. The shoes took forever, as Jimmy Choos are wont to do, but she opted for light grey slip-ons, which added a necessary touch of personality without compromising her team-player presentation-of-self. A string of cultured pearls, a pair of matching earrings and her favourite black rose brooch, a beautiful gift from a gentleman admirer, completed the dashing designer ensemble. She double-checked her make-up and close-cropped hair in the hall mirror, threw the Aquascutum trench coat over one arm, hooked her Chloé Paddington handbag around the other, briskly opened the front door and bounced down the wonderful wooden staircase that she shared with the apartment above and that abutted the apartment below.

The three-storey house was old and Victorian and filled with exquisite original features, not least the gleaming mahogany banister rail that generations of descending hands had turned silky to the touch. Big Victorian families were few and far between in the 21st century and the house had long since been converted into three separate apartments. Irascible top-floor neighbours notwithstanding, this arrangement didn't bother Abby in the least. On the contrary, it offered a modicum of company and companionship, while enabling her to live in a neighbourhood that she couldn't otherwise afford. Colenso Parade was not only the most desirable street in the Stranmillis area of South Belfast, because it overlooked Botanic Gardens, but Abby's end-of-terrace property was the most desirable house at the most desirable end of the most desirable street in one of the most desirable parts of the city. Immediately adjacent to Queen's University, the Stranmillis district was chock-a-block with young professionals, resting actors, undiscovered artists, bohemian media types, middle-aged divorcees, spritely empty nesters and an eclectic mix of oddballs, weirdos, academics. Its steeply sloping streets – some tree lined, as God intended; others as naked as insurance companies with subsidence concerns insisted – were dotted with gigantic university buildings and gorgeous little shops and restaurants and rinky-dink retail outlets. Stranmillis, in short, was the perfect place for a singleton, close enough to the university to benefit from its intellectual buzz and hectic social life, yet far enough from the centre of the party-animal action to guarantee residents their full eight hours.

She'd almost reached the communal vestibule when one of Abby's ground-floor neighbours appeared at her front door, with a "we need to talk" expression on her face. Esther Island and her partner, Penny Farthing, were the polar opposites of the bolshie bruisers on the top floor – petite, reserved, demure, immaculately groomed in a fusty, old-fashioned, twinset-and-Tweed perfume way and probably impossibly pretty during the war when eligible bachelors were few in number and marriage-worthy men were completely non-existent. No change there, then. Abby assumed Esther and Penny were step-sisters, though she sometimes joked that she lived in the Zuider Zee. Surrounded by dykes.

Still, it was unusual to see either of them at this time of the morning and almost unprecedented for one to initiate a conversation. "Oh, hello Esther," Abby said, as she eased open the vestibule door, a William Morris-ish wonder in stained glass and leaded lights.

"It's Penny."

Whoops. "Sorry if my singing disturbed you, Penny."

"You didn't disturb us, Miss Maguire. Compared to the clod-hoppers on the top floor, you are as dainty as a…"

"Rogue elephant?"

"Hardly," she smiled. "I just… we just… wanted to wish you well in your new job."

Understandably, Abby was a bit taken aback. Not only by the

19

forwardness of her ordinarily unforthcoming neighbours, but by the fact that they somehow knew it was her first day. "How did you find out?"

Still smiling, Penny's cornflower-blue eyes shone with good neighbourliness and with what, well, seemed to be you-go-girl, what-glass-ceiling, women-are-winners solidarity. "We're not completely out of touch, Miss Maguire."

"No, no, I didn't mean…"

"And, anyway, we read the morning paper. There's a piece about you in the early edition of the *Belfast Telegraph*."

"Not *another* article," Abby joked.

"Anyway, we simply want to wish you well. Esther worked there for a while and found it very… ah… bureaucratic. Hopefully you'll shake things up. Rattle a few cages, as they say. Watch your back, though."

"I'll do that, Penny. Thank you."

"No, thank *you*… Abby."

Touched by the old lady's support and the fact that a formerly stand-offish neighbour had used her forename for the first time, Abby closed the vestibule door behind her, opened the heavy front door with its enormous brass knocker in the shape of a lion's head, and skipped down the three granite steps to the fog-wreathed street.

"Belfast City Council, here I come."

Little did she know what horrors lay in wait.

20

Chapter Two

On a Hill Far Away

The old rugged cross rose slowly, cubit by cubit, to its final resting place. The multitudes roared their approval. The ceremony was about to begin. The moment of reckoning was at hand. The dome of the temple glinted in the distance. The spear of destiny was poised and ready. The idolaters would pay the price of iniquity, ere long. Crucify them. Crucify them. Crucify them.

Ecstatic, the crowd cheered ever louder as another heavily laden cross was hammered into position atop the rocky outcrop. Up, up, up, they cried, as a third wooden rood was heaved heavenward with the aid of rope, tackle and human horsepower, not to mention brute force and ignorance. Ignorance especially.

The stench of kerosene was overpowering. The burlap-wrapped crosses were primed and ready, silhouetted menacingly against the threatening sky. After saying a short prayer of thanksgiving, which carried across the entire clearing in the cool evening air, Grand Dragon Stephenson set light to the old totemic timber. The flames spread rapidly, racing up the central shaft and across the armature. The second and third fiery crosses followed suit.

A forest of arms rose in unison, waving side to side like a wheat field on a storm-tossed day. The silvered scene was almost ghostly, as hundreds of white-clad worshippers swayed as one. Their shin-length robes were white. Their loose cotton leggings were white. Their conical cowls were white, albeit with ominous ink-black eyeholes. The only things that weren't white, apart from the imperial purple vestments of Grand Dragon Stephenson, were the blood-red logos on their left breast pockets. A yin-yang circle within a square over a fiery Maltese cross, they wore the mark of the Ku Klux Klan. And wore it with pride.

What a day it had been! One of the biggest Klonklaves that the state had ever seen – 15,000 participants packed into Island Park – had gone off without a hitch. The free food, the marching bands, the aerobatic display by a squadron of Klan-liveried biplanes, the incredible sight of a fully robed and hooded tightrope walker, with a flaming cross in one hand and Old Glory in the other, had made the 1924 South Bend rally a high point in the organization's illustrious history. Seventy years after the brotherhood's ironic inception – when it was founded as a Halloween joke by seven Scotch-Irish pranksters in Pulaski, Tennessee – the KKK boasted five million members in the United States and 350,000 in the Hoosier state alone. Indiana was the diadem in the crown of the Klan, the state where one in four adult males was a member and most of the remainder were sympathetic to the cause.

Good as the wire walker was, impressive as the flypast had been and easily as the barbecued beef had slipped down, the warm-up events were small potatoes compared to the cross-burning ceremony. When the flames were at their height and when the white-robed multitudes locked arms and joined together in a rousing chorus of "The Old Rugged Cross", the Klan's signature psalm, there wasn't a dry eye in Island Park, South Bend, Indiana. God bless America. God bless the Hoosier state. God bless the Invisible Empire.

Sherwood Forrest hadn't intended joining the KKK. Even though he was a direct descendant of Nathan Bedford Forrest, the charismatic Confederate general who was the Klan's first Grand Wizard, Sherwood Forrest had no quarrel with his Negro neighbours, nor his Jewish neighbours, nor indeed his Roman Catholic neighbours, who were the main target of the Klan's campaign of intimidation and suppression. Yes, he was worried by the ever-rising tide of Catholic immigrants from southern and eastern Europe. Yes, he feared that White Anglo-Saxon Protestantism, the rock upon which America's greatness rested, was being undermined by the new arrivals. Yes, he had been to see Sister Helen, a runaway nun who told lurid tales of priestly perversion, convent concubinage and drunken diocesan orgies to scandalized audiences of straight-laced Evangelicals, who feared God almost as much as they hated the Pope and his heathen minions.

But the good book said "love thy neighbour" and if those

neighbours were Roman Catholics or Jews or Negroes or whatever, Sherwood Forrest loved them indiscriminately. It was good for business. According to President Coolidge, the business of America was business. And that was good enough for him. As the owner-manager of a small-fry general store, Sherwood Forrest couldn't afford to alienate any customers, irrespective of their nationality, denomination or fraternal affiliation. Faced with price-cutting, nationally advertised chain stores like A&P and Woolworth's, as well as the insidious competition of mail order giants Sears Roebuck and Montgomery Ward, the lot of main-street businessmen like Sherwood was getting harder and harder. Nowhere was that lot harder than in Indiana, a state that suffered grievously in the recent post-war slump, where money was tight and unemployment was rife. Mom and pop operations, if not quite dead and buried, were wending their way to Boot Hill.

That's where the Klan came in. The Klan took care of its own. Klansmen and women were encouraged to patronize stores and services and small businesses belonging to fellow fiery cross followers. The TWK movement – Trade With Klansmen – was firmly established in Indiana, from Evansville in the south and Indianapolis in the centre to South Bend way up north. How could Sherwood resist the Klan, despite his righteous reservations? Not only would he lose out on invaluable TWK business, but refusing to join meant ruination, because many Hoosier consumers boycotted non-Klan businesses, most famously the Fuller Brush company. Membership of the Invisible Empire meant money in Sherwood's empty pockets and bread in the mouths of the Forrest toddlers.

Although Sherwood was hesitant to swear allegiance to the Klan, commercial common sense dictated that he should seize his opportunity. The bottom line is top priority for small businesses. So he worked hard as a Kleegle and sold memberships all over the state. He rose rapidly through the organization and, to his eternal shame, conveniently ignored the anti-Catholic rumour-mongers who maintained that holy war was about to be declared on Protestants, that every time a male child was born to a Catholic family the local Knights of Columbus contributed another rifle to the RC arms dump, and that the extensive sewer system of

Notre Dame University was actually a gigantic Catholic arsenal filled with explosives and weapons and heavy artillery.

Notre Dame was a major headache. A thorn in the side of God's own country, it was the cockpit of Catholicism in a 90 per cent Protestant state. It was the home of the Fighting Irish football team, which was attracting favourable national publicity thanks to its unbeatable coach, Knut Rockne. With 7,000 students, Notre Dame was a sufficiently powerful state-within-a-state for the Klan to send out tentative peace feelers, a broad-minded delegation who explained that the KKK didn't have a problem with Irish Catholics, as such. It was those Roman Catholics they objected to.

Notre Dame had it coming. Hence the Klonklave in Island Park. Hence the show of strength. Hence the burning crosses that presaged a torch-lit parade to Sacred Heart Basilica, the black heart of the South Bend campus. The gilded dome of the main building would be torn down like the Temple after the crucifixion. The papist munitions would be removed from their infernal underground bunkers and made safe for God-fearing Christian folk.

The day of deliverance had arrived!

As the Exalted Cyclops of the local klavern, it was Sherwood Forrest's sacred duty to lead the klavalcade on its march to everlasting glory. Resplendent in his dragon-embroidered robes, he mounted his Klan-caparisoned horse – complete with eyeholes in its equine hood – and raised his left arm in the Ku Klux salute. As if on cue, his mount reared magnificently, an Indiana re-enactment of the recruitment advertisement that appeared in newspapers nationwide. The crowd of Klansmen roared its approval. They swiftly formed into regiments of white-sheeted warriors and followed the Exalted Cyclops as he exited the park, heading east along Jefferson Boulevard before turning north towards the sinners' godless campus. The front row of twenty good men and true carried tasselled American flags, which they swished in figures of eight to energize the rank and file. A mighty column of burning torch-bearing Klansmen filed through the gates of Island Park, wheeling right in perfect time. The individual klaverns were interspersed with fife-and-drum Klan bands, uneven lines of chugging Model Ts, painted white for the occasion, and impressive flatbed floats sponsored by local businesses who knew what side their cross was burning on. Bringing up the rear, with an electric light bulb-studded cruciform on its front fender, was the great gleaming Cadillac of the Grand Wizard himself. Switching the cross on and off at will, Stephenson sat in the back seat, surreptitiously sipping his "holy water" to keep out the night-time chill. Prohibition be damned. Stephenson's law was the only law in Indiana, Volstead Act included.

Soon the singing started. "Onward Christian Soldiers", followed by "Battle Hymn of the Republic", followed by "Stand Up, Stand Up for Jesus, Ye Soldiers of the Cross". Curious crowds of onlookers gathered at the sidewalks as the procession passed through town and headed up Notre Dame Avenue, towards the great Catholic college at its apex. The locals didn't look happy. "Go home, Klan, Klan go home," one shouted. "Goddamn the Klan," another yelled. "Stephenson is a philandering fornicator," roared a third, to the amusement of many bystanders.

Sherwood Forrest pressed on regardless. He couldn't lose face, well covered though it was. South Bend may be the seat of Catholicism, but Indiana was a Protestant state. The crowds didn't concur. On the contrary, the baying mob got uglier and more vociferous as the enormous white slowworm wound its way towards the campus. A knobbly potato – Ireland's iconic root vegetable – whizzed past the Exalted Cyclops's head. "Missed me, you crossback hayseed," Forrest snapped unwisely. A fusillade of Idaho's finest was the hayseeds' considered reply. The spuds were supplemented with eggs, tomatoes, corncobs and suitably bruised fruit.

Bright white outerwear, albeit intimidating when pristine, proves much less terrifying when spattered with tomato juice, egg yolk and pomegranate pulp. Emboldened, the belligerent crowd of college boys raised the stakes with rocks, bricks, shingles and lumps of lead piping, which were hurled into the klavalcade like deadly Aboriginal boomerangs.

The column wobbled, as crowd psychology kicked in. Fight or flight? Christian doctrine said turn the other cheek, but the battle hymn of Protestant fundamentalism said get stuck into the toe-kissing, wafer-worshipping, irreligious acolytes of the Scarlet Harlot. In a revivalist state like Indiana, where hellfire and brimstone preachments were part of the born-again furniture, it was no contest.

With a communal cry, the Klan charged. Fists flailing, feet swinging, heads butting, the hooded hooligans of the Invisible Empire broke ranks and attacked. Its cavalry, led by Sherwood Forrest, slammed into the swirling crowd at the corner of La Salle and Hill Street. Its tank regiment of Model T Fords revved up and roared into the milling multitudes at a fearsome seven miles per hour. Its commander-in-chief, Grand Wizard D. C. Stephenson, turned and high-tailed it out of South Bend before the first gunshot broke the stillness of the night.

As is so often the case with pitched battles, from the blood-soaked pass at Thermopylae to Blücher's belated arrival at Waterloo, the outcome hinged on a single incident. The Klan was carrying the day. They had seventy years of bullying and brutality to draw upon. The student phalanx at Cedar Street was starting to crumble, when Knute Rockne's undefeated football team arrived, hotfoot from the training ground. Kitted out in their emerald green uniforms, the famous Fighting Irish stretched across Notre Dame Avenue at Sorin Street, directly between the cavalry of the Klan and the gilded dome of their home from home. They crouched, resolute, in the first down position. The famous Four Horsemen of the Apocalypse, Don Miller, Elmer Layden, Jim Crowley and Harry Stuhldreher, faced the pale riders of Indiana's Ku Klux Klan.

Like his glorious forerunner Nathan Bedford Forrest, the greatest cavalry officer of the American Civil War, Sherwood Forrest reared his white-suited steed and led the charge at Rockne's revered line. Afterwards, many reported that the entire melee fell silent, though that seems highly unlikely. Almost everyone claimed to have heard the shout, the snap, the ferocious whirr of the football-sized boulder as it homed in on its target. The missile struck Sherwood between the eyeholes of his ceremonial cowl. His steed reared again as the unconscious, if aptly named, Exalted Cyclops toppled to the ground, like a sack of Idaho potatoes.

The pale riders retreated in disarray. The Klansmen rapidly evaporated. The Fighting Irish remained undefeated. God was a Roman Catholic, after all.

Chapter Three

Ku Klux Dan

"So, what do you think?"

The silence spoke volumes. Dan Brown took a deep slug from his ice-cold Diet Coke and burped slightly as he set his beverage down on the plastic table top. Despite the background hum of a busy city centre, just getting into gear for another money-making day, Simon Magill could hear Dan's drink fizzing in the pregnant interpersonal silence. Idly pulling at the constrictive neck of his trademark black turtleneck, Dan gazed around Piazza di Sant'Agostino, a compact, church-dominated square within easy walking distance of Piazza Navona, the Pantheon and the imperishable Trevi Fountain.

"Another reject, then?" Simon asked, impatiently demanding an answer. The problem with Dan, Simon Magill firmly believed, was that he was just too nice, too polite, too painfully aware of what rejection feels like. Hence, he tended to hum and haw and hesitate and murmur meaningless remarks like "interesting", "challenging" or, infuriatingly, "we'll see".

"We'll see," the multimillionaire author finally replied, with downturned eyes and an awkward smile.

Simon Magill was not a happy bunny. When he signed on as Dan Brown's factotum – though he much preferred the title "new product development manager" – he naively assumed that he'd be sitting at the feet of the master. Or picking up a few writing tips, at least. But every time he suggested a scenario or pitched a "taster" for the next Robert Langdon novel, the mega-selling author of *The Da Vinci Code*, *Angels and Demons*, *Deception Point* and *Digital Fortress* merely smiled benignly, nodded his approval, fidgeted a little or sipped on a Diet Coke until the eloquent silence made his opinion painfully apparent. He then returned to his Samsung netbook with a weary sigh. He was always working on something, though God alone knew what it was. It had been seven long years since he started writing the 60-million selling *Code*, five since its tumultuous publication and four since he last topped bestseller lists worldwide.

Tact reserves running on empty, the Englishman tried again. Reddening slightly, he broke their tacit contract, where Simon suggests and Dan decides. "The KKK is perfect," he insisted, to his employer's evident astonishment. "It's got everything a Langdon novel needs. The Klan's a secret society, closely affiliated to the Masons. With all the symbology and terminology and secret handshakes and stuff there's plenty of scope for introducing enormous slabs of spin-it-out backstory. The bizarre story behind the name. The fact that it was inspired by a Sir Walter Scott novel. The fact that its guiding light was a lingerie salesman, specializing in garters and stays…"

"Enormous slabs?" Dan spluttered. "Spin-it-out?" he huffed. "My novels don't have *enormous slabs* of unnecessary backstory. Judiciously interwoven historical material that helps propel the plot forward, perhaps."

Magill ignored the author's self-exoneration. In for a penny. "There's all sorts of splinter groups within the Klan, Dan. Organizations within organizations. Power struggles. Hidden secrets. Ruthlessness. It has all the elements of the Dan Brown formula."

"Formula? *Formula?* I am an *artist*, I'll have you know!"

Simon Magill had started, so he'd finish. "The Notre Dame riot *really happened*, Dan. It took place on 17 May 1924. It's the *truth*. Your novels are true, aren't they Dan? That's what you claim in the prefaces."

In his red setter-like enthusiasm, Simon Magill had unwittingly crossed a line in the sand. The truth or otherwise of Dan Brown's novels was a major bone of contention, a literary stick that his critics beat him with incessantly. Entire books had been published debunking the claims in *Da Vinci* and *Angels and Demons*. Their nit-picking authors were happy to garner enormous sales on the back of Dan's books while mocking them unmercifully. Jealous bastards. Parasitic bastards. Slimy bastards, one and all.

Wincing from the withering insinuations, Brown looked his underling in the eye. "My novels are based on the truth, Simon.

Based. On. The. Truth. I don't claim they are the gospel truth. They are truth-full, not truthful."

Whatever. Magill took another tack. "Think of the market, Dan. Think of the controversy. Think of the reaction of the Catholic Church. It'd welcome you with open arms. You'd be their blue-eyed boy for a change. As the people who defeated the Klan in '24, they'd be falling over themselves to endorse you."

Partial to true-blue American beverages, everything from Starbucks and Budweiser to E&J Gallo and an occasional Jack Daniel's, the chart-topping author drained his Diet Coke in stony silence.

"Notre Dame'll give you an honorary degree," Simon laughed. "Dr Dan. Dan the Klan. Dan the Klan Killer."

Lips pursed, Brown tugged on his Redsox cap and promptly changed the subject. "We should never have come here."

Magill begged to differ. He had never been to Rome before and the past two days had been nothing less than an eye-opener as amazing architectural tableau after amazing architectural tableau unfolded before him. The Eternal City was aptly named, because it would take forever to explore its incomparable delights. Better yet, this was his first time on a movie set, though nothing much seemed to happen for most of the time. The set-ups were interminable and the "action" was over in an instant. Still, the crew was full of fun and he'd got to meet Tom Hanks, who was as affable in person as he appeared to be on screen. No doubt it was all an act but in fairness to the two-time Oscar winner, he acted himself fairly well.

"Dan, you have to be here," Simon said, stepping into his secondary role as Brown's personal assistant and general dogsbody. "You're contractually obliged to contribute an on-set interview for the DVD extras package."

"Yeah, I know."

Most authors would give their right arm to be sitting on a film set in Rome, where their bestselling novel was being turned into a big-budget blockbuster by Columbia Pictures Inc. True, most novelists couldn't afford to lose their right hand, unless of course they were one of those left-handed creative geniuses like Leonardo da Vinci. Yet, despite the glamour and the excitement and the delicious additional sales of the tie-in edition when the movie opens big, the little balding man in the black turtleneck and tweed jacket was unhappy with his lot. The fresh-faced author who'd rocked the world with his ground-breaking conspiracy thriller was a distant memory. The strain of fending off all sorts of crazies – crank callers, threatening letter writers, burn-in-hell religious zealots, Opus Dei devotees who vowed to "make him pay" and many, many more – had taken its physiognomic toll, as had the plagiarism suits and the struggles with Hollywood over movie mal-adaptations. They'd even decided to make the Camerlengo an Ulsterman. Huh?

"There are worse places in the world to be, Dan."

"Yeah," he barked, "like back home waiting for a bunch of hooded Hoosiers to turn up, with lynching in mind."

Magill couldn't believe what he was hearing. "Don't be daft, Dan. You've nothing to fear. The Klan's a joke nowadays. When D. C. Stephenson was sent to jail in 1925, after being convicted for rape and murder, the Indiana Klan imploded. Membership fell off a cliff, then fell further during the Second World War when the organization's Nazi leanings were exposed, then fell again thanks to their heavy-handed opposition to civil rights in the 1960s. The KKK is dead and buried. There may be a few recidivist Klansmen in the Deep South and among the wild and woolly mountain men of Montana. But that's about it. The Klan's an easy target, Dan. Sufficiently controversial for marketing purposes but not sufficient to cause sleepless nights. And you still get to make disparaging remarks about Roman Catholics!"

The all-American author glared at the ginger-haired Englishman. "The Ku Klux Klan is just a joke, is it?"

Simon smiled to himself. Doubtful Dan had just handed him a glorious conversational gambit, one he wasn't going to forgo. Humour was his boss's soft underbelly. His novels were full of quips, puns, one-liners and all the rest. But nobody ever mentioned Dan's rib-ticklers. Not a single freakin' reviewer on Amazon or anywhere else. Whereas everyone talked about J. K. Rowling's humorous asides, merry japes, sense of fun and so forth, the Danster's side-splitters were roundly ignored. It rankled. It *really* rankled. The man had written two joke books before becoming a famous novelist (though some heartless cynics said all his books were joke books). "Exactly, Dan," Simon said, with a grin. "They're a joke. A complete joke. Think of the fun you could have with their fatuous rituals, their absurd outfits, their spurious symbology, their kompletely krazy nomenklature – klavern, kleagle, kludd, klectoken, kligrapp, klexter. Just think of the alliteration, Dr Dan."

The best-selling author looked up sharply.

"You love a bit of alliteration," Magill inveigled.

"Whatever do you mean?"

"Come on, Dan," he joshed. "Your character names alone are an arresting agglomeration of alliterative appellations, if I may be so bold."

"I did not know that."

"Vittoria Vetra, Gunther Glick, Tyler Tingley, Midge Milkin, Sister Sandrine. I could go on."

"I did not know that," Brown repeated in an unnatural monotone.

"And then there's Senator Sedgewick Sexton," Magill continued blithely, warming to his theme, "the bad guy in *Deception Point*. What was it you said about his love of alliteration?"

"I can't recall right now."

"You said he adored the musical quality of his own name." Grinning, Magill was beginning to enjoy himself. "Hey, who cares that excessive alliteration is a literary no-no? What do Strunk and White know? You're the king of the airport novel. Not a bed-wetting Man Booker wannabe."

Dan cleared his throat.

In his enthusiasm, Simon Magill failed to take the hint. How was he to know that Dan had suffered grievously from the swarm of artsy-fartsy literati who poured scorn on his stylistic malapropisms. How was he to know the anguish Dan suffered every night, writhing at the chatter about his literary infelicities – infelicities that enormous royalty cheques couldn't quite assuage. How was he to know that Dan had spent the best part of two years writing *Moby Dicker*, an exquisite sequel to the greatest American novel of all time. Then there was that other Langdon novel he'd already written but refused to publish, though there was a very specific reason for that. A reason that was… well… too horrid for words.

"I haven't told you the best bit, Dan."

Brown rolled down the neck of his rollneck sweater and started scratching his throat distractedly. "You know, Simon, I really think this, er, conversazione has gone on long enou…"

"The hotties, Dan. The hotties!"

Taken aback, the king of the conspiracy thriller looked askance at his irresponsible assistant, whose dog-with-a-bone exuberance would be commendable if it weren't completely overwhelming. "What hotties?"

"The Lotie hotties!" Magill laughed. "All your books are blessed with bootylicious hotties. Vittoria Vetra, Sophie Neveu, Rachel Sexton, Susan Fletcher, Gabrielle Ashe, the Hassassin's hos in *Angels and Demons*."

"Yeeeeessss," Dan said warily. "I hope you're not suggesting that I put the ho in hokum."

The uncrowned king of quips had cracked another. Magill guffawed appreciatively. "The Klan had a female subsidiary called the Ladies of the Invisible Empire. Loties, Dan. Lotie hotties, Dan. The eternal feminine, Dan. Okay, not the skimpiest negligees in the world. But, hey, Big Bobby Langdon isn't choosy. As long as they have a hood over their heads, right? Is that a burning cross in Robert's pocket or just his Zippo lighter?"

It was time to call a halt. Dan had had his fill of Magill. As someone who had once written books under a female pseudonym, Brown had to be extra careful when gender reared its medusan head. "Enough!" he barked, looking round anxiously as if seeking an escape route. "Goddamn it, Simon, let's keep women out of this!"

Drawn by the raised voices, several nearby lighting technicians looked over. "Simon," one simpered camply, "let's keep women out of this." The rest laughed uproariously, delighting in the opportunity to bring "the talent" down a peg or two.

Magill waved over at the peasants, adding a "got me" grin for good measure. Dan, by contrast, pushed back his plastic chair and promptly stalked off set. Head down, he hurried in the general direction of the crowd control barriers, where black-suited security guards regulated access to the production unit. Simon raced after the rapidly disappearing figure. "Dan," he shouted, "you're not supposed to go off the set unaccompanied." The production company's insurance policy contained stipulations to that effect, on account presumably of the possibility that psychotic priests or crazy cardinals might instigate an armed assault on the heretical movie makers.

Diminutive at the best of times, Dan instantly disappeared into the milling crowds. As ever, the environs of Piazza Navona were filled with sightseers, souvenir sellers, quick-fire caricaturists, blue-uniformed *carabiniere*, reproduction oil painting vendors and lots of loitering local onlookers, hoping to catch a distant glimpse of the movie stars. Despite the height advantage that Magill had over the masses, there was no sign of a Brown tweed jacket.

"In the name of Jesus," Magill muttered. "What on earth's eating that guy?"

Chapter Four

Obelisk

Atlas shrugged. The name wasn't on the list and the wuss didn't have a laminated pass with photo ID. There was no way the jerk was getting through. It was more than Chas's job was worth. A veteran minder with twenty-five years' experience on movie sets, plus provision of personal security to the stars, he recognized a crank when he saw one. Stalkers, crazies, obsessives, weirdos, psychos, sociopaths, get-a-lifers, he'd dealt with them all during his time, mostly politely, though some were so insistent that a bit of subtle muscle was called for. The small guys were the worst, oddly enough. You'd think that the sight of a 6′ 2″, 200lb, shaven-headed, black-suited slab of obsidian would be enough to dissuade them. But dinky little dudes were always the first to put up their dukes and start swingin'. If Chas had an ambition, other than to work the red carpet on Oscars night, it was to place a hand on some small guy's head and hold him off while he took airshots beneath. Just like those old silent movies he'd seen as a kid. It was never going to happen, though, not on this set anyhow.

"Please step away from the entrance, sir," Atlas said deferentially, motioning up the next in line.

Arms akimbo, the jerk refused to budge. "I have an appointment," he announced. "I'm expected, bozo. I'm already running late," he added with asperity.

In ordinary circumstances, Chas Atlas would have beat the shit out of the uppity SoB. But his instructions were strict. Keep it low key. The producers had been denied access to key locations like St Peter's and the local bureaucrats were making life difficult, despite the tourist dollars that would flow into Rome next May, when the blockbuster was released. The movie was being shot on a catch-as-catch-can basis, with various buildings standing in for the Vatican. The Biblioteca Angelica, at the edge of Piazza di Sant'Agostino, was a prime example. Surrounded by temporary security fencing, the piazza was off limits to visitors without appropriate accreditation. Such as this one.

"What's your name again?" Atlas said, pretending to peruse the list on his clipboard. "Dick Dribble, was it?" There's only so much low-key a man can take.

"Richard Quibble, actually. Dr Richard Quibble."

"Well," the security guard retorted with relish, trying not to laugh in the mendicant's pasty face. "We have a Dick Nibble, a Dick Nipple, a Dick Dabble, a Dick Drabble and a Dick Wad. But no Quibble." He'll be swingin' any second now, Chas calculated. Then he'd hold him off politely, call for assistance, escort him down the side alley opposite and "explain" a few home truths. "Hold on a mo. Did you say *Doctor* Dick Quibble?"

The get-a-life nodded eagerly.

"Well, doc, I've got this terrible pain in my ass."

"I'm not that kind of…"

"And I'm looking at it!" Atlas snarled. "If the little haemorrhoid doesn't get the fuck out of my face, he'll get my size 15 Gucci loafer up his butt-crack. And I get kinda angry when my Guccis get dirty. *Capisce?*"

Momentarily confused by the security man's unnatural anatomical outburst, Dr Quibble allowed himself to be eased aside by the door-bitch, who was already dealing with the next in line. A prim Italian porn star – prim or porn, it was hard to tell them apart in this place – was let through on the nod.

Quibble made his way to the nearby Piazza Navona, site of Emperor Domitian's infamous chariot races. A rethink was sorely needed. Perched on the rim of Fontana dei Quattro Fiumi, where Robert Langdon once grappled with the heinous Hassassin and employed his sub-aquatic skills to good effect, Dr Richard Quibble considered his options. He wasn't going to let a bloated blowhard stop him, not this close to his goal. For four long years he'd maintained his Dan Brown tribute website, WhollyBloodline.com. It was an unofficial celebration of all things Brown: biography, bibliography, lists of characters, places, technologies, artworks, conspiracy theories, as well as potted plotlines, critical reactions to the great man's books and countless other nuggets likely to be of interest to Dan's fans. Naturally, the website also contained sections on the plagiarism suits, the movie adaptations, the soft rock albums that Dan released before his career change and the plethora of parasitic publications that attached themselves to Brown's bestsellers, like barnacles on a battleship. There were more than one hundred *Code*-clone novels at the last count, not including puerile parodies (most of which were a bad joke, frankly). There were almost as many tribute websites.

From Quibble's perspective, the principal problem with this proliferation of parasites was that it was practically impossible to stand out from the i-Brown crowd. Yes, his website was more complete than its competitors, though being the best was no guarantee of visitor numbers, much less click-throughs to his increasingly antsy advertisers. Yes, the release of the movie would raise interest in the Dan Brown brand generally. But the uptick in interest would be spread very thinly, unless a new angle was available, another inducement was offered, a fresh bit of bait was dangled in front of the media's insatiable maw.

Quibble knew exactly what that incentive should be. Except an Armani-wearing obelisk stood his way. All he needed was a ten-minute interview with Dan. All he needed was a quick answer to the questions everyone's asking: when's the next book coming out?; what's happening with *The Solomon Key*, Dan's *Da Vinci Code* sequel?; why is it taking so long? Was Brown beset by writer's block, as some said? Had he choked, as many overnight successes tend to do, when faced with writing an impossible-to-follow follow-up? Had he lost his edge now that he had millions banked and no need to work again? Or was there something more sinister afoot? A conspiracy, perhaps?

Given ten minutes with the man, Quibble was convinced that he could get the answers out of him. Even a "No comment" could be parlayed into a "Brown Blocked?" posting that the media'd snap up come the premiere of *Angels and Demons* and that'd lead in turn to talking head appearances on TV, assorted History Channel specials, opportunities to review low-brow conspiracy fiction for high-brow periodicals – with a U Penn doctorate, he was perfect for the job – and, most important of all, a surge of interest in the website, where traffic had thinned to a trickle.

There were two ways of handling this frustrating situation: bluff or bribery. Fortified by a couple of glasses of Lambrusco, which he purchased from La Dolce Vita, a piazza-side wine bar, Quibble crept back to the set-access gate. Chas Atlas was still holding the fort.

"Back again, bozo? Dr Dribble, wasn't it? You're still not on the list. We got a Dick Head, a Dick Dastardly, a Dick Turpin and an Officer Dibble, but that's it."

Quibble smiled, letting the arrows of mockery bounce off harmlessly. "I'm Officer Dibble," he lied. "There must be a typo. I have a hush-hush appointment with a very important person. Need to know. You know how it is."

Atlas played along, since nothing much else was happening and the pass-less lines of movie set mavens had long since dispersed. "Oh yeah, I know all about need-to-know. But, as you know, I need to know who you need to know on a need-to-know basis. That's my job, you know."

"Well… Dan Brown, since you insist."

"There's no one of that name on set."

"Well, I know and you know that's not true, because Tom Hanks's latest twitter, posted twenty minutes ago, states that he's talking with Dan about his motivation during the Vatican Archives scene."

"Don't know what you're talking about, man. There's no Tom Hanks here. There's no Dan Brown. This isn't the Vatican, or hadn't you noticed. Here's something you need to know, buddy. The Vatican's about a mile thataway. You've got the wrong movie set. This is called *Obelisk*." Atlas raised his laminated pass. The walrus-oid photo did him no favours. A single word was emblazoned across the top of the plastic rectangle: Obelisk. He waggled the pass in front of Quibble's face, a smirk the size of Trajan's Column wrapped around his Burger-Kinged countenance.

Quibble struggled to keep his composure. He was well aware of the movie's working title – changed from *Angels and Demons* to confound possible protestors – but the Vatican slip-up had cost him dear. "My captain won't like this, Mr Atlas. We bear grudges in the Agency."

"What agency would that be, Officer Dibble?" Chas Atlas was

on a rollicking roll. "FBI? CIA? NSA? LAPD? William Morris? That Top Cat dude, is he still giving you trouble, Officer Dibble? Wanna show me your badge, Officer Dibble? You packin' heat, Officer Dibble?"

Quibble knew what was coming next. Questions about height restrictions on the force. Bluffing wasn't his strong point, as he'd discovered when he tried to talk his way into CERN, to double-check Dan's description in *Angels and Demons*. The door-bitch's good humour could be used to his advantage, though. It was time for Plan B. "Look… er… dude, I'm sorry we got off on the wrong foot. Guess I'm in the wrong place. No hard feelings?" He held out his hand. Chas Atlas responded in kind. As they shook, the webmaster slipped a large-denomination note into the security guard's gigantic paw, which was the size and consistency of a baseball glove.

"What's this?" Chas said suspiciously.

"Just a little something to apologize for my pugnacity."

Atlas sized up the opportunity, then succumbed to temptation. "But you *lied* to me, Dribble."

Quibble slipped another 100 euros into his massive mitt.

Chas considered the offering, examined his conscience and decided to do the right thing. "But you refused to step aside when I asked you politely, Dabble."

A third donation was directed towards the amply oiled baseball glove.

"You also called me a bozo, Babble."

Quibble's heart sank, because he was clean out of euros. The nearest ATM was three blocks away and common sense suggested that it was now or never. Defeated, the diligent Dan-fan turned to go, 300 euros lighter and no better off. He trudged back towards Piazza Navona for one last look at Bernini's imperishable water-feature.

"But I'll forgive you for that," Atlas called out to the downcast, stoop-shouldered dwarf. He swivelled on a sixpence – five cent piece, rather – and bounded back, stature increasing with every stride. "Look, I can't let you through, man, 'cos I'd lose this gig if I did. However, if you come back in forty-five minutes, when the shooting stops for the day, I'll let you on to the set. You can walk around for a while until we lock down for the night."

Quibble weighed up his options. What options? There was nothing to lose. There might be a "Where's Dan?" posting in it, plus exclusive on-set photos courtesy of his trusty camera phone. "Thank you, Mr Atlas. Thank you. I'll see you shortly… dude."

Elated, the great Brown-hunter celebrated his good fortune with a few additional glasses of Lambrusco, then slipped on to the set when Chas gave him a wave. The place was pretty much deserted, since technicians tend not to hang around when there's bars to hit and babes to hit on. He picked his way through the lighting rigs and camera cases and set dresser detritus, then slipped into Biblioteca Angelica, which was doubling for the Vatican Archives. Commandeered by the production company, the ordinarily busy public library was empty… echoing… eerie, almost.

An incredibly realistic recreation of an hermetically sealed library vault rested in the middle of the rococo reading room. Quibble stepped inside, strangely fearful that he'd get trapped in the air lock like Robert Langdon, even though he knew it was only a movie set and that there was no air lock and that there was nobody around and that if the worst came to the worst he could kick over the book-laden shelving and trigger the domino effect, as stack crashed against stack and the Vatican's vellum volumes smashed through the plate glass for fresh air and freedom. He laughed at his own stupidity, as he wandered among the "secret archives", occasionally picking up and examining the ancient leathered volumes made from the finest cardboard, then returning them to their rightful place. The whole scene, he knew, was lifted straight from *Indiana Jones and the Temple of Doom*, but it would still look incredible on screen.

Quibble was still smiling when a knife-wielding figure appeared from behind the final stack, at the very back of the vault. He continued to smile as the razor-sharp blade lanced across his unprotected throat. He had no time to do anything else. He tried to speak, to yell, to ask why his attacker was taking photos of him as he went down in what felt like slow motion. No answer was forthcoming as Quibble struggled for breath. A big, bright red puddle appeared on the floor beside him. What was that all about? It's only a movie, isn't it?

Chapter Five

Belfast Means Business

"I'm going to kill that arrogant bastard." Abby Maguire switched off her Compaq desktop – tempted though she was to smash the thing – and got ready to head for home. "Oh for a pump action blunderbuss, something that'd splatter his smirking face all over the place." Pausing only to say goodnight to the git through gritted teeth, she gathered up her things, grabbed her Burberry gabardine, slung the Mulberry Roxanne over her left shoulder and stormed out of the office. "Another day in paradise? I don't think so!"

Six weeks on from her auspicious start at Belfast City Council, Abby was beginning to have second thoughts. As well as third and fourth thoughts about the wisdom of her career change. It wasn't the actual work that got her goat. On the contrary, she loved the job. As the public face of the Belfast Means Business campaign, she was constantly out and about, meeting and greeting businesspeople from all walks of life. She'd visited factories and offices and everything from corner shops to haulage contractors. She'd played golf with Rotarians, glad-handed investors from the USA, clapped politely at countless self-congratulatory award ceremonies and eaten more lukewarm chicken dinners, with cloying crème caramel to follow, than her rowing training could cope with, let alone counteract. All in all, it had been a busy yet invigorating time. Whether she could cope with much more of it – much more of *him*, to be exact – was another matter entirely.

On closing the office door with a satisfying click and a sigh, Abby started to have second thoughts about the blunderbuss scenario. A pump-action shotgun, she decided, was too quick, too messy, too good for the so-and-so. An enormous bear trap under his desk would be better, ideally one with gigantic, razor-sharp teeth that'd snap shut on his unprotected nether regions. Then grind for a bit. Several hours, say.

Or perhaps she should just inform him that as a former abattoir worker she knew how to disembowel pigs in double-quick time. The male chauvinist strain especially. However, the supercilious sod would probably use the abattoir information against her, in his wily weaselly style. What was that word they used to describe Malcolm "Call me Mal" Montgomery? Machiavellian, wasn't it? Malignant, maybe? Whatever it was, it was nothing a machete couldn't handle.

Within half-a-dozen steps of the office door, Abby's mood lightened immeasurably. How could it not when the central dome of Belfast City Hall soared 173 feet above her. Whatever the frustrations of working for a self-anointed Marketing Mastermind – though their Integrated Communications Unit was basically a PR department with delusions of grandeur – there was one particular employment perk that never failed to raise her spirits. The City Hall itself. Constructed at the start of the twentieth century, when the city was in its pomp, money was no object and a monument befitting Belfast's industrial, commercial and civic glory was a necessity not an indulgence, the council's headquarters was a Baroque Revival confection in gleaming Portland stone, with an enormous burnished dome and similarly gilded domelets at each corner. Situated slap bang in the middle of the mighty metropolis, surrounded by efflorescent Edwardian office blocks, the City Hall sat in immaculately manicured, statue-studded gardens, like an opalescent urban jewel. True, the architect had to sue the city council for his fee and the then Lord Lieutenant of Ireland, on hearing that the foundation stone cost a whopping £500, sarcastically commented, "It's a precious stone, I presume." But a century on from the Edwardian overspend, the City Hall was the one bona-fide architectural gem that Belfast possessed.

If the colonnaded and pedimented exterior of the City Hall was simply magnificent, its interior beggared belief. Far from becoming blasé about its marble floors and Carrara staircases and stuccoed ceilings and scrollwork pilasters and vermicular spandrels and stained glass windows and bronzed busts of local worthies and unprepossessing oil paintings of former Lord

Mayors, Abby found that her workplace was becoming more and more fascinating. As she slowly acquired the lore and legends that adhere to all landmark buildings and heard some of the stories that circulated around its panelled corridors and splendid state rooms, she found herself falling hopelessly in love with the place. It was an example, apparently, of Wrenaissance architecture, inspired to the point of plagiarism by St Paul's Cathedral. Its council debating chamber was modelled on Pugin's House of Commons, even down to the sword-length separation of the opposing benches. Its central rotunda was the setting for the signing of the Ulster Covenant in 1912, when half a million men and woman pledged to resist Irish Home Rule. It survived a direct hit by a Nazi incendiary bomb during the big bad Blitz of 1941. It was the venue of the Peace Accord concert where Bill and Hillary Clinton saluted hundreds of thousands of well-wishers and listened to a set by the Belfast cowboy himself, Van Morrison. Characteristically, the grumpy old rock star played songs from his latest album rather than the greatest hits that the crowd and the Clintons and the world-wide television audience were hoping for. If ever a gesture was symbolic of Belfast, Morrison's curmudgeonly contrarianism was surely it.

Belfast was its own worst enemy, Abby often thought, though she had her own worst enemy to worry about. As her love for the City Hall increased exponentially, so her detestation of Mad Mal accelerated asymptotically. Part of the problem with her permanent pain-in-the-posterior was his slippery superciliousness and part of it was down to the fact that she, as an entrepreneurial free spirit, found it difficult to come to terms with the bureaucratic mindset that bedevilled the place. Namely, the preoccupation with status and hierarchy, the interminable meetings about angels on a pinhead, senior employees' small-minded obsession with individual entitlements such as personalized stationery, office furniture specifications, reserved car parking spaces and the rest of the mammalian male mindset, which sets enormous store by suitably embossed envelopes and filing cabinet allocations.

However, Abby's real problem was Mal's father-knows-best manner. The casual sexism she could cope with, but the fact that he treated her as the face not the mind of Belfast Means Business

43

was very, *very* irritating. She was a political pin-up basically, the professional equivalent of scantily clad models draped over car bonnets at motor shows. Her photogenic features and on-camera articulacy were the sum total of her contribution to the city's FDI strategy, as far as her infuriating boss was concerned. Whenever she tried to contribute to council policy, or made suggestions based on feedback she'd received from company visits or evening soirees or media contacts, she was patted on the head – metaphorically – and told not to concern herself with such weighty matters. Leave that to the professionals, the heavy hitters, the movers-and-shakers, the big-picture people like "Call me Mal".

The ultimate insult was when Abby innocently asked about the Belfast branding campaign. For some time, the council had been concerned about people's perceptions of the place. In the ferociously competitive world of city region marketing, where image was all important and potential investors were both few and fought over, it was necessary to keep the brand fresh, the offer relevant, the package appealing, the slogan snappy, the logo up to scratch. Teams of external consultants had pitched their place marketing panaceas. Reams of qualitative and quantitative research were gathered by fee-gobbling agencies at great expense. Logos were focus-grouped, slogans were pre-tested, strategies were, well, strategized, what-ifs were wrestled with, pseudo public participation exercises were mounted in the name of crowd-sourcing, we-think or whatever the latest consultancy buzzword was.

The self-important Pooh-bah at the centre of this honey-pot was Field Marshal Montgomery. He was in his element, surrounded by fawning supplicants in expensive suits, all mouthing meaningless gobbledegook about positioning, USPs, Delphi projections, structural equation calibration and strategic scenarios going forward. After all the rigmarole, they would probably come up with something mind-bogglingly banal like a cartoon bumble bee that captures the essence of "buzzing" Belfast. When Abby asked to have a look at the consultants' recommendations, Mad Mal responded with dismissive remarks that weren't so much crushingly condescending as actionable under sex discrimination legislation. Top secret. Need to know. Above your pay grade. Learn to walk before you can run. Let's stick to the meeting and greeting, shall we. And just about everything short of "don't worry your pretty little head about it, now sit on my lap and let's discuss the first thing that comes up". Jesus. It was all Abby could do to resist yanking him out of his ergonomic executive chair by the lapels, dragging him across his leather-topped executive desk and beating the runt to a pulp with his hand-engraved executive nameplate.

As if that weren't enough, Mal then tried to mollify her by suggesting a profile in one of the local newspapers, a piece of fluff about Abby's exciting working day that'd show off the council's roster of fresh-faced talent, draw attention to the sagacious mentoring she was receiving from wiser heads and showcase the City Hall's non-discriminatory, gender-neutral, anti-sectarian employment practices. "You *are* a Catholic, aren't you?" Little wonder Abby found it difficult to be civil to the man. Even the architectural attractions of the soaring dome and the geniality of the local councillors, most of whom were blessed with the common touch that the bureaucrats conspicuously lacked, were insufficient recompense for the "pleasure" of working with Mal. Six weeks was more than enough time to realize that red-tape swaddled, pecking order-preoccupied organizations weren't for her.

As she stomped across the chequer-board marble floor of the rotunda, Abby ruminated on her professional options. Fight, flight or feather her nest like the rest? Smiling at the uniformed security man as he held the door open, Abby knew she couldn't be seen to fail again, not so soon after WeeTube's implosion. She had to persevere for a wee while longer. She'd give it six months. Maybe Mal'll get knocked down by a speeding Citybus. Wonder where you sign up for bus driving lessons…

Fingering her beloved black rose brooch, Abby was seriously tempted to scratch it along the side of Mal's Porsche 911, which sat mockingly in an executive parking space within the exclusive inner courtyard of the City Hall. But she resisted the temptation. Just.

Ordinarily, Abby'd head straight for the Stranmillis Road bus stop. However, the day's frustrations dictated that she browse a while at the Continental Market. From mid-November through to Christmas, the grounds of the City Hall were given over to vendors from all over Europe. Brightly lit, canvas-covered stalls sold French cheeses, German sausages, Italian pastas, Spanish tomatoes, Greek olives, Norwegian salmon, Turkish delight, Belgian chocolates and every imaginable gastronomic stereotype. What it lacked in post-colonial, politically-correct provender, the temporary market more than compensated with excitement, exuberance and joie-de-vivre. The swirling crowds of bantering, boasting, benevolent Belfastians, all wrapped up against the winter chill, would raise anyone's spirits. The atmosphere reminded Abby of the Hauptmarkt in Nuremberg, where she'd spent an unforgettable few hours, a fear-filled interlude that didn't leave much time for sightseeing. Except from a Citroën MPV, driven by a crazy, kilted Scotsman.

Abby nibbled some free Brie at the fromagerie and chewed the fat with a posse of passers-by who seemed to think that they knew her from somewhere – school? college? church? – though they couldn't quite remember where. Abby loved being half-recognized because she always played along, asking about their families, their holiday plans and the like, knowing they'd be struggling for hours trying to work out who they'd been talking to. There must be some perverse psychological process going on there, she surmised, making a mental note to ask her tutor at the next evening class.

The next evening class? Abby suddenly realized that she'd a class that very night! Worse, she hadn't done this week's required reading. Her lecturer was a stickler for reading round the subject and often started his class with a "cold-call" interrogation session, designed to expose those who hadn't followed instructions. Drat, drat, double drat!

Checking her Chopard, Abby politely thanked the stall-holder for the Brie, serpentined through the crowds of happy shoppers, dashed past the giant Ferris wheel that afforded elevated glimpses of the sparkling city to thousands of excited children – and their long-suffering grandparents – and leapt on to the Stranmillis Road bus just as the driver was closing the doors and releasing the clutch with a hiss of hydraulics.

Fifteen minutes of sluggish traffic later, she jumped from the Citybus and hurried down the hill to Colenso Parade. Just time for a workout, hairwash, M&S ready meal and a speed read of her class handout. Hey, who cares about the Belfast Brand?

Chapter Six

The Fenian Ram

15 November 1887

"Dive. Dive. Dive."

The submariner pitched his craft into a steep descent, the most dangerous manoeuvre in the book. Captain Harry Ramsden tried to remain calm and businesslike in front of the novice crew. They were nervous enough as it was. And with good reason. It was twenty-five years since the *Monitor*'s attack on the *Merrimack*, in the mighty war between the States, and ironclad technology had improved immeasurably. But the loss of the entire crew of the *Huntley*, in its pyrrhic victory over *Housatonic*, and the unending catalogue of fatal accidents ever since, ensured that submersibles remained a high-risk billet. They were the future, though. Completely undetectable by surface shipping, which had no defence against submarine marauders, and equipped with an array of lethal weapons – most based on that terrifying new-fangled technology known as "dynamite" – the submersible represented a potentially massive shift in the balance of maritime power. The strongest navies in the world were susceptible to undersea attack, even the imperious Royal Navy. Naturally, the top brass didn't see it that way. They dismissed such devices as Jules Verne fictions, children's toys for dandies and dilettantes. However, recent advances in submarine propulsion, particularly the replacement of pedal-power with diesel engines, were a whisper on the wind. Just as steam was superseding sail and wooden hulls were being replaced by steel plates, so too surface crawlers would be soon surpassed by the "sub".

Captain Ramsden's craft plunged deeper and deeper, the angle of descent growing steeper and steeper. He blew the forward ballast tank as a precaution. This was only an experiment, after all. The ship's centre of gravity suddenly shifted aft, tilting the vessel into a precipitous dive. Terrified, the novice crewmen screamed like little children as the submersible canted out of control. The commander's frantic attempts to level her off proved fruitless. She hit the bottom with a booming crash, the shuddering impact of which was psychologically and physically magnified by its abruptness. Thrown forward from his insecure seat in the cramped cockpit, Harry Ramsden hit his unprotected head against a protruding cast iron flange. Knocked unconscious, with a limited air supply and two panicked crew members unfamiliar with the intricacies of the new technology, time was running out for the captain and his complement…

A chill wind swept in from the west as Walter Wilson checked his pocket watch. Wrapped in several layers of protective clothing, Wilson was as cosy as a man could be in the middle of a cold November night. However, the chill that gripped his heart was palpable as the minutes ticked by and there was no sign of the submersible. The new generation "subs", he knew, could remain underwater for several hours or more. But Ramsden was under strict instructions to take her down to the bottom and bring her up right away. The Clarendon Dock was only 30 feet deep. Even at its slowest rate of descent and ascent the submarine should have surfaced by now. The object of the exercise was to check the prototype's protective seals, not run an undersea endurance test.

Decision made, Wilson clicked his fingers at the two shadowy figures on the dockside. One was wearing a full John Brown, the iconic diving suit with a bulbous metal helmet invented by Augustus Siebe in 1837. The other assisted with the compressed air pump, the necessary guide ropes and the heavy brass helmet, which had to be painstakingly bolted into place. "Get down there, Sammy. See what's up."

"She's not comin' up, Mr Wilson," the gnarled Ulsterman replied, trying to inject a bit of black humour into the deadly serious proceedings.

"Just get down there," Wilson ordered. He lit up a stogie as the diver clumped in his weighted boots to the quayside and, with the aid of his apprehensive assistant, clambered laboriously down the wrought-iron ladder that descended into the dock. Mercifully, the anchorage was free of heavily laden cargo vessels, despite the city's insatiable demand for imports. Forty years ago, Belfast was an insignificant place, mean and dirty, with no natural resources to its name. Now, thanks to go-ahead industrialists like himself, as well as a commercially minded town council and harbour commission, the conurbation had grown at an astonishing rate. Belfast was the first city of Ireland, having bypassed Dublin a dozen years before, and along with Glasgow and Liverpool formed part of the Lancashire-Lanarkshire-Ulster industrial triangle that was one of the wonders of the modern world. All was at risk, however, unless appropriate steps were quickly taken. Everything rested on what rested beneath the gently lapping waves of Clarendon Dock.

Fifteen agonizing minutes later, Sammy the Sealion emerged from the dock's murky depths, clanking up the ladder, seawater cascading off his globular headgear.

"Well?" Wilson asked, when the heavy helmet was removed.

"Nothing, sir."

"Nothing at all?"

"Oh, I found her all right. She's on the bottom about ten yards out from the quay. But I couldn't hear a thing, Mr Wilson, sir."

"How could you possibly hear a thing, man, with that monstrosity on your head?"

The diver raised his right arm, wearily. "I hit her with this spanner, sir. If the crew had banged back, I'd've felt the hull vibrate. There was nothing, sir. No response at all. They're goners."

"They are *not* goners," Wilson snapped. "Get down there again and don't come back without them." Even as he said it, the industrialist knew that he was being irrational, that his desire for a successful outcome was clouding his judgement, that the prototype should never have been tested in the first place. He called a halt to the futile exercise, swore the diver to silence with folding money and a fearsome threat, then repaired to his waiting brougham for the short ride home.

Chastened, Walter Wilson reported his failure to fellow board members the following morning. Meeting in the resplendent

Harbour Commission building, the commercial conclave listened glumly as their chief designer summarized the state of submaritime science. The world's foremost builder of submarines, Wilson reminded them, was John P. Holland, an Irish-American based in New York City. Whereas most rival designers were working on even-keeled descent and ascent, Holland's "sub" was able to rise and dive at an angle, while ensuring that the vessel's centre of gravity remained stable. How this was achieved as the air and fuel ran down was anybody's guess. What was not in doubt was its manoeuvrability. Holland's submersible was as nimble as the porpoise that inspired its design. His experiments with diesel engines and periscopes and torpedo tubes and explosive projectiles were the talk of the industry, though the US Navy hadn't yet woken up to the porpoise's prodigious potential.

The ill-humour around the boardroom table was palpable. Alongside his esteemed colleagues Edward Harland, Gustav Wolff and William Pirrie, Walter Wilson had built the greatest shipyard in the Empire, if not the world. Yet Harland & Wolff's four leading lights were baffled by the behaviour of a one-man band in New Jersey.

"Are you sure he won't come to a suitable financial arrangement?" Gustav Wolff, the company's chief accountant and source of the financial package that got their great shipyard off the ground, found it hard to grasp that Holland wasn't motivated by money.

"You could offer him the Crown Jewels," William Pirrie replied in his effortlessly superior manner, "and he'd still prefer to remove the head that wears the crown than pocket Her Majesty's diamonds and pearls."

The fundamental problem, the patricians ruefully recognized, was that Holland was a fire-breathing Fenian, a fully fledged member of *Clan-na-Gael*, the Irish secret society that plotted against the Empire, that bombed Britain's cities with impunity, that launched an abortive invasion of Canada, that sprang six Irish convicts from imprisonment in Australia, that brutally murdered two British cabinet ministers in Phoenix Park, Dublin, that tried to assassinate Queen Victoria during her diamond jubilee year, only to be thwarted by the British Secret Service, that possessed an enormous war-chest, which funded Holland's "salt-water enterprise" to the tune of £100,000, and, most despicably of all, that demanded Home Rule for Ireland, even though independence would be disastrous for industrialists and populace alike. Harland & Wolff's continuing success depended entirely on its access to British markets, British financial institutions, British steamship companies, British colonial possessions that the sun never set on – and never would.

Holland's so-called *Fenian Ram* was not only technologically superior to anything in Harland & Wolff's armoury, it was a threat to the Great British Empire itself. If his submarine performed as well as rumour had it, the Irish republican warship could wreak havoc almost anywhere in the world. Easily transported in the hold of a tramp steamer, then surreptitiously launched while the fleet lay at anchor, the *Fenian Ram* could undermine the Royal Navy's nautical hegemony and with it Britain's commercial suzerainty. The latest lamentable failure of H&W's replica "sub" – the aptly named *King Billy Goat* – indicated that something had to be done. Urgently.

"We need to look at this issue afresh," Sir Edward Harland said sagaciously, if somewhat redundantly. "Conventional wisdom is no use to us now. Aslant thinking is called for, gentlemen."

Aslant thinking? Wilson had never heard the term before, though it had an imaginative ring to it. Must be one of Pirrie's. "If you will permit me, Sir Edward," he interrupted, seizing the moment. "I have a man waiting outside, who might abet our deliberations. He's been sworn to secrecy, rest assured."

The triumvirate around the table exchanged uncertain glances, then nodded their approval. Wilson slipped out of the boardroom and returned a few moments later with someone who looked like a bookkeeper. Slim, sallow, moustachioed, neatly turned out with a well-pressed suit and freshly starched collar, he could be any one of the countless colourless clerks who worked in the company's commodious drawing office. Only his steely grey eyes, which appraised the plutocrats warily, bespoke anything other than due deference.

"Gentlemen, may I introduce Mr Archibald Carmichael. You may not be aware of it, but he has worked for us in the past. He helped bring the labour disputes we suffered some years back to an – how can I put this? – impressively speedy conclusion."

Carmichael listened in silence as Sir Edward Harland, speaking on behalf of his younger thrusting colleagues, spelled out the *Fenian Ram* situation in suitably pithy prose. After carefully considering his response – and spurning a proffered cigar, due to the filthiness of the smoking habit, which was almost as Satanic as imbibing strong liquor – the flint-eyed bookkeeper succinctly laid out their options. "You could remove Holland from the equation," he observed laconically.

The grandees exchanged glances that were outrageous only in their absence of outrage. That possibility had certainly been entertained in the recent past. Holland was a known associate of unscrupulous Irish assassins and, in the great scheme of things, blood-thirsty wretches who plot against the Empire generally get what's coming to them.

"But that would be a mistake," Carmichael continued with clinical dispatch, "because there are two superior options. One, you could steal the *Fenian Ram* from its moorings. If Holland is a one-man band and if his 'sub' fits into the hold of a steamship and if you create a small diversion, you could whisk the infernal machine from under his nose, analyze it here at your leisure, uncover the technological secrets and, given the superior resources of your world-renowned shipyards, monopolize the market for submarine torpedo boats, as well as sending the *Ram*-less Mr Holland back to the *Clan-na-Gael* drawing board."

The Harland & Wolff quorum was uniformly impressed by Carmichael's adroit analysis and incisive plan of action. Murmurings of assent scampered around the boardroom. Even the manifold oil paintings of Protestant Ascendency noblemen, which filled every wall in the chandeliered, oak-panelled chamber, seemed to concur with the consensus.

"Second, you could follow the foregoing proposal then add an extra component." Archibald Carmichael hesitated momentarily, evidently unsettled by his own train of thought. "If preservation of Belfast's place in the British Empire is your ultimate aim, then you could use the *Fenian Ram* to sink Queen Victoria's flagship when she visits our fair city next year. The *Ram* would then be abandoned and captured by the authorities. *Clan-na-Gael* and their Irish-American henchmen would be held responsible for the assassination of our monarch, and war would almost certainly be declared on the United States, which has encouraged the Fenians for decades, largely because Britain supported the southern states in their late fight against northern oppression. The Confederacy would rise again in revolt, loyal Canadians would invade from the north, the rapidly growing American Empire would be nipped in the bud and the hostilities would be beneficial for the shipyards, engineering plants and munitions manufacturers of Belfast. Indeed, even if the Great British Empire was so affronted by Ireland and the Irish that it cut us loose, the loyal, faithful, true-blue north of Ireland would probably remain exempt."

A stunned silence greeted Carmichael's exposition. So shocked were the industrialists by the grotesqueness of the book-keeper's cold-blooded plan that Pirrie could only mutter, apropos of nothing, "The partition of Ireland? Inconceivable, dear boy!"

The meeting broke up not long after, leaving only Harland and Wolff with their whiskies and sodas and cigars. The fixer and financier sat in companionable silence, puffing and sipping and weighing up possibilities.

"What do you think?" Harland asked.

"She's an old woman," Wolff observed, "sixty-eight at the last count."

"Her diamond jubilee was the pinnacle of a glorious reign," Harland mused. "Impossible to surpass."

"Business is business, Edward."

"Belfast *means* business, Gustav."

Chapter Seven

Erin Go Brown

"What's the verdict?" Simon Magill already knew the answer. He'd been here before. Too many times before. When the Danster took the Englishman under his wing, he made it perfectly clear that the bulk of Simon's scenarios, treatments and digests would be unceremoniously spiked. Ruthless winnowing's the way of the creative world, Dan said.

Knowing that rejection's the norm doesn't make it any easier to handle, though. Brown's continuing refusal to entertain any of Simon's ideas, and his increasingly frequent exhibitions of "artistic temperament", were deeply dispiriting, to say the least.

Biting his lip, Simon Magill waited for the hammer to fall. There was usually a pregnant pause before the inevitable thanks-but-no-thanks.

"Loved it, bro. Your best yet. You even remembered to include the date at the start, like proper thriller writers."

The approbation shot straight over Simon Magill's head, because he immediately started apologizing and prevaricating and pointing out ways in which the "taster" could be improved.

"Simon, Simon, Simon," Dan said, waving his hands in front of the gofer's glazed eyes, trying and failing to get through. "Earth to Simon. Paging Simon Magill."

"Sorry?" Magill murmured, his focus finally reined in. "What was that again?"

"I thought it was great. For the first time, I wanted to continue reading. You might make it as a writer, after all. Compared to some of the stuff that gets published, bro, it's pretty darn good."

If it weren't such a literary cliché, Magill would have pinched himself. He couldn't believe what he was hearing, though he *so* wanted to. Not only was the world's bestselling author endorsing his treatment, but he was giving him marks for style, in addition.

Magill's natural pessimism quickly kicked in, on mental override as always. The maestro's words weren't heartfelt – they couldn't possibly be – they were a consequence of their current circumstances. It had been a good day in Salt Lake City. Everything had gone to plan. The tourist chief was very helpful. More than very helpful, in fact. Unbelievably helpful. Hardly surprising, really, because the business that a Dan Brown book can bring to its host city, à la Paris and Rome, was not to be sneezed at. Their guided tour of the Temple Square complex had obviously stimulated Dan's imagination, as had their side trip to the gigantic LDS genealogy archive in the Wasatch Mountains, overlooking the city. The so-called "secret" documents that their liaison generously supplied were decidedly intriguing too, though Dan didn't seem especially interested. Perhaps he was playing it cool.

All things considered, the Danster was in as good a mood as Magill had ever seen. He'd been testy of late, not least in Paris where he threw strop after strop and kept stalking off to Starbucks, but he was almost back to the old Dan Brown, the guy Simon had hooked up with in the aftermath of their Las Vegas "adventure". Magill sometimes wondered if they'd ever get back to the lazy, light-hearted days of casual code-cracking, playful piphilology and general goofing around. Maybe Dan's new-found amiability was an indicator of things to come, a new stage in their personal/professional relationship. Or maybe it was a result of the Budweisers Brown was downing in Spanky's, a sweaty rock'n'roll club in central Salt Lake City. The place was filling up rapidly. It'd be mayhem when the band came on. The last thing Magill expected to find in Salt Lake City was a lively nightlife. Surely the latter-day saints eschewed coffee and alcohol and, polygamy aside, the pleasures of the flesh. As Simon was quickly discovering, not everyone in Salt Lake City was Mormon, and things had moved on from polygamy a-go-go.

The maestro pulled deeply on his Bud and set the bottle down with a sigh of satisfaction. He wiped his mouth with the back of his hand, in an exaggeratedly manly way – it was that kind of club – then beamed across at his companion. "There's only one problem with it, Brother Magill."

"What's that, Father Brown?" he parried, while dreading the inevitable.

"I can't see how Robert Langdon fits in. Even if we do a Kate Mosse and run the past and present stories in parallel, it'll be a stretch to squeeze Big Bobby into this one. There's not much scope for symbology, either, as far as I can make out."

Amazed that his mentor was missing the obvious, Magill pointed out that *Clan-na-Gael* was a secret society with all the accompanying codewords and handshakes and ciphers and cod-Celtic symbology that were meat and drink to Robert.

Brown looked unconvinced.

"Well... to tell the truth, Dan, I don't see this as a Langdon project. I see it more as a separate franchise set in the nineteenth century, a second string to your literary bow. Just as James Patterson and Iain Banks and Peter Carey and Terry Pratchett and Alexander McCall Smith run several storytelling franchises in tandem, so you could do the same. Maybe."

"Oh yes?" Brown said noncommittally. He gazed idly around the heaving club, a compact space at the best of times, but sure to be a sweatbox when The Crunge, a Led Zeppelin tribute band, started its set. "Convince me, Simon."

Rising to the challenge, Brown's new product development manager made his case. "Retro is big nowadays. Far from being a passing fad at the turn of the millennium, the nostalgia boom shows no sign of stopping. In troubled times, people like to look back to happier days, especially people stranded in middle age. America's population is aging, as are the population profiles of most western nations. Demography demands a retrospective perspective, not least in its literature. There's a whole bunch of retro police procedurals and retro detective stories out there – C. J. Samson's Sheldrake series, Boris Akunin's Fandorin mysteries, Gyles Brandreth's Oscar Wilde collection – but nothing much in the way of retro conspiracy thrillers. Given your facility with historical material, as the Langdon books brilliantly demonstrate, a full-blown Brown franchise seems like a natural step."

"I see."

Having completed his elevator pitch and having salted the story with a necessary dollop of flattery, Magill ordered a couple more brewskis from a passing hostess. Amply tattooed, with a surly, heavy metal attitude, she scowled, scribbled and stomped off towards the bar, bawling their order to a biker chic-bedecked bartender. "Two Buds for the bozos by the door."

"Well, bro," Dan announced, weighing his words carefully. "I think we should focus on the Langdon franchise for the time being. However, I definitely reckon the, er, *Fenian Ram* is worth pursuing at some stage…"

The ambrosial beverages clattered and clinked across Spanky's and landed with a clank and a cuss on their empties-strewn table.

"… it reminds me a little bit of *The Day of the Jackal*, but in an historical setting. I like that."

"In an Irish setting too, Dan."

"*The Day of the Wolfhound*, perhaps?"

"Good one," Magill said unctuously. Obsequious ass-kissing was against his principles, as a rule, but bearing in mind that James Patterson and Tom Clancy and the late great Robert Ludlum wrote their second-string series with co-authors, who were entitled to a sizable slice of the royalties – presumably – a little bit of buttering up might pay big Brown dividends.

"Yeah, an Irish setting has possibilities. I can see that. Perhaps we should check out the place sometime soon. Dublin rather than Belfast, though, since that's more likely to appeal to the Irish-American market."

Magill was tempted to explain that there were far more Americans of Protestant, northern-Irish descent than Catholic, southern-Irish extraction and that Belfast's brutish aura of violence was better suited to thrillers than Dublin's limp-wristed cosmopolitanism. But there was plenty of time for persuasion.

"I'm Irish myself," Brown confessed. "My family's of Scotch-Irish descent. I've been in Belfast before. I spent some time there a few years back in the bad old days when the books weren't selling."

"Oh really."

"It wasn't a happy time, Simon," Brown added. He drew deeply on his brewski. "I love the city's black humour. But Belfast has painful memories for me. Let's stick with Dublin."

End of discussion.

A couple of burly roadies, wearing T-shirts way too small for them, ambled across the empty stage, acting as if they were the stars of the show. "Onetwo. Onetwo," they mumbled imaginatively. The Crunge, if the sound levels were any indication, were a tribute band in ear-splitting amplification as well as head-banging repertoire.

As a momentary miasma of moroseness had descended on the duo's beer-fuelled debrief, it fell to Magill to lighten the mood. "It's a great opportunity, too, for anachronistic *bons mots*."

Brought back to brute reality with a burst of gobbledegook, Brown looked a little lost. He shook his head, as if to dispel the Bud-instilled bewilderment. "Excuse me?"

"Think about it, Dan. The nineteenth century setting gives you lots of opportunities for quips about new technology. Nickelodeons will never catch on! Bicycles are a passing fad! Heavier-than-air flight? Impossible, dear boy! You could include horseless carriage chases at dangerously high speeds…"

"Fifteen miles per hour?"

"Steady on, Dan. I was thinking of ten, myself, though you do like your high-velocity modes of transportation. You speed-freak, you!" Simon did an impersonation of someone struggling with a giant steering wheel. "And then there's the hotties in whalebone stays with bustles and petticoats and pantaloons and attacks of the vapours."

"Wearing scandalous outfits that suggestively swirl…" Brown bit his knuckle for emphasis. "… two inches above the ankle!"

"Stop it, sir! Desist. Forsooth. You rake. You blackguard. You malapert." Magill cooled himself down with an imaginary fan, while fluttering his eyelashes. Perhaps it's as well he refrained from "you gay blade", because Spanky's wasn't that kind of bar, though its moniker could easily be misconstrued.

"I'm lovin' this more and more, bro," Brown laughed. They clinked beer bottles in contractual celebration. "As soon as the next Langdon's taken care of, we'll get on to it."

With the Danster in as serene a disposition as Simon had ever seen, he took the opportunity to broach a hitherto taboo subject. "Whatever happened to *The Solomon Key*, the Langdon novel you were working on after *Da Vinci*? There was a lot of talk about it at one stage. Why did you decide not to publish, Dan? Did it fall below your usual high standard or was there something else going on?"

Grimacing glumly, the multi-millionaire author shot his assistant a sorrowful look that said you're-better-off-not-knowing. Then opened his mouth to reply.

A sudden flurry of activity erupted on-stage. A beefy Bonzo Bonham lookalike took his seat behind the drum kit. A drunken shout went up from the crowd. He did a quick snare roll and cymbal skim of acknowledgement. The bassist, channelling John Paul Jones's legendary anonymity, stood stoically stage left. A replica Jimmy Page and parody Robert Plant, with a wig like a coil of tumbleweed that had been dragged through a thorn hedge backwards, bounded on and launched straight into the stuttering riff of "Black Dog". The noise was excruciating. Even though Zeppelin were his way-favourite rock band, Dan immediately waved his arms in sonic surrender and shouted through the tumult that he was heading for the restroom, then back to the hotel. Simon watched him go, then reluctantly decided to follow suit. Although, at twenty-eight, he wasn't too old to endure brain-bludgeoning rock music, he was loath to entertain the singer's tune-challenged screeches. Exiting the sweaty club, he stood outside for a few minutes waiting for Dan to emerge. Then they started back down Main Street towards the Grand America Hotel, a local landmark. The thoroughfare was impossibly clean, not a cigarette butt in sight, much less discarded Coke cans or mounds of Mormon trash. Nothing besmirched Salt Lake City's immaculate shopping district. A retro-tram chugged past, clanging its bell in the cool of the November night.

Looking uncharacteristically flustered, Dan declined to continue their confessional conversation. He abruptly changed the subject. "Incidentally, Simon, I'm not happy with the title of your treatment. *The Fenian Ram* smacks of odd agricultural pursuits, possibly illegal agricultural pursuits. Couldn't you come up with something better than that, bro?"

"Sorry Dan," Simon laughed. "I'd come to that conclusion myself and I've thought up a cracking alternative."

"I presume it's *Day of the Jackass*."

"I'll have you know, Father Brown," Magill said faux-officiously, "it's much better than that."

"Oh yeah?"

"*The Hunt for Green October*."

Dan stopped dead and looked around balefully. "What did you just say?"

"*The Hunt for Green October*. It's loosely based on Tom Clancy's old technothriller. You know, the submarine showdown shoot-out scenario. Except that it's a retrothriller set in the nineteenth century and includes *Clan-na-Gael*'s plot to assassinate Queen Victoria."

"Did you say Tom Clancy?"

"Yup. Surely you've heard of him, Dan. You of all people! He was the big chief technothriller writer till you came along with *Digital Fortress* and *Deception Point*."

"I. Know. Who. He. Is."

Magill prepared to walk on but Brown grabbed him by the collar and pulled the 6' 4" Englishman down to his own height. "Don't ever mention that fucker's name to me again. If you so much as breathe his name in my presence, you're fucking fired." Dan shoved Simon away and sped off.

Simon was too shocked to follow. In two years, he'd never heard Dan utter a four-letter profanity. Then two in as many sentences. Jesus H. Christ. What the fuck was that all about?

Chapter Eight

Bony Moroni

What just happened? Four hours after the meeting ended, Thomas Trespass was still at a loss. The all-day event had gone well – amazingly well – but the queasy feeling in the pit of his stomach boded ill. Very ill.

Neat, tidy, tall, carrying a few midlife pounds around the midriff, Thomas Trespass made his way to the picture window of his apartment on Fairfax Road. The sight of distant storm clouds sweeping in over the Wasatch, while he watched in comfort from his cosy front room, never failed to ease his worried mind. The view towards central Salt Lake City, where the magnificent Temple Square compound bespoke power and tradition, was the perfect counterpoint. Together, they were the visual balm that reassured him after another fraught day at the Salt Lake Tourist Office.

But not on this occasion. A single shaft of evening sunlight lanced through the storm clouds and caught the gilded statue of Angel Moroni on the topmost spire of the Temple. It was a sign, an unwelcome reminder of his impending meeting with Gideon Devine. The second councillor to the president, Gideon Devine was the most forward-thinking member of the Quorum of the Twelve Apostles and a veteran of the Church Radio, Publicity and Mission Literature Committee. Shrewd, scheming and saturnine, Devine was not a man to cross. Much less disappoint.

The day had gone pretty much to plan. He'd met Dan Brown and his lanky PA at the International Airport. He took them on a tour of the city and its surroundings, as prearranged, though they insisted on one or two stops that hadn't been agreed beforehand. The weather was perfect – cold, sunny, bracing – and, even as a life-long resident of Salt Lake City, he'd never seen the place looking so beautiful. Viewed from the Wasatch, in that crystal-clear light that seared the eyeballs and forced everyone to wear shades and made the place look like a cross between Celebrity City and Hitman Central, the conurbation seemed to hover above the intermontane basin that encircled it. He'd also delivered the "carrot" document to Dan Brown, as instructed. From his reaction to the gift and indeed general demeanour throughout the day, he'd clearly been impressed with the city, the set-up, the arrangements, the honest answers he'd received to what many Mormons would consider impertinent questions.

Yet Thomas Trespass remained uneasy. He feared they were dicing with disaster. Yes, the Dan Brown multiplier effect – the additional tourists that would flood into the city in the wake of his Salt Lake-set novel – would be worth millions to the local economy. Yes, the inevitable movie of the book would generate many millions more, both during production and after its release. Yes, many other cities were competing for the Dan Brown dollar, in an airport thriller equivalent of bidding for the Olympics. And yes, the PR opportunity was simply too prodigious to ignore.

But he wasn't so sure about the rest of the Quorum's rationale. The Twelve Apostles seemed to think that if Dan Brown did his worst, if he gave the LDS a drubbing on the founder's "eternal feminine" failings, and even if he made a meal out of Joseph Smith's manifold extra-marital affairs, their church would still come out on top. His condemnation of Opus Dei in an earlier Langdon novel had only served to increase membership of the organization and helped re-ignite the faith of millions of Roman Catholics worldwide. The LDS would likewise benefit from the public debate, no matter how negative the initial publicity.

In his heart of hearts, Trespass suspected that Gideon Devine and his fellow patriarchs had misjudged the situation. After a day with the Danster, as his stringy sidekick insisted on calling him, he sensed that the man was much less predictable than the Second Councillor imagined. The case for cooperation with Dan Brown – pithily put to him as the 3Cs of commerce, converts, conversation – was compelling at first, but without the fourth C of control, the Quorum was playing with fire and in danger of getting burned. If the imminent debrief didn't go well, Trespass feared, he'd be first in line for the fiery furnace.

Almost time to go. Doubting Thomas freshened up, slipped on a clean white shirt and a black two-piece suit. He then composed himself with a short but heartfelt family prayer alongside his kneeling wife and eight tiny Trespasses. Outside, the sun slid ominously behind the Wasatch ridge, its indigo shadow creeping ever further across the shallow bowl that contained the cleanest, safest city in the United States. Reportedly.

As Thomas Trespass swung his cherry Chevy on to vertiginous Virginia Street, only fifteen minutes and four miles from his meeting with Gideon Devine, he was fifteen years and four thousand miles away, carried back to the bleakest days of his missionary work. A callow nineteen-year-old, he'd naively assumed that south London was a plum place to spend time proselytizing on behalf of the Jesus Christ Church of the Latter-day Saints. The inhabitants of Brixton, however, were very well versed in Mormon matters, especially Brigham Young's notorious invective against black people in general and interracial relations in particular. Two full years of vituperation and abuse were hard to take at the best of times, but when combined with the isolation, the self-abnegation, the renunciation of all fleshly pleasures, LDS missionary work was nothing less than hell on earth.

But this was worse. Trespass felt physically sick as he turned into Crossroads Plaza parking garage, a few blocks from Temple Square. Floodlit, the glorious neo-gothic monument to Mormonism looked like a giant wedding cake, though some unfairly compared it to a Vegas casino circa 1973. Only more kitsch. As directed, he made his way to the basement of the Temple, then to the chilly cubicle where he'd undergone the Endowment ceremony sixteen years before. He felt just as naked as he was that fateful day and feared that the coming indignities would make the groin-grappling he endured during Endowment seem like the kiss of angels' wings.

Perched imperiously on a high-backed wooden seat, Gideon Devine rose to greet his guest. He extended his right hand, fingers splayed. They exchanged the "Sure Nail of the Cross", a secret handshake that guarantees Mormons' admission to Heaven, since God puts new arrivals through the same tactile test. Having performed the requisite formalities, Devine motioned towards the wooden stool opposite and, without further ado, interrogated Trespass on the day's activities. Nervously, the tourist officer explained that the visit had gone pretty much as planned and that the dignitaries appeared impressed by the immaculate city and its exquisite setting, and that he had passed on the "secret" document, as instructed.

"Pretty much?" the patriarch repeated quietly, his widow's peak, conjoined eyebrows and lowering frown giving his sallow features a vampiric aspect. "What do you mean 'pretty much as planned'? Where and why did you deviate from the itinerary?"

"He, um, insisted on going to certain places and I could hardly deny him. Similarly, he expressed interest in certain, ah, unanticipated matters and ignored some of the, erm, salient topics that you – sorry we – were expecting."

"Such as?"

"He asked to go to Brigham Young's Beehive House, showed great interest in the State Seal and demanded we stop off at the UU campus, that infernal den of sodomites."

Deep in thought, Devine steepled both index fingers against his lips while hooking his thumbs under his trenchant chin. "Did he ask to see your underwear?"

"Y-Y-yes. Yes, he did," Trespass stuttered, both embarrassed by the question and by the ridiculous undergarments themselves, which he wore religiously. "Though obviously I refused."

"Fool! You should have stripped. He's working on the Masonic angle. Our holy ritual owes much to the Masons. Joseph Smith was a Freemason, as were many of the Founding Fathers. The symbols on your underwear are Masonic in origin, as is the Sure Nail of the Cross. The Beehive is associated with Freemasonry, hence his interest in the State Seal and Brigham Young's abode. The University of Utah was once called Deseret College, as per the newspaper. Deseret means honeybee, as even *you* must remember from reading the Book of Mormon."

"I'm sorry… I didn't think…"

The second councillor to the president – thus the third most powerful man in the church – dismissed Trespass's apology with a curt wave. "Brown's main character is an expert in symbolism. If he focuses on our symbols we have nothing to fear."

With an enormous sigh of relief, the tourist officer prepared to take his leave of the elder. But was cut off in mid grovel by Devine's brittle enquiry. "What *didn't* he do? You said Brown ignored some anticipated issues. Which ones, Thomas?"

Disconcerted by Devine's use of his Christian name, Trespass couldn't think. "He, ah, he, ah, oh yes, he ah, disregarded gender, strangely. He didn't ask a single question about the, ah, subordination of women."

"Impossible!" the cranky churchman spat. A nonplussed look crossed his sardonic countenance. "Celestial marriage is *certain* to figure in his novel. The eternal feminine is what he is famous for. It's one of his trademarks. He's bound to focus on our founder's alleged promiscuity and the utterly unfounded allegations of child molestation."

Trespass shook his head in sympathetic bewilderment. "I broached the subject with him and he said the eternal feminine was old hat. The gender seam had been exhausted by his second-rate imitators and third rate copy-cats. He accepted the secret document, but I don't think he's particularly interested, to be honest."

"Impossible! The man's obsessed with secret documents. *The Da Vinci Code* is full of them. *Les Dossiers Secrets*, pah!" The church elder couldn't hide his irritation, nor did he try to. With a face like thunderclouds over the Wasatch, he sprang from his "throne" and began muttering all manner of blasphemous imprecations about Brown, imprecations that Trespass pretended not to hear.

Ten minutes later, the tempest passed. The second councillor smiled conspiratorially at his pliable accomplice. If not quite evil incarnate, Gideon Devine was Iago reborn, the imperturbable personification of premeditated unpleasantness. "Where else did Brown go? What else did he talk about, Thomas?"

"Business mainly. Money matters. Tithing. LDS assets. Our real estate portfolio. Media interests. Banking institutions. The alleged links with the Mob in Las Vegas. Joseph Smith's failed financial adventures. He specifically asked to be driven past the Deseret Management Corporation's offices on East South Temple. To get a good look, he said."

Once again, the Machiavellian elder was perplexed by the

unexpected angle of their visitor's inquiries, though he was of course cognizant of the anti-business undercurrent in Brown's books. In today's credit-crunched world, an exposé of LDS business practices might not cover the church in glory, especially if the novelist was looking into the Las Vegas connections. Worse, it might jeopardize the "unveiling ceremony" they'd planned in the aftermath of Brown's gendered revelations. The secret document could be revealed as a forgery at any point of their strategic choosing, thereby crushing the interfering fool like a cockroach.

"I have another task for you, Thomas," he said with an air of cordial intimidation that was almost imperceptible but not quite. "I want you to retrieve the secret document from Dan Brown. Promise him another... a better one instead... one that deals with monetary matters."

"I'll try, though he might not be amenable. I'm seeing them off first thing tomorrow. I'll speak to him then."

"You'll speak to him tonight. You'll get that document back. You'll make sure he agrees to swap." The Second Councillor smiled coldly. "If you know what's good for you, that is."

Trespass gulped audibly. He was sweating into his ritual underwear, despite the chill of the sub-basement cubicle. "Brown's assistant said something about catching a show at Spanky's. I'll try there first."

Gideon Devine frowned at the mention of Spanky's nightcub, a festering sore on the face of the city. "You do that. Don't let me down." With that he rose abruptly and departed the Endowment ceremony cockpit, leaving Trespass alone with his stool.

Revolted by the naked exhibition of power politics, Doubting Thomas struggled to compose himself. Sick to his stomach, he departed the Temple compound, collected his Chevy from the parking garage, and drove seven blocks up State Street, where he found a space close to Spanky's on Main. A sizable crowd, mostly inebriated, was milling around outside and heavily amplified howling emanated from within. He used his tourist office credentials to talk his way past the long-haired, tattoo-covered creature at the box office, if you could call it that. He ventured into the belly of the beast. He covered his ears with his hands, and looked around with distaste. Even if he found the pair of them, there was no way he could converse in this hellish racket, much less request the return of a gift. Brown and his ginger minder were nowhere to be seen, though the tightly packed bodies made it impossible to see anything clearly. Billowing clouds of stinking dry ice didn't help either. He'd go straight to their hotel instead and wait for them to return from their unchristian escapades.

His gorge rising, Trespass dived into the bathroom before departing. He was going to be sick. It was empty, thank goodness. The facility was less than spotless. Gagging, he chose the least objectionable stall. There was a strange scuffling noise behind him, though he had other things on his mind. Four horrid heaves later, he finished and flushed and turned to leave. But that was as far as he got. A razor-sharp blade slashed across his throat and, before it quite registered, he found himself on the floor of the festering cubicle, watching his life ebb away, wondering why someone was waving a Dan Brown book in his face.

Chapter Nine

The Brand That Never Was

Field Marshal Montgomery, the *real* Field Marshal Montgomery, was an arrogant little Ulsterman who believed that he knew best. He was high-handed with his general staff. He infuriated the Allies, one and all. He took credit for others' achievements, most notably Auchinleck, who laid the ground for El-Alamein. He was so busy polishing his reputation for posterity – the Monty brand – that to this day he is revered as a great tactician, when he was anything but.

Abby closed the Wikipedia entry, while wondering whether Call Me Mal was any relation to the chippy Ulster warrior. Probably not, though she suspected that her hateful boss was using the legendary commander as a role model. When she made Michael O'Leary's acquaintance a couple of years back she was struck not only by his vast collection of Winston Churchill biographies, but also by the fact that Ryanair's marketing tactics were so blatantly Churchillian. We shall fight Easyjet for the beach-goers; we shall fight British Airways on the landing charges; never in the field of low-cost airlines have better deals been offered to so many travellers for so few surcharges.

Although she wasn't militarily inclined – what women were? – Abby's Guerrilla Psychology class made her realize that she needed wartime tactics to get the Belfast Brand info out of need-to-know Montgomery. She didn't really *want* the information, but being continually denied access to it only increased her determination to peruse the consultants' recommendations.

As she sipped her first cup of coffee – aesthetics aside, the principal perk of the City Hall job was the office Gaggia – Abby recalled her lecturer's remarks from the night before. When he put up the first PowerPoint slide, "Guerrilla Psychology: The War Years", her heart sank. The prospect of a wasted evening loomed large. But, before long, all thoughts of Christmas shopping fell

71

away as she was swept up into another world. Deception, Abby discovered to her amazement, was not only imperative in many walks of life – without little white lies like love-the-dress, you've-lost-weight, that-colour-suits-you, civil society couldn't function – but it was of paramount importance during wartime. From the infamous Trojan Horse to the doctored WMD evidence behind the invasion of Iraq, deceit has been central to successful military action. At no time was it more necessary than during the Second World War, when Britain stood alone and had nothing to defend itself with except pretence.

The stunts Churchill's wizards came up with! They ranged from everyday decoys like dummy tanks, airfields and artillery – which were bombed to hell in a handcart by the Luftwaffe, thereby wasting precious munitions – to an elaborate ruse involving "the man who never was", a dead body planted with fake D-Day invasion plans who was deposited on a beach in Spain. Better yet were the rumours that the British managed to spread among German troops prior to the mooted invasion of England in 1940. Unfamiliar with amphibious warfare, the stormtroopers were susceptible to suggestions that the British had imported two hundred man-eating sharks from Australia and had released them into the English Channel.

Abby couldn't help laughing at the thought of that. She needed something similar to get the gen on Belfast's top-secret branding plans. Is there a man-eating shark supplier in town, she wondered. Better yet, a PR-man-eating shark supplier?

The telephone rang. Oh. My. God. It was only Spike Holden, a newspaper reporter from the features department of the *Belfast Telegraph*. Field Marshal Montgomery had only gone and arranged the fluffy-bunny profile, even though she'd specifically asked him not to, even though she'd made a point-by-point refutation of his daft idea, since it would undermine her credibility with serious businesspeople. This means war…

"Hi Spike," she said in that cheery PR manner which conveys bosom-buddyness among complete strangers. "What can I do you for?"

"I'm trying to set up an interview. Mal said you'd be game for it."

"Did he?" Abby stonewalled. "Didn't mention it to me, Spike."

"Really," he sympathized, then continued as if nothing were amiss. "Well, obviously we'll do the usual isn't-she-wonderful spiel, with some anodyne stuff on your educational and employment background. But instead of the, yawn, photograph of you sitting at your desk, yawn, we're thinking of snapping you abseiling from the dome of the City Hall."

"I gather abseiling from the dome is forbidden."

"Hmmmm." Abby could hear his wheels grinding. "What about one of those saucy Calendar Girls snaps. Every organization's doing an all-naked spread nowadays."

"You mean like me sitting starkers behind my desk reading the *Belfast Telegraph*, which luckily covers my bits and bobs?"

"Just as well it's a broadsheet, eh Abs? Did you say bobs or boobs? Can I quote you on that?"

"You just blew it, Spike. You had me tempted for a second. By the way, this call is being recorded for training purposes… training and sexual harassment purposes."

Spike laughed uproariously. "Okay, okay, you win. What about you dressed up as Santa Claus, giving presents to homeless children outside the City Hall?"

"Love the sentiment, Spike. It's good to know that the features department has its heart in the right place. Why stop at homeless children, though. What about a couple of cripples?"

"Crippled homeless children. I love it, Abs. If you can rustle up one or two with facial disfigurements, so much the better. Not too disfigured, mind you. Don't want to frighten the readers."

"Blemished rather than deformed, Spike?"

"Exactly! When's best for you, Abs, sometime later this week? I've got a window Friday afternoon."

Taking a leaf from the wartime deception book, Abby closed in for the kill. Knowing that the journo's diary was certain to be chocka around Christmastime, she responded eagerly. "What about this afternoon, Spike? Say 2.00 p.m. It's such a great idea, the sooner we do it the better. I'll get on the phone right now to the council's Home for Ugly Crippled Kids."

"Arrggh, I'm tied up this afternoon. Busy time. You know how it is, Abs. Ummm… let me see."

Now firmly in the interpersonal driving seat, since Spike was the one who couldn't make it, Abby apologized profusely and explained that she was going away for a wee pre-Christmas holiday. Leaving tomorrow. What a shame. She was so looking forward to the interview and photo-shoot. "The New Year, maybe?"

Triumphant, Abby heard him groan and moan as he checked his schedule, to no avail. Churchill's wizards have nothing on Ms Abby Maguire! Now for Field Marshal Montgomery...

"The New Year it is. I'll give you a bell to set things up."

"Okay then, Spike. Lookin' forward to your call. Happy..."

"Before I go, Abs," he interrupted, trying to salvage something from the conversation. "Can you tell me about the Belfast Brand?"

"What about it?"

"Well, I hear the branding sub-committee's due to meet *in camera* this afternoon. Any inside information you can give me? An exclusive on the new strategy? Come on, Abs, throw me a bone."

Abby couldn't believe her ears. The committee is meeting this afternoon? First she'd heard of it. "I'm afraid I'm not at liberty to discuss that," she replied.

"At least give me some idea. Tell you what, I'll read out the shortlist of contenders and you can, ahem, cough whenever I get to the winner. You know the drill, Abs."

"You're familiar with the shortlist?" Abby gasped. So much for hush-hush, need to bloody know.

"Of course. Aren't you?"

Abby didn't like the way this was going. Having outmanoeuvred him over the interview – without resorting to flat rejection, which is a no-no in media relations – she was suddenly on the back foot. Like a shark in the English Channel with a whiff of Nazi blood in its nostrils, the reporter could sense her discomfort.

"You don't know, do you? You're out of the loop! Mad Mal's kept you in the dark, hasn't he? My, my, my. That's *very* interesting."

Flummoxed, Abby was uncertain about her next move. No comment was the obvious rejoinder but no serious corporate communications officer would ever resort to such a feeble statement, one that's reserved for the legal representatives of disgraced politicians or professional footballers caught dogging in the undergrowth. What would Churchill's wizards do? "Yeah, you're right," she quipped. "The old git always plays his cards close to his chest. And you can quote me on that."

"Might just do that, Abs. I can see the headlines now. City Council Communications Cock-up. Belfast Demeans Business. Anyone Know What the Belfast Brand Means? The City Council Doesn't, Either!"

"Very good, Spike. I like it. It would be a shame to cancel our interview, though, especially if the disappointed disfigured kids write letters of complaint to your editor, despite their dyslexia and learning difficulties. Anyway, I thought you were in features, Spike. Feature writers don't get credit for ferreting out exclusives."

Nine weeks in harness and she was playing hardball with the best of them. "Okay, Abs, you win. The interview it is."

"Glad we reached a mutually satisfactory arrangement."

"Later this week with the Calendar Girls pose. Wasn't that it?"

"Don't push your luck, Spike."

"Abseiling?"

"And disappoint all the little kids like that? Surely the *Telegraph* wouldn't want that on its conscience, especially if rival newspapers found out."

"Crippled kids it is. I'll call to confirm."

That went well, Abby groaned, as she replaced the receiver. She checked the time. There was still no sign of his nibs, her boss, the lazy so-and-so. Sorely in need of a nibble, since she'd skipped breakfast for an early morning sculling session, Abby slipped on her Jaeger overcoat, slung the Gucci Babouska over her left shoulder, took her leave of the City Hall, and shimmied across Donegall Square to Apartment, a fashionable bistro-cum-bar with an unparalleled view over the Continental Market and Garden of Remembrance. She ordered a small skinny latte and a low-fat blueberry muffin and tried to make sense of what had just happened.

Idly fiddling with her black rose brooch, as she was inclined to do when deep in thought, Abby sipped and munched and mulled over the options. Churchill's wizards' success, she'd discovered the previous night, was based on mixing gobbets of truth with the deceptions they practised. Big lies grew best when seeded with grains of truth. The credibility of ostensibly German radio stations, set up to broadcast British propaganda to the Fatherland, was established by describing Churchill as "a flat-footed bastard of a drunken old Jew". The CIA camouflaged its catalogue of post-war disasters – from the Bay of Pigs debacle to the Iran-Contra catastrophe – by interlarding little bits of truth with big dollops of deception. Or so their lecturer claimed, though he might have been deceiving them...

The solution was obvious, Abby realized. She'd tell Mad Mal the truth. She'd explain that Spike Holden called first thing. He made cunning enquiries about the Belfast Brand strategy. She'd told him she didn't know and, even if she did, she couldn't say. The scheming sod then threatened them with lurid "Need to know" headlines. However she had talked him out of it by agreeing to an exclusive interview, even though it'd interrupt her holiday plans. Not only would she have told the truth and shown loyalty to her boss, but Montgomery'd be reciprocally obliged to fill her in on the branding strategy.

This wasn't quite how Abby hoped to winkle the brand plan out of Call Me Mal. But an ability to improvise was the hallmark of a guerrilla psychologist.

Sated, Abby finished her muffin and left a hefty tip. The snow was starting to fall as she scurried across Donegall Square, dodging the buses and side-stepping through the crowds, grateful for the temporary shelter they provided as a cold west wind scoured down Bedford Street, driving the snowflakes straight into her face, adhering to the front of her coat. Even though it was less than one hundred yards to the sanctuary of the City Hall, it was Abby the Snowman who shuffled through the double doors, stomping and flapping and shaking her uncovered head, while the security guard looked on, laughing.

Still flapping, she walked into her office, only to see the Deputy Lord Mayor sitting in her seat.

"Ah, there you are," the council's second-in-command said testily. "Nice to know someone's holding the fort." He slowly moved her computer mouse around, scrutinizing the flat screen display carefully. "Even better to see that computer security is taken so seriously by our Integrated Communications Unit."

Damn! "I've been here since 8.30, councillor. I just nipped out for a quick coffee break."

"Well," he said, looking pointedly at the expensive coffee-maker in the corner, "I hope you're feeling energized, Ms Maguire, because you're on at 2.00 p.m."

"What do you mean, on at 2.00 p.m.?"

"The sub-committee meeting about the Belfast brand. We're looking forward to hearing your analysis of the alternatives and listening to your recommendations concerning the best way forward."

"But Mal. Sorry. But Mr Montgomery is leading that discussion."

"Mal's in hospital. He had a heart attack this morning. Lucky he has such an able deputy."

Chapter Ten

The Classic Comedy Collective

W. C. Fields was feeling grumpy. Grumpy with a small "g". He used to be grumpy with a big "G" when he worked at Disneyland as part of the Snow White Tribute Troupe. Those days were long gone. Today, he bore the look of a dyspeptic dipsomaniac whose secret hoard of bootleg hooch's been discovered by a Prohibition Officer. Then emptied down a drain. "My little chickadee," he griped, prior to taking his tip-up seat, "do we really have to do this? It's not a good idea."

"Goodness has nothing to do with it," Mae West purred in her best *femme fatale*, as she settled one seat away from him. "If we don't freshen up the show, WC, it will be goodnight Vienna."

"This ain't Vienna, sister," Fields growled. "It isn't even Philadelphia. And don't call me WC." The sun was out, the sky was blue, the birds were twittering in the branches. But Fields was in no mood for Twittering birds. He didn't like sparrows with cellphones. "This could damage our cover," he grumbled. "Our cover comes first."

"The show *is* our cover," Mae West hissed. "Unless people come up and see it sometime, our cover is over." Sensing resistance, she changed the subject. "WC means bathroom in Britain. Everybody knows W. C. Fields was British. We should use it as a running gag."

Fields bristled. "And what proportion of our box office are Brits? Zilch. Zero. Zip. If that's the best you can come up with, sister, no wonder audiences are down."

"Is that a ticket stub in your pocket, WC, or just a tiny penis?"

"And you, my dear, are as pure as the driven sulphur dioxide."

That was it. A zinger too far. Mae West balled her mitts to knuckle-sandwich the nincompoop. This was one sucker who was getting an even break, plus a compound fracture or two of the proboscis. Though it'd be hard to spot the difference.

If it weren't for the shuffling arrival of Charlie Chaplin, the peevish bank dick and the irascible inflatable lifejacket would've been at it hammer and tongs. Immaculately dressed in his Little Tramp outfit, he sat between the warring factions, twiddling his toothbrush moustache in that trademark manner. "First," he shouted, clapping his hands for silence and action.

The audition commenced.

A lanky, long-haired figure ambled on stage, looking for all the world like a laid-back hippie throwback. He paused to take in the open-top auditorium, a five-hundred seater or so, then focused on his audience of three. "There are some people," he said, "who aren't into words. There are some people who would rather you didn't use certain words. Yeah, there are 400,000 words in the English language and there are seven of them you can't say on television. You know the seven, don't you? Shit, Piss, Fuck, Cunt, Cocksucker, Motherfucker and Tits."

"Oh, oh," Charlie Chaplin stage-whispered to his co-stars on either side. "Not exactly what the Classic Comedy Collective's looking for."

"Give the guy a chance," Mae West cooed coquettishly. "I like George Carlin."

The Carlin clone continued, running smoothly through the legendary Seven Words routine. "Shit, Piss, Fuck, Cunt, Cock-sucker, Motherfucker and Tits. Wow," he intoned, "Tits doesn't seem to belong on the list, you know. It's such a friendly sound-ing word. It sounds like a nickname. Hey, Tits, come here. Tits, meet Toots. Toots, Tits. Tits, Toots. It sounds like a snack, doesn't it? New Nabisco Tits…"

The routine rolled on for the full seven minutes. "Give the guy his due," West said, as Carlin-lite concluded on the unforget-table line: You can prick your finger but don't finger your prick. "He was word perfect on Seven Words."

W. C. Fields cut across her. "Tell me something, George," he snarled up at the Carlin-alike, who was still standing centre stage. "What do you hear?"

The feedback wasn't quite what the comedian expected. He

looked a little lost, then attempted a one-liner. "You're hired, would be nice." The silence said it all. Thrown, he tried again. "Um... a train whistle. Some shouting in the distance. Is that an oompah-oompah band? Animal noises from the petting zoo. Oh, and I think I heard a roller-coaster during my set... I'm not sure, I was concentrating." He smiled self-consciously behind a curtain of lank hair extensions.

"What you hear," Fields went on icily, "is the sound of American children enjoying themselves, with their protective parents in tow. Do you really think we'd include an act that incorporates such profanities? Are you out of your fucking mind?"

"That's rich coming from you," Carlin retorted, holding his ground. "I thought W. C. Fields hated children. What's that legendary line of yours? Children should neither be seen nor heard from – ever again."

Fields corrected the misquotation then continued his harangue of the hapless tribute act. "You might be able to say Shit, Piss, Fuck and Tits on television these days, and get away with Motherfucker and Cocksucker in the movies. But you can't say them during a stage show at a theme park, you cunt!"

Grinning goofily, Carlin was untroubled by the tirade, which was pretty much par for the course at auditions where the supply of acts vastly exceeded the demand. "No problem, I can do Bob Newhart too." He launched straight into his deadpan Newhart patter, complete with trademark stutters and tics. "I don't like country music but I don't intend to denigrate those who do. And for the people who like country music, denigrate means 'put down'."

"Sorry, George," Charlie Chaplin piped up. "Most of the visitors to this vacation attraction are aficionados of country music. Aficionados means fans."

"Next!" W. C. Fields roared. A moon-faced bejeaned loafer mooched on stage as Carlin/Newhart stalked off. The troika of comedy titans looked at each other, wondering who this was supposed to be. Moon-face pulled out a cigarette, lit up and let fly. "If anyone here is in advertising or marketing, kill yourself. Just a little thought. There's no rationalization for what you do. You are Satan's little helpers. You are Satan's spawn filling the world with bile and garbage. You are fucked and you are killing us. Kill yourself…"

Fields's face was puce with indignation. "Tell us who you're supposed to be!" Equally unenlightened, Charlie Chaplin checked the master list, informed his colleagues that it was Bill Hicks, whoever he was, then suggested that maybe Bill was big in Britain. Fields looked fit to be tied.

Moon-face rampaged on regardless, determined to get as much of his routine in as possible, before the metaphorical hook of rejection scooped him off stage. "I know what all the marketing people are thinking right now. Oh, you know what Bill's doing? He's going for that anti-marketing dollar. That's a good market, he's very smart. Oh man, I am not doing that, you fucking *evil* scumbags! Ooh, you know what Bill's doing now? He's going for the righteous indignation dollar. That's a big dollar. We've done research – huge market. Goddamn it, I am *not* doing that, you fucking *scumbags!*"

Bringing up the mighty marketing dollar wasn't bogus Bill Hicks's best move. Aside from the impermissible profanities, drawing the audience's attention to the hefty entrance fee they'd paid earlier – to say nothing of the dollar-hoovering devices that lay in wait for them throughout the theme park – wasn't what West, Fields and Chaplin wanted to hear. "Next!" they shouted in unison.

A tiny African-American with a Zapata moustache and an extravagant Afro – the kind of hairdo that hadn't been seen since the days when Starsky and Hutch were shagging Shaft – bounced on stage, and hit it big-time. Nigga this. Nigga that. Mutherfuckin nigga the other. The threesome had forgotten how edgy Richard Pryor was in his prime; far, far too edgy for their family-friendly cavalcade of comedy. In fact, just about every comedy tribute act that beautiful, blue-skied, early December morning was unacceptable. Chris Rock, Eddie Murphy, Sarah Silverman, Rita Rudner, Ellen DeGeneres, Beavis & Butt-head and dozens of others drifted across the stage only to receive a "Next" for their efforts. There was a Steve Martin lookalike, who was neither wild nor crazy. There was a Jack Benny cardboard cut-out who couldn't tell the difference between pregnant pauses and narcoleptic catatonia. There was a pitiful troupe of Monty Python lumberjacks whose dead parrot sketch was DoA. There was a copycat Robin Williams who had the original's coke-fuelled, crack-filled, amphetamine-rushed routine off pat. Too pat.

Only one of the wannabes passed muster, a lumbering lug of a Canuck who performed a John Candy soliloquy from *Trains, Planes and Automobiles*. It wasn't particularly funny. It wasn't funny at all. It was tear-jerking, heart-breaking, lump-in-the-throat stuff, if truth be told. However, the routine was performed with such conviction that it stood out from the rest, which may have been word perfect but lacked an all-important ingredient called soul. "There's our Oliver Hardy," W. C. Fields murmured to his comedic confreres. "Mr Chaplin, do you think you can handle Stan Laurel?"

One act was scant reward for a full day's auditions. Fields was getting testy now that the sun was over the yardarm, which it always was somewhere or other, according to the classic comic's calculations. The final act shimmied on stage. It was a Marilyn Monroe mimic, wearing the skin-tight, Swarovski crystal dress from "Happy Birthday Dear President". She went into a stunning boop-boop-be-do sequence of "I Wanna Be Loved By You", "Diamonds Are a Girl's Best Friend", "Running Wild" and several similar sex-kitten classics. Both Fields and Chaplin were on their feet at the end, applauding loudly. Mae West demurred. A muted argument broke out among the principals. Hissed accusations of petty jealousy and middle-aged adolescent arousal were exchanged. Ms Monroe was told that they'd get back to her. She removed the blonde wig with a flourish, bowed deeply and revealed a waterfall of rich red curls. "Lucille Ball, lookin at'cha," Fields sighed. "Ginger Rogers," Chaplin added; "I can do a passable Fred Astaire."

Mae West wouldn't budge. "This is a classic *comedy* collective, in case you guys hadn't noticed." They were still arguing backstage, where Fields cracked open a bottle of oak-barrel bourbon and passed well-filled tumblers of harmony replacement therapy to his co-stars.

The communal dressing room of the Globe Theatre was big, bright and beautifully appointed. But not with the usual array of costume racks, hothouse flowers, brimming fruit bowls, naked bulb-fringed mirrors and you-were-wonderful-darling syco-phants, four hangers-on for every principal. On the contrary, it was fitted with humming workstations, flickering monitors, whirring colour printers, wall-mounted display screens and ye olde fax machines that looked like something out of the IT ark. There wasn't a sycophant in sight. They already knew they were wonderful, darling.

Schnozzle aglow, W. C. Fields rapped the top of the Xerox machine with his empty tumbler, assuming command of a bus-tling backstage operation where interpersonal equality no longer prevailed. "Right, let's get down to business. Have you read the latest bulletin from Big C? I forwarded it earlier."

"Yes indeedy," Chaplin chirruped. The ordinarily taciturn Chinese-American, whose Little Tramp was by far their biggest crowd-puller, was ready for the fray.

Fields peered impassively at Mae West. "Make it so."

His statuesque African-American co-star, whose quip-filled act was out of this world, nodded her hesitant assent.

"What about the other matter, Charlie?"

The little man's moustache wiggled wanly. "I can only do one thing at a time. Unless you want to cut back on my performances..."

"Once Hardy and Monroe are on board," Fields announced, "we should have more time to spare." He glowered at West, daring her to dissent.

"It's almost showtime," his little chickadee warbled, with the merest hint of distaste.

"In more ways than one," Fields affirmed.

Chapter Eleven

Barnum Brown, Dinosaur Detective

7 June 1907

Bleak and intimidating, the badlands of south-east Wyoming rose before them in rolling waves of adversity. Only the foolhardy ventured into this butte-buttressed territory without good reason and only the intrepid survived. But bone hunters were a special breed. No canyon walls were too steep, no boulder fields too rocky, no scree slopes too slippery, no mudslides or flash floods or swollen river crossings were too intimidating, perish the thought. Nothing was allowed to stand between bone men and a Brontosaurus or a Stegosaurus or a Triceratops or an Iguanodon or the veritable king of the dinosaurs, a Tyrannosaurus-rex. The swarms of mosquitoes made life difficult, the rattlesnakes were always ready and willing to strike, the grey wolves circled menacingly at the edge of the campsites, the mountain lions were out there somewhere, biding their time, weighing their prospects, licking their lips. Then there was the ever-present threat of a break-out from the reservations, rampaging war parties of Sioux or Shoshones, who slaughtered settlers without mercy. Barnum Brown didn't blame them. Their treaties had been torn up by greedy white folks and unscrupulous politicians back east, their land had been overrun before their very eyes – fenced, farmed, filled with flat-board townships, full of floozies and firewater – and their most sacred places had been desecrated by pyrite prospectors, whose furious mine workings and mounds of spoil were scars on the spirit-, ghost- and forefather-filled landscape.

Dinosaur hunters made a mess too. That was different, though. Their expeditions and excavations and dynamiting and diggings were in the name of science, betterment, the growth of knowledge. The natives' belief that dinosaur bones were the last vestiges of their ancestors – giants who walked the earth when the world was young – was demonstrably absurd. Preposterous, in point of fact. It could thus be ignored in the never-ending quest for intellectual enlightenment and the attendant march of progress. The canyons around Como Bluff contained the greatest concentration of dinosaur bones on the North American continent, possibly the world. It would be criminal to leave them be.

Brown chucked the reins. The roans moved forward, pulling the equipment-laden wagon effortlessly. The going was good along the pine-topped ridge, though the descent into the thickly wooded valley floor was steep and treacherous. Most members of the expedition walked behind, casually shooting at deer for the dinner pot, observing the wildlife like good naturalists do, or simply drinking in the clear, fresh, cedar-scented air that prevailed several thousand feet above sea level. This was God's own country, albeit a vengeful god's own country.

They set up camp in a clearing beside a rushing stream of ice cold water and enjoyed a hearty supper of boiled potatoes, fried rice, corned beef hash, canned mutton stewed with onions, followed by flapjacks swimming in syrup. Ample appetites sated, they quaffed coffee round a sweet-smelling fire of cottonwood logs – the dryness of the mountain valley climate meant that they burned particularly brightly – while Barnum Brown regaled his frisky party of student palaeontologists with horror stories of Como Bluff. When the dinosaur bone fields were first discovered, way back in the early 1870s, the two greatest palaeontologists in the country fought over the fossils. Deadly rivals Edward Drinker Cope and Othniel Charles Marsh ransacked the deposits in a mad competitive rush to collect and claim and catalogue and classify the incredible finds that the precipitous canyons contained. Formerly fast friends, Cope and Marsh weren't so much dinosaur hunters as glory hunters. Their unrelenting feud was the bitterest in the entire history of science, which has never been short of flint-eyed rivalries. So frantic was the adversaries' excavation of anything and everything – all of which was shipped back to their antagonistic institutions – that some of the rivals' finds remain un-catalogued more than thirty years after the Bone Wars. To this very day, they sit undisturbed in dusty crates in dark corners of the Academy of Natural Sciences in Philadelphia and the Peabody Museum at Yale.

"The Como Bluff dinosaur deposits," Brown reported to his rapt audience, eager faces ruddy in the firelight, "were damaged irreparably by Cope and Marsh's unconscionable activities, activities that were close to criminal."

"But didn't their duel draw attention to dinosaurs and palaeontology generally?" The speaker was a wispy-bearded, cowboy-hatted, blue-jeans-wearing sophomore student, whose personal trust fund was doubtless bigger than New York University's entire endowment. "Didn't their intellectual fisticuffs attract more responsible scientists into the field?"

"You mean people like you, Mr Astor?" The circle laughed as one. A combustible mixture of nerves and excitement, the students sat on the cusp of their first day proper on an actual dinosaur dig led by the foremost palaeontologist on earth. "Scientific competition is a good thing, Astor, providing it is conducted in a gentlemanly fashion. Cope and Marsh's embittered feud led inevitably to muddled thinking, hasty conclusions, precipitate publication, falsification of evidence, public denigration of the other's work, unedifying exchanges in the gutter press and, ultimately, attempts to sabotage each other's excavations. Cope actually unearthed a T-rex skeleton, though he failed to recognize it in his unseemly rush into print."

"Lucky for you, Professor Brown."

"Lucky for me, Astor." Brown couldn't help grinning at the thought of his own good fortune. The ruinous rivalry of his data-diddling, findings-fudging predecessors had provided an opportunity for professional advancement that he'd seized with both hands. "Lucky for all of us, perhaps, as we'll see tomorrow."

The morning was chill. Rain had fallen overnight, soaking the groundsheets of the open-air slumberers. But the damp didn't dampen the students' spirits, as they breakfasted hurriedly on sausage and beans and bread and butter. They were on a mission. They were crusaders for science. They were palaeontological evangelists, martyrs for Megalosaurus.

Well rested after his night in the tent, Barnum Brown divided up the party, issuing strict instructions to the neophyte bone hunters. Half of the six-man party walked one side of the slope – each participant appropriately positioned at top, middle and canyon bottom respectively – while the remainder did likewise on the opposite slope. Together, the human chain moved slowly up the valley, ensuring that all the ground was scrutinized for fossils. Everyone knew what to look for, though discussing geological layers in class was vastly different from identifying fossil beds in reality. Still, they were an observant bunch and this area was so rich in dino-plunder that even Blind Pew could find a femur or four.

The trouble started mid-morning. Unseasonal rain was falling steadily, hampering the students' progress. When he first heard the tremulous shout, Brown assumed that someone had either slipped and fallen – a broken leg was no laughing matter, not when it was many miles to the nearest medic – or that a Brown Bear, or some such wild creature, had emerged from the foliage and frightened the silly city boys. It was likely more scared of them than they of it. "Come quickly. Come quickly," Orville Astor called out. He rushed into camp, his aristocratic face flushed with excitement.

"Calm down, Astor," Brown said, reluctantly setting aside his pile of paperwork. If nothing else, student expeditions provided ample opportunity to catch up with professional pursuits. While the youngsters scampered around the hillsides, working themselves into a fossil-hunting frenzy, expedition leaders could write to their hearts' content, free from the administrative demands that dominated life on campus, back east. Well, they could if it weren't for the incessant interruptions…

"I've discovered a hominid. I think it's a hominid. Come and see. Come and see." He was practically tugging on his professor's shirtsleeve. Astor ran off into the cedars, then rushed back to see what was keeping the old timer. "Quickly, sir. Come quickly!"

Barnum Brown was in no rush. Hominid skeletons in dinosaur beds were not only inconceivable but completely impossible in scientific terms, since one was extinct for millennia before the other appeared on the scene, barely able to stand upright. With the naivety of youth, however, Astor assumed that he'd made a discovery of monumental significance, perhaps the greatest palaeontological discovery of the decade. Of all time, dagnabit. Hominids and dinosaurs together. Humph. He'd been reading *The Lost World* or some such penny dreadful a tad too assiduously.

Astor's discovery *was* of monumental significance, though not in the way he'd anticipated. As Brown looked at the human skeleton, half-covered by rock chippings, and coprolites and bleached bright white in the dry mountain air, he sensed immediately what had happened. He picked up the gleaming skull and turned it around in his hands, like Hamlet, Prince of Dinosaurs. The back of the cranium had been staved in, as if hit repeatedly by a pick or a shovel. "This man was murdered," he said to the surrounding crowd of students, all shocked, all taken aback, all of whom had abandoned their duties, all of whom were anxious to high-tail it back to what passed for civilization.

"The rivalry between Cope and Marsh was much worse than we thought."

Chapter Twelve

Tie Me Kangaroo Down, Brown

"What's a coprolite?" Brown asked, looking up from his Samsung netbook with a surly expression. "Remind me, *bro*."

"It's a fossil," Magill replied, disappointed that Dan had interrupted his reading of the taster to query the vocabulary. That didn't bode well. Another strike-out in prospect, dammit.

With an irritable tug of his baseball cap – a tug that said "I can tell it's a fossil from the context, you klutz" – Dan repeated the question in a disgruntled manner. "What kind of fossil is a coprolite? It's not that dinosaur dung, is it?"

"Fossilized faecal material is extremely important scientifically," Magill objected, attempting to seize the intellectual high ground. "It contains a record of the diet, constitution and indeed the environment of the creature responsible. The so-called Lloyd's Bank deposit in York reveals that the Viking warrior who, er, extruded the ten-inch, um, artefact was riddled with tape worms and suffered from TB."

"Hold the fort," Brown barked, his eyes red-rimmed, almost incandescent. The fiery look owed much to a 20-hour flight to Sydney, which even the sybaritic service of the first-class cabin couldn't quite erase. But the great man's bloodshot glare was still unpleasant to behold, let alone apprehend from the receiving end. "Are you seriously suggesting that Robert Langdon, professor of symbology at Harvard University, should stick his aquiline nose into dinosaur poop? This is complete and utter shit, Simon." He snapped shut the netbook with a peevish click.

"Fossilized shit, I think you'll find," Magill said, trying to make a feeble joke of it. "The world's foremost collection of coprolites is held at Yale. So what's your Harvardian's problem?"

"Yalies," Brown sniffed, scratching his neck absent-mindedly. "Why does that not surprise me?"

"And anyway," Magill continued diplomatically, "we can drop the droppings. They're not important."

Dan rose from the sofa in the Intercontinental Hotel's sumptuous reception area and adjusted his rumpled tweed jacket, ready for the off. "Oh, they are if your surname's Brown and critics consider your books to be crap, with a turd on top."

"I never thought of that," Magill said bashfully, while struggling to unfold his long legs from under the imprisoning leather armchair. "Actually, I wasn't thinking of it as a Langdon novel," he went on. "The adolescent market is wide open, Dan, now that Harry Potter has finished. Little boys of all ages love dinosaurs. They adore Victorian gentlemen adventurers. They lap up tales of derring-do in the Wild West. Abandoned silver mines, swirling snow storms, herds of stampeding bison, packs of ravening wolves, flooded rivers that are impossible to cross, deadly rivalry between ruthless desperadoes…"

"So you see Barnum Brown as a teenage franchise?"

"Precisely," Magill enthused, looking down on his red-eyed and floppy-tailed superior. "The beauty of it is that Barnum Brown really existed. That's his real name. He discovered the T-rex. He dug up dinosaurs in India, China, Canada and, get this, a place called Hell Canyon in Montana. He was a spy in the First World War, for goodness' sake. He got involved in industrial espionage on behalf of big oil companies. He's a gold mine, Dan."

The literary lion lost the rag. "He's a fool's gold mine, you mean! He's a doltish distraction, a crapulous confection of pathetic pulp fiction clichés." Dan was on an alliterative roll. "What did I tell you, Simon? What did I specifically say to you?"

Magill pursed his lips, refusing to respond to his employer's ferocious onslaught. Go ahead, Dan, get it off your chest. I know you're tired and crotchety. I felt the same way when I got here, three days ago.

"I told you to focus on the Langdon franchise. I told you our top priority was a sequel to *Da Vinci*. I told you to come up with Langdon treatments not potential franchises for the dim and distant future. Focus, Simon. That's your problem. You never focus."

Spitting with rage, Brown vented his spleen for a full five minutes, ignoring the embarrassed stares of passing hotel guests inadvertently exposed to the toxic sonic spill-over. When the tiny typhoon had almost blown itself out, Simon suggested they repair to a nearby Starbucks.

The magic word had a soothing effect on the ranting writer. "Someone said there are no Starbucks in Australia."

"I found one," Magill said. "It's less than five minutes' walk from here."

As they sat slurping in the Queen Victoria Centre, a former fish market that had been adroitly converted into a four-storey wonderland of designer boutiques, upmarket souvenir stalls and expensively decorated restaurants of dubious culinary merit, Simon outlined his latest thinking on the long-awaited sequel. Vittoria Vetra, last seen tending manta rays in the aftermath of *Angels and Demons*, has taken up a post at the Sydney Aquarium. While diving off the Great Barrier Reef, she hears stories of shipwrecks dating back to the Second World War. Rumours abound that they are German vessels stuffed with secret weapons en route to Antarctica...

"This is all documented," Simon insisted, when the latte-tranquillized tyrant raised a sceptical eyebrow. "Anyway," he went on, "Vittoria dives to the sunken wreck, wrestles with a great white along the way, discovers indecipherable religious relics in the hold and calls her friendly neighbourhood symbologist, Big Bobby Lang..."

"What religious relics?" Brown interrupted.

Magill hadn't thought of that, since conspiracy-related objects were Dan's speciality. His job was to propose the basic outline. If it tickled the master's fancy, the master would take things from there. But he obviously wanted an answer. "I'm not sure," Simon confessed, then took an educated guess. "The Spear of Destiny, maybe. It's right up there with the Holy Grail and Veronica's Veil, isn't it? Doesn't it have special powers of some kind...?" Magill's prattle petered out under Dan's indignant stare. He looked as though he'd eaten a bran muffin with senna pods sprinkled on top and was about to participate in a Lloyd's Bank coprolite-laying competition.

"No Spear of Destiny," he scowled. "Forget the freakin' Spear of Destiny!"

Well used to Dan's artefactual obsessions, Magill let the comment pass. He decided not to make a case for the Spear's obvious "masculinity", which would complement the "femininity" of Langdon's previous escapade. That was Dan's job. His task was to pitch ideas, tasters, treatments and simply plant the acorns from which a mighty Langdon oak would one day emerge.

Smiling grimly, Simon suggested that they move on to the first location. The site of a possible chase sequence, he'd scouted it out earlier. The Danster agreed. Commenting idly on the ubiquitous Christmas decorations, which were somewhat incongruous in the summer sunshine of the southern hemisphere, the discombobulated visitors exited the grandiose shopping mall and strolled down the hill to Darling Harbour, a glittering cove surrounded by restaurants, bars, hotels, Imax movie theatres and analogous tourist traps. The Aquarium was one of the Harbour's most popular attractions, understandably so. It comprised a catacomb of Plexiglas fish tanks, where awe-struck visitors watched schools of sharks, stingrays, snappers, sea serpents and assorted marine animals of savage mien circle lazily overhead, well within easy chomping distance.

The Danster was transfixed. Not simply by the exhibition itself – the penguin pen proved particularly appealing – but by the thrilling possibilities it triggered in his mind's eye.

"I see a shoot-out of some kind," Simon said.

"Then the glass breaks," Brown enthused, "thousands of tons of seawater filled with ferocious, thrashing, snapping creatures cascades everywhere, covering everything and everyone."

The maestro's juices were flowing. Simon could sense it. Dan could sense it too. But the euphoria of their breakthrough was brought to a sudden halt by an onlooker, a nosy parker who'd been listening in on their excited conversation. Unlike most Australians, who are renowned for their decorum, tact, reticence and natural reserve, this particular specimen butted in without a by your leave. "Sounds like *Mission Impossible* to me, mate. Didn't a fishtank explode in that un?"

Belittled by a Bruce, Simon had never seen Dan deflate so fast. It wasn't just that the bubble of inspiration had been popped so brutally, or so publicly, since several of the other onlookers laughed and nodded agreement with the loudmouth, but that he spent the next ten minutes picking at the scabs of scenarios past. As they tramped across the monorail-bearing pedestrian bridge that crossed Darling Harbour, en route to the next port of call, Dan launched into a brutal deconstruction of the KKK treatment. *O Brother, Where Art Thou*, wasn't it? He then turned savagely on the Victorian retrothriller, accusing his plot-plotter of plagiarizing *The Day of the Jackal*, even though that was part of its appeal at the time. Fortunately, perhaps, Simon couldn't hear the details of his employer's tirade. They got separated in the swarming crowds on the bridge. By the time Magill caught up with the Danster, he was complaining that Barnum Brown was Jack London lite. *Crock of the Wild*, he called it.

There was no talking to him, especially during a squall of the wild, so Simon steered him towards the Maritime Museum, which sat in splendid isolation at the cusp of the cove, its architecture evoking sail-filled schooners of days gone by. Three historic vessels were moored alongside this magnificent monument to Australia's seafaring heritage: Captain Cook's *Endeavour*; a wartime destroyer, HMAS *Vampire*; and the *Onslow*, a cadaverous Cold War submarine. Magill envisaged a chase sequence where rampant Robert Langdon and sultry Vittoria Vetra were pursued by very bad guys, the usual Brownian assortment of malformed assassins, religious zealots and renegade researchers with "possums on the roof" (as some call crazies in Oz). Simon pitched for all he was worth but Brown wasn't biting. He carped about the low ceilings and cramped quarters on *Endeavour*, since Robert wasn't partial to confined spaces. He pooh-poohed the destroyer, since he'd already done the navy in *Deception Point*. He flatly refused to board the submarine, though he eventually relented after a delicious plate of Sydney scallops at the Museum's quayside restaurant, plus a glass or three of Hunter Valley Pinot Grigio. It wasn't a patch on E & J Gallo's finest Californian chardonnay, but it wasn't unpleasant either, Dan said.

The submarine tour was going quite well until they reached the Operations Room, where a board game with counters was set out on the old ops table. It was probably intended as a bit of fun. It may even have been what submariners played during down time at sea. But the sight of the Hunt for Red October board game sent Brown absolutely ballistic. Scratching his neck like a madman, he cursed his assistant up and down in language that only the saltiest of salty sea dogs could comprehend.

Simon Magill had had enough. "Listen to me, you little shit," he retorted angrily. "Stop blaming *me* for your creative shortcomings. I'm not the cause of your bloody writer's block. *You're* your problem. Stop making excuses for the absence of sequels. Oh, there's a movie to make, Mr Magill. Oh, there's a screenplay I must check, Simon. Oh, I need to do more research before putting pen to paper, *bro.*" Magill had already gone way too far and should have stopped right then and there. But he'd put up with the tantrums caused by Brown's procrastination and he ploughed on past the point of no PA return. "You've choked. You're history. You don't have another novel in you. You're a busted literary flush!"

The Danster looked distraught. Home truths are never pleasant, but being told home truths in the cramped hull of a submarine, several thousand miles from home by a person you'd not only nurtured but taken under your professional wing was very hard to take. Without a word, Brown turned and walked away, climbing up the clanging stepladder to the submarine's superstructure, a couple of decks above.

Although it had been good to get everything off his chest – responding in kind was refreshing in its way – Magill instantly regretted his intemperate remarks and the lack of gratitude he'd shown to the world-renowned novelist who'd treated him like an equal, by and large.

There was no sign of Dan when Simon emerged topside. At a loss now the Vittoria Vetra scenario was kaput, he spent the rest of the day moping around Sydney's magnificent tourist attractions. He took in the Opera House, the Harbour Bridge and Hyde Park Barracks, where he found that one of the first fleeters – the convicts transported to Van Diemen's Land when it became a penal colony – was called Dan Brown! He made a note of the serendipitous nugget, with a view to making it his peace offering.

There was still no sign of Simon's patron when he got back to the hotel. Dan had checked out already and taken a taxi to the airport. There was a little note for him, though. Magill dissolved into tears as he read Dan's handwritten words, thanking him for all the hard work he'd put into the Langdon projects and the remarkable creativity he'd shown. He had real literary potential. However, an inner voice was telling him that it was time they went their separate ways. He wished his ex-employee well. If he ever needed a book-jacket blurb, he only had to ask.

Simon was so choked up that he almost threw away the envelope, with the Danster's parting gift. It wasn't a cheque or anything so callow. Wrapped in his pink slip, it was a toll-free telephone number. Simon had never heard of the Patton Writing College.

But it had heard of him.

Chapter Thirteen

The Curious Incident of a Dan in the Daytime

I remember the day I met Tina. It was the day they closed the orphanage down. I liked the orphanage. It was okay. The nuns were nice. Father Flynn was nice too. But they closed it down all of a sudden and then Tina turned up. Why not come and join us, she said in that big sister way of hers. She said they had a programme. Opportunities for people like me. You mean dirty smelly stupid boat people, I said to her. No, she said to me, in a nice voice, I mean people who love books. She could tell I loved books, she said. She could see that from the photograph in the paper. I think I was holding a book. Pretending to read it, probably. I didn't read much back then. It's funny when you think about it.

I started in the stockroom. I really liked it there. Big cardboard boxes of books came in on Monday mornings. We cut them open with a Stanley knife. Sharp it was. We bent the flaps back and all the books were beautifully piled up. Perfect. Packed tight. It was the smell I loved more than anything. It was nice to touch them too, especially the ones with bumpy lettering on the front. Gold letters usually. Imbossed, Bill called it. That's what I thought he said. It was years before I knew it was Embraced. Embraced letters. Describes it perfectly, because you so want to touch them.

I liked Bill. He was quite a character. That's what everyone said about him. He grouched. He barked. He complained about the idiots upstairs. Well, he said they were f-ing idiots upstairs. He used very bad words. All the time. The nuns would've been angry if they knew I was working with a blasphemer – is that the right word? – like Bill. But he was okay to me. He slit the boxes. I piled the books on the big metal stockroom shelves. He ticked his sheet. He was always ticking sheets. Except when there was a difference between the number on the sheet and the number of books. Then he started cursing and shouting and telephoning people and cursing and shouting some more.

The staff from upstairs used to come down and see Bill. The staff from the shopfloor. They were nice too. They came down to smoke a cigarette with Bill and shoot the breeze. Shoot the breeze is another word for cricket, I think, because that's all they ever talked about. Smoking cigarettes, talking cricket, while I moved the books. That was okay, though. I moved the books from the boxes to the shelves, then from the shelves to the trolleys that went up in the lift. Then the old stock came down and I did the same thing again. Only in reverse. It was sad packing up the books to send them off. They looked sorry to be leaving. Bill said they were returns. Or was it remainders? He didn't care for them much. But I did. I cried sometimes when the cardboard flaps covered over their little faces. Then I had to seal their coffin with the packing case dispenser thing. That was fun to use, because it made a great noise as the sticky tape stretched out. But I was sad to see them go.

Sarah caught me crying one day. She asked what the problem was. I said the cardboard coffins made me sad. The books were being buried alive. She laughed at that. She said I had a vivid imagination. I must have done because she started coming down to see me. At lunchtime mainly. She was nice. She was okay. She gave me a pair of magic glasses that might help me with my reading. That's what she said. She was the boss of the children's department, where there were lots of books on magic spells, magic beans, magic glasses and stuff. So she knew all about magic. She knew all about reading too. Because the magic glasses worked. The words that used to sort of swim on the page stopped moving. They stood still for me while I was looking at them. While I was wearing the magic glasses, that is. When I took the magic glasses off they started swimming again. Sometimes I put the glasses on and took them off quickly, just to see if I could surprise the words and catch them in the act. But I never could. The words were too fast for me. Swim. Still. Swim. Still. I never caught them once.

It was about then that they moved me upstairs. To the children's department. Sarah said she wanted to keep an eye on me. That's a good thing, I think. Sometimes she kept her eye on people in a bad way. But her eye on me was okay. It was nice. I helped display the kiddie books. Big books they were with lots of pretty pictures. She said I had a way with display. I didn't know what that meant to start with, because I just set out the books where she told me. But everyone in the store used to come and look and say that my displays were special, that I had a gift, that I was a shop-floor prodigy or something. I don't know, though. I just set them out on the big table close to the cash register.

So they moved me from children's and put me on display. I did all the displays – fiction, non-fiction, travel, cookery, window displays, counter displays, aisle end displays, displays of pens, pencils, writing accessories. They used to photograph my displays and send them to the other stores, where they made copies of my displays. That's what they told me. I didn't see any of them myself. They used to send photographs of the other displays. They looked like the photos we sent them. I thought maybe they were sending our photographs back to us. But Tina wouldn't let that happen. She sacked people who didn't tell the truth.

The problem with working on displays was that customers kept asking about books. Did we have this in stock? Did we have that in stock? When's the new Stephen King coming out? Would I order it for them? I couldn't answer most of the questions. They got angry. Very angry sometimes. It was like being back at school again, when everyone called me a dirty stupid boat person. Some of the customers complained to Tina, I think. They said I was being unhelpful and she should do something about it.

I sort of lost interest after that. Doing the displays got boring and people stopped saying how nice they were. So I used to sneak off down to the aquarium at Darling Harbour. I sat and watched the sea anemones, the big zebra eel, the tiny sea slugs, the beautiful blue and yellow tangs. Sometimes I looked into the platypus pen, the alligator den, the seal sanctuary and the place where they kept the penguins. But mostly I sat beside the glass wall at the Barrier Reef tank. It was filled with the colourful little fish that I'd seen in children's books – clown fish, lion fish, mandarin fish, sea urchins. It was just like being there, in an undersea Aladdin's cave, only with angel fish.

That's when I saw him. I'm sure it was him. I recognized him right away. I knew him from the signed photograph he sent me. Well, he sent it to Tina and she passed it on. It was such a surprise. The display was nothing special, just piles of his books really. I recreated the cover of his book using the covers of his other books. Tina, or someone, took a snap and sent it to the publisher who passed it on to the author who sent me a signed photograph. He looked very nice, especially for an old guy.

He looked even older in the aquarium, though still very nice. He had a friend with him, a tall thin man with ginger hair. Really ginger. They were talking in very loud voices, something about blowing up the Barrier Reef tank. Then a man said something to them. He told them off for talking about the aquarium like that. Everybody laughed. There were lots of people there. It was lunchtime. The author and his friend started arguing among themselves. Shouting really.

So I followed them. I wasn't being nosy or anything. I just wanted to check that it was really him and to thank him for the photograph. I wasn't snooping. Is that the right word? I like snooping. It's a good word, a cartoon word, though it's a bad thing to do. That's what Mother Superior said when I found her with Father Flynn. They were playing a game together. A game with whips and handcuffs. They locked me in a cellar for snooping. But it was okay. It was nice. I don't snoop any more, though. I wasn't snooping on the small man and his tall friend.

I followed them across the bridge to the ship museum, where they walked around for a while and had lunch. Then they went back on the long black ship whose name I can't remember. Oh, that's right, a submarine. There are books on submarines in the shop. Military history section. That's where all the old men go.

Not long after, the little guy popped out of the submarine. On his own. There was no sign of his big ginger friend. He was all alone really. He looked strange, funny, the kind of look customers have in the shop when they ask me about Stephen King's new book. Or when they're lost and can't find the biography section.

So I asked him if he was lost. He sort of smiled and said he was a bit. He'd lost his way a couple of years ago, he said. So I offered to show him round. He said yes, he'd like that. He was a nice man. We walked from the ship museum to Paddy's Market, past the fountains, beneath the bridges, dodging the little-biddy train for kiddies. We stopped at McDonald's for a McFlurry. It was okay.

I told him about my job in the bookstore and he got so excited. He loved books too. He loved the feel of them, the smell of them, the musty smell of second-hand bookshops. I don't know what musty means. It's not a nice word. It's too like mucky. He told me he wrote books as well as read them. I said I know. I told him I knew who he was. He looked like Sarah did when she saw my first display. He looked so funny, I laughed. I told him about the display and the signed photograph that sits by my bed. He said he remembered. He remembered the photograph of my display. He remembered signing his photograph and sending it to Tina. He said I had a special gift. Everyone says I have a special gift. But I don't really. He said he wanted to go to the bookshop to tell Tina to treasure me. He wanted to go and meet her and say hello and sign a few books, maybe.

So we walked through Chinatown, past QVC, then down George Street to Dymocks. Tina was at lunch. Sarah was in a meeting with a sales rep. Only Bill was about and he chewed the fat about cricket. Dan said he didn't understand cricket. I don't either I said. He laughed at that. Said we had something else in common besides books.

He said he was heading for the airport. But he bought some writing paper before he left. He bought me a copy of his own book – the really expensive one on lovely smelly paper with colour photographs – and wrote a message in it about my special gifts. He said he'd send me his next book, if it ever comes out. He shook my hand and said goodbye. He was very nice really.

Tina came back from lunch and I told her what happened. She was all smiles. But sad-faced too because she'd missed her chance. That's okay, I said, he said he liked Sydney and he'd be back soon to say hello. She was all smiles again. She said I could take the rest of the day off.

So I took the signed book to my favourite place. The Botanic Gardens beside the Opera House. I sat near Mrs Macquarie's Chair and looked out over the Harbour and looked at the photographs in the book he bought for me. I tried to read it but it was too hard. Then he reappeared. Just popped up, right in front of me. He looked a bit different, though. Did you forget something, I said. He said nothing. He just looked at me. He pulled a sharp knife out of his pocket. That was okay. You have to be careful with sharp knives, I said. That's what Bill told me when I worked in the stockroom, unpacking the new books and sealing their coffin lids.

He swung his hand at me. It was so quick. It wasn't sore, not really. It wasn't nice either. It was okay.

Why, I said. I couldn't hear what he said. Not really.

Chapter Fourteen

So Not Narnia

More of a pragmatist than a panicker, Abby was nonetheless struggling to remain calm. Having to face a notoriously pernickety sub-committee was bad enough, but the hospitalization of Mal Montgomery less than 24 hours after her vicious maledictions was somewhat unsettling, to say the least. It's not every day you can put a curse on someone and the hex works faster than ibuprofen. She'd be lying if she said she was emotionally distraught by his predicament. However, just because she wanted to kill him didn't mean she wanted him dead.

After ringing the City Hospital to see how Mal was doing – sitting up, apparently, full recovery likely – she checked in with the Town Clerk. Surely the committee should be postponed as a mark of respect for Mr Montgomery. Not a bit of it. Mal would want the show to go on. The council is keen to make an announcement immediately after Christmas thereby getting the New Year into gear with lots of good publicity. The meeting was the last on this year's calendar. Postponement was inconceivable, short of an outbreak of bubonic plague. Or a state visit by Paris Hilton. And anyway the councillors were keen to see Abby in action. She was their in-house celebrity, fronting the Belfast Means Business campaign. Who better to lead the discussion of the Belfast brand?

Okay, she said to herself on discovering there was no escape, you've handled much worse situations that this. She thought back to the moment in Edinburgh where she invented and defended a complete PhD thesis during an interrogation by suspicious policemen. She recollected her encounter with Michael O'Leary, the obdurate CEO of Ryanair, when he not only caved in completely but collapsed whimpering before her very eyes. She summoned up the games of bluff and double-bluff that were played when getting WeeTube off the ground and coping with its serio-comic collapse.

Better yet, she'd been studying Guerrilla Psychology since her fraught encounter with WeeTube's nemesis. Surely she could handle a piddling city council meeting. Couldn't she?

Abby's confidence evaporated on entering her boss's office. Far from finding a neat and tidy file containing Mal's recommendations, plus PowerPoint presentation, she discovered a bulky folder stuffed full of scribbled notes, market research reports, random letters and emails from concerned citizens, as well as doodle-covered beer mats, traffic violation citations, Chinese carry-out menus and flyers for lap dancing clubs. The cause of his cardiac comeuppance, she surmised cynically, while cursing the so-and-so who'd left her in the lurch. The milk of human kindness curdled quickly at City Hall.

The sod was going to wing it, Abby surmised. Well, two can play at that game. She sifted through the debris, trying to make sense of Belfast's adventures in branding. Extensive and expensive programmes of market research had been carried out by highly paid teams of London-based consultants. One organization, QuantEx, had undertaken a rigorous analysis of matched samples of residents and non-residents. The residents regarded Belfast as friendly, lively, welcoming, good-humoured, a post-Peace Process place on the up and up. Non-residents considered it a hell-hole of fighting Irishmen, where bombings were a nightly occurrence and drive-by knee-cappings were not unusual, a city they'd no sooner visit than make an appointment for root canal work with a Parkinson's-afflicted orthodontist. No mention of the fact that when the latter group actually visited the place, they changed their opinion in line with the locals.

Abby set the report aside.

A second consultancy, EthnoAnswer Inc., had spent weeks prowling about the city's sink estates and leafy suburbs, getting down with the kids, in-dwelling with the rugger-buggers and deep hanging out with the hoodies. They were astounded by the affability and post-pub extroversion of the citizens, to say nothing of the richness of informants' suggestions for Belfast's branding strategy. Unfortunately, EthnoAnswer failed to realize that their informants were taking the Mickey. Brands are bullshit, branding consultants are bullshitters and, if it's bullshit you want, you've come to the right place. Surely, Abby sighed, they should have twigged that the suggested slogans and strategies were tongue-in-cheek. Belfast: It's Not as Bad as You Think. Belfast: Try It If You're Tough Enough. See Belfast and Die (Literally). Belfast: As We Only Hate Each Other, Visitors Are Pretty Safe (Most of the Time). Belfast: The Hometown of C. Day Lewis (But So Not Narnia).

Abby filed that one in Mal's wastepaper bin.

A third research report, from a crew of Hoxton charlatans called Archetypecast, was based on in-depth qualitative interviews with unspecified "key informants". In all likelihood these were well-oiled local worthies, questioned during happy hour at the Merchant Hotel oyster bar. Deep-penetration projective techniques had revealed, apparently, that black is the colour most people associate with Belfast, that punk is the symbolic soundtrack of the city, that if Belfast were a painting it would be *The Scream* by Edvard Munch, that if Belfast were an animal it would be a black panther on the prowl, that if Belfast were a celebrity it would be Amy Winehouse in her cups, that if Belfast were a motor car it would be (Abby turned the page) stolen by joy-riders and set on fire…

Actually, Abby thought, that one makes a bit of sense. Most locals would agree with parts of that, the blackness certainly, as well as the Amy Winehouse comparisons – her *Back to Black* years, naturally – if not necessarily the oil painting or the motor car. The stolen car would definitely be a BMW. A black BMW!

She set Archetypecast to one side and picked up the next insightful offering by Beyond the Box. The name of the organization alone was off-putting, but their proprietary research approach beggared belief. Eschewing all empirical evidence, a cadre of creatives, futurists and brainstormers interfaced, synergized and primal screamed at one another until something meaningful emerged, something beyond the box of convention, something so far out of this world that it was orbiting Jupiter while taking holiday snaps with its iPhone. Their counter-intuitive suggestion? Change the name of the city. Just as Marathon became Snickers, just as Opal Fruits morphed into Starburst, just as Andersen hid its face behind Accenture, just as Royal Mail flirted with Consignia before common sense prevailed, so too Belfast badly needed a new brand name. The Belfast brand was so freighted with negativity, so weighed down with unwelcome images of death and destruction, that the only option was to wipe the slate clean and start again. Ever mindful of their client's needs, Beyond the Box helpfully supplied a list of exhaustively focus-grouped alternatives: Harmony, Happiness, Prosperity, Progress, Pillow, Placenta, Funtown, Balmville, LaganLove, Whisper-by-the-Sea.

She filed it next to Ethnoanswer.

The final offering was from CrowdSource, which wasn't so much a marketing consultancy as a comment-sifting software package. In the spirit of public participation, the council had set up a brand suggestion website, with a view to eliciting citizens' ideas. These were moderated to keep out pranksters, profanities and politically charged comments of sectarian stripe. The proposals were sorted into themes and topics, plus running totals of the "votes" for each. Inevitably, these comprised the usual array of city positioning conventions, ideas adopted from successful campaigns mounted elsewhere. I heart Belfast. Belfast's Miles Better. Belfast is for Lovers. Some of the suggestions were undeniably original: Belfast's Faster, which captured the speed and zest of the contemporary city, while evoking Glasgow's classic strapline; Simply the Best, an allusion to the late great soccer star, George Best, who wasn't exactly immoderate; Belfast Says Yes, an apt inversion of the old obdurate slogan that prevailed prior to the peace process, while referring to the welcome that awaits investors, tourists and anyone with time or money to spend; We Can't Wait to Say Bout-ye, which aped Australia's iconic words of welcome, duly adapted to the local vernacular. However, the obvious problem with echoing existing slogans or appropriating popular song titles was that they communicated an absence of originality, a metropolitan me-tooism that set the city back rather than burnished the brand.

Abby closed the folder and covered her face with her hands. The committee room challenge that loomed before her was troublesome enough, but the waste of resources that the whole exercise represented was, if not quite obscene, pretty close to X-rated. Hundreds of thousands of ratepayers' hard-earned cash had been squandered on a bunch of fee-padding con artists when it could have been used to help fund hostels for the homeless. Or ugly crippled kids, at least.

For the first time in her life, Abby was seriously tempted to bash her head against the wall. Looking around Field Marshal Montgomery's militaria-encrusted office, she had a better idea: requisitioning one of his wall-mounted sabres and running amok in the committee room, slashing and hacking at the spend-thrift councillors who sanctioned the Belfast Brand expenditure. She was pretty handy with a blade, as anyone would be after four years on an abattoir killing line, and the court of ratepayer opinion would undoubtedly declare her not guilty. The fire alarm caught her eye. Maybe there was an easier way. Alarm goes off, building gets cleared, committee meeting is cancelled. Abby gets sacked for flouting Health and Safety regulations.

"Of course!" the wannabe arsonist said to herself. "Why didn't I think of that earlier?" Mal's best mate was the Health and Safety Officer. They were as thick as thieves with special needs. If anyone was party to Mal's brand plans, it would be Howard Knox. Energized, Abby hurried across to the City Hall's west wing, where the senior administrators had their offices. She hesitated outside the heavy panel door, understandably deterred by the sign above his nameplate. "School of", it said. Abby rat-tat-tatted on the off-putting portal. This was no time for timidity.

"Come," came an officious voice from within.

Chapter Fifteen

Zinging in the Rain

The rain came down in torrents. Cold rain. Dark rain. Brutal rain. Snow was the norm for Virginia at this time of year. Big puffy flakes of snow – flakes the size of softballs – usually settled gently on the state's Historic Triangle. They unfailingly covered Jamestown, Yorktown and Colonial Williamsburg in a duck-down duvet of delicious silence and Christmas cheer. The tourist trade responded accordingly and although Williamsburg in winter wasn't a patch on Aspen's celebrity après ski, let alone sunbathing on a Palm Beach lounger, there were sufficient Yuletide vacationers to justify opening the big attractions. In a world of single people – lonely occupants of one-bedroom apartments – the concept of a traditional Colonial Christmas had considerable emotional appeal. Granted, the concept of Christmas as consumers now understand it didn't exist during the pre-Revolutionary era that Williamsburg skilfully evokes, but that is neither here nor there. Not when there's money to be made and ye olde coffers to be filled.

Rain was bad for business, though, torrential rain especially. The segment of vacationers who yearned for the Yuletides of yesteryear – mulled wine, crackling log fires, robin redbreasts on snow-covered wooden fences – did not take kindly to bitterly cold sheets of stabbing rain that cut deeply into dreams of times past and present-day profits alike. The spin-off attractions that cluster around the Williamsburg money machine were particularly hard hit by snowfall shortfalls. When Colonial Williamsburg shivered, they came down with hypothermia. Busch Gardens suffered less than most, since its raft of indigenous attractions – French restaurants, German beer halls, Italian coffee bars, half-timbered British taverns – could cope quite well when outdoor's was impassable. The snug-as-a-bug stables of the world-famous Clydesdales also appealed to intrepid visitors, though seeing them in situ was no substitute for the iconic beer-wagon parade. The Budweiser dray horses were as much part of postmodern Christmas celebrations as Coke's vintage delivery trucks. However, there's a world of difference between a beer parade over ground that's deep and crisp and even and sloughing through lashing, slashing rainstorms with mud up to the withers.

And that's just the tourists.

If the Clydesdales were hobbled by the weather, open-air concerts were cut off at the knees. Comedic talents, no matter how finely honed, can't warm the cockles when winds are chill, sleet is strafing and rainwater runoff is cascading down the aisles. As the show must go on, the Classic Comedy Collective repaired temporarily to the Bavarian beer hall, which had been converted into a comedy club. The replica routines transferred well to an intimate setting though some of the bigger production numbers, such as "Springtime for Hitler and Germany", had to be scaled down considerably.

Small though they were, the crowds were determined to have a good time – hey guys, it's Christmas! – and the comfort blanket of enforced camaraderie helped the new cast members settle into their allocated roles. Mae was still unhappy about Marilyn's usurpation of her top billing and Charlie Chaplin was having trouble playing second banana to Oliver Hardy's big kahuna. But the range of comedic options that the multi-talented newcomers made available more than compensated for the inevitable teething problems and necessary adjustments in the ego department.

The security risk was something else again.

Fields shivered involuntarily as a drip landed on the back of his neck. He hated water at the best of times, but an unprovoked assault by the stuff was tantamount to persecution. Worse, he wasn't convinced that the newcomers were convinced by Chaplin's cover story – namely, that the computer equipment facilitated communication with performers at the other theme parks, thus ensuring a standard Busch Gardens experience. It didn't hold water.

"Is this meeting really necessary?" Mae moaned, looking round with a my-life-has-come-to-this expression. The roof leaked and there were puddles of rainwater on the dressing room floor. "Can't it wait till the Great Flood subsides?"

"'Fraid so. 'Fraid not," Fields said. "We've had our orders from Big C. D-Day is less than three weeks away."

Chaplin twirled his bowler nonchalantly. "Who's the target?"

Speed-reading the email, Fields couldn't disguise his bafflement. "Business schools in general and marketing departments in particular."

"But why?" West asked, equally bemused by the bombshell.

Fields scrutinized the message, while fingering his frock-coat for the extra-capacity hip flask he carried at all times. "Because business schools are the curse of American capitalism. They've led our best creative minds astray, with their stupid theories and unworkable ideas. They've made us weak and vulnerable to foreign competition. They bear ultimate responsibility for the credit crunch, the collapse of the car industry, the cataclysmic decline in our country's reputation..."

"George W. was an MBA," Chaplin announced, nodding his head in approval. The attack made perfect sense to him. "As were many of the monkeys around him, as were many of the malefactors of great wealth, as were most of the investment bankers, the hedge fund managers, the vulgarians in venture capital. They all absorbed the same absurd ideas. They all drank from the same well of Kool-Aid. And that well was poisoned."

"Well, I can see that seizing the snake by the head makes sense," West said, subtly but effectively changing the figure of speech. "And that decapitation is the simplest and quickest solution. However, as snakes in the grass go, business schools aren't particularly poisonous..."

"And why marketing," West went on, "when neoclassical economics and debt-is-good finance professors bear much more responsibility for the ideas that brought down western capitalism?"

"Because marketing's the most important business function." Chaplin was giving as good as he got. "It's the integrating mechanism that brings the component parts of business together in a customer-facing formation. It's the head of the head of the snake. The brains, rather..."

"Spot the marketing major." Hard-bitten to the bone, Mae remained sceptical. "I still don't get it, WC."

Wisely, Fields refused to rise to the nickname bait and descend into a debilitating interpersonal squabble. Their future rested on this mission going to plan. He skimmed the rest of the message. "Hmmm, it seems that marketing is the vulnerable underbelly of the B-school cobra. Marketing professors are so desperate for intellectual respectability, academic kudos and so forth that they'll fall for everything."

"Yeah, I can see that," Mae conceded.

Fields took a big slug from his giant hipflask – it was the size of a cocktail shaker – before continuing. "When marketing professors fall for our ruse, every other discipline will have their prejudices confirmed. Only marketers would fall for something so obvious, something that they as economists or strategists or even HRMers would never be foxed by. Thereby ratcheting up their smug, self-satisfaction and making them vulnerable to the second phase assault."

If less uncertain than before, Mae remained unconvinced. "Why is January 12 D-Day?" she asked, determined to check the carious condition of the gift horse they'd been given. "What's so significant about that?"

"Read for yourself." Fields placed the hard copy on Mae's dressing room table. It bubbled and crumpled as an imperceptible patch of damp seeped through. "Our responsibility is to follow orders."

Disdainfully, Mae peeled the soggy directive off her slap-stained table then held it up, pinched between finger and thumb. Like most glamorous women of a certain age, whose 20/20 vision had gone the way of the 24-inch waistline, Mae refused to admit that long-sightedness was an issue, let alone be seen dead in a pair of spinsterish spectacles. "Hmmm. January 12 is the nadir of the year for most people, the day when the Christmas credit card bills begin rolling in, New Year diets and resolutions are all-but abandoned, the weather veers from unpleasant to miserable and back again, and just about anything that raises the spirits is seized upon with alacrity."

"Makes sense to me," Fields said.

"Me too," Mae conceded. "Will we be ready in time? Charlie?"

Chaplin twiddled his moustache cautiously, which was quite a feat. "The Fulcanelli Code has been written. I'll be stress testing it later this week. Even if it needs tweaking, we'll still be ready come 1/12. There's only the accompanying email to compose, though that's of paramount importance."

"Okay," Fields said. "Sounds good. What about the other matter, Mae?"

"The shit has hit the fan," she said. "Four times, to be exact. Won't be long now."

"Can we trust him?"

"Dannyboy'll do exactly as he's told. He knows the price of failure."

Fields looked lugubriously round their damp, dreary and decidedly unprepossessing accommodation. "I never drink water," he announced. "You know why?"

"Fish fuck in it," Charlie and Mae said simultaneously.

Chapter Sixteen

Brand It and They Will Come

Howard Knox had the look of a know-it-all. He was one of those unpleasantly over-zealous individuals who knows the price of everything, the value of nothing and the Victorian by-laws that pertain to the sale. Although homely in general appearance – well fed, well watered, well padded, well dressed – Knox's eyes betrayed the bigot within. Not only was he a jobsworth with real power and the law on his side, but he had a finger in every civic pie, allegedly. The scuttlebutt among the secretarial staff was he knew everyone's little secrets. He was Mad Mal's eyes and ears and the source of his committee-room clout. It was rumoured that he kept a black book – more likely a spreadsheet – on the peccadilloes, perversions and padded expense claims of each and every city councillor, which was hinted at when a vote was tight or looked like it was going the wrong way. The right way was Mal's way.

Despite his everyman mien, Howard Knox was the kind of person who pretended to partake in the pub with the lads, while listening carefully to their liquor-loosened conversations. Abby was understandably wary of him. But sometimes you have to sup with the devil before the main course is served. After exchanging anxious remarks about Mal – Abby was going to see him after work, Howard had already been – she let slip how worried she was about the branding sub-committee meeting. She did not want to let Mal down. She owed her mentor so much. She didn't know enough about branding.

Nodding sympathetically, Knox had the demeanour of a back-street bookie appraising a profligate punter, before quoting improbable odds. He sat back in his swaddling executive chair, clasped his hands behind his bulbous head, with elbows spread-eagled, and gazed up at the intricate plasterwork ceiling. "There's an awful lot of nonsense talked about marketing and branding," he pontificated, with all the assurance of an amateur. "I come from the school of hard knocks." He smiled. Abby reciprocated. "I spend a lot of my time talking to market traders, small shop-keepers and entrepreneurial types, such as your good self, Ms Maguire. I know the reality of front-line marketing and it's a world away from the claptrap that's spouted in lecture halls and seminar rooms and, especially, by expensive management consultants. They overcomplicate things for their own fee-earning ends."

"What's the nub of it?" Abby interrupted. Time was passing and he was obviously winding up for a long-winded peroration on the pseudo-philosophy of branding.

"Follow your nose," he said.

Relieved that there wasn't more to it, Abby said what anyone would've said in the circumstances. "Follow your nose?"

"Trust in your instincts in general," he smirked, "and rely on your nose in particular."

At a loss, Abby could only grin back at him.

"NOSE is Mal's branding acronym," Knox explained. "Surely he mentioned it to you? The essence of branding is in NOSE. N refers to the all-important brand name, which distinguishes it from every other competitor. O refers to the offer, the product or service that the organization provides and should be on a par with best-in-class. S is the slogan that should stick in the minds of everyone who hears it, ideally for ever more. E is for emblem, the logo which depicts what the organization stands for, how it sees itself and how it is seen by others. Name. Offer. Slogan. Emblem. N.O.S.E."

"Now I nose." Abby's quip received a cold stare for its trouble, as did the follow-up. "I don't suppose you nose what Mal was planning to say at the meeting?"

Knox remained strangely silent, as if pondering his next move.

"Well, I better head on," Abby sighed ostentatiously. "I want to buy some flowers for Mal while the shops are still open. I'm sure the committee meeting will go on for quite a while. There's a lot of market research to go through with them and I'm pretty sure the councillors will have pet slogans of their own. The Sleeping Giant Awakes. Once Seen, Never Forgotten. The Gritty City. Belfast is IT. A Titan Takes Time…"

"The basic problem with the Belfast brand," Knox opined, clearly relishing the sound of his own voice, "is the gulf between spoken and unspoken. Everyone knows what the rest of the world really thinks of this city. Most of the tourists who come here want to see the places associated with the Troubles, where people were killed or shot at, where murals depict the obdurate opinions of our warring tribes, where the so-called Peace Line still divides our antagonistic communities. But the councillors can't be seen to exploit death and destruction, especially as some of them were responsible for the death and destruction in the first place. So we displace our collective necrophilia on to the *Titanic*. We trumpet Belfast's association with the big beautiful boat, even though it was the greatest new product failure in history. It's a mass manifestation of Freudian transference. We attach ourselves to an ancient failure while boasting that the city is bright, energetic, dynamic, go-getting and fast forwarding into the future. No wonder we send out mixed messages. No wonder branding Belfast is an impossibility. No wonder our NOSE is out of joint." He smiled the smile of a bureaucratic basilisk.

Although she knew better than to trust the man, Abby couldn't help agreeing with Knox's assessment. "What can we do about it?"

There was a very long pause before he answered. Abby could hear hailstones clattering and battering against the window panes of his spick and span office. "The name is fixed, irrevocably; the offer can be improved, considerably; the slogan is up for grabs, inevitably; and the emblem needs a makeover, because the city's heraldic crest is too old-fashioned to function effectively. We need a new logo."

"No pressure, then," Abby lamented. If not quite time to face the music, the orchestra was certainly on stage and tuning up.

Shuffling the papers on his desk, Howard Knox raised his eyebrows conspiratorially. "I have a little idea you can use, if you think it's worthwhile."

"All donations gratefully received."

"The emblem should be a bull's-eye. The slogan should be Targeting Tourists With Taste, though obviously you can adapt that to each separate segment. Targeting Citizens With Services. Targeting Investors With Ambition. Targeting Companies With Can-do. Targeting Entrepreneurs With Advice."

"Ah, so you simultaneously allude to people's perceptions that they'll get shot in Belfast while using management speak to suggest that Belfast is on the ball and open for business." Abby may have been a novice when it came to the amoral machinations of senior administrative officers, but she could recognize a career-killer when she saw one. "What a brilliant idea, Mr Knox! I'll definitely put it to the committee. You'll receive full credit, rest assured."

"Oh, there's no need for that," he replied, with a rictus grin. "It's yours, Abby. If you think it's worthwhile. You take the credit. Good for your profile."

"I may be a media whore, as some people have unkindly described me. But I always give full credit to the people I work with and for. It's only a pity that Mal can't be here. If only I knew what he was planning to say. I'd hate to steal his thunder with such a compelling campaign."

"You know," Knox said icily. "Mal did mention something this morning that might be pertinent to the committee meeting. He was heavily medicated at the time and his mind was obviously wandering. However, in light of our conversation, I can now see the relevance of his remarks."

"Really. That's wonderful."

Knox pulled a Post-it pad out of his desk drawer. With a look that said you'll pay for this, miss, he scribbled a couple of words on the sticky wad and passed the yellow memo across to Abby.

"Thank you so much," she said, trying to keep her face straight. "Perhaps I'll see you later at the hospital."

"Perhaps."

Abby galloped out of his office, surrender document in hand. She could now face the committee with confidence, certain that Montgomery would back her up if necessary. His best friend had spilled the branding beans, after all. Oh. My. God. Abby stopped dead at the bottom of the Grand Staircase, as if struck by a tine of fork lightning. She stared at the Post-it with disbelief. There was a cartoon of a rabbit with big floppy ears and a gormless expression. Beneath it were the bloodcurdling words "The Belfast Bunny".

Abby reeled over to her office and collapsed into the chair. Bunnies must be the most overworked cliché in history. Just what the city needs, an asinine anthropomorphized animal. She could hear the councillors' comments already, remarks about bunny boilers, bunny clubs – where's your uniform, Abby? – bunny promiscuity, Bugs Bunny, Energizer bunny, were rabbits, brer rabbits, Ann Summers Rabbits. The list was endless. Oh. My. God. What was Mad Mal thinking of? It's official, Mad Mal is the Mad March munchkin.

Abby really was about to bash her head against the wall when she heard a strange scuffling noise from her boss's office. He's back. He's okay. Thank God!

She nipped next door and peeked in. There was no sign of the invalid. There was only a statuesque Scot with bushy beard and kilt combo.

"Hello there, lassie. Long time no see."

"B...b...but you're dead," Abby gasped. "They told me you'd been... m...m... murdered."

"Alive and kicking, lassie. Alive and kicking. Do you have a wee dram around here, lassie?"

Chapter Seventeen

The O. C.

A bright yellow school bus chugged up California towards Peltason, the four-lane ring road around UC Irvine's campus. It paused at Academy junction, as if trying to decide which way to turn. Left to the looming sports complex or right to a chain-link fenced facility? It turned right, as did the rest of the canary yellow convoy. Passing under an automatic metal barrier, which rose to greet them, the belching, bustling buses made their way through the pines to an asphalt-surfaced open space at the rear, out of sight.

Low-slung shoeboxes, the PWC buildings were just like every other O. C. edifice. Despite the synthetic glamour of the television series – and notwithstanding the architectural distinctiveness of The Irvine Spectrum, South Coast Mall and the money-no-object confections on Newport Beach front – the vast majority of Orange County buildings were nondescript constructions in cinderblock and stucco. This was especially the case in Irvine, a ticky-tacky new town of bewildering conformity, situated on the southern edge of the Los Angeles basin. If it weren't for the prodigious eucalyptus, wandering wisteria, superabundant succulents and balmy SoCal climate, Irvine would be as bleak as its inhospitable Scottish namesake.

The PWC facility was bland rather than bleak. Tucked behind doughty stands of marine pine, it squatted on the periphery of the Irvine campus, within a triple jump of the UCI athletics track. It lurked, aptly, on the wrong side of the tracks, where the mani-cured lawns of academic civilization met the intimidating natural landscape of mesquite-clad semi-desert. Only the scalloped ranks of rooftop satellite dishes – like a low-rent Sydney Opera House – suggested that PWC was anything other than a University of California science park, a site for spin-offs from the biochemistry department or the engineering school. Most of those who drove past the clinkered shoe-boxes on the way to UCI's sports stadium assumed it was a local outpost of the multinational accountancy firm, the one that hadn't changed its name in the post-Enron orgy of nomenclatural self-flagellation.

Flagellation, however, was the speciality of this particular PWC, the Patton Writing College. The General George S. Patton Writing College, to be precise. Also known as Book Camp.

The school buses stuttered to a reluctant stop at their designated spaces. The late-afternoon heat rose from the scorching surface of the parade ground. It shimmered like an underground furnace stoked by Old Nick himself. Old Nick's ornery younger brother greeted the new arrivals as they tumbled out of the vehicles, grateful to escape the pizza ovens on wheels. Ranging in age from twenty-something to sixty-plus, the hot and bothered arrivals were a mixture of nerd and jock, male and female, black and white, trash and class. There was one common denominator, though, apart from the military issue, camo-coloured kitbag. They were writers. Wannabe writers. They aspired to best-sellerdom, they dreamed of literary prizes, they longed to have their masterpieces piled up on display tables in Barnes & Noble, they wanted to write for a living, revel in royalties, read flattering articles about themselves in *USA Today*, *LA Times*, *Chicago Tribune* and the *New York Review of Books*. The front cover of *Time* wasn't beyond the bounds of possibility.

"Line up over here, you goddam sons of bitches," shouted Drill Sergeant Leroy Crush, the veins on his temples knotted with menace. "This may be college but it ain't Harvard college, you fuckfaced buttbrains. This is Hardass college, and I'm doing the butt kickin'. Got that?"

The new arrivals looked around at each other, wryly amused. This was some kind of joke, right? Writer's retreats were places of calm and balm, where peace and productivity prevailed, where creative juices flowed with the aid of long, lazy lunches and copious glasses of chilled Chardonnay and where literary chit-chat was exchanged with like-minded aesthetes in the effortlessly intellectual milieu of Harvard, Groton, Yale.

Not here, however. The clue was in the title. Military of mien, brutal of bearing, the Patton Writing College was the antithesis of warm and fuzzy, soft and squidgy, wine and cheesy, group and huggy writers' retreats. It was more poison ivy than Ivy League. Less Big Ten than *Dirty Dozen*. Closer to *Platoon* than Princeton.

But, by God, PWC produced the goods, delivered the results and made men of its raw writing recruits. Even the women. *Especially* the women.

The drill-sergeant's welcome-to-California routine was lost on the bone-weary travellers. Still disorientated from their cattle-class flights from Buffalo Breath, Kansas, Moose Poop, Saskatchewan, and All Points East, West Virginia, they shuffled into three straggling lines, kitbags at their feet. DS Crush walked slowly through the ranks, carefully appraising the college's intake. He wasn't impressed. "You've heard of Fort Bliss?" he snarled. "You've heard of Fort Plenty? Well, this is Fort Payne, spelt P-A-I-N."

Self-conscious smirks absented, there was no response from the recent arrivals.

"You. Old-timer," the sergeant shouted into the face of a big, bulky, well-nourished man of advanced years, who was wearing mottled military fatigues, mirrored aviator sunglasses and looked as though he'd done several tours of duty at the International House of Pancakes. "What's your name?"

"Jack Clark, Sarge."

"It's Sergeant Crush, you fat fuck."

"Sir, yes, sir!" Clark yelled, in a perfect imitation of boot camp idiom. Presumably culled from countless viewings of *An Officer and a Gentleman*, *Full Metal Jacket*, *Navy Seals* and suchlike, it was too word perfect for the recruit's own good.

Bristling, almost crackling with aggression, the drill sergeant snapped, "You fuckin' with me, fat Jack Clark?"

"Sir, no, sir!" the chunky arrival replied at full volume, looking through the NCO as military handbooks advised.

The sergeant slowly slid the forage cap off his gleaming pate, as he evil-eyed the veteran of countless All-You-Can-Eat counters. It was over in an instant. Head butt; busted nose; floods of blood; and a slack sack of potatoes on the boiling asphalt. Clark undulated like a lumpy waterbed. Sounded like one too.

One of the others broke ranks and rushed to his aid.

"Leave him, soldier," the drill sergeant ordered, while carefully replacing his forage cap and adjusting it just so. "Get back into line and wait for my command."

Simon Magill ignored the order, as any Good Samaritan would. Quickly removing his T. K. Maxx safari jacket, the ginger man eased it under the fallen hero's head and pressed Clark's bleeding nose between thumb and forefinger. "It's okay, Jack. Let me clean that up for you." He whipped a white cotton handkerchief from his cargo pants pocket and wiped away the worst of the blood-streaked snot.

The little drill sergeant grabbed Magill by the scruff of the neck and with a mighty heave pulled the putative paramedic upright. "What's your name, Dr goddam Dolittle?"

"Simon Magill, sergeant."

"Well, Simon Magill. Do you know what happens when someone disobeys my orders?"

"No, sergeant."

The whippet-thin, shaven-headed NCO cracked an evil grin. "Hit the deck and give me fifty."

"No problem, sergeant." Simon Magill adopted the push-up position and, despite the fearsome heat on his bare hands, started pumping like a Muscle Beach stud muffin. At number 25, he felt the weight of an army boot on his back, a boot that kept pressing harder and harder and harder. Magill pushed for all he was worth. He wasn't going to be beaten. Thirty-one… thirty-two… thirty-three… thirty-… Arms wobbling uncontrollably under the strain, the ginger man gasped and panted aloud. The sweat poured off him in cascades, sizzling as it hit the scorching asphalt.

"All right, sergeant," a voice piped up from the third rank of recruits, most of whom were silently urging the athlete on, "you've made your point. We're all very impressed." The voice was educated, aristocratic, east coast, New England, Boston, Back Bay, old money. It made JFK sound like a Hoboken stevedore.

The sergeant kicked Magill in the ribs with a "Good try, soldier," then made his way to the back row. Antagonism was his pheromone of choice. "Who spoke?"

There was no reply. The line stood silent, staring straight ahead.

"Unless the sonofabitch who spoke owns up, we're all going for a five-mile run."

Silence.

"Kitbags included."

"It was me, sergeant." The speaker was dark and nebbish with black-framed, owl-rimmed glasses. He had East Coast pseudo intellectual written all over him: button-down Brooks Brothers shirt; voluminous chinos, neatly pressed; tasselled leather loafers, perfectly polished; light brown herringbone jacket, loose fitting, somewhat shapeless.

Sergeant Crush sized up the uppity recruit. He eased his forage cap off again. The freshers stiffened in anticipation. However, the lion of Harvard Yard didn't bat an eyelid. He held the sergeant's gaze.

"And you are?"

"Ishmael Meriwether Washington."

Even the line laughed at that.

"Ishmael Meriwether Washington," the drill sergeant echoed, with exaggerated incredulity.

"The Fourth, sergeant."

"Ishmael Motherfucker Washington the Fourth."

The aristocrat looked impassively at the angry NCO, smiling like he'd heard it many times before. A stick of well-chewed Wrigley's spearmint, the jibe had long since lost its flavour.

"Well, Motherfucker the Fourth," the drill sergeant said, replacing his forage cap at an even jauntier angle than before, "I've got a little job for you, something that says welcome to book camp." He glanced at his watch – plain face, military webbing. "When the colonel completes his welcome address, asshole, remain on parade. Got that, Motherfucker?"

Tipperary O'Shaughnessy had heard enough. A sassy platinum blonde from Knobbly Potatohead, Idaho, who'd earned a part-time MBA at community college while holding down two miserable McJobs, then went on to start her own publishing business, she wasn't prepared to put up with this macho horseshit. "I'm outta here," she announced, breaking ranks. She picked up her knapsack, pulled out a cellphone and, turning her back on the dishevelled parade, started calling a cab.

The call never got through. A uniformed arm plucked the Motorola from her grasp and single-handedly crushed the plastic clamshell – like an aluminium Coke can – in front of Tipperary's astonished eyes. Sergeant Crush slowly opened his palm. The cellphone chaff tumbled earthwards. "Thinking of going someplace?"

"Home, sergeant," she said with an upper-midwestern lilt that evoked waving cornfields, clapboard farmsteads, bulbous water towers and bright red grain silos.

"And where would that be, sugar tits?"

"Idaho."

Leroy Crush looked her up and down. "Idaho," he spat. "I'd a ho from Idaho once and, do you know what, she looked just like you. You're a ho from Idaho. Isn't that so?"

Sensibly, Tipperary remained silent. Tempted though she was to kick him in the stones, she refused to rise to the troglodyte's bait.

"Or are you a fucking female faggot? Faggots and maggots are the only things that ever came out of Idaho. Apart from potato-eatin', pig-kissin', piss-drinkin', shit-shovellin', skunk-fuckin' retards, that is. Which one are you?"

"All of the above, sergeant."

Crush placed his swagger stick under O'Shaughnessy's pert chin and pushed steadily upwards. He leaned over and whispered into her ear. "I've got something special lined up for you too, sugar tits. See me after the colonel's speech."

Glancing menacingly from side to side, the drill sergeant returned to the front of the bedraggled parade. "Straighten yourselves up, you cocksuckers. Tenshun!"

At 4.00 p.m. exactly, a pair of plate-glass doors opened in the main PWC building. A six-man colour party of US Marines, in full dress uniform, appeared from within and snapped to attention on either side of the doorway. A bugle sounded. Weapons were shouldered with syncopated aplomb. A striking figure emerged from the gloom.

Chapter Eighteen

Old Blood and Guts

Ugly was one way to describe him. Grotesque was another. But grotesquely ugly hardly did justice to the misshapen apparition that limped, gimped, hobbled and tottered out of the PWC administrative block. Appearance-wise, Colonel Cyrus C. Clamber was a hybrid of *Halloween*'s Michael Myers and Cecil B. de Mille, with perhaps a genetic twig or two from John Merrick's family tree. One side of his face looked as though he'd been dunking for apples in napalm, whereas the other was merely horribly disfigured. His right ear was missing completely; his left hand had been replaced by a metallic claw; and, as a massive prosthetic boot bore witness, his right leg was six inches or so shorter than its withered sidekick.

It was the humungous hunchback, however, that took the breath away. The camp commandant's mother may well have loved him. But only if she was a dromedary. The mutant lovechild of Quasimodo and Miss Piggy, he was a shoo-in for the Texas Chainsaw Massacre sequel: *Leatherface Gets Ugly*.

Hunchback aside, Colonel Clamber cut a commanding figure. His dress uniform was immaculately pressed, with knife-edge seams, razor-sharp cuffs and nary a wrinkle at elbow or oxter. Gleaming medals, burnished buttons, flashing epaulettes and highly polished riding boots, which enclosed a pair of puffy pants that resembled inflatable jodhpurs, combined to convey an impression of power, of indomitability, of human dignity in the face of adversity. The colonel also carried a riding crop that he thwacked against his left boot while lurching to the centre of the parade ground, callipers jingling like spurs on a coked-up cowpoke with Restless Leg Syndrome.

A small podium had been placed in front of the new recruits. Clamber mounted with difficulty, spurning the assistance of two eager aides de camp. After pausing for a moment's respectful silence – a moment many used to take in his copious campaign medals, including the HarperCollins Cross, the Penguin Purple Heart, the Doubleday Medal of Honor, the Dorling Kindersley Croix de Guerre and the Mills & Boon Order of Merit, with bar – he ferociously slapped the riding crop into the palm of his robotic claw.

"This," he said, holding the leather-handled scourge between both hands, "is the secret of literary success, a symbol of what's in store for you at Old Blood and Guts Book Camp. It stands for drive, discipline, determination, do-or-die. It stands for pain, pain, pain and more pain. It stands for militarism, merciless-ness, mental strength and, above all, marketing smarts. Literary success has nothing to do with your ability to compose a well-turned phrase or capture the human condition in pellucid prose. Success comes from hard work, long hours, physical fitness, mental agility, gruelling training, total commitment and an ability to stand out from the slack pack of lazy SoBs. The world is full of would-be writers. There are more unpublished manu-scripts in bedroom drawers than grains of sand on Laguna Beach. At low tide. Everyone may have a novel in them but very few get those novels into bookstores, and fewer still on the best-sellers list. If you pay attention, do as you're told and give 110 per cent at all times during the next six weeks, you too will be part of that special breed, the blood and guts breed, the George S. Patton Writing College breed."

He fixed a baleful eye on Tipperary O'Shaughnessy. "Failure to follow orders can be fatal."

In sharp contrast to his grotesquely disfigured body, Cyrus C. Clamber's voice was rich and resonant, with a light southern twang, possibly affected. Its rolling cadences conveyed an unmis-takeable air of confidence, conviction and good old-fashioned can-do. It energized by intonation alone. "Who," he said, point-ing his buggy whip at Ishmael Meriwether Washington, "is your literary role model?"

"Herman Melville, sir," he shouted. "I fully intend to write the next Great American Novel."

"As do we all," the colonel observed laconically. "And

yours?" he continued, gesturing disdainfully at Jack Clark, the overweight sexagenarian whose nose had stopped bleeding but continued to swell.

"Jabes Joyce," he snuffled, like a victim of terminal rhinitis.

Clamber frowned fractionally then turned his attention elsewhere. "Yours?"

"Sylvia Plath," Tipperary O'Shaughnessy hissed at the cyborg-in-chief.

"She died young," the colonel observed. But before the Idahoan could respond, he returned to his inaugural address. "Your role model for the next six weeks is George S. Patton Jr, the greatest soldier of the twentieth century." He raised the rugged riding crop above his head, for all to see. "This whip is Patton's personal property. It saw action in the Spanish-American War, the First World War, the North Africa campaign, the invasion of Sicily, the Battle of the Bulge, the first Rhine crossing at Oppenheim and the blood-drenched liberation of Nuremberg. It will belong to one of you by the end of this course. Providing you survive." He slapped the crop against his claw, a pistol-shot in the mid-winter sunshine.

"You're all aware of this, I imagine. What you may not know is that Patton was a first-class writer, whose success owed as much to the pen as it did to the sword. He was also an astute marketing man. He sold himself constantly, mainly though eye-catching magazine articles on military matters. He dressed ostentatiously – pearl-handled pistols were his calling card – and was always willing to strike his trademark scowl when photographers were present, as they usually were. He coined all sorts of attention-grabbing slogans because he knew that the media would publish them eagerly and polish his halo thereby."

Silence reigned. Only the chirruping cicadas and rustling treetops broke the breathless hush. "Let me ask y'all something," the colonel said softly. "How many Second World War commanders can you name? Think about it for a moment. Most people manage two or three at most, but one of them is always George S. Patton, a Californian cut-throat, a warrior, a writer, a war poet, whose family owned the very land you're standing on."

The raw recruits looked around, half expecting the four-star general to come striding round the corner, cussing and quipping and pistol-whipping innocent bystanders.

"Eyes front," Drill Sergeant Crush yelled at the top of his voice. The ranks complied instantly. Several tried to stand to attention, though they needn't have bothered. The NCO's eyes glinted with anticipatory malice as he took in the slovenly sight.

Reverentially, Clamber doffed his gold braid-covered cap, placed it over his medal-strewn heart and bowed his bare head. Many non-combatants might have tittered at his tufts of thick grey hair painstakingly plaited into incongruous cornrows. But such was the colonel's Patton-channelling presence that no one noticed the cranial caterpillars crawling across his sunburned pate.

"Your country," he announced to rapt attention, "needs you. America is in crisis. Our great nation is going to hell in a hand-cart. Our government is corrupt. Our legislature is log-jammed. Our lawyers are venal. Our schools are failing. Our colleges are depraved. Our hospitals are unaffordable. Our cities are sink-holes. Our waste is shameful. Our landscape is polluted. Our sick society is obsessed with shallow celebrity. Even our all-conquering military has lost the will to win. Shock and awe has become aw shucks, this sucks. We're the cowardly lions of combat. Old Blood and Guts Patton must be cussin' in his casket."

Despite the dramatic call to arms, the new recruits stirred uneasily.

"But that's not the worst of it," Clamber continued. "Our economy is a basket case. Our hedge funds are postmodern Ponzis. Our CEOs' avarice knows no bounds. Our banks are swindlers, one and all. Our stockmarkets are suppurating cess-pits, filled with cheats and embezzlers. Our biggest growth sectors are pornography and gambling and recreational drugs. Our economy increasingly depends on the cultural industries. And the cultural industries depend on great storytellers. This great country has a great history of great storytellers. It is the country of Poe and Stowe and Longfellow and Lovecraft and Fitzgerald and Hemingway and Steinbeck and Bellow and Cheever and countless others. Literary giants no longer walk the earth, however. Today's storytellers are pale imitations of their

132

forebears. Today's storytellers are either solipsistic wimps who whine about their unhappy childhoods, drug addictions and yeast infections or, like the Kings and Grishams and Barbara Taylor Bradfords, they've been recycling themselves for years. Our premier storytellers are fat and lazy and rolling in royalties and, in the cases of chickenshits like Dan Brown, are stricken with what they call writer's block and everyone else calls cowardice in the face of a deadline."

Simon Magill winced when his literary mentor was mentioned in unflattering dispatches, though he couldn't deny that there was a tincture of truth in the commanding officer's diatribe.

Continuing with his sorry state of the nation address, Colonel Clamber turned his ire on identikit college courses in creative writing, which were producing cadres of supremely ambitious authors with nothing to say, all of whom said nothing in exactly the same way. Hollywood, he went on, was a morass of aesthetic mediocrity, unnecessary committee meetings and scripts in development hell that shouldn't have been developed in the first place. If not remakes or sequels, they're feature films of Broadway shows based on Disney cartoons or comic books or long-dead, best-forgotten television series. "American storytelling," he roared, "has lost its way. If it weren't for our country's marketing muscle we'd be in the can with the rest of the western world and even our once magnificent marketing muscle is rapidly atrophying thanks to knuckleheaded professors in our business schools, Ivy League schools especially. They over-intellectualize what is an inherently straightforward activity, provided it's pursued with vigour and vim and victory in mind. They dither and debate and endeavour to decide, when what's needed is blood and guts and a bold bayonet charge. They build a tower of Babel when a wigwam would suffice. They can't even sell their ideas about selling, because nobody understands the godforsaken things."

A ragged cheer went up from the recruits, if only because arrogant ivy leaguers were getting it in the neck and, Ishmael Meriwether Washington excepted, the Ivy League was out of their league.

With shaman-like aplomb, Colonel Clamber dropped to one deformed knee and importuned his audience. Arms outspread, buggy whip in one hand, peaked cap in the other, it was almost as if he were making a proposal of marriage – plus a little light S&M – or doing an impromptu Al Jolson impersonation. "This is where you come in," he said, with a convincing catch in his throat. "You are the cream of the crop. You have been spotted and scrutinized and specially selected. You come highly recommended. The stories you tell and sell will get this once great country back on its feet and out of the clutches of business school buffoons. You are the future. You are on the fiction fast-track. You are our last best hope. But only if you listen up, work hard, abandon your artistic ideals, focus on realistic role models, do exactly as your DS tells you, and do it at the double. When Drill Sergeant Crush says jump, you don't say how high, let alone how often, you say how's that, sergeant?… and that, sergeant?… and that?… and that?"

Staggering unsteadily to his feet, the military showman pressed his peaked cap to his chest yet again. "The PWC book camp awaits," he cried. "Are you up for it?"

"Yes," the raw recruits shouted in unison.

"Yes, what?" the commandant asked, cracking a grisly grin, a bit like Mickey Rourke after an implantathon had gone awry.

"Yes, sir," they bellowed as one. "Sir, yes, sir!"

"Carry on, sergeant."

Chapter Nineteen

Way to Go

While Colonel Clamber limped back towards the administrative block, with much clanking of callipers and accompanied by snapping of salutes and cheering from raw recruits, DS Crush addressed the parade. "Right you sons of goddamn bitches. Double-quick time to the RECBN for uniforms and haircuts. Then double-double quick time to your billets for shower, shit and shave. No beards, moustaches or facial hair are permitted on camp. Especially you women of Russian or Mexican extract. Chow's available at DFAC from seventeen-hundred. Anyone caught in possession of contraband – that is, alcoholic beverages, non-prescription medication or communications equipment of any kind, including laptops, MP3 players and cellphones – will be shovelling shit for the next six weeks. Do I make myself clear?"

"Yes, sergeant," the motley crew mumbled.

"Do I make myself goddamn clear?"

"Yes, sergeant!" the squad shouted with half-hearted gusto.

"I can't goddamn hear you, you motherfuckin' pieces of shit. Do I make myself clear?"

"Yes, sergeant!!"

"O'Shaughnessy and Washington, stay where you are. The rest of you asswipes, dismissed."

The writing unit ricocheted off with a whoop and a holler. Left alone on the empty parade ground, Tipperary O'Shaughnessy and Ishmael Meriwether Washington remained in place, facing forward.

With a malicious grin, DS Crush reached into his breast pocket and pulled out an old blue toothbrush. Most of its bristles were missing, the rest were curled over. He waved it under the Ivy Leaguer's imperious nose.

The east coast aristocrat remained expressionless. A tempestuous teenager who'd driven his Boston Brahmin parents to distraction, Ishmael Meriwether Washington had done time at a military school. Donald Trump was one of its distinguished alumni. Butt-bustin' drill sergeants held no fear for him. He'd been "smoked" many times before, restroom duty included.

"I promised you a punishment, you cock-suckin', chicken-shit, fuck-me-two-times faggot."

Icy calm, Washington knew better than to respond to the prick's provocation, because that's exactly what the NCO wanted. "Yes, sergeant."

"Report to DFAC after chow." He tucked the toothbrush into the top pocket of the recruit's Brooks Brothers button-down. "You'll be scrubbing the food service containers with this. They better be gleaming, soldier. Otherwise, you'll be running in full kit up there." He gestured towards the mesquite-covered San Joaquin Hills, which rose steeply behind PWC. "So will the rest of your squad."

"Yes, sergeant."

Dismissing Washington with a wave, Crush turned to the other mutineer. "Right, potato face, follow me."

"What about my kitbag, sergeant?" she inquired, hands on hips.

"It'll be waiting for you when you leave, Ida Ho." Ramrod-backed, Sergeant Crush marched his insubordinate off the parade ground, along an asphalt track through the manzanita trees. A troop of literary grunts jogged past in sweat pants, the leader holding a fluttering guidon and presiding over the tuneless singing: *I just know what I been told/Rowling's pussy's freezing cold; Updike's dead and Houellebecq's not/tie his pecker in a knot; Stephen King he ain't no quitter/his writing, though, is in the shitter.*

Turning off the access road, the DS and his charge speedwalked towards a low-slung, Mission-style, adobe rancher, with a picture postcard veranda hung with unmilitaristic swags of purple bougainvillea. They filed through an anteroom staffed by keyboard stroking, telephone juggling adjutants in full dress uniform, to an inner sanctum where several gilded standards stood sentinel. Small-scale maps with large thrusting arrows covered three of the four walls and a desk the size of an Abrams tank held a commanding position in the centre of the room. A tiny figure sat behind the desk, head down, writing rapidly, ignoring their arrival. With a flick of the wrist, he directed O'Shaughnessy into an army-issue aluminium chair. Two burly MPs took up position behind her. One was an escapee from the WWF circuit, the other was chiselled from a slab of mob-supplied Colorado marble: pale, pock-marked, possibly psychotic. He smelt of brilliantine and broken limbs.

Drill Sergeant Crush saluted and departed, shutting the office door behind him.

Colonel Clamber looked up, his horribly mutilated face a mask of avuncular concern. "Ah," he sighed sorrowfully, folding his hands on the desk in front of him while stealing a glance at the paperwork, "Ms... ah... Plath. You don't feel you can participate in our, ah, project?"

"It's O'Shaughnessy, sir. And no sir, I don't."

He stroked his scabrous chin. "That's your prerogative. We'll arrange transportation to the airport, momentarily. But perhaps you can tell me why our mission is unacceptable to you. Our profiling suggests you're an ideal candidate. Your unhappy family background, your pain-filled personal life, your desperate struggles to get that little publishing company off the ground and keep it in the black, as well as your unfortunate dalliance with expensive, business-school trained, MBA-medallioned solutions suppliers, led us to believe that you'd want to, ah, join our crusade."

"It's not the project itself, Colonel Clamber. I agree that business school graduates are full of it and that business school professors are even more full of it. I too worry about Brand America. But I also think that gung-ho, top-gun, kick-ass, neo-Nazi, macho-man militarism is a mistake."

Clamber scratched his good ear, as if weighing up his words before slipping into a set speech. "Business is war. War to the death. It's savage, brutal, ruthless, relentless. It's kill or be killed, dog eat dog, survival of the fittest. You know this from your own experience. The secret of success in business, as in war, is to destroy the competition and spit on their graves. According to General Patton, the only way you can win a war is to attack and keep on attacking and after you've done that keep attacking some more. American business has gotten soft. It's paid too much attention to yellow-bellied, hug-the-customer, corporate-social-responsibility spouting professors, who get tenure for writing unreadable horseshit and wouldn't last five minutes in the real world."

"That's true, Colonel. But it's also true that General Patton was a fascist, who abused his troops, allowed Nazis to hold on to positions of power, talked about ruling the world, and aspired to be American president by ballot, or dictator by force. My publishing house commissioned a book about him once. I know all about General George S. Patton, Jr. The man was mad. He believed in telepathy, reincarnation, déjà vu and all sorts of hocus-pocus. He thought he was a Roman legionary in one of his past lives and was channelling Napoleon Bonaparte. He's hardly a 21st-century role model."

As a psyops pioneer, Clamber didn't take kindly to exhibitions of ignorance. But he was too urbane to let on. "Patton was many things. Mystic, yes. Mad, on occasion. Full of blood and guts, always. But what else can you expect from a feisty Irishman, Tipperary?"

It was O'Shaughnessy's turn to bridle. "Our country has moved beyond crude racial stereotyping, sir, though many military men seem to have trouble acknowledging that. Men like Patton."

"Yes, he was a rough diamond. I don't deny it. However, he was one of the greatest soldiers this country has ever produced. He was one of the greatest managers this country has ever produced. Have you any idea of the management demands placed on military commanders, especially those committed to speed, boldness and never-look-back attack? The logistics alone are almost unimaginable."

Patton-like, Tipperary refused to budge. "He was a blood-thirsty, self-regarding, glory-hunting tyrant," she said defiantly. "I'd prefer not to participate in a project that has a madman as its figurehead."

Without further ado, the commanding officer opened his drawer and extracted a single sheet of paper. Holding it steady with his claw, he signed the discharge chit with a that's-that flourish and slid the official document across the desk, for her countersignature. "I'm truly sorry we can't convince you, Tipperary. We'll arrange transportation to the airport. I'd see you off myself. But I have other matters to attend to. You are free to go."

"Shun," the WWF escapee barked. Taken aback, Tipperary leapt up automatically. The aluminium chair fell back with an embarrassing clatter. She was frogmarched out of the office. A golf buggy was waiting outside. The driver, a jovial, red-faced, sandy-haired corporal from Brooklyn, had Irish-American written all over him. Her kitbag sat in the back seat.

"Top of the morning to you, Tipperary," the NCO beamed.

"It's 4.30 p.m.," she snapped, still unsettled by the super-swift exit. "Don't you have cabs around here?"

The corporal beamed again. "No cabs allowed on camp, ma'am. Bad for morale. We have a treat for you, though. You're going back by the scenic route, a little boat trip across SoCal's crown jewel, the Upper Newport Bay Ecological Preserve. A limo will meet you on the other side and take you to the terminal. All part of the service, ma'am. The customer comes first round here."

"I think I'd rather take a cab."

"It's this or walk, ma'am."

Reluctantly, Tipperary settled into the rear seat. The cart set off with a whine. Three minutes later it pulled up at a small jetty. The jetty jutted out into a narrow, reed-fringed lagoon, which ran all the way from Irvine to Balboa peninsula. It was exquisite, an eco-friendly gem. The late afternoon sun glinted off the gently rippling surface, as waterfowl skittered on top. Only the hum of distant traffic on the San Diego Freeway, and the howl of commercial airliners taking off every two minutes from nearby John Wayne International, spoiled the bucolic scene. A small, strangely painted speedboat bobbed by the jetty. If Pablo Picasso had worked in a Californian boatyard during his Cubist period, he'd have come up with something similar.

"What's with the boat?"

"The ferryman will explain, ma'am." The big man beamed as before and whined off with a cheery wave. Tipperary hefted her kitbag and started along the rickety quay. The water lapped peacefully against the wooden supports. A light on-shore breeze lifted her shiny, shoulder-length hair.

"We've got a little parting gift for you. Just to show there are no hard feelings." The speaker was Drill Sergeant Crush, standing arms akimbo, with Colorado marble behind. He held out Patton's legendary riding crop. "It's only a replica. All we ask in return is that you remain silent about our facility. Do we have a deal?"

Tipperary's internal alarm bells started ringing. "You know, I think I'd really rather take a taxi. Much as I appreciate your hospitality, I'd feel safer in a cab."

"No cabs on base, Ms O'Shaughnessy. What is there to worry about? The lagoon is surrounded by expensive houses, as you can see." He indicated a line of trophy homes, perched on the bluffs above the nature reserve. "The rich folk on Back Bay Drive are in their hot tubs, enjoying the sunshine, sipping their spritzers and looking out over a superlative suburban paradise. You can wave to them from here."

Distant sounds of laughter and rattling glasses drifted down from the nearby cliff top. Tipperary remained hesitant.

"It's all an act, you know," Crush smiled, revealing a gleaming set of movie star veneers. "People have seen *An Officer and a Gentleman* and all the other grunt movies. They expect a ballbusting drill sergeant. They're disappointed if they don't get their butts kicked, big time." He held out the riding crop, with look of no-hard-feelings. "Hey, you're in California, Tipperary. Everyone's an actor here." He paused for dramatic effect. "You can swim across if you like."

Unconvinced, she stepped into the boat gingerly and settled herself down on one of two leatherette seats. The drill sergeant sat next to her. The MP sat behind gripping the throttle of the outboard. As they chugged across the languid lagoon, a heron flashed by with a cry. It was beautiful, peaceful, so unlike her grid-locked, smog-filled image of southern California. "What's with the crazy paint job?" she asked, since the interior of the craft was as Cubist as the exterior.

The drill sergeant swished his riding crop lazily. "Planning on going back to Shit Sandwich, Idaho?" he asked. "Or is it Roadkill Canyon?"

140

"Knobbly Potatohead." She corrected the DS with mounting asperity. "I live in Knobbly Potatohead."

"Planning on going back to the books business?" He grinned cruelly. "The little publishing house on the prairie?"

"Something like that, asshole."

The DS reached across the vessel and, in a flash, snapped a steel manacle on to Tipperary's ankles. Its chain was attached to a block of concrete ballast, situated in the stern. Before she realized what was happening, the MP heaved the block into the water. As the chain uncoiled rapidly, Tipperary started to scream. But was prevented from doing so by the plastic bag over her head. She struggled for breath. The harder she inhaled, the tighter the transparent mask became. The concrete block yanked one foot over the side, then the leg, then the torso. Scrabbling frantically, she somehow managed to cling on to the gunnels, dragging the boat over at an ever-increasing list as the concrete block pulled, pulled, pulled her down.

Thwack. The riding crop came down on her desperately grasping fingers. The blood spurted from her knuckles. Thwack. Thwack. Thwack.

Balancing himself against the list, DS Crush leaned down and stared Tipperary in the face. "You asked about the paint job, sugar tits. It's camouflage. Developed during the First World War. Makes the boat impossible to see from the cliffs or anywhere else for that matter. It's better than stealth technology. The old ways are the best. Give my regards to Roadkill Canyon."

Thwack. Thwack. Thwack.

Chapter Twenty

He Came, He Saw, He Counselled

"So, what happened?"

Abby had misjudged Peter Holden. She'd checked him out before the interview. Googled him. He wrote very well, classic features journalism. He had a knack for penning readable profiles of local worthies, which is no trivial achievement in a region renowned for no comments, say nothings, silent soundbites and an uncommunicative manner generally. While sober, that is. Spike Holden, she'd discovered, had a degree in Media Studies from Hustler University, as did most people in Northern Ireland's communications cabal. He'd studied at Coleraine while she was there, apparently, though she didn't remember seeing him. "This *is* off the record, Spike?" with a subtle but firm emphasis on the "is".

"No problem," he said, switching off the old-fashioned mini-tape recorder that lay between them on the cluttered table, alongside the usual post-prandial detritus of empty coffee cups, complimentary breath mints and dessert plates with the remains of what seemed like a good idea after a glass of white wine.

Abby knew better than to stop at Google and Facebook. She did the time-honoured thing by actually talking to Spike Holden's colleagues at the *Tele*. Being part of a PR department had its privileges. And contacts. Spike, it seemed, was known in the newsroom as Holden-the-Front-Page. He was considered an extremely ambitious journalist on the make, looking for a big story to break, the exclusive that'd catapult him to the ranks of Woodward or Bernstein (which was some shot given that the *Washington Post* and *Belfast Telegraph* were 3,000 miles apart, in both geographical and reputational senses).

Understandably, Abby was on her guard, even after a delightful meal at The Northern Whig and long list of fluffy bunny questions. She was *especially* on her guard after the long list of fluffy bunny questions, because bunnies were notorious tricksters of myth and legend. She'd read up on rabbits in the aftermath of Mal Montgomery's branding bombshell, just in case she'd missed anything important. Untrustworthy creatures that they are, bunnies may be a perfect symbol for disingenuous journalists and sneaky media types. But they're no good for a city on the up and up. "They're all off, aren't they?" she said, gesturing towards the collection of communication equipment on his side of the table.

"Everything's off, Abby," he laughed, "apart from the secret microphone taped to my manly chest which is recording every word of this conversation. It is admissible in court and may be used in evidence against you."

Abby laughed too. "You're wired, Spike?"

"Wired up, Abby!" He looked like a mischievous little boy, albeit a little boy with bags under his eyes, deeply furrowed worry lines and the twitchiness of a nicotine addict who's been lighting his cigarettes with a candle burning at both ends. Deadlines could be very stressful things. But only in the newsroom. Features were, if not quite sedate, blessed with longer than average lead times. Unless, of course, you were constantly searching for a career-defining scoop.

"As long as everything's off."

Hurt, Holden replied with his best what-do-you-take-me-for expression. "So, what happened when you got back to the office?"

Abby wasn't quite sure how their conversation had worked its way round to the Belfast Branding campaign. The bulk of the questions during their two-hour interview were about Abby's life and times. He was very well informed about her family background. His questions about her father's suicide and mother's madness were asked with commendable tact, as were his inquiries about Abby's struggle to bring up her brother and sister while working in an abattoir to supplement their miserable income from the family farm. He'd obviously done his homework. When he broached the ticklish matter of the infamous lost weekend, the occasion when Abby went missing from a student placement project and a country-wide gender-neutral manhunt was launched, he did so in a sincere and serious manner. And when Abby refused to talk about the topic, Holden moved on to WeeTube without missing a beat. He'd actually been to WeeTube on several occasions and had a great time. Inevitably, he raised the delicate question of the alleged insurance scam, the fact that WeeTube burned down at a very convenient moment, just as the fateful legal action was pending. Abby batted his queries away, as she had done on many occasions since the incident. There was no conspiracy. The reason was much simpler. Patiently, she explained that a "Guitar Hero Night" went awry when one of the contestants set light to his instrument, *à la* Jimi Hendrix. The plastic guitar proved highly inflammable and the old building went up like thunderflashes at a Metallica gig. Everyone got out safely and, after the inevitable investigation, their insurance company paid up. In full. No questions asked.

Satisfied, Holden moved on to Life-After-WeeTube – the television appearances, the sudden media career, the appointment as PR czar of Belfast Means Business. All good stuff, all soft soap, all easy-peasy, all falling-off-a-log questions. Human interest in mind, he even asked about her hobbies, favourite books, marital status and so forth. She gave him her Guerrilla Psychology course, threw in W. B. Yeats's *All Fall Down* and, instead of mentioning the not-so-small matter of dastardly Dave Kelley, made her joke about Zuider Zee.

Howling, he almost wet himself at "surrounded by dykes". He called for the bill and, as the conversation was winding down, they turned to other inconsequential matters. Abby of course was well aware that idle chit-chat with journos was extremely dangerous. Hence her insistence on off the record. Although she was responsible for the Belfast branding breakthrough, a stroke of creative genius that did for Belfast bunnies what myxomatosis did for Melbourne's rabbit population, Abby knew better than to take full credit. It was a city council decision. It was a testament to the Lord Mayor's inspirational leadership. It was clear evidence that Belfast was big, bold, brave, brilliant, a city that refused to conform to the diktat of the focus group or the conventional wisdom of city branding consultants. However, as the formal announcement was due to be made at tomorrow morning's press conference – Abby'd been preparing media packs since 7.30 a.m. and even Mal road-to-recovery Montgomery had got out of his sickbed to assist – there wasn't much Holden-the-Front-Page could do with the inside information. Not even if he held the front page, which he'd never be allowed to do. "Well, as you know, a Belfast Bunny idea was being bandied about. I was all set to present it to the sub-committee."

"Now, *that* idea was daft."

"Crazy, Spike, completely crazy." Abby rolled her eyes, stuck her tongue out at an angle and, with her hands behind her head, did a fair-to-middling wiggly-fingered imitation of a big-eared bunny. "Anyway, I went back to my office to prepare the pitch when I heard a strange noise from Mal's office."

"Mal's empty office?"

She nodded, while polishing off her second glass of house white. "Anyway, I heard this noise and, lo and behold, there was someone in the room. It was *only* someone I met a couple of years back in Germany, *only* someone who was one of the world's greatest brand whisperers, *only* someone who died an extremely gruesome death."

"No way."

"Way."

"A brand whisperer, you say?"

"I thought everyone knew about brand whisperers."

Holden looked as though he'd seen a ghost getting ready for a night on the town. "So, he was like a whispering zombie, sort of decomposing and stuff like *Sean of the Dead* or *American Werewolf in London*. Just as well it wasn't a *Donnie Darko* thing with the big rabbit, right?"

"Nooooo," she chided, punching him playfully on the shoulder. "He was perfectly normal. Apart from the kilt, that is."

"A kilt? The ghost was wearing a kilt?"

"It isn't as crazy as it sounds."

"I guess not."

"Believe me, Brodie was as real as you are now. And when I bounced the bunny idea off him…"

"Brodie?"

"Yep. Professor Pitcairn Brodie. Edinburgh University

symbologist. Big in brands. Or used to be." Abby didn't have all day to chew the cud, not with dozens of media packs still to assemble. She cut to the chase. "Anyway, we talked through the Belfast bunny thing."

"You and the whispering ghost?"

"Correct. Do keep up, Spike." A gentleman, Holden tipped the dregs of the carafe into Abby's empty wine glass. Stuffing media packs was thirsty work. "Brodie started with the advantages, funnily enough: the tie-in merchandise, the cute character factor, the lucky rabbit foot thing, the serendipitous link between the Easter Bunny and the timing of the Lord Mayor's show."

"This, erm, whispering ghost must be pretty well informed about Belfast if it knows the date of the Lord Mayor's show."

"Yeah, he used to live here. As I was saying…"

"Haunt here or live here?"

Abby humoured him. For all of five seconds. "Naturally, I outlined the disadvantages. The mythological tricksterism, the perceived promiscuity, the not so lucky rabbit's foot thing – I mean, cutting off appendages in a city famous for appendagectomies – and of course the truly horrific slogan."

"Bibbity Bobbitty Belfast, wasn't it?"

Abby didn't know that had leaked out. But no matter. "Yeah, you can just imagine what an unscrupulous journalist might do with the whole Bobbit amputation scenario. No offence," she added quickly.

"None taken," Spike replied, with a knowing wink.

"Anyway, talking it through with Brodie helped clarify matters. We looked at some of the market research reports. The word association stuff was very insightful."

"And that's when you came up with the radical branding strategy?"

"No, no. He asked about a brooch that he'd once given me as a parting gift."

"That brooch, the one you're wearing now?"

Abby stroked her favourite item of costume jewellery, as if for luck. "Yeah," she smiled, "this brooch. I nipped next door to get it from my jacket and when I got back to Mal's office, Brodie was gone. He'd disappeared into thin air."

"Not even an, erm, whispered farewell?"

"Nope, all that remained was a single rose on Mal's desk."

"A black rose."

"The black rose that's about to be announced as Belfast's brand slogan, brand symbol, brand identity, brand everything. The black rose that's strangely beautiful, extremely rare, studded with thorns, part of Ireland's ancient heritage, both Protestant and Catholic. It refers to the colour that most people associate with the city and is enshrined in places like Black Mountain, Blackstaff River, the Black North generally. It alludes to Belfast's world-famous rose festival and taps into all the symbolic roses of Judeo-Christian culture – from rose windows in medieval cathedrals to the Troubadours' romance of the rose – and, in the legendary language of flowers, it's a symbol of overcoming, transcending the trials and tribulations of a troublesome journey. The black rose is a symbol of tough love."

"Belfast to a T."

"Yes. Precisely. It's a totally unique approach to place branding. It connects our dark past and burgeoning future. There's even a great song of that title by Thin Lizzy, one of whose members was from Belfast. We're thinking of using it in the TV ads."

Holden started pocketing his bits and bobs and BlackBerries. "Amazing."

"What's even more amazing is that it couldn't have taken me more than thirty seconds to get to the coat rack and back. Even if he'd left Mal's office at the same time as me and sprinted for the exit, he'd still have been under the rotunda when I returned. I couldn't have missed him." Abby picked up her Moschino trench and Marc Jacobs tote. "Oh well, there you go. Will you be at the press conference tomorrow?"

"Hardly," he said, politely acknowledging the smiling diners at an adjacent table. "I'm features, that's news."

Abby smiled too. She knew what it was like to be on the B-team. Mal Montgomery's B-team, anyway. A-team here we come. Tomorrow at 10.00 a.m. Belfast: The Black Rose. "When will the profile appear?"

"Next Thursday. Probably. That's our Day-in-the-Life night."

"No photograph?"

Spike paused, slapping his pockets to check all was shipshape and *Belfast Telegraph* fashion. "Ah, we got one from the council. Studio portrait. Looks good."

Abby had never sat for any such portrait. Oh well. There'd been so many snaps in recent years that doubtless they'd dozens to choose from. Wouldn't want to look bad in the local rag.

Chapter Twenty-One

Assault and Battery

"An advertising executive for J. Walter Thompson, James Patterson hit mid-life with a crisis-shaped keyboard. He wrote his first Alex Cross novel in a couple of days and, unlike the angst-ridden outpourings of most middle-aged men, *Along Came a Spider* had blockbuster written all over it. Good, you might think. Bad, Patterson thought, when he saw the crap cover his publisher was planning. Real bad, the adman concluded, when he heard that his novel had no advertising budget. Dr Alex Cross was being thrown into the potboiler piranha pool with a concrete block tied to his feet."

Simon Magill saw the frisson of unease cross the instructor's face. He didn't know why Lieutenant Lance Spearmann had a problem. Jack Clark was a natural raconteur. Massive yet myopic, ponderous yet passionate, clumsy yet crack-em-up funny, he was blessed with the rare ability to hold a seminar room enthralled. He may have been hopeless on the rifle range or when running five miles before breakfast, but when it came to delivering a seminar paper, Jack Clark had the right stuff. In spades. Ever since that first day, when Simon hit the asphalt and gave Crush fifty on Jack's behalf, they'd been official Battle Buddies – inseparable, interchangeable, indivisible. Even if Clark were crap, which he wasn't, Simon'd be there for him. Theirs was the military way, the honourable way, the book camp code of conduct.

"So, faced with the choice of sink or swim," Clark continued, his fleshy face suffused with boy's-own bravado, "Patterson chose to take flight. He used his contacts in the design community to redo the cruddy cover and spent a small fortune of his own money on an advertising campaign." Clark peered myopically at his spellbound platoon, scattered around the Spartan seminar room in full metal fatigues, listening like little children during a captivating bedtime story. A shambling bear of a man, Clark rose to his full height. "It was a huge risk. It was all or nothing. It was…" He paused for effect. "… A moment of book marketing genius. Patterson's damn the torpedoes decision propelled him to the top of the bestsellers list, established Alex Cross as an iconic detective, ripe for sequel after sequel after sequel, and made James Patterson a literary brand name alongside Cussler, Crichton, Child, Coben, Cornwell and Clancy. Fortune favours the brave. Though an advertising campaign helps, too!"

The seminar room burst into a round of spontaneous applause. Abashed, Clark scissored his beefy arms in the "cut" signal. "You haven't heard the best bit yet."

Although it was only three weeks since that memorable induction day, it felt like a lifetime for Simon Magill. The bad old days of Dan Brown's dithering – the constant chant of no, no, no – were behind him, happily. Old Blood and Guts Book Camp, by contrast, was nothing but go, go, go. One thing followed another like a literary Gatling gun. Lectures, seminars, route marches, assault courses, speed writing classes, creative marketing classes, book idea brainstorming, unarmed combat training and all manner of FTXs (fitness training exercises), everything from bogus Borders patrols to simulated dawn raids on City Lights, were part of Magill's daily round. There was no time for relaxation, let alone agonizing over the perfect adjective. As for slumping in front of the television of an evening or watching the latest high-octane DVD, that kind of malingering was strictly verboten. The nearest they got to entertainment was illicit, after-hours card schools, though Magill's infallible memory for numerical sequences put the frighteners on most poker players. When pressed, he'd reluctantly recite pi to the one hundredth decimal place or list the nine-digit ID numbers of every person in the platoon. He called Clark 321 for short. He was his best Battle Buddy, after all.

Old 321 was giving it the ABC: Author Brand Cultivation. "Most writers would be content with one bestselling brand name character. But not Patterson. He developed a series of sub-brands, most notably Maximum Ride, Michael Bennett and Woman's Murder Club, which are written with other authors under the

Patterson label. His literary factory is supremely well organized, cranking out five or six new novels per year, all of which can be read during a single transcontinental flight. The chapters are kept short to allow for constant interruption, the plots are paper thin in keeping with the pressurized air at high altitudes, which doesn't permit high grade mental processing. Not since Michelangelo's workshop has so much great art been produced in such a systematic manner."

Three weeks previously, Magill would've assumed that Clark's concluding comment was ironic. But not any more. When it wasn't disbursing useful information on human anatomy, serial killer MOs, scene of crime protocol, safe breaking, lock-picking and suchlike – all vital tools for wannabe blockbuster writers – Old Blood and Guts Book Camp celebrated authors who cranked out their manuscripts in a methodical manner. Its heroes were Anthony Trollope, Terry Pratchett, Agatha Christie, Georges Simenon, Barbara Cartland and Joyce Carol Oates. Its villains included James Joyce (thirty years writing *Finnegans Wake*), Herman Melville (gave up after *Moby-Dick* bombed) and Sylvia Plath (went mental writing about going mental). The cruellest invective was reserved for alleged victims of "writer's block", an entirely imaginary condition that didn't exist except among literary loafers, lead swingers and lazy sons of bitches.

"Many thanks, Private Clark, for your inspirational paper." Lieutenant Spearmann, an angular man with angular ideas, led an additional round of applause. "Okay, who's next for the hot seat?"

A forest of hands shot up, like vegetation after a rainstorm in Death Valley. Spearmann settled on the only soldier whose arm wasn't raised aloft, Ishmael Meriwether Washington. Eyes rolled and feet shuffled as Washington started to speak. For all his bravado on parade and for all his obvious intellectual gifts – gifts that were even more obvious to their possessor than the dispossessed around him – Washington had done little to endear himself to the others. He was secretive, condescending, egotistical, someone who looked after number one and only number one. He didn't pull his weight, frankly. Some suspected that he was writing his Great American Novel, in secret, on a contraband item of electronic equipment that they'd all be punished for, if discovered. Others reckoned that he was taking note of everybody else's ideas, with a view to exploiting them on graduation. Magill refused to get involved in the bad-mouthing, because he had more important things to worry about than the paranoia of the unpublished. He'd endured the paranoia of the published – Dan Brown's paranoia – and knew it was needlessly debilitating.

He had Sergeant Crush to worry about.

Ever since their push-ups face-off on the first day, Crush had sought to crush Magill at every opportunity. Any infraction by anyone in the platoon meant a smoking for Magill. The smokings were getting tougher and tougher, moreover. It wasn't so much the physical side of things – on the contrary, the push ups and star jumps and leg thrusts had buffed him up as never before – it was the malicious accompaniments to every repetition. Hit the deck and give me twenty…titles of books by Charles Dickens…famous first lines…famous last lines…famous advertising slogans…famous brands beginning with the letter F… famous porn movies based on books by E. M. Forster. Every failure, and Magill always failed at some point, meant that the exercise started all over again, only with a new tacked-on task. The slightest mistake also sent Magill back to square one. How was he to know that *Howard's Rear End*, *Back Passage to India* and *A Womb With A View* weren't proper porn movies? He was guessing, frankly. He wasn't a big fan of Forster.

Washington's seminar paper was on J. K. Rowling. Angry murmurings greeted such an unimaginative choice. Everyone already knew the story behind the boy wizard brand and was well aware of the author's marketing savvy. Spearmann had to ask for quiet while Washington prattled on about the penniless author in a coffee bar, the rejection by numerous publishers, the take-off, the controversy, the movies, the merchandise, the lines of fans outside bookstores at midnight, the yada, yada, yawn.

The rumbling grumbling stopped when Washington wrapped up his perfunctory presentation. Despite Spearmann's attempts to get some discussion going with an expert diagnosis of the Potter brand's potentially troublesome future – now that the core story was over, whither the theme park and movies?

– the seminar adamantly refused to engage with Hogwarts this, Hagrid that, Hufflepuff the other. Stiffening in silence was a long established army tradition, the military equivalent of sending certain officers to Coventry. Washington's seminar paper was getting the silence it deserved.

If it hadn't been for the silence, they'd never have heard the cat-like arrival of DS Leroy Crush. He burst into the seminar room with a spontaneous FTX up his sleeve, as he was entitled to do under book camp regulations. Instead of a sprawling roomful of laid-back layabouts, the sergeant found a perfectly formed line of military personnel, fit and ready for the fray. Crush could barely hide his disappointment. Lieutenant Spearmann could barely hide his smile, though both abided by the respectful rigmarole of power transference.

"Right, you cock-suckin', faggot-fuckin', finger-lickin' numb-nuts," the drill sergeant said when the troop reassembled outside, "this time it's personal. The assault course. Now. Double quick time." In four ranks of four, the unit power-jogged across the campus, past the administrative block, round the parade ground, through the springy palm trees and stands of peeling eucalyptus towards the start line of what PWC cadets called Hellboy. The assault course rose steeply through scrub-covered hillocks to a mesquite-matted plain strewn with boulders, barriers, barbed wire, rope bridges, tree swings, tyre pulls, log carries, snake crawls, splash-and-dashes, arm-over-arms and plank-spanned shit-pits. It concluded with a downhill sprint to the finish. Four minutes thirty-two was the record, though Jack Clark once clocked an incredible 5.10. Although he suffered terribly on five-mile runs, his bulk was perfectly suited to Hellboy's demands and Clark took great pleasure in showing the whippersnappers a clean pair of heels. He couldn't match the squad's real speed merchants, but he had the beatings of his British Battle Buddy.

"This time we're doing it with live ammunition," Crush announced, to discreet glances of consternation. "I'm lookin' for five flat. If anyone exceeds 5.45, they'll be cleaning the DFAC restrooms for a week, with only their tongue for wipe-down. Do I make myself clear, douchebags?"

The troop took their marks at the start line, jostling for

position. The "Go" was drowned in a fusillade of heavy machine gun fire. The angry ordnance either whizzed overhead with a terrifying whine or thudded into the bare earth on either side of the well-worn path, sending showers of sun-baked mud over the helmeted heads of the greenhorn grunts. Disconcerting to start, the bullets were soon ignored as the initial uphill sprint stretched out the field. Apart from taking two attempts at the 18-foot wall and an unavoidable fall off one wobbly plank, Magill made it in 4.52, three seconds behind his big Battle Buddy. Not bad, but no cigar. Not even a cigarillo. Come 5.10 everyone was home and dry, with one noteworthy exception. Ishmael Meriwether Washington. Magill asked if anyone had seen him drop out. Magruder, an aspiring police procedural writer from Dallas who'd delivered a dynamite seminar paper on Harold if-it-moves-hump-it Robbins, gasped that he'd last seen him at the tree swing.

Ignoring the "fuck Washington" comments of his fellow recruits, all of whom agreed that a spell of latrine cleaning would do the WASP bastard a world of good, Magill ran back on to the course. He dashed up the final descent, skirted the big wall, ignored the log carry and scurried through the mountain pines to the tree swing. Washington lay on a bed of mesquite, clutching his ankle.

"I twisted it, Simon," the chastened Ivy Leaguer said, stating the obvious.

"Not a problem, Ish. Leave it to me." With the benefit of his smoking-honed upper-body strength, Magill heaved Washington over one shoulder and carried him in the classic fireman's lift position. Twenty-four seconds later, they crossed the line together. As one, the grunts slapped Magill on the back, though he was too exhausted to appreciate the comradely approbation.

DS Crush cast an expert eye over the penitent patient's twisted ankle. "It's not broken," he said. "If it were broken, boy, I'd have to shoot you." Washington laughed uneasily, since Crush was more than capable of carrying out the threat.

The sergeant stood and stalked over to Magill. "You crossed the line at 5.54, soldier, nine seconds after the deadline. You know what that means."

A mutter of protest went up from the men, since their buddy

had been fifty to the good when he first crossed the line. Crush glared them into silence. Magill had a fair idea of what lay in store. On top of the restroom detail, this likely involved another lap of the assault course, possibly with full kitbag, plus rifle and lead-weighted boots. Failing that, it was sure to be fifty star jumps reciting the names of Civil War generals or Strunk and White's rules of grammar or 21 marketing Ps in addition to the big 4. "Yes, sergeant, I know what it means. I'll report for latrine-licking duty immediately after chow."

"No you won't," the DS said. "Because you'll be enjoying a beer bust with the rest of your buddies."

The implications of the sergeant's incongruous remarks took several seconds to sink in. But when the squad finally twigged, the spontaneous shout of delight carried all the way back to the seminar suite.

Crush waited for the unit to settle before delivering his homily. "The regular army never – repeat NEVER – leaves a man behind, no matter who he is or what he has done. The seventh commandment of the soldier's creed is 'I will never abandon a fallen comrade.' I don't know whether Mr Magill is much of a writer, but he's a damn fine soldier."

The grunts couldn't believe their ears. They couldn't believe their luck. They were dreaming, weren't they?

"Alright, you goddamn sons of cunts. Dismissed!"

Chapter Twenty-Two

Albertson's Associates Against Anti-Christian Activities

The trucks arrived at zero five-hundred. Big Macks. Canvas covered. Painted desert-theatre taupe. The entire platoon scrambled on board, rapidly filling the hard wooden benches on either side of the vehicles, huddling together for warmth. Southern California was balmy for most of the year – often unbearable in August – but the first few weeks of January could be freezing before dawn. It was chillier still at Irvine, on the outer edge of the LA basin. It was chilliest of all on account of the Wal-Mart associates' apparel. The grocery store outfits had appeared in the barracks twenty minutes earlier, just as the grunts were towelling themselves down after showering or otherwise holding their heads, still muzzy from the previous night's beer bust. Beer busts were unheard of in boot camp, especially extra-intensive boot camps like book camp, where the physical demands of standard army operating procedures were combined with literary seminars, marketing case studies and such.

Theirs was not to reason why. Twelve well-chilled cases of Budweiser were stacked in the centre of the barracks on their return from the assault course. The first sip of beer was one of life's little pleasures at the best of times, but on a hot afternoon after vigorous exercise and three full weeks of total alcoholic abstinence, it was the nectar of the gods. Beer bust was a misnomer, though. Beer bond was better. Never had the troop felt closer. Camaraderie flowed like champagne at a society wedding. Simon Magill was "the man". Jack Clark led the fulsome eulogies. Ishmael Meriwether Washington, of all people, was toasted on at least ten separate occasions, since he was the root cause of their ambrosial kegathon. His ankle strapped, his misdeeds forgiven, the patrician Ivy Leaguer was carried shoulder high, much to his amazement, delight and indeed shame for being such an asshole in the past.

The king of beers' piper had to be paid, however. And wearing thin Wal-Mart uniforms was the start of it. The few recruits capable of speech – or approximations of speech at 5.00 a.m., after a bellyful of Bud – concurred that they were heading off camp, hence the disguises. They weren't far wrong, though there was more to it than blending in with the local service economy. The trucks started up with a mighty roar of the six-cylinder engines, coupled with great gouts of stinking tailpipe smoke. They lined up astern and the three-truck convoy set off along the perimeter road, through the guarded gatepost, past the UCI sports complex and, after a few twists and turns and stoplights and access ramps, settled into the slow lane of the 405, heading north. Even at the butt crack of dawn, the interstate was busy. Come rush hour it was the ninth circle of Dante's Inferno. By that time, the convoy had tacked on to the I-110 and was nearing its destination in the San Gabriel Mountains, several miles east of Sunset Boulevard.

Its vistas familiar from innumerable Hollywood movies, the Huntington Library and Museum was one of the must-see destinations in a destination-rich city. A robber baron of the old school, who made his pile in streetcars and property speculation, Henry Huntington had purchased himself immortality with a priceless collection of paintings, an incomparable haul of books, including the Gutenberg Bible and Shakespeare's First Folio, an enormous mansion plus annexes to house the immemorial artefacts, and an exquisitely landscaped park dotted with statuary, monuments, belvederes, exotic gardens and folly-filled prospects.

The Wal-Mart associates didn't have time to appreciate the pristine Pasadena panoramas, much less savour the sweep of the San Gabriel Hills as they rolled in wooded folds towards the distant Pacific. They were hurried into the Library, a great, red-roofed annex adjacent to the main building. Pausing only to appreciate the exquisite display cabinets – as any book lover would – the bibliomanes descended two flights of marbled stairs to an underground auditorium, where they took their seats without fuss. At least the heating was on.

As the lights dimmed, the rationale for the cloak-and-daggery became apparent. A black-suited, black-shaded "operative" took centre stage and started talking in a barely amplified whisper about conspiracy theories. Instead of working through the list of usual suspects – the Illuminati, the Knights Templar, the Rosicrucians, the Freemasons and so forth – he focused on the rise and fall of conspiracy theories per se and what it meant for novelists. Conspiracies, evidently, were as prone to crazes and fads as the fashion industry or children's toy market. The present decade was dominated by religious conspiracies, largely on account of Dan Brown and Dan Brown wannabes. The nineties were dominated by celebrity conspiracies, in the wake of Princess Diana's, Kurt Cobain's and Biggie Smalls's untimely deaths, all of which boosted interest in the Elvis Presley, Jimmy Hoffa, JFK and Rasputin assassination industries. The eighties were the military conspiracy years, thanks to the black ops adventures that leaked out in the aftermath of the Iran-Contra hearings – Operation Paperclip, Grillflame, Stargate, Condor, Artichoke, Echelon, etc. – not forgetting the notorious Tonkin Gulf incident that precipitated the Vietnam War.

Magill was only half listening to the Man in Black. Having worked for Dan Brown, he'd studied every conspiracy theory this side of Roswell, with a view to developing Langdon vehicles. The heat in the Huntington lecture hall was oppressive. Magill felt himself nodding off, though he jerked to attention from time to time, like many of his sleep-deprived beer buddies. He pretty much missed the operative's theory that a thirty-year conspiracy cycle existed. The conspiracies of the eighties were likely to come back into vogue, as were those of the fifties. Recent advances in neuroscience and consciousness studies meant that there were lots of opportunities for aspiring thriller writers. Remote viewing, the intelligence community's alleged ability to traverse the astral plane and spy invisibly on the enemy, was ripe for rediscovery. MK Ultra, the infamous *Manchurian Candidate*-style experiments in brainwashing, were due for a Mark 2 makeover. Subliminal advertising scams, dismissed for decades as complete and utter hogwash, were not only under serious reconsideration but being actively pursued by Madison Avenue's neuromarketers. Psyops had perfected the ability to kill sheep, goats and assorted small rodents with a single lethal look. That could come in handy, Magill mused. When the hamster invasion force lands at Laguna Beach, we'll be able to take them out with a good hard stare.

The perfunctory applause had barely died down when the comatose booklovers were jerked into life by a loud shout of "Shun!" Rigid, DS Crush razored a salute as Colonel Clamber gimped through the auditorium, pleats perfect, medals displayed, flanked by two flint-chinned military policemen.

After waiting politely for the conspiracy theory theorist to depower his PowerPoint and depart, Colonel Clamber addressed his troops. "You may be wondering why you've come all this way to listen to a lecture, when we have perfectly good lecture halls back home. You may be wondering why you are dressed in Wal-Mart uniforms instead of regulation BDUs. As inveterate storytellers, no doubt you'll be able to invent enough conspiracy-filled yarns to keep you amused all the way back to Irvine."

The audience smiled politely.

"There are three main reasons why you're here. Two of them are cosmetic, one is crucial to your future as bestselling novelists. Cosmetically, we want you to pass within touching distance of the world's finest literary accomplishments, if only to remind you that you are not in the business of producing museum pieces. Your task is to write books that'll be read by millions, millions who are free to read millions of other equally good books. Cosmetically, we also want you to look around the grounds as you leave, because this very land was once trod by your military, marketing and literary role model, General George S. Patton, Jr. George S. Patton Senior sold this land to the Huntingtons in 1903 and was their general manager while this library and the museum were being built."

None of the recruits looked around for the swaggering ghost general on this occasion – Old Blood and Guts' belief in reincarnation notwithstanding – because standing to attention in Wal-Mart uniforms was a sufficiently creepy experience.

The colonel removed his peaked cap as he was prone to do when things turned serious. "Take a seat, soldiers, while I explain the crucial task that awaits you."

"Rest easy," the sergeant shouted, in response to Colonel Pickett's command. The lecture hall's stalls groaned and squeaked as butts were settled and booze-wearied legs were relieved of their standing orders.

"What is the biggest threat to the novel today?" the colonel asked, once the room had fallen into respectful silence.

"DVDs," a voice volunteered from the back. "Computer games." "iTunes." "Wii." "Google." "Facebook." "Guitar Hero." "Monday Night Football." The manifold alternatives to recreational reading rose up thick and fast. "MudWrestlingMormonMamas dotcom," someone yelled during a pregnant pause. Everyone turned to look at the Latter-day Saint lover. "It's a website," Suzy Swaggart said sheepishly, "that an ex-boyfriend told me about." The entire platoon laughed, while making a mental note of the URL and imagining Sexy Suzy in a muddy clinch with Mormon Mamas.

The colonel allowed the moment of barrack room humour to pass, before continuing in deadly earnest. "The greatest threat is not electronic alternatives to reading, though their unstoppable proliferation isn't helpful. Nor is it electronic supplements to reading like Kindle or Google's digitization project, since they're making books easier to access than before. The real threat is the supermarket, the Wal-Marts and K-Marts and Safeways and Albertsons of this world. They cherry-pick the bestsellers and slash their prices, which renders bookselling uneconomic for both mom and pop bookstores and Barnes and Noble alike. They not only stock a very limited range of titles, diet and cookery mostly, but pretty much dictate what books get published in the first place. The chief book buyer for Wal-Mart has more influence on the trade than the CEO of HarperCollins. The types of books that Wal-Mart and Albertson's carry – and therefore that publishers and agents are commissioning – are getting more and more restricted by the day. Your room to manoeuvre, as aspiring authors, is getting narrower and narrower." He paused to let the information sink in. "And, as you'll recall from your seminars in military strategy, that calls for a Patton-patented reaction."

"Breakout!" the fighting men and women of PWC shouted as one.

"Exactly," their commandant responded with approval. "We require a breakout action that'll shift the balance of power in favour of ambitious authors like yourselves. But Wal-Mart is impregnable, isn't it? If we attack the Arkansas sidewinder head on by, say, Semtexing some of their stores…" A frisson of excitement surged through the room as the prospect of real military action raised its head. "… That'll only increase public sympathy for the terrorized organization. So what should we do instead?"

A smattering of unrealistic suggestions rose from the floor. But the colonel's question was rhetorical. He'd already decided what to do. "Comrades, we will be taking our cue from the Tonkin Bay incident, as discussed by our psyops officer earlier." He turned a bloodshot eye on Magill's squad, whose snoozing had obviously been noted with disapproval. "As you'll recall, our navy launched an attack on itself, pinned the blame on communists in North Vietnam and duly declared war on the gook sons of bitches. Analogously, we shall attack a selection of New Age bookstores; surveillance cameras will spot our Wal-Mart finery; Wal-Mart will deny any such action; and in so doing will focus media attention on its totalitarian book stocking policies. Two days from now, we shall release a statement from Albertson's Associates Against Anti-Christian Activities, claiming responsibility for the attacks on Satan-worshipping bookstores. Albertson's naturally will not only deny all responsibility, thereby focusing attention on their totalitarian book stocking practices, but point out that the bookburners were wearing Wal-Mart uniforms. Albertson's and Wal-Mart will fight it out between them, both stressing their bookselling broadmindedness, which of course they'll be effectively forced to adhere to for a time. Time enough for your first books to be published and stocked in Wal-Mart, regardless of your chosen genre or storyline."

The fiendish brilliance of Clamber's book breakout couldn't be denied. It was an opportunity for everyone to strike a blow for freedom and forge their own future with a single decisive act. Every grunt was game. Except one.

"Colonel Clamber, sir," Simon Magill spoke up. "Did you say that we'd be burning the books in the four target stores? That is, burning physically, as opposed to metaphorically."

"Yes, Mr Magill, that's exactly what I'm suggesting. No one likes to burn books, of course, but it's a small price to pay for the bigger plan."

"I'm sorry, sir, but I won't be party to book burning of any kind."

"Sacrifices must be made in wartime."

"That's a sacrifice I'm not prepared to make, sir."

"This is not Nazi Germany," the commanding officer said acidly. "Do you know how many new books are published in the US each year? Two hundred thousand. And if each receives a minimum print run of, say, one thousand copies, that's approximately two hundred million. Do you know how many books are remaindered and pulped and pressed into service as recycled paper, ceramics and even highway resurfacing materials?"

"No sir."

"About as many as get published each year. Burning a few thousand new age volumes is a drop in the ocean."

"But it's a symbolic act, sir. I used to work for a symbologist and I have some understanding of the power of symbols. I can't, in all conscience, go along with this. It is wrong. I won't do it. My mind is made up."

"In that case, young man, you must withdraw from book camp, forthwith. See me in my office tomorrow morning, when you'll receive your dishonourable discharge."

Chapter Twenty-Three

Yes, We Have No Piranhas

There was no raid. There was never meant to be. The exercise was a test. It was designed to discover whether the ill-disciplined rabble of three weeks earlier had been forged into a lean mean writing machine. Or was willing to follow orders, if nothing else.

Gratifyingly for PWC, the answer was in the affirmative. True, the new rabble army wasn't exactly Delta Book Force, much less the Marketing Marines. But they'd been prepared to sack bookstores on command, which was an indicator of how far they'd progressed.

With one exception.

Magill was still in a state of shock as the truck rumbled back to base, via the I-5 and the Costa Mesa Freeway. He'd refused to follow orders. He'd been insubordinate. He had to go. He wondered what would happen during the dishonourable discharge ceremony. Stripped of his Moleskine notebook in the middle of the parade ground? Parker pen ceremonially broken in front of the entire book camp? Placed up against an administrative block wall and read to death by a Proustian? Would he be allowed a few last words, possibly a heart-wrenching speech about freedom of expression and America's constitutional right to buy ghost-written celebrity memoirs?

Was burning a bunch of R. L. Hubbards really so bad?

Yes, it was.

Reveille sounded at zero five-hundred, as usual. Instead of grumbling and cursing and getting into chilly PT gear, Magill gathered his stuff, emptied his locker, packed his kitbag, stripped his bunk down to the bare mattress – as per regulations – and exchanged love-you-forever farewells with his Battle Buddy, Jack Clark.

Magill felt like an abject failure. Again. He'd failed his father.

He'd failed his brother. He'd failed his first mentor, Pitcairn Brodie. He'd failed his second mentor, the Danster. He'd failed his third mentor, Big Jack Clark. Even though he'd only known him for a few weeks, he'd learned a lot from Big Jack. The guy had a natural flair for storytelling. He was a damned decent man, to boot.

With a final backward glance, Magill said goodbye to the empty barracks, then joined the MPs outside. They escorted him to a camo-coloured golf cart, which one drove as the other sat shotgun. Magill squeezed into the back, his kitbag beside him. The whine of the electric engine, unmilitary though it was, couldn't drown the stirring sounds of the awakening book camp. Marketing marching songs drifted through the manzanita trees, something about Kate Phillips's sorry ass. A group of newish recruits wilted under the withering tongue of an ornery drill sergeant, performing push up after push up in synchronized time as their taskmaster shouted a homophobic quatrain of unforgettable marketing doggerel: *Product, place, price, promotion/move your body to the motion/else you end up in the ocean/rub my butt with suntan lotion.*

The golf cart – Gulf cart, rather – pulled up outside Colonel Clamber's wisteria-sheathed office, just as the golden shafts of dawn aroused a bed of birds of paradise, the beautiful sharp-faced flower that symbolizes so much of southern California's incomparable appeal. Falling in behind, the adamantine MPs marched Magill up a short flight of steps, across the veranda and into Colonel Clamber's vestibule, where he was told to wait until the commanding officer could see him. Fifteen minutes passed, with only back issues of *Lock and Load*, *Shock and Awe*, and *Guns and Buns* to distract him. Another fifteen minutes passed, sufficient time to scrutinize the Roll of Honor, a great gilded plaque listing the names of famous authors who'd delivered BGDLs – Blood and Guts Distinguished Lectures – to the assembled alumni. Gore Vidal and Tom Wolfe, Toni Morrison and Amy Tan, Umberto Eco and Cormac McCarthy and, somewhat incongruously, Tom Clancy and Dan Brown. The latter pairing was listed for 2004, the year of Dan's greatest literary triumph, when he was on top of the world and a long line of Langdon sequels beckoned. It wasn't to be.

It wasn't to be for Simon, either. For as long as he could remember, he'd wanted to be a writer. He helped write his father's sermons when he was seven years old – the kiddie homilies, admittedly. He loved writing essays at school and had a natural flair for them, or so his English teacher said. He also had a flair for mathematics, though it was closer to precocity. His teenage years were a blur of math bees, piphilology competitions and party tricks with prime numbers. He'd rediscovered writing at university, where it came in handy at exam time and assignment deadline down-to-the-wires, of which there were plenty. Writing also had its place when he went into web-wizardry, since the home pages of his e-commerce ventures required rhetoric of the highest order, otherwise no click-throughs. Writing, he'd discovered, was central to business life, everything from marketing plans to outgoing emails. Yet they'd never discussed writing once during his Masters in Marketing. Heaven only knew how reluctant writers coped with marketing's literary demands.

"Hoo-ah," Sergeant Crush shouted, on bursting into the colonel's waiting room. What was he doing here? Shouldn't he be grinding the squad's nuts in a vice?

Magill jumped up on the DS's command and followed him into the colonel's office, where the great man was reading the latest issue of *American Prosthetics*. He set aside his favourite glossy with considerable reluctance and motioned Magill into the seat opposite. Drill Sergeant Crush stood behind, impassively. The colonel leaned forward, planting his elbows on the army-issue, two-drawer desk, the spit and polished surface of which was completely empty except for a faded photograph of Second Lieutenant Clamber posing beside a Humvee in his salad days before he trod on a M14 land mine during a game of kickin' chicken, an outdoor form of Russian Roulette. "Mr Magill," he said, "have you ever read *Trilby* by George du Maurier?"

Although he didn't quite know what to expect from a dishonourable discharge interview, the very last thing the wannabe writer anticipated was an inquiry about his light reading. "No sir, I haven't."

"Don't bother. It hasn't stood the test of time."

Thanks for that, Magill thought. I'll delete it from my list of one thousand books to read before I die. Jesus, where do I sign to get out of here?

"*Trilby* was a huge hit in its day. All sorts of tie-in products capitalized on its popularity – chocolates, cigars, corsets and of course the Trilby hat that's still with us. It was turned into a highly successful stage show and a new town in Florida was named after the novel."

Magill was at a loss. Where was this going? "Are you suggesting, sir, that the time is ripe for *Trilby Two*?"

"No, Mr Magill. I'm telling you this because du Maurier's book introduced a character that everyone has heard of, even if they've never read the novel. Svengali, he's called. He's the alien enchanter who has Trilby, a prostitute turned opera singer, in his power. He controls her hypnotically, mesmerically, and when Svengali dies backstage during a gala concert, Trilby immediately loses her ability to sing like a nightingale."

Much as he loved to chew the literary fat, Magill was starting to lose patience. "What, you reckon Simon Cowell is mesmerizing *American Idol* contestants?"

"Who knows. What I do know is that the enchanter archetype finds expression in many walks of life – sports coaches, orchestra conductors, political leaders, faith healers, corporate CEOs… commanding officers. Their orders must be obeyed for the team or orchestra or party or therapy or company or battalion or whatever to operate effectively. If the spell is broken by insolence or insubordination, disaster befalls everyone involved."

"I see."

The colonel grimaced, having finally gotten through to his obtuse recruit. "The thing I can't understand is why you failed to follow orders. Your background reveals a succession of influential father figures. Yet you refused to do as you were bid by your commanding officer, even though you swore an oath on arrival."

"It's very simple, sir. I have a thing about burning books. My father was a minister in a little place in Ireland called Eden. One night, while he was away at a brass rubbing convention, a gang of yobs attacked the church. They didn't burn the building down, as such, they gathered up all the hymnbooks and psalters and Bibles and suchlike and torched them in front of the manse."

"Did no one try to stop them?"

"My mother did. They beat her up. Called her a papish bitch. Threatened to burn her along with the books. Told her to get out of town."

"And you were a baby at the time?"

"No, no. I was nine or ten. I was afraid of them. I hid in the house while my mother was kicked around."

"I see."

"My big brother had just joined the army. I was the only man in the house. I was derelict in my duty. My mother forgave me. My father never did. The thought of burning books brings that night back to me. Reminds me of my cowardice. I guess General Patton would've horsewhipped me, as he often did with fight-shy soldiers."

The colonel said nothing. The nothing said everything. He pulled a sheet of paper from his top drawer, held it steady with the claw and signed at the bottom using his good hand. He passed it across to Magill. "Countersign at the bottom and be on your way."

Magill didn't bother reading his dishonourable discharge statement. He got to his feet and followed the NCO through the outer office and on to the veranda. The winter sun was up. The view through the golden-edged eucalyptus towards Santa Ana Heights was magnificent. An invigoratingly gummy smell assaulted his nasal passages. Magill asked about ordering a cab to the airport. Sergeant Crush explained that that wasn't permitted. However, an alternative mode of transport was available. They rode the golf cart to the jetty. A ferry boat and its simian Charon were waiting. Crush outlined Magill's transportation options. Swim or sit. As anyone would, Magill sat, shaking his head at the ridiculousness of PWC's top secret bullshit. He was already retreating from the military mentality.

Magill spied the concrete ballast. "Let me guess," he said sardonically, recalling the seminars on storytelling structure, plot arcs and narrative progression. "You attach that block to my ankles and throw me overboard midstream, where I scream and shout and struggle desperately but eventually go under."

"Don't be absurd," the sergeant replied, idly swishing a

replica of General Patton's riding crop. "We put a plastic bag over your head to drown the sound, otherwise it upsets the neighbours." He pointed out a line of expensive houses on the bluff above the nature reserve.

Magill laughed. It was a good joke. Drill sergeants have a way with repartee. "Don't tell me. The dead bodies are conveniently eaten by a ravening pack of barracudas that flourish in these sheltered waters."

"Piranhas, hereabouts."

The dishonourably discharged recruit was still chuckling when the craft stopped in the middle of the watercourse. He could sense the simian breathing heavily behind him. He could hear something rustling. "You know what, Mr Magill," Crush said quietly, flicking a glance at the ferryman. "General Patton wouldn't have horsewhipped you. He too was a cowardly child, a wimp, the runt of the litter. He overcame his cowardice by willpower and training. He would have recognized himself in your story and sympathized. If he'd seen what I saw the other day, when you went back for a fallen comrade, he'd've mentioned you in dispatches, not slapped you around. You are not yellow, Mr Magill."

"Thank you, sergeant. That means a lot to me."

Crush looked around, taking in the scene, watching the sunlight play off the choppy water. The waves slapped against the side of the boat. Birds wheeled overhead, chittering, chattering, cawing, calling out warnings. "Here's where we say goodbye…"

"Oh really," Magill said, tensing himself for what he thought was a joke but was proving all too real. "Spare me the plastic bag at least. They're bad for the environment, you know."

Crush nodded appreciatively. "Let me finish, boy. Here's where we say goodbye… to most dishonourable dischargees. But not you, Mr Magill. You may not graduate Blood and Guts Book Camp, but you're a soldier in my book." He shook Simon's hand vigorously. He had a grip like a manacle. "Start her up," he said to the ferryman.

Magill didn't know whether to be grateful or to laugh at the patently obvious psyop stunt. Putting the frighteners on him, eh? He said nothing. The drill sergeant asked about Magill's mathematical prowess. He'd heard talk of it from the grunts. The dischargee recounted the serial numbers of his entire platoon and, on examining Crush's dog tags, informed the astonished NCO that 354767453 was a palindromic prime number.

The drill sergeant looked at his dog tags with delight, as if he were seeing them anew. "There's someone you should talk to," he said. "A big name author who's looking for collaborators with math smarts. He has a sideline, a subsidiary brand, called Net Force."

"Who is he?"

Crush pulled a tiny, spiral-bound notebook from his top pocket, jotted something down using his knee for support and handed the fluttering sheet of paper to Magill. "He'll tell you himself. Ring this number."

The speedboat nudged through a bed of reeds on the far bank of Newport Bay Ecological Preserve. Magill stood up, shouldered his kitbag and stepped awkwardly past the MP, who looked vaguely disgruntled. Regretting missing his breakfast, no doubt. A black Chrysler minivan was waiting to take him to the airport. Magill glanced at the paper and pocketed it. "Thank you, Sergeant Crush."

The drill sergeant stood at the stern and saluted. "Good luck, Mr Magill."

"Want me to hit the deck and give you one last fifty?"

"Get the fuck outta here, you cocksuckin' cunt."

Chapter Twenty-Four

No-go Dumbo

Mae West snapped shut her Sony Ericsson then returned to her touch up. She double-checked her mascara in the dressing room mirror, while humming a sultry show tune.

W. C. Fields and Charlie Chaplin had got the gist of the curt conversation. "Trouble?" Fields inquired brusquely.

"Nope," Mae replied, pouting and preening and admiring her ravishing reflection. "No trouble. Dannyboy's in Dublin. He's identified a suitable target. She's reading *Digital Fortress* as we speak. He's waiting for the go-ahead. He's keen to get started. He's getting a bit irritated, that's all."

"Tell me about it," Chaplin chipped in.

Ever the perfectionist, Mae removed a tiny speck of lipstick from her front tooth. She arched her eyebrows, fluttered her eyelashes and applied another touch of lascivious lip gloss. "Our quarry's tougher than we thought," she said with a so-it-goes shrug. "Not as tough as Big C, though."

Fields took the hint. Redirecting his ire, he turned to Chaplin, who was twiddling his moustache and rolling his eyes in that infuriating manner. "What's your latest excuse?" he growled at the diminutive thespian.

Chaplin fiddled with his bowler hat. "The Fulcanelli Code works perfectly. I tested it using a mailing from Disney's World-Wide-Website. Everything went to plan. Every customer who opened the free-gift attachment experienced complete HDD meltdown. Drivers immobilized, memory erased, archive wiped, keyboard crippled, control-alt-delete deleted. Fulcanelli's the IT equivalent of Ebola. I once promised you I'd take computer viruses to places they hadn't been before. And that's what I've delivered."

"What about the old switch-off-and-on-again subroutine?" Mae asked, wondering if his high-tech mindset had overlooked the low-tech reactions of many ordinary computer users. She picked up a powder puff for one last dab on the end of her nose.

"Rebooting only makes things worse," Chaplin snickered. "That'll teach them to trust Mickey and Minnie. Beware rodents bearing gifts, especially at Christmas."

Exasperated, Fields had had enough of his self-satisfied co-star. "Yes, that's all very well. Doubtless Dumbo's coming down with deadly dengue fever, next stop the elephants' graveyard. But what proportion of the recipients actually opened the attachment?"

"Eighteen," Chaplin confessed. "It was double that in the States, where consumers are more gullible in general and more besotted by Disney in particular. So they let their guards down, unsurprisingly. Japan and China also did okay…"

"I don't consider 36 per cent okay," Fields barked. "It's a disaster. What was the attachment opening ratio in France?"

"Ten per cent."

"Big C won't be pleased. Didn't you read the latest e-screed?"

Chaplin shook his head. "No. No. I've been too, uh, busy with the Fulcanelli Code."

"Well, let me read it to you," Fields continued, opening a hard copy of their employer's most recent communication. It was yet another rant about the iniquity of business school professors who were pointing western corporations in the wrong direction. Salespeople were no better, because somebody sold all those CDOs and CMOs that got western capitalism into its current mess. By God, marketing would pay for its misdeeds.

The curmudgeon's recitation was interrupted by a knock on the dressing room door. "Five minutes to curtain."

"It goes on like this for four more pages," Fields said, shuffling through the sizzling sheets of paper. "If we don't find a way of upping that percentage, it'll be curtains for us all. Curtains with a capital C."

Mae West lit a cigarette, dragged deeply and exhaled through her nostrils. She looked like a beautiful bad-tempered bull in a sequinned dress, plus platinum blonde wig. Not so much lipstick on a pig as pancake on a Pamplona participant. "Hmmmm, that's what I call a B-school in the bonnet."

"Listen up," Fields said. "I want the pair of you to work

together on this. With your *femme fatale* infallibility, I'm sure you can think of something, Mae. At least 80 per cent of B-school professors are men. If anyone can get to grips with their peripherals, it's you. As your side of our assignment is almost over, you can help Charlie from here on in."

Mae shot him a glare that said do-I-have-to-do-everything-around-here? But Fields was in a Ben Franklin mood – hang together or hang separately – so there was no dissuading him.

A second knock, louder this time. "Two minutes. Two minutes to curtain up."

Fields's cellphone tinkled. "My little chickadee," he cried, as the great incorrigible slipped into character. He listened attentively, muttering on occasion. "Felicity! Serendipity! Providentiality! Inestimability!" all in that signature sing-song voice. He rang off. "Good news, accomplices."

"Oh yeah," West drawled, stubbing out her cigarette. Chaplin waddled up and down the dressing room, feet splayed, cane twirling, saying nothing, focusing on his act.

"Our quarry has finally cracked and it's a big one."

"Yessss," West hissed, flipping open her Sony Ericsson. She hit redial and listened distractedly as the electronic tonic sol-fa plinked out its one note tune. "It's a no-go. Repeat, it's a no-go." Once again, her co-stars could detect a tone of trans-Atlantic protest. "Yes, you'll get paid in full. No, you must leave her unmolested unless I rescind this order within the next 24 hours. I don't care how much you were looking forward to it. You will follow instructions in a professional manner, otherwise our association is over. Leave her alone for now. Got that?"

The murderpreneur was trying his best to extract something from the arrangement. Clearly this was someone who enjoyed his work.

"Do you think we're barbarians? Do exactly as you're told, Dannyboy. Or else!" Infuriated, Mae snapped shut her cell. She tucked it into her cleavage, checked her butt in the mirror and wiggled her hips like she hadn't a care in the world. "Showtime, Charlie. Showtime, Claude."

"Showtime," they said as one, slapping high fives, as they always did before the curtain rose.

Chapter Twenty-Five

The Streisand Effect

"Can I help you?"

The nerve of it. The guy was just sitting there. As large as life. Larger, in fact, because he was taller than average. Better looking too. Sculpted face. Honed bod. Still, that didn't give him the right to sit behind her desk. Maybe it did. Perhaps he's her replacement. They don't hang around, do they? Sods! "You might at least have waited until I cleared my desk," she said in a bark that hovered somewhere between Staffordshire Bull- and Yorkshire-Terrier. Professional politeness is so over.

He looked up, blue eyes appraising her coolly. A slight smile flickered at the corner of his mouth, not exactly cruel but not far off. "I'm here for our date," he said, in an impossibly polite English accent.

Definitely a PR type, though his ginger buzz-cut was unusual, to say the least. Affected eccentricity was not unknown in the "creative" community. At least he wasn't wearing a bow tie or, worse, a cravat. Abby ran through her mental appointments book. Definitely no lunch dates for today. No lunch dates for the foreseeable future, come to think of it. "You must be mistaken. Perhaps you're in the wrong department. If you tell me who you're looking for, I'll escort you to the appropriate office." Professional service had been resumed. Almost. "Where you can sit behind someone else's desk..."

"You don't recognize me, do you?"

Damn. The worst insult in the PR industry, where everyone assiduously remembered everyone's name, everyone's spouse, everyone's dog's birthday – albeit only for show. Abby was past all that. She had ceased to care. She was unwilling to pretend any more. "Yes..." she said.

A look of genuine surprise crossed his chiselled face.

"… I don't recognize you."

He smiled ruefully. "You look different," he said. "You look very well," he went on. "But you still owe me lunch."

"Is that right?"

He threw a newspaper on the desk. *The Irish Times.* They'd reproduced the photo, the one where she was rolling her eyes, sticking out her tongue, waggling her hands behind her head, doing her crazy city councillor impression. They seem to have reproduced the entire article. So much for a local storm in a local teacup. She was the laughing stock of the entire country now. The British broadsheets were probably running it too. What a nightmare.

"It says here that you got the idea for WeeTube from someone you met in Scotland. That someone was me, I suspect, because we tossed i-ideas around over lunch one day."

Abby looked at him again. He seemed vaguely familiar. But different. Of course, the gangly geek who worked for Pitcairn Brodie. God, he'd filled out in the interim. In a good way. It was a long time since she'd seen a man so muscular. It was a long time since she'd seen a real man, full stop. "Yes," she said. "I remember you now. Simon… Simon… Simon something."

"Magill," he said, putting a stop to her struggle. "Simon Simon Simon Magill, at your service."

Abby smiled. "Ah yes. Do all your extended family have triple-barrelled Christian names or is it a deed-poll thing?"

"Nah," he replied. "Our minister had a terrible stammer, that's all. Caused havoc at the christening, though. My sister's called P-P-P-P-P-P-Paula Ma-Ma-Ma-Ma-Ma-Ma-Magill."

She shouldn't have laughed, since mocking the verbally afflicted wasn't exactly P-P-P-P-PC. But the PR industry had a black-humoured underbelly and, given what Abby was currently suffering at its hands, she'd earned the right to make m-m-m-mock. "I don't recall agreeing to buy lunch, Simon Simon Simon. We *had* lunch in Edinburgh's National Gallery. Lunch that was paid for by *me*, if memory serves. We didn't arrange a second date."

"Ah, but we did. I told you that I'd taken up a lectureship at the University of Hustler. We agreed to meet and eat when I got here."

"That was a couple of years ago," she said, reverting to a bantering mode of conversation that she hadn't experienced since the good old bad old days with Dave Kelley. "The statute of lunchtime limitations has expired."

"I'm buying."

"You're on."

He laughed uproariously at that. Abby's somewhat unimpressed memories of a giggling ginger geek who'd be eaten alive in Ulster were dispelled in a great gust of good humour. Hustler University had obviously been good for him, which was more than it ever was for her. As they set off from the City Hall, in search of a suitably anonymous eating place – somewhere where Abby didn't have to cope with cruel finger-pointers – she asked him about the good life at HBS. He succinctly, if cryptically, recounted that he'd left Hustler under a cloud and was living and working in the States. The under a cloud comment was strangely comforting, Abby found. Maybe this was going to be an interesting lunch date, after all.

They bought a pasta bake and club sandwich at a Mace convenience store and took a turn on the Big Wheel, which afforded impressive views across the River Lagan towards Titanic Quarter and the snow-spattered Holywood Hills beyond. They had a cabin all to themselves and, wrapped in their heavy winter woollies, tucked lustily into lunch.

"Whatever happened to WeeTube?" he asked with a sympathetic smile. "Sounds like a great idea, if I say so myself."

"You didn't read the article, then?"

"Oh, I read it. That's why I'm here."

"Well, Simon Simon Simon, if you're pursuing your intellectual property rights, you're wasting your time. WeeTube collapsed pretty much as the piece reported. Things were going pretty well. The themed evenings were particularly popular, as were the live gigs, air guitar evenings and so on. It was Wii that did for us."

Magill fiddled with his plastic fork. The last of the pasta pasta pasta was playing hard to get. "I'm surprised they were so hostile, especially as it was all good publicity."

Abby munched for a moment or two then swallowed. There's

181

only one thing worse than talking with your mouth full and that's talking with your mouth full of club sandwich. "Guess the device was so popular that Nintendo didn't feel the need for any more publicity, especially the sort of publicity that we provided."

"WeeWii was too much for them, then?"

"I thought it was very funny myself. We thought of calling it Wii at WeeTube, but WeeWii's so much more… evocative… don't you think?"

"If a tad… um… urinal."

"Anyway, they sued. Trade mark violations, damaged brand equity, blah, blah, blah. We thought of fighting it, because the court case would have meant lots of sympathetic press coverage. But then we had the fire and that was pretty much that."

"The accidentally-on-purpose fire?"

Abby felt a fit of pique coming on. However, the playful look in Simon's eye took the edge off her testiness. WeeWii was ancient history. What did it matter any more? "Don't believe everything you read in the paper, Simon Simon Simon."

"So you didn't really describe your next-door neighbours as lesbians?"

"That was a joke."

"So you didn't really describe city councillors as crackpots?"

"Well, they are. Let's be honest."

"So you didn't really approve of the Belfast Bunny branding campaign?"

"No, and I still don't. The Black Rose was agreed. The press packs had gone out. They changed their minds at the last minute. The Lord Mayor had second thoughts because someone told him that the black rose symbolized death, which of course it does. But in a good way, a death and resurrection way. My boss dropped me in it. Got his own back on me. I thought he'd come in from his sickbed to help. To help crucify me, more like."

"So the council won't forgive you, then? They can't complain about the publicity their branding campaign's generated, that's for sure."

"Are you enjoying this?" she snapped. "For your information, our esteemed city fathers don't take kindly to employees who hog the headlines, especially if they're headlines involving crackpot councillors and their daft branding ideas about bunnies, bunnies that are hippity-hopping across our city's publicity material, as I speak."

"Bibbity Bobbitty Abby's a very funny headline, you've got to admit."

Ordinarily, she'd have stalked out of the room at this point. However, with a 200 ft drop to the nearest fall-breaking surface, she had second thoughts about flouncing off.

"I'm sorry, Abby. I didn't mean... I was only teasing... I thought you'd see the funny side..."

"For your information, I was about to clear my desk when I met you earlier. That's how funny I find it." She was still haunted by the look on Mal Montgomery's face when he set the *Belfast Telegraph* in front of her, conveniently open at Day in the Life. The glee in his eyes was not far short of fiendish.

"Why don't you make a formal complaint to the press commission? The photo was taken without your permission. The video on the *Belfast Telegraph* website was obviously captured by an iPhone or similar hand-held device. Presumably you were speaking off the record."

"I was," Abby sighed. "Well, I thought I was. Spike Holden had confederates at the next table, taking photographs of someone mugging in a public place. He even told me that he was recording the conversation. I thought he was joking. The slimy sod was after a scoop. He got one. I hope he's happy."

"So why didn't you complain to his editor."

"The Streisand Effect."

"Sorry," he said, with a confused expression. "The what effect?"

"Barbra Streisand once sued a freelance photographer when he posted aerial photographs of her house on his homepage. The resultant publicity meant that countless thousands of people visited the guy's website and searched on-line for additional pictures of her house. Her attempts to prevent the publicity only perpetuated the publicity. It always does. It's a law of nature."

Magill smiled with recognition. "I know what you mean. When I was at Hustler, a very senior academic sent a round-robin email to all members of staff, ordering them not to talk about his allegedly drunken antics during committee meetings. It was the first most members of staff had heard of his carry-on and, by trying to quash ugly rumours before they went critical, he ensured everyone talked about them."

"Aye. Well. There you go. If I were to complain about Holden's underhand behaviour, it'd only redouble the bad publicity. I prefer to let sleeping dogs lie, though if I ever get my paws on one particularly poisonous pooch, he'll be Holden his testicles in his hands."

"Quite," Magill said, unsettled by an image that was too close to his brother's untimely demise for comfort. An awkward silence threatened to descend. "I didn't realize the Streisand Effect was a proper syndrome."

"Well, that's not the clinical name. That's just what we call it in Guerrilla Psychology class."

Magill looked embarrassed. "I've never heard of guerrilla psychology, let alone the Streisand Effect. What's guerrilla psychology?"

Abby brightened. One of the few pleasures she had left in life – apart from rowing – was her evening class. "I never finished my marketing degree at Hustler."

"Don't blame you."

"But I was intrigued by consumers' perverse reactions to WeeTube promotions. The things I thought would go well, like the porn nights, completely flopped. Other events that seemed certain to fail, such as the poetry recitals, packed them in. So I started to wonder about the psychological principles behind consumer perversity. I met an old guy one evening and he turned out to be a lecturer in, of all things, guerrilla psychology. He talked me into signing up for his part-time course at the OU. It's great. He's great, though a wee bit obsessed with the Freemasons, conspiracies and suchlike."

As a former lecturer himself, if an ineffective one, Magill knew how hard it was to inspire part-time students. "Oh yeah, what's his name?"

"Ian Kane. Dr Ian Kane. Have you heard of him? He used to work at Hustler."

Magill blanched. Ian Kane, his buddy, his so-called mentor,

his goddamn nemesis. "The fat guy? Fond of a fry up? I think I know who you mean. Didn't know he had a degree in psychology, though."

Abby could tell that there was something he wasn't telling her. She changed the subject, subtly as ever. "You said you were here for a reason, Simon. What is it you want with me? If it's the inside scoop on the Belfast brand, I'm afraid I'm out of the loop."

"I want you to come to Dublin with me. I've got a problem and I need your help. I need someone I can trust. Professor Brodie told me about you, one night in The Beehive, not long after he'd returned from Nuremberg and the day before he… well… you know what. He spoke very highly about you, said you were a remarkable young woman, someone worth cultivating when I got to Ulster. It's a bit late, but, well, here I am and I really need your help."

Abby swallowed hard. She felt the tears prickle her eyes. "I saw him, you know. Pitcairn *was* in Mal's office that day. I saw him with my own eyes. That stuff in the paper about Mad Maguire seeing ghosts at work. That's so not true."

"I'm sure you saw something," Magill said benevolently. "But Pitcairn Brodie is dead. I discovered the body, Abby." Their lunchtime skyride concluded in silence. A gentleman at heart, Simon offered her a helping hand as she exited the cabin. "I guess it's time I headed back to Dublin. Are you coming? Or is clearing your desk top priority?"

She mulled the offer over for a second. She had no work to go back to. She didn't want to face her neighbours anytime soon. Getting out of town while the dust from Bunnygate settled seemed like a good idea. There were worse places in the world than Dublin. Bibbity Bobbitty Belfast, for one.

"Okay, Simon Simon Simon. Let's go go go."

Chapter Twenty-Six

It Takes U2 to Tango

The Enterprise Express slithered into Belfast's Central Station, arcing like an aluminium anaconda around the final bend. Even before it had come to rest, the doors of the high-speed train were thrown open, as thrusting tribes of travellers descended, determined to go about their business. They surged across the platform, scampered up the escalators, stampeded along the covered walkways, squeezed past the unmanned ticket barrier and, after getting their Belfast bearings, sallied forth into the welcoming metropolis. They weren't there for the architecture, much less the impressive public buildings or even the restful riverside walkway. They were there for the shopping. The drastic fall of the pound against the euro, in the aftermath of the global banking crisis, meant that consumers from the south of Ireland could pick up unbelievable bargains in the cheap and cheerful north, where sterling still held sway. Despite the near-collapse of Ireland's own economy, the lucky few with euros to spare found that they went far, far further north of the border. Hence, they were prepared to travel far, far further than they ordinarily would and even when transportation costs were taken into account, a day trip to Belfast was well worth the outlay.

Belfast Means Bargains.

Apart from the obvious economic benefits, this consumer carpet bombing of Ireland's second city had another unanticipated advantage. The mid-morning trains returning to Dublin were almost completely empty. Travelling north, the Enterprise Express was akin to a Punjabi inter-city service – packed carriages, standing room only, swarms of free-riders on the rattling, swaying roof. Heading south, the Enterprise was like a real-life ghost train, complete with strangely abandoned half-eaten meals and slowly cooling cups of coffee. If not quite the *Marie Celeste* of rolling stock, the trains were a postmodern inversion of coffin ships.

As they took their comfy seats in the empty carriage and waited for the train to depart, Abby and Simon exchanged carefully expurgated back stories. She told him about her experiences in Some Like It Hot, St Stephen's Retreat House and the dark heart of the Carlton Hotel in Nuremberg. He reciprocated with his own edited highlights, from Brodie's body via King Billy's hospitality to the showdown in show town, followed by his internship at the Danster's.

"What's he like to work for, anyway?"

"I guess some would call him a pretty hard taskmaster. Every time I pitched an idea, he shot it down in flames."

"Pitch an idea?"

Magill smiled modestly. "Yeah, I was a kind of scenario man. Well, okay, I was employed as his PA but that evolved into making suggestions, such as identifying potential locations and possible plot progressions for future novels. Other times, I concocted chase sequences, pitched gory killing sprees and suchlike." Amused by her takes-all-sorts expression, he elaborated. "You know, tuk-tuk chases in central Bangkok, gelignite-filled gondolas grappling on the Grand Canal, bad guys being eaten alive by ravenous fire ants atop ancient Mayan temples in Mexico."

"Sleep well, do you?"

"I do now."

"Why's that?"

The train was picking up speed as it left the back yards of Belfast behind. Snow-covered, the Ulster countryside huddled under its blanket – strong, silent, surly. Magill explained that he was no longer in the Danster's employ. He told her how a series of second-rate scenarios had precipitated his fall from grace: KKK, Green October, Barnum Brown.

Unused to the turmoil of the creative process, Abby innocently asked, "So what was his problem with them?"

Simon shrugged. "I'm still not sure. He didn't fully explain his rationale for rejection. He just went ballistic. The tantrums got worse and worse and worse, what's more. I'd never seen anything like it, certainly not from Dan. He's the most mild-mannered man, believe it or not, the nicest person you could meet. Given the head-turning adulation he received in the aftermath of *Da Vinci* – and despite all the vituperation and plagiarism suits and movie adaptation machinations and pressure to deliver a block-buster sequel – he always managed to keep his feet on the ground. Except when he was hanging from his gravity boots, of course."

The joke was lost on Abby, who'd only ever read Brown's books and knew nothing about his famously eccentric working habits. "Sounds to me like you're better off without him."

"I'm not exactly without him," he sighed.

"What exactly do you mean by not exactly, Simon?"

Like a dam breaking, Magill started speaking rapidly. It was pouring out of him. "Dan's holed up in the Clarence Hotel. That's where we're heading, Abby. He's had a breakdown of some kind, a complete mental breakdown. When I saw him yesterday morning, he was curled up in the foetal position, muttering crazy stuff to himself. It's a terrible sight, Abby. I badly need your help. I'm really grateful for your assistance."

Abby was nonplussed. She took several moments to gather her thoughts. "Simon, if you no longer work for him, how come this is your problem? What's wrong with the medical facilities in Dublin? Why are you grateful for my assistance? There's nothing I can do for him. I study guerrilla psychology, not clinical psychiatry."

It was Magill's turn to look nonplussed. He had ready answers for part one and two, but the third question was a problem. "Well, when Dan sacked me in Sydney he gave me a priceless farewell gift and said that if ever I got into trouble, he'd help me. I'm duty bound to reciprocate. He's in trouble. Therefore, I'm going to help him."

"This was a man who sacked you on the spot, Simon."

"I know, but he's still a friend in need." Ignoring Abby's sceptical glance, he continued on his pre-prepared justification. "Hospitals are like leaky buckets. If Dan is admitted, every newspaper in the country will be reporting the fact. You can just imagine what they'd do with something like that. There's nothing we Irish love more than a 'writer cracks up' story."

"Hotel rooms are safe from prying reporters, are they?"

"The Clarence is," Magill said. "Bono makes sure of it. All sorts of celebrity shenanigans go on there. U2 operates an *omertà*, from what I can gather. It's stronger still when the boss man's involved."

"Why's that?"

Thrown by the naivety of her question, Magill wondered whether it was wise to rely on this woman. Surely she can't be that obtuse. "Because Bono's a buddy of the Pope. Brown's in the Pope's bad books. Bono and Brown are best buddies, too. Two's company, three's a schism."

"I see."

Magill checked his Mickey Mouse watch, a birthday present from the Danster. "Good. We'll be there in forty-five minutes." He pulled a mobile out of his voluminous Ulster overcoat and hit speed dial. "Hi Bono, Simon here."

"Bono?" Abby mouthed, her reservations rapidly evaporating in the white heat of A-list celebrity. "As in *the* Bono?"

Phone pressed against his ear, the ginger man ignored her. "No, not Simon Cowell, Simon Magill. You know, the friend of your friend in the penthouse suite. Uh-huh. Uh-huh. How's the patient? Okay. Okay. Got ya. That's right. That's right. Tom Hanks's hairstyle *is* based on your mullet. No, really. *Joshua Tree* era, I think. No really. Sure thing. No problem. Peace."

"Simon," Abby said, "much as I'd like to meet Sir Paul Hewson, or whatever Bono's called nowadays, I still don't see how I can help. I was once asked to join a band as drummer, but Larry Mullen's doing a pretty good job, as far as I can see. Mind you, if hot bot Larry's in town, I might be tempted to hang around."

Long since inured to the so-called charisma of celebrities – the film set in Rome had cured him of that, though Hanks was a pretty regular guy, considering – Magill had more important things to worry about. "Dan's been shouting and screaming and stuff, apparently. Had to be given a shot. Bono's worried."

"Sounds bad. I still can't see..."

Shaken by the latest twist in Dan's spiral of decline, Magill stared into space as the drab lowlands around Drogheda flashed past. The snow had mostly melted in the Boyne Valley's sheltered microclimate. The steely grey Irish Sea lay flat and taciturn. "He's screaming something about the Priory of Ryan, the Protocols of the Elders of Ryan…"

An overactor would have gasped, groaned and clutched her chest at this point in the proceedings. But Abby made do with a sinking heart and a sudden frisson of fear. She'd hoped the Priory of Ryan days were behind her. She should have known better. Named after a secret society in *All Fall Down*, a potboiler penned by W. B. Yeats, the Priory was some kind of fraternal front for the commercial activities of the IRA, the UDA and God only knows who else. Its tentacles stretched around the entire world – the underworld, rather – and presumably they were putting pressure on Magill's ex-mentor.

Face set in an authors-say-the-craziest-things demeanour, Magill continued with his unwitting whinge. "What on earth's the Priory of Ryan, when it's at home? Maybe Dan said Sion. His New England accent can take a bit of getting used to."

Regretfully, Abby enlightened her unsettled travelling companion. She told him some of the things she'd omitted earlier, most notably Dan Brown's apparent plagiarism of his greatest literary hit. Magill looked as though he'd been hit in the face with a skillet – something, she'd discovered earlier, he'd had empirical experience of.

"It wasn't supposed to be like this," he groaned.

"What do you mean, Simon?"

"The plot."

"What plot?"

"The plotline," he mumbled. "The twelve stages of the narrative journey. You were supposed to Refuse the Call but you agreed to come along anyway. We're facing the Ultimate Ordeal and we haven't even reached the First Threshold yet. This can't be right. It's not possible. It's madness. It's…"

"Simon," she snapped. "Simon," she snapped again, snapping her fingers under his nose. "Simon," she snapped a third time, slapping him across the face sharply. The crack of his hollow cheek echoed around the empty carriage. "Calm down, Simon. Explain yourself."

Magill's eyes swam into focus. He rubbed his face distractedly. "Ow. That was sore. Do you do that to all your patients?"

Jesus. Abby was beginning to think that Dan Brown wasn't the only crackpot in the plotline of this particular narrative journey. Patiently, she extracted the storyline behind the storyline. Magill told her about PWC, about the classes on narrative structure. All stories follow the same basic outline, according to Joseph Campbell's monomyth, only the setting and characters and incidental details differ. She tried to tell him that this was real life, but he insisted that real life was mediated by the stories we read, the movies we see, the TV programmes we watch, the computer games we play, all of which are predicated on the monomyth. The pattern is immutable, inviolate, pretty much universal.

Bowing to Magill's experience of such matters, Abby let sleeping Dans lie. "So, what's with the patients?" she asked him as the outer Dublin suburbs of Donnybrook and Drumcondra blurred by.

"The patients? There's only one patient. I hope. We'll be seeing him soon enough."

Abby strongly suspected that there was more than one patient, but she qualified her remark. "You asked me did I do that to all of my patients. What patients would that be?"

Magill stared at her, uncomprehending. "*The Irish Times* said that you were a faith healer, a woman with the healing touch, the seventh son of a seventh son, as it were. That's why I need your help. I want you to heal Dan, just like it said in the paper. I want you to lay your hands on him or whatever it is you do."

"Simon, that was my mother. The newspaper article got it wrong. I told you the report was garbled gibberish. Its facts were all over the place. You should know better than to believe what you read in the paper."

Looking as though he'd been hit by a scalding skillet this time, Magill's jaw dropped open. "You're supposed to be the wise woman archetype. This is not good."

"Sorry," she said with asperity. "I'm the woman-who-used-to-work-in-an-abattoir archetype. If you want me to eviscerate Dan's entrails, I can help you. Other than that I don't have much to offer. Maybe I should get the next train back to Belfast."

"Yeah, maybe that's for the best. I'm sorry I dragged you into this."

"Not a problem Simon. Perhaps we can hook up for another lunch sometime." Like sometime around never, she thought, trying to force a smile.

Embarrassed, he started pulling on his scarf and gloves. The train was decelerating prior to its arrival at Connolly Station. "You'll keep this to yourself, won't you?"

"Not even a world-class hypnotist would get it out of me."

Magill started, as the words of Colonel Clamber came back to him. Command, he claimed, was a form of mesmerism, as was the relationship between faith healer and patient. "Hypnotist? What do you know about hypnotists?"

"Studied them in guerrilla psychology. Wrote an assignment on hypnotism, in fact. Fascinating subject."

"Abby," Magill said, making up his mind. "Why don't you get a later train back instead."

"I guess this is where I refuse the call, Simon."

"I'll introduce you to Bono."

"Tough call. But no thanks."

"Larry might be there, too."

Abby weighed up her options yet again. Face the music in Belfast or face the musicians in Dublin? "You talked me into it, Simon."

"Guess I got myself a wise woman archetype."

"A parky type, perhaps. It looks freezing out there."

"Lucky Larry's hot to trot, I hear."

"It takes U2 to tango."

Chapter Twenty-Seven

Pro Bono

For all the talk about Ireland's economic woes, Abby found it hard to tell. At first glance, Dublin looked as busy as ever. If ever a town bustled and hustled and greeted visitors with a display of urban braggadocio, it was dirty auld Dublin. Abby wanted to walk to the Clarence, since it was only a fifteen-minute dander to their destination. Dublin was a city that begged to be walked through. But Magill manoeuvred her into a waiting taxi. Twenty minutes of taxi-driver tourist blather later, they pulled up outside the Clarence on the lip of the Liffey. Formerly an 84-bedroom flophouse, with fleas and flushless toilets, the Clarence had been turned into a 42-bedroom wonder, with hot and cold running opulence, plus a pair of hip hoteliers who epitomized everything brand Ireland stood for during the glory years of the Celtic carnivore, Bono and the Edge.

The Witchery aside, Abby had never seen such luxury. The Clarence was ye olde Witchery with a modernist minimalist twist. It also had architectural ambitions that made Rameses II look like a little boy building sandcastles on the beach at Bray. Dublin's town planners maintained that Bono's grandiose plans for a great glass superstructure were out of keeping with the area, but as Temple Bar was a kitschy cobbled congeries of touristy knicky-knacky and stag night hanky-panky, perhaps that wasn't such a bad thing.

Even as it stood, though, the Clarence Penthouse was pretty impressive. Stretching the full length of the Wellington Quay frontage, it consisted of two floors, three bedrooms, a leather-lounger-strewn TV room and an Alessi-equipped kitchenette, as well as a rooftop terrace that looked out across the river towards the Northside. Magill was well used to such splendour. Thanks to Dan's inspiration-seeking wanderlust, he'd stayed in the Raffles, the Savoy, the Crillon, the Mandarin Oriental, the Waldorf Astoria and many other landmark hotels. The sybaritic was second nature. So much so, that he'd happily return to PWC's bunk-lined, snore-rattled, flatulence-filled barracks.

Never one to wallow in wow factor, Magill looked around for his former mentor. There was no sign of Dan in either of the main bedrooms, much less the TV lounge or the kitchen. Suddenly fearful, he strode on to the terrace, wondering whether Dan had decided to end it all. There was no evidence of bloody disturbance on the snow-slicked street below. Relieved, he stepped back into the warmth of the suite, locking the double French doors behind him.

"We're upstairs," a mellifluous Irish voice called from the second floor. Abby and Magill clumped up the tiny winding staircase to the upper level of the penthouse, where an additional bedroom, with en suite and walk-in closets, was neatly tucked under the mansard roof. A Catholic cardinal, complete with bright red cassock and scarlet galero, sat by the side of a king-sized bed, reading the good book to a pitiful figure curled on top of the duvet. The cardinal was also wearing Brand Red loafers and Bulgari wrap-around shades.

Magill did a double take. "Bono, is that you?"

The cardinal stood up and floated towards them, hand extended in friendship. Abby got down on one knee, as per tradition, preparing to kiss the ring. "Hey babe," he said, grinning, "don't kneel in front of me like that. My missus might get the wrong impression."

Abby looked around, expecting to see Ali Hewson with hatchet in hand. Looking back, there was only Bono, a big grin plastered across his fashionably stubbled features. "I guess you're the chick with the healing hands. Nice to meet you, Abby."

"You too, Mr Hewson."

"Hey, babe," he laughed, "there's no need to call me that. Saint Bono of Ballymun will do nicely." He held out his fist for a hip-hop knuckle-knock greeting.

Abby curtseyed, crossed herself, then presented her palm in a paper-wraps-rock gesture. Bono looked at her hand for a second, taken aback by the effrontery, then roared with laughter, pushing up the wrap-arounds to wipe his streaming eyes. Superstars are so rarely greeted with cheek – even in Ireland where interpersonal abuse is the norm – that a little bit of audacity can go a very long way.

"How's the patient?" Magill interrupted, trying to shift the focus back towards their cause for concern. "Forgive me, Saint Bono of Ballymun, but do you think it's wise to wear your uniform when the invalid's received death threats from the Catholic hierarchy?"

Bono gestured towards the bed, where the good book lay beside the glassy-eyed patient. "Oh, I don't know, Simon. He's been a bit calmer since I started reading extracts from *Angels and Demons*." He winked at Abby. "In costume," he added archly.

The banter was interrupted by a wail of anguish from the king-size. For a second, Abby thought that it was the prelude to a thunderbolt from above – or Ali Hewson at least – but it was desperate Dan in the direst of straits. He rolled from side to side, muttering, jabbering and clutching something to his chest.

"He won't let go of the manbag, man." Bono tried his best to comfort Magill, who was standing over the prostrate author, a worried expression on his face. "It seems to be a talisman of some kind."

Abby looked again at the babbling patient. He was holding an old black haversack in a limpet-like grip. If it's full of fake fivers, she thought, I am so out of here. She took her place beside Simon and pressed a palm gently across Dan's forehead. He was burning up. His face was covered in scratch marks, as was his throat and neck. Self-inflicted by the look of them. She didn't quite know what to do. However, having calmed wild animals in the past, usually with a reassuring word or two, Abby knew the therapeutic score. Or parts of it, anway. She hunkered down beside the distressed thriller writer and said a few nice things about his literary ability, his adoring fans, his downright decency as a human being. To no avail. He stared at her blankly. If anything, he tightened his grip on the grip. She tried again, only this time telling him how hot he was, how handsome, how most authors are plug ugly but Dan the Man, Brown the Babe was bootylicious. That didn't work either. So much for female wiles, let alone the eternal feminine. "Of course!" she murmured, turning to reverse psychology. She urged him to scream as loud as he liked, to hold on to his satchel for grim death, to ignore any sympathetic entreaties or readings from fourth-rate books like *Angels and Demons*. She further intimated that he was a complete prick, a shitty writer, a stunted dwarf, a dickless wonder, understandably fearing that she'd gone too far. Far from it. He sat up, sharply. He held out the haversack with both hands rigid. Abby took it. He flopped back down again and fell instantly asleep.

"Praise the Lord and pass the paracetamol." Bono looked gobsmacked. He raised two crossed index fingers in a vampire-be-gone gesture. Abby responded with the heavy metal devil's horns she'd learned from Dave Kelley. "Gotta go," the superstar said. "We're going on tour soon, babe. If you need a gig, we could do with a pair of healing hands."

Abby thought for a moment about lubricating Larry's gluteus maximus. Then thought for another moment about a rock entourage offer she'd spurned in the past. "I'm not the backstage type."

"I can see that." He had to go. "If you need anything else, just give me a shout. In the meantime, I'll get one of my minders to keep an eye on you."

"You really are a saint, Bono."

Reverentially, he bowed to the worshipping multitude of one, then funny-walked away whistling "It's a Beautiful Day".

Starstruck, she gazed longingly at the departing holy man, only to be brought back to earth by the sound of someone taking the Lord's name in vain.

"Jesus H. Christ," Magill gasped, pulling book after book after book from Dan's manbag. Abby couldn't see the need for the profanities until she looked more closely at the state of the novels. They were all tattered and torn and ripped from their bindings. The spines were broken. The pages were buckled and brutally bent. They were covered in crazed scribbles, bright yellow highlightings, mad marginal notes with lots of asterisks and exclamation marks. Some of the paperbacks had scorch marks, others had what looked like teeth marks and at least one or two had stab marks. It was as if someone had plunged a big bread knife into the still beating heart of the novel and twisted it without mercy.

An inveterate bibliophile, someone who'd sooner face death than deface a book, Magill was in a state of shock. "These are all Langdon-alikes," he said, looking through the pile of savaged softbacks. Without exception, they were thrillers in the *Da Vinci Code* mould, many with covers that copied Dan's original. They included a couple of ripped Raymond Khoudrys, a brace of butchered Sam Bournes and a mutilated airport edition of Kate Mosse's *Labyrinth*, with "plagiarizing bitch" scratched across the front in blood-red felt tip. Magill opened Michael Cordy's *Messiah Code* and scrutinized the marginalia carefully, almost forensically. "Looks like Dan's handwriting."

"What does it say?"

Despairing, Magill flicked through the novel, pausing at random, reading his mentor's considered words of literary criticism. "Thieving bastard, exclamation mark," he said. "You'll burn in hell, you SoB, double exclamation mark," he added. "Asshole, asshole, asshole, triple exclamation mark, pen piercing the paper on the third." He set the book on top of the others and placed his head in his hands. "I knew the Danster was unhappy about the copycats. Who wouldn't be? He's been ripped off more royally than investors in Madoff's pyramid schemes. He established the market for theological conspiracy thrillers but when he paused for breath after *Da Vinci* – a pretty big breath, admittedly – the imitators ate his lunch. He took all the flack from the Catholic Church, to say nothing of death threats from fundamentalists, only to find that the clones were coining it while he was in hiding." Sorrowfully, Simon re-examined the stab wounds on *Labyrinth*. The knife had cut all the way through to page 495. "I'd be miffed too," he moaned. "But this is madness."

Abby couldn't disagree. "Is there anything else in there?" she asked, nodding towards the danbag, which lay on the bed beside Brown. "No Nazi bayonets, I trust," she added, taken back to an earlier unhappy encounter with decommissioned weapons.

He shook his head, pulling the empty holdall towards him. "Don't think so, Abby." Magill squeezed the cheap canvas container, just to make sure there wasn't anything untoward in the lining. "Hold on, there's something here." He unzipped an outer pocket and extracted a tiny notebook. Not a Moleskine-style notebook but a pygmy notebook computer. "It's Dan's netbook," he said.

"His what?"

"His netbook. They're the latest thing in convenience computing. Began as a kid's toy, cost next to nothing, have very few functions, little or no memory and rely on cloud storage."

Wisely, Abby refrained from asking what cloud storage was. From her days at WeeTube, she knew that boy's toys, especially e-toys, can give rise to inordinately lengthy one-sided conversations. "What do you think's on it? Should we check?"

Magill shrugged noncommittally. "I've seen him using it from time to time. I'm pretty sure it's his *silva rerum*." Catching Abby's blank expression, he continued. "A little book of ideas, idle thoughts, snatches of dialogue, names of characters, descriptions of places, general observations about human behaviour. They're jottings, basically. Every writer has a *silva rerum*, though most prefer pen and paper to Word and Notepad."

"And every author treats books with respect, right? Book mutilation is second only to child molestation in the thriller writers' chamber of horrors, correct?"

"Yeah," he said, prising open the netbook, "And children's book mutilators are the lowest of the low." He switched it on and waited for Windows XP to open up. "Password protected, I'm afraid."

A left-justified cursor blinked in the password box. Abby turned the tiny screen round to look. "Presumably you know what it is. You *were* his PA, after all."

Using his upper thighs as a table, Magill sat at the end of the bed and touch-typed LANGDON. "It should be straightforward enough. The Danster's fairly predictable." Access denied. He tried again with NEVEU, VETRA, LOUVRE and LEONARDO, all unsuccessfully. He tried the titles of his books, with variations. He tried Dan's name, his wife's name, his brother's and sister's names. He even tried TOMHANKS and OPUSDEI and POPEONAROPE, again without success. "Hmmm. This is harder than I thought."

Suddenly struck by inspiration, Abby cried, "I've got it, Simon. I've got it. Didn't *The Da Vinci Code* contain a scene where the characters type passwords into a bank account?"

Magill knew exactly where she was going. "Of course. Of course. You're right. It was the Rue Haxo sequence, in the vault of the Depositary Bank of Zurich."

"Do you remember what the password was?"

"You're looking at a piphilologist. Mathematical sequences are my bread and butter. It was Fibonacci," he added, happily hammering the keys 1–1-2–3-5–8-13–21.

Access denied.

Magill glanced over his shoulder at the recumbent figure on the bed. "Tell you what, Abby, why don't you ask him."

"I think we should let him sleep, Simon."

"Yeah, I guess so." Fifteen minutes later, he asked her again. She demurred, out of respect for the patient. Then again, after another ten fruitless minutes of putative passwords had passed.

"Impatience will be the death of you, Simon." Reluctantly, Abby whispered a few words of casual invective into the Danster's ear. He sat up, instantly alert, eyes wide open, on the point of panic. "The Big C. The Big C. The Big C's after me, bro." He reached out for Magill and wrapped his arms round the astonished redhead.

Abby struggled to calm Dan down, pausing only to fire Simon a look of disapproval. "Happy now?"

"The Priory of Ryan," Dan shouted. "The Protocols, bro. The Priory. The Protocols."

"Take your pick," Abby said acidly, gently pressing the patient's head back down on the pillow, whispering sweet nothings for all she was worth.

Magill picked, but soon wished he hadn't.

Chapter Twenty-Eight

Include Me Out

Simon felt sick. He rushed into the bathroom, but apart from a few unpleasant dry heaves, his gag reflex managed to keep the pasta pasta pasta down down down. After a few recuperative breaths of chill winter's air on the terrace overlooking Wellington Quay, he crept back inside. Momentarily reminded of the last time he'd gathered his thoughts on a river-view terrace after an unspeakably grisly experience, he checked around the penthouse to ensure that no intruders were in hiding. Reassured, he poured himself a big Bushmills from the complimentary bottle at the bar and downed it in one. "Like a drink?" he called up to Abby.

"Not for me, thanks," came a voice from behind him. Abby had moved to the little sitting room in the centre of the suite, letting sleeping Dans lie. "I reckon there are four victims in total," she said calmly.

Unsteadily, Magill poured himself another shot and slumped on the sofa beside her. "You're very blasé about all this, Abby."

"I've seen arterial blood before," she observed, in a matter of fact manner. "I used to slit throats for a living." She re-opened the first of the jpegs. "Still photographs are a lot less unpleasant than the wriggling reality."

Jesus, Magill said to himself, taking a quick peek at the horrors on screen. So much for the military making a man of him. Drill Sergeant Crush would not be impressed by his rapid regression from warrior on parade to wimp about town. He stole another hesitant glance at the tiny screen. High resolution close-ups of murder victims with their throats cut weren't what he expected to find on Dan's netbook. A complete manuscript of his legendary unpublished novel, *The Solomon Key*, several additional draft novels that appear to have been abandoned, and a complete collection of his own Robert Langdon scenarios with annotated comments, some quite complimentary. Those he could understand. He could likewise comprehend the My Music folder full of Led Zeppelin, U2 and Aerosmith downloads, since the Danster was a hard rocker at heart, despite his inability to break into the music business. But the unspeakable images in the My Photographs folder, alongside family snaps, the location collection – Sydney, Salt Lake, Rome and more – were so far out of character that Magill initially assumed they were posed by actors, something that was part of the thriller writing process alongside rough notes, chapter summaries, plot twist listings and pen portraits of possible characters. However, Abby soon disabused him of that idea. She'd seen sufficient death in her life to tell the difference between fake blood and real. He too had seen his share of cadavers at close range, Pitcairn Brodie, Carlingford O'Connell and Barton Brady among them. There was no mistaking the waxy pallor, let alone the gore, the gristle, the viscera, the staring eyes, which seemed horror-struck with the unimaginable thought that this was *the end*.

Abby angled the tiny screen slightly, so that he could see more clearly. They squeezed together on the Starck sofa, transfixed by the unspeakable sight. There were twelve photographs in total, three for each victim. One close-up of the head and neck, one medium shot of the upper torso and one full-length image of the corpse in situ – behind a car wheel, in an old library, across a park bench, on the floor of a toilet stall.

Grisly as the sight of the throat slittings were, the killer's calling cards were more horrific still. Each of the victims had the front cover of a paperback novel driven into their chests. Worse, the titles were instantly recognizable – *Digital Fortress*, *Deception Point*, *Angels and Demons* and *The Da Vinci Code*. Worst of all, the covers were covered in strange occult symbols, drawn in bright yellow highlighter.

"This is one sick puppy," Abby said, stating the obvious.

"I think I've seen those symbols before. They're definitely not the Tarot, nor Freemasonic from what I can tell. They might be Rosicrucian, possibly Order of the Golden Dawn...."

"There's never a symbologist when you need one," Abby said drily, cutting him off mid-babble. She stared intently at the overwritten covers – an eight-pointed star; the sun, with sardonic human features; an all-seeing-eye inside a crescent moon; a quartered shield, each field containing the letter A. Half-remembered thoughts of Rosa Alchemica Caledonia, a Scottish antique shop filled with immemorial images of good and evil, came back to her unbidden. She shuddered at the memory, while struggling to keep cool, calm and collected. She'd been here before. She could cope with whatever fate threw at her. She was a survivor. So far.

It was hard, though, to cope with the depravity. Each of the thumbnails in Dan's folder of death had an unforgivably callous caption, drawn from popular culture. I'd Rather Kill in Philadelphia. Come Up and Slay Me Sometime. The Little Tramp Deserved to Die. Is That a Novel in Your Pocket or a Thriller in Your Thorax? And others too revolting to read. "Dan's a very sick man," she murmured to her aghast companion. "I think we should call the police."

"Dan had nothing to do with this," Magill stated with finality. "I know him. He's the nicest, kindest man imaginable. Dan's totally incapable of killing someone."

"He's a man who spends his life writing about people dying horrible deaths. That kind of thing can warp someone's mind. There's a dark side to all of us, Simon. The serial killer within is never far from the civilized surface."

Infuriated, Magill crashed his empty whiskey glass on the Philippe Starck coffee table. "Learned that in your guerrilla psychology class, did you? Or was it *Star Wars* reruns? You'll be telling me that the Force is with us in a minute."

"It is. It will be. I'm ringing the police right now."

The penthouse suite fell silent, apart from the patient's occasional sleep-crazed shout from the bedroom above. Magill placed his hand on Abby's knee. She flinched. He squeezed. "Don't do anything rash. I beg you. You know what the police are like. You know how they react when a celebrity's involved. You know they'll be straight on to the media. You know what the press'll make of Dan the madman in St Bono's hotel." Magill stared intently into Abby's face, looking for some signs of sympathy. "I *know* Dan didn't do this. He's been set up. He has a lot of enemies. You have no idea what he goes through. The crazies who constantly hassle him."

"Like the Big C, you mean?" Abby felt her resolve crumble under Magill's conviction. His vestigial devotion to someone who'd sacked him unceremoniously was admirable in its own way. Would that she had a faithful friend like that. She knew only too well what policemen were capable of, as an encounter with the Edinburgh constabulary once demonstrated, and the media hellhounds' bite-marks were still discernible on her pert posterior.

"I don't know who or what Big C is," Magill replied, with an emphatic shake of the head. "It's just something Dan'd mutter from time to time. I asked him about it once, but he said I'd be better off not knowing. I tried every 'C' I could think of, the Catholic Church, Columbia Pictures, Clive Cussler, the Credit Crunch, Communists, Castro, Santa Claus. I got the feeling it was something to do with Catholicism but it was no more than a feeling."

"You think the Catholic Church is behind this?" Abby asked, as indignant as he'd been earlier, when Dan's bona fides were called into question. "The killings? The book covers? The symbols? Pinning it all on Dan?"

Magill didn't mince his words. "Four murders mean nothing to the organization behind the Inquisition, the Crusades, the Cathar holocaust, the Knights Templar slaughter, the counter-reformation, the witch-burning craze, the betrayal of the Jews during the Second World War, the assassination of their own Pope, Paul IV, the murder of Jacques Saunière in the Louvre, the strangulation of Sister Sandrine in St Sulpice, the slaying of Leonardo Vetra, a former priest, in CERN…"

"Actually, Simon, I think the last lot were fictional, the outcome of a certain someone's warped imagination!" She rolled her eyes heavenward.

"Chuck Palahniuk once said that fiction tells the truth better than the truth does."

"Aye," Abby countered, "Chuck Palahniuk's a sick puppy too. I tried reading one of his books once. It was disgusting."

Coming from someone who used to work in Some Like It Hot – someone who'd handled more sex toys than Ann Summers herself – Abby's benchmark comments could not be lightly dismissed. Magill didn't try to argue. He tried to change tack. "You know, there's a very simple way of finding out who Big C is and who's behind the killings."

"What's that?"

"We'll ask him. Let's ask the Danster."

"Simon," Abby countered, as politely as she could. "He's not exactly *compos mentis*. And, if he wouldn't tell you who Big C was when he was himself, what chance is there he'll tell you in his current state?"

"He will if you hypnotize him."

Shaking her head at the stupidity of the suggestion, Abby sat back in the luxurious leather settee. It smelled of wealth and squeaked softly with pleasure as she sank into its U2-pian embrace. "I know the theory, Simon, but I've never practised."

"You did a pretty good job of calming him down earlier. Your mother was a hedge-row healer. That sort of stuff runs in families. It's in the genes. There's no harm in trying." He poured himself another Bushmills then tilted the bottle towards her. "Join me?"

She surrendered. "Just a wee one. Don't want to be drunk on duty."

"You'll give it a go then? Cheers!"

They clinked glasses. "Before I break out the healing hand of the eternal feminine, let me ask you something."

Magill swallowed and gritted his teeth as the whiskey worked its volcanic magic. "Anything," he wheezed.

"Did you recognize any of the victims?"

"No, of course not. Why do you ask?"

"Well, you've been Dan's constant companion for the past two years and if he were slashing throats with gay abandon, you might have noticed something or someone. Calling cards aside, I can't quite grasp the perp's MO. The victims of serial killers usually have something in common – courting couples, prostitutes, geographical locations and the like – but here we have a jumble of ages, sexes, ethnicities, hair colours and so on. I can only assume that they're… I don't know… well… um… known to the killer."

"Watch a lot of *CSI*, do you?"

"Yes… yes… I do, as a matter of fact. I like *Silent Witness* too. And *Waking the Dead*. And of course *Wire in the Blood*. Pretty much everything by Lynda La Plante. To be perfectly frank, Simon, I'm much better qualified in forensic pathology than I am in hypnotherapy."

Forcing himself to focus on the facial features of the victims, which were horribly contorted in the throes of violent death, Magill went through the vile files once again, slowly, systematically, scrupulously. The middle-aged woman behind the wheel of the Renault. He'd never seen her before. The little man in the library stack that looked like the movie set in Rome. Never seen him either. The young Asian girl on a park bench with bizarre kangaroo motifs in wrought iron. She too was unfamiliar. The final one of a besuited, clean-cut man indecently spread-eagled in the stall of a public restroom. "Christ," Magill gasped. "Christ, that's the guy from Salt Lake City visitors' bureau. We met him last October. Jesus, those tiles in the background. They're just like the ones in Spanky's night club. Dan and I went there after our meeting with…" Magill screwed up his face, struggling to remember. "…What was his name again? It was very distinctive. Trespass, that's it. Thomas Trespass."

"I wonder when this photograph was taken."

"That's easy." He returned to the thumbnails, right clicked on the image, scrolled down the menu to properties and suddenly stopped in his tracks. "This was taken on the night we were in the club, the day before we left town."

"But obviously you were with Dan the whole time. Presumably the pair of you didn't see anything suspicious."

Magill pinched the bridge of his nose, endeavouring to concentrate on the time-warped memories of their Salt Lake trip. "Actually, Abby," he said slowly, almost reluctantly, "Dan went to the bathroom just as we were leaving the club. I waited outside."

"Was he carrying his manbag, the one with the stabbed and ravaged novels?"

He nodded, disbelievingly. "It rarely left his sight, though he forgot it once while we were staying at the Crillon. He came back for it in a panic, then stormed off in a strop to Starbucks. The one in the Louvre. He loved going there, watching the Da Vinci Code tours passing through."

"When was that, Simon?"

Magill frowned, trying to remember. "Let me just check Dan's diary." He opened Outlook, clicked on Calendar, flicked back to September and cross-referenced against jpeg properties. The dates coincided, as did the dates for the deaths in what seemed to be Rome and Sydney. With a quiet sigh of despair and a quick glass of Bushmills' misery muffler, Magill confirmed that the Danster had gone off on his own in Rome and disappeared in high dudgeon during their short Sydney sojourn.

"I think maybe *you* should ring the police," Abby said with regret. "Or at least talk to Bono about it. He's obviously well connected and capable of pulling just about every string in this place."

"Yeah, I'll do that."

"Do you want me to leave, Simon? If I'm here when the police arrive, the Belfast press will have a field day."

Magill threw back his head and groaned aloud. "Aaaaaarrrrrgggghhhh."

Abby got up to go.

He grabbed her by the wrist. There was desperation in his voice. "At least try the hypnotism."

"It won't work."

"Please."

"It won't work, Simon. I'm sorry."

Chapter Twenty-Nine

The Big C

It didn't work. Nor would it. As Abby explained to desperate Dan's disappointed companion, the nonsensical idea that
"hypnos" tell all under the spell of a swinging watch fob is derived
from second-rate stage shows. Stage shows are just that; a form
of entertainment where the mildly suggestible are persuaded
to perform in accordance with a well-established repertoire of
crowd-pleasing stunts. Most times, it involves confederates who
are known to the hypnotist and who are prepped accordingly. It's
showbiz, plain and simple.

"Try again. Please."

Staring deep into the Danster's eyes, Abby murmured a
selection of sweet nothings. Without success. He sat on the
edge of the bed, ignoring Abby's sleepy-time lullabies, talking
to himself, rocking to and fro, clutching the empty manbag to
his chest.

Disappointed by Abby's obvious lack of commitment to the
cause, Magill was less than impressed by her half-hearted performance. Lack of conviction, surely, would communicate itself
to the patient. "I always thought that you were supposed to
swing a focal object from side to side," he carped, "thereby tiring
the eyes and putting them under."

Abby was tempted to tell him to stuff it. But she knew that his
bad temper came from a good place. She patiently explained that
the therapeutic side of mesmerism doesn't necessarily involve
the swinging fob watch of legend. Some of the earliest practitioners made passes with their hands over the recumbent bodies of
their patients, but before long this was abandoned for a penetrat-
ing stare or a single touch or thought transference at a distance
or simply holding a shiny object in front of their faces or indeed
audio tapes with embedded messages that subliminally convince

patients to stop smoking, quit gambling or go on a diet. "Most of it is nonsense, of course."

"Is that fact?"

"Yes it is, sadly. There have been hundreds of scientific studies of subliminal persuasion and they agree that there is no solid evidence to support the idea. The famous subliminal scare of the 1950s, when a marketing consultant allegedly persuaded people to drink Coke and eat popcorn, was a hoax. We held a subliminal advertising night in WeeTube once. The movie that the 1950s audience was watching – the one supposedly spiked with persuasive subliminals – was called *Picnic*. The increase in sales of Coke and popcorn had more to do with images of people feasting on-screen than the subliminal messages hidden in the movie, if there were any. Subliminal advertising is an urban myth, beloved by conspiracy theorists." She looked at Magill accusingly. "And by writers of conspiracy thrillers."

Abby got up off her hunkers, ready to abandon the attempt. Her knees cracked loudly as she stood up. The patella pistol-shot jerked Dan fully awake. Eyes staring wildly, he started scratching at his face and throat, while shouting maniacally about Big C coming to get him. His hair was dishevelled. He looked distraught. He didn't seem like a serial killer, though serial killers seldom do. The moustachioed villain of Jack the Ripper stripe or the cellar dweller of Hannibal the Cannibal kidney was almost as far from reality as it was possible to be, except inasmuch as real serial killers often imitate movie, book or TV show portrayals and feel obliged to leave clues to their identity. Killers read thrillers too.

"I hate to tell you this," Magill quibbled, while gently persuading Dan to take a sip of Ireland's favourite cure-all – extra-hot hot whiskey, with extra whiskey – "but your Guerrilla Psychology lectures aren't up to date. I know for a fact that the US military has been working on subliminals since the 1950s. Psyops didn't end with the Cold War. Do you really think they'd announce to the world that they'd made a breakthrough? Basic military tactics suggest the opposite. They'd spread rumours to the effect that subliminals don't work. Call yourself a guerrilla psychologist?"

"You're talking like a crazy conspiracy theorist," Abby

answered angrily, though as soon as she sounded off she knew she was denying her own experiences, experiences which could be repressed but not eradicated. True, she'd never actually seen the legendary Spear of Destiny, but she'd sufficient experience of the Priory of Ryan to know that conspiracies did exist and that the greatest cover-up of all was the cover-up that cover-ups were cover-ups.

"I want to show you something," Magill said, making for the bedroom door. "I'll give you crazy conspiracy theorist." He clumped downstairs, where his overcoat lay draped over a chair. He'd thrown it there on arrival. He returned a couple of minutes later with something in his tightly balled fist. Before he could say anything or "prove her wrong", in that mucho-macho, ultra-competitive, men-know-best manner, Abby cut him off at the pass. "Did Dan ever mention Citroën at all?"

"No, why do you ask?"

Abby puffed out her cheeks and exhaled expressively. "Thought it might be Big C." That took the wind out of Simon's sails. She told him about Nuremberg, when she met Pitcairn Brodie after his encounter with Citroën's "personnel" department. She told him about the Dan Brown connection, how the late great Brodie was being blackmailed into acts of anti-Brown sabotage, how the car manufacturer planned to make Dan suffer for his attempted publicity stunt.

"I always thought there was something odd about Citroën," Magill admitted, with a faraway look on his face. "My first thought on discovering his body back in Edinburgh..." He paused to gather his thoughts, as the full horror of Kames Road came back to him, "... was that Citroën was behind it. I don't know why that was. Intuition, I suppose. However, it was a very powerful feeling. And whenever I heard of André Citroën's Masonic connections..." Magill drifted off, lost in the enfeebling fug of prefer-to-forget recollections.

"You said you had something to show me," Abby inquired gently.

"It doesn't matter. It'll only bring you bad luck. I bring everyone bad luck. Quit now, Abby, while you're ahead." Hesitantly at first, then with greater and greater self-loathing, he poured out his heart, telling her about his father, who blamed him for his brother's murder, his betrayal of Pitcairn Brodie's memory, his failure to prevent Barton Brady's untimely death, his amorous adventures with May Day, Hustler's own Mata Hari. "And now this," he said with piteous self-detestation that bordered on woe-is-me narcissism.

Tenderly, Abby tried to prise open his left hand. He resisted, clinging on tight. "We all have our shame-filled back stories, Simon. Surely you learned that from your classes in narrative structure, as well as sitting at the feet of the master." She nodded towards their prostrate patient, the libation having worked its narcotic magic. "At least yours is private. Mine was splashed all over the newspapers."

Duly chastened, Magill unfastened his fingers.

In her astonishment, Abby's eyes were the size – and the shape – of Philippe Starck saucers. "That's absolutely beautiful, Simon." A bright blue, lapis lazuli locket sat in the centre of his palm, its delicate chain coiled alongside like a display in a museum or upscale jewellers. Carefully, almost reverentially, Abby picked up the exquisite object. "Your mother's?" she asked.

"No, no. It was given to me by an acquaintance, a very wise woman. It's supposed to be an object of enormous power. I thought perhaps you could use it on Dan. I appreciate that the trance-inducing object is irrelevant, but some objects are more powerful than others."

Abby held the locket up to the light, which lanced in from the penthouse windows, intensified somehow by the snow-covered cityscape. It glowed and glistened and near-enough throbbed as it revolved slowly at the end of the chain. Ordinarily, she would have scoffed at the idea of a force field – though a bayonet she'd once encountered possessed a kind of malign power – but this represented a completely different order of magnitude. "If it works, do I get to keep it?"

"I don't know," Magill replied cryptically. "The object chooses its own owner. I feel it doesn't belong to me. I'm just keeping it safe until the right person comes along."

Taken aback by the portentousness, Abby was tempted to say "Yes, Obi Wan." However, there was something about the locket that stilled any such cynicism. "You'll be telling me it's the Holy Grail next."

"Keep your voice down, Abby. Dan still thinks the grail's a bloodline."

Curled up in the foetal position, with eyes fixed on the far wall, the patient started muttering madly to himself. "2–3–5–7–11. The Big C. 2–3–5–7–11, bro."

"What's he saying, Simon? Is that another password, do you reckon?"

"Could be. They're the first five prime numbers, though. Dan's very fond of mathematical sequences. We used to recite them to each other for relaxation. Brain training," he added, catching her sceptical look. "Pi is my speciality. He'd call out 3.141, bro, and off we'd go."

Having witnessed the weirdness of all human life while working in Some Like It Hot, Abby wisely kept her own counsel. She sat Dan up, albeit with difficulty, and set to work. She raised the locket, twisted the chain and let it unfurl in front of his face. The bleary-eyed patient reached out for the shining, spinning object a couple of times, but refused to slip under. For someone who peddled conspiracy theories to the susceptible public, Dan was decidedly unreceptive to suggestions. She tried again. His madly staring eyelids seemed to droop for a second but he fought back, refusing to grant access to his innermost thoughts.

The bedside telephone rang, breaking the spell. Abby grabbed the receiver angrily. "Oh, hello Bono. It's good to hear your voice, as well. The patient's still a bit below par. We're working on him. Uh-huh. Uh-huh. Ooooooooookay. Whatever you say. I'll try. Will do. Oh, you cheeky monkey. Really? How dare you! Righty ho…"

Magill felt like a spare part in a two's company, three's a crowd situation. He picked up the locket and, without thinking, tried it on Dan. As the incandescent locket twisted, turned and unwound in front of his former friend's troubled features, he could see the mad light in his eyes diminish and a limpid pool of empathy take its place. It was almost as if he was connecting with the very consciousness of the creator of literary classics like *The Da Vinci Code* and *Deception Point*. It was almost as if *he* was the one being hypnotized, not the other way around.

"Oh, my, God," Abby laughed, setting down the receiver. "Bono only wants a mention in Dan's next book. The music industry's in such turmoil that all sorts of unconventional promotional tactics are being considered. Apparently, product placement in movies, plays, TV programmes and novels is the most successful mode of communication, the only thing that today's marketing-literate consumers trust. However, he wants control over what's said about the band. Apparently he got a name check in *American Psycho* way back in the early nineties. It wasn't very favourable. This time they want oversight."

"Really?" Magill responded absent-mindedly, heaving himself from the momentary mind-meld. He'd always believed Bono to be a self-serving SoB, an astute marketer of his band's brand of CSR. In fairness, though, he'd been pretty decent in person. He gave the dude the benefit of the doubt. "What else did he say?"

"Apparently, U2 has done deals with a bunch of big-name authors – Stephen King, Sophie Kinsella, John Grisham, Tom Clancy – so expect to read a lot of references to Bono's selfless charity work, as well as his band's monumentally breathtaking music."

"Smart move. He's one smart cookie."

"If this were a book, like you keep saying, Simon, I'd be going on at great length about Bono's incredible philanthropy, the band's totally brilliant new album, the forthcoming world tour, which…" Abby never completed the sentence. She was staring at their patient, who was gazing wistfully into the distance. "What have you done with him, Simon? He's under. He's definitely under. We watched videos in class. I recognize the look. You put him under yourself. The establishment of trust is the key to success. He obviously trusts you with his life, Simon."

Astonished, Magill turned back to the Danster. He had a distant yet beatific expression on his face. He smiled up at Simon, like a little lost child. Magill felt tears of love and admiration prickle the back of his eyes. No matter what the photographic evidence suggested, he knew Dan was innocent. There was no way this kind-hearted man would hurt a hair on anyone's head, though he must have been sorely tempted. The pressure he'd been under since *Da Vinci* exploded into public consciousness would've turned lesser men into monstrous egomaniacs or psychotic monsters or both. Dan hadn't succumbed. He knew it in his heart of hearts. No matter what the future held in store – screaming headlines, police interrogation, worldwide condemnation – he was going to stick by the man he'd bonded with at the Bellagio. He'd get them through this no matter how long it took. Someone who can recite every Fibonacci prime up to 1636007 can't be all bad.

"He's saying something, Simon." Abby pressed her face close to Dan's, trying to make out his mumbling.

"What? What's he saying?"

"Ssssshhh."

"Still the mathematical sequence?"

Abby's face was completely blank, completely devoid of emotion. "Listen for yourself."

Magill sank to his knees beside the bed and gently raised his former mentor's chin. The words, though slurred, were unmistakable. "Tom Clancy. Tom Clancy. Big C. Tom Clancy. Big C. Big C. Tom Clancy's Big C."

Chapter Thirty

Knick-knack Paddy-whack, Give a Pair a Clue

"It doesn't make sense," Abby said, as they cut through Temple Bar's narrow streets en route to Waterstone's in Dawson Street. Despite the recession and the inclement weather, the Oirish restaurants, paddy-whack pubs and Celtic-script-covered souvenir shops seemed to be doing good business, even though January is traditionally the lowest point of the fair city's tourist cycle. The chain stores along Dame Street were even busier, as the seasonal sales were in full rub-a-dub Dublin swing.

"It makes a lot of sense to me," Magill replied. "Artistic types are famous for their spats. Consider Gore Vidal versus Norman Mailer, Terry Pratchett and J. K. Rowling, Sam Beckett and James Joyce, Martin Amis and just about everyone. It makes even more sense if you bear in mind that Tom Clancy was the king of the thriller until Dan Brown deposed him, that Tom Clancy's espionage- and Cold War-based novels lost traction when theological thrillers took off, that Tom Clancy hasn't had a big hit since *The Da Vinci Code* came out, that Dan Brown started off as a Clancy clone with *Digital Fortress*, then reverted to the Clancy model with *Deception Point*, when *Angels and Demons* failed to sell. *Deception Point* was a blatant attempt to out-Clancy Clancy. Talk about red rag to a bull. Dan was easy to ignore when his book didn't sell but when *Deception* became a huge retrospective hit in the aftermath of *Da Vinci*, it must have hurt big time."

Abby stopped to throw some change in the begging bowl of a rag-covered street person, whose pitch beside the Central Bank spoke volumes about the state of Irish society. "There's a world of difference between an artistic spat and setting someone up as a serial killer."

"You obviously don't know the artistic mindset, Abby. Thriller writers spend their lives thinking up ways to kill people, the more gruesome the better. They spend their lives fretting about sales figures, publishers' lack of marketing support, the nasty reviewers on Amazon, and their thieving, conniving, utterly unscrupulous rivals, who steal their ideas and make millions from them, while their own books languish in remainder bins, charity shops and overstock retailers or on unsold piles of returns, which go back to the publishers as a kind of literary 'don't call us, we'll call you'. That sort of thing can drive a man to extreme measures, to whack attacks, to ice-capades, to ultimate sanction, as they call it in the espionage industry."

"Seems a bit excessive to me," Abby said without much conviction, since she'd put forward the same theory a few hours earlier.

Dodging the busy traffic on College Green, as he jaywalked with the invulnerable insouciance of the *idée fixe* fixated, Magill spoke rapidly over his shoulder to his Louboutain-shackled companion, who couldn't keep up with the striding redhead. "There's something you must understand about Tom Clancy, Abby. His reputation hit rock bottom just as Dan's was rising rapidly. In 1994, he wrote a book called *Executive Orders*, which featured terrorists crashing passenger jets into US government buildings. When his prediction came to pass in 2001 – it's even alleged that Bin Laden is a big Clancy fan – the author compounded the problem by saying that the US only had itself to blame on account of its penny pinching attitude towards the military. He may have been right but that wasn't the time to say it. His reputation has never fully recovered."

"I can see how that might precipitate a mental breakdown, but it doesn't justify an unprovoked attack on an innocent competitor."

"True, but if you'd just published a thriller about an assassination attempt on the Pope and had it roundly denounced as your worst book ever; if your principal character made his name with a book called *Agents and Agency* and suffered from a debilitating phobia akin to Langdon's fear of enclosed spaces; if you invented the word 'symbology', only to have it misappropriated by a copycat who makes millions from your coinage, you'd be pretty ticked off too."

Abby was beginning to find Magill's logic, if not quite compelling, then undeniably plausible. However, she had learned to be wary of a man with a bee in his bonnet, because the buzzing drowned the sound of commonsense. More importantly, she couldn't keep up with the ginger enthusiast, as he galloped towards their destination on Dawson Street. "Simon," she shouted after the fast-moving figure, arms waving wildly as he conversed with himself, "can you hold on a wee minute?"

He stopped, turned round and waited for her to catch up. Abby stood her ground, like a Lacroix-clad rock in the middle of a mountain stream of harried office workers, swirling and eddying on either side. With a disappointed frown, he drifted back, his great overcoat hovering a couple of inches above the pavement.

"What do you see, Simon?" she said, before he could open his complaining mouth.

He raised his palms heavenward. "Looks to me like a very attractive woman, throwing a strop."

"If you had stopped halfway through that sentence, I might be more accommodating. But, since you didn't, let me tell you what you see. You see a woman who is built for comfort not for speed, a woman who is wearing fashion-forward footwear in this fashion-forward, footwear-conscious city, footwear that is not designed for hiking, yomping or indeed sprinting from one end of the city centre to another. Why are we even going to this bookshop anyway, when the information is probably available on-line? I thought you were an IT whiz. Surely we should be back in the Clarence, surfing the web and keeping an eye on your bosom buddy."

"But you have to keep running from place to place, otherwise the narrative loses momentum. And momentum is all in a thriller."

Arms akimbo in Nassau Street, Abby stood resolute, hands on hips. "This is not a novel, Simon, let alone a thriller."

"Well, it won't be if you don't get a move on! We're close to the Inmost Cave."

Abby had had enough of his narrative nonsense. There was Streat coffee shop three doors down, not far from the inmost cave entrance. She knew which one she was heading for. Joseph Campbell's acolyte followed, albeit with great reluctance. "So," she said, sipping a revivifying hot chocolate, "what was it you were saying about Clancy's contract on Dan the doppelgänger?"

"It doesn't matter," he huffed, looking enviously at Abby's sizable chunk of coffee cake. She cut a forkful and reached across the table, tempting Simon to take a nibble. In he-man fashion, he stiffened indignantly and pursed his lips as tightly as he could. Abby rubbed the hi-cal delicacy across his perma-sealed orifice. Inadvertently, he licked the smear of icing sugar off his lower lip and, having succumbed to the tantalizing temptress, opened his mouth for the remainder. Abby promptly popped the forkful into her own mouth and mmmmmed loudly. She was tempted to do the full *When Harry Met Sally*, though Simon didn't deserve that degree of cruelty.

The lanky redhead laughed sheepishly. She cut him another slice and, with it, some slack. He immediately launched into a silly Sally-says-yes performance, complete with table thumping and embarrassing orgasmic groans, though no one said I'll Have What He's Having when he finished. Understandably.

"Do you think Dan'll be okay?"

"Bono seemed happy enough to babysit."

"At least he took off the cardinal's outfit," Abby observed.

"Thank heaven for small mercies."

Suitably refreshed by the coffee cake break, Abby encouraged her mocha-mollified companion to continue with his literary conspiracy theory. Casual observers of the couple, as they walked arm-in-arm up Dawson Street, might have inferred that love was in the air. However, Abby was only interested in keeping a grip on Simon's enthusiasm, which made its presence felt in stride length and ever-greater ground speed.

"The thing is, Abby, I know for a fact that they've met. I also know that Dan's exactly the sort of person Clancy hates. Clancy's books are full of get-up-and-go military types barking orders, jumping to attention, following the chain of command without question. Small men, unmilitary men, tweedy academicians, private school types, Ivy League types, Phi Beta Kappa secret-handshake types are anathema to him, as is the entire White

Anglo-Saxon Protestant establishment. Clancy is a self-made man, who comes from an underprivileged, Roman Catholic background, who didn't go to a good school or shine at college. He's also driven by high achievement. All his characters are angling for promotion, an extra general's star or climbing to the top of the greasy pole of professional life. His chief protagonist started off as a no-name college lecturer and ended up as President of the United States. So you can imagine how he felt when he was blown out of the literary water by his worst nightmare, a weedy WASP with a whiney voice, a privileged upbringing and a private school education, a slacker who bummed around in the music business before becoming a schoolteacher."

"And who ripped off his ideas."

"Exactly," Magill said, as they entered the bottle green portals of Waterstone's, a stone's throw from its deadly rival, Hodges Figgis, directly across the street. They made their way through to the Crime, Mystery and Thrillers section, where Magill pulled out a copy of Clancy's *Executive Orders*. He flicked through to page 1269. "There's something I want to read to you."

All this way for a reading, Abby thought, as her insteps howled in anguish and bunions keened for their country.

"It's called The Ryan Doctrine."

"Ryan, as in Priory of Ryan, as in Protocols of the Elders of Ryan?"

"The very same. Jack Ryan is Clancy's main man, the protagonist of all but two of his thrillers and nothing less than the 33rd President of the United States. On his accession to the presidency, Ryan sets out a policy directive." Magill read out a couple of pages of chest-beating bombast that basically boiled down to a declaration that if anyone ever messed with Jack Ryan, he would hunt them down and kill them without mercy, whether they be presidents or generals or terrorists or CEOs of multinational companies. "The Ryan Doctrine formed the real-world basis of George Bush's axis of evil policy, his bomb Afghanistan policy, his invasion of Iraq policy, his shock 'n' awe policy, his kill Saddam policy, his take out Osama policy."

"Are you saying it's the basis of Clancy's author-of-evil, bring-down-Dan policy?"

"That's exactly what I'm saying."

"How, exactly, would he arrange it? You can't just go around whacking people without someone noticing."

Magill snorted derisively. "Well, the US military got away with it day and daily in Iraq. They picked up innocent people, flew them back and forth all over the western world, while torturing them cruelly aforethought. Abu Ghraib and Guantánamo Bay weren't exactly beacons of civil liberties. Do you really think they'd think twice about deep-sixing four nobodies in Paris, Rome, Salt Lake and Sydney?"

"So you're saying that Clancy has some kind of hold over the US military. Why would they do his bidding?"

"I don't know for sure. I do know that he's very well connected to the military-intelligence complex. He couldn't have written his thrillers otherwise. When *The Hunt for Red October* was published, there was mass panic in the Pentagon. They thought state secrets had been leaked to the author. President Reagan himself was caught up in the kerfuffle."

"Really?"

"Really. It was Reagan's endorsement that sent *Red October* to the top of the charts. By chance, a newspaper reporter asked him about his holiday reading and the president joked that he was reading *The Hunt for Red October*. He added that it was a great yarn. It shot to the top of the bestsellers list, as did all of Clancy's subsequent books. He's been a pretty good recruiting sergeant for the US military, to say nothing of his contributions to Republican policy. They owe him, Abby." Magill slipped the book back into place. The rest of the so-called Ryanverse sat resolute on either side: *Sum of All Fears, Clear and Present Danger, Cardinal of the Kremlin, Patriot Games, Red Storm Rising.*

Although she wasn't entirely convinced by Magill's case, there was no denying that he made it persuasively. "How come you know so much about Clancy anyhow? Have you studied his works for a thesis or something?"

"No. It's much simpler than that."

"Oh yes?"

"I work for him, Abby. I'm a Clancy man."

Chapter Thirty-One

J'Acuzzi

The scales fell from Abby's eyes. A set up! She was about to get whacked by Clancy's henchman, in a public place like the other four. Dan wasn't the only person in Paris, Rome, Sydney and Salt Lake City. Simon Magill was there too! He'd been a cuckoo in the nest all along, feeding information back to his butt-kicking boss on Brown's movements. Every one of Dan's trips, according to his diary, had been marked by the death of an innocent civilian. Why would Dublin be any different? Had Magill groomed the others, with promises of meeting the celebrity author, before slitting their throats? Or had he asked them for help too and they'd fallen for it hook, line and slaughter? Was, now that she thought about it, Magill behind the untimely death of Pitcairn Brodie? He discovered the body, did he? He slew the scholar, rather!

Well, Abby wasn't going to be anybody's victim. Not without a fight. She'd bested a brace of psychotic paramilitaries in the past, as well as a gun-toting priest, to say nothing of a pair of sausage-faced henchpersons in Nuremberg. She'd give a good account of herself now that the Priory of Ryan had finally come a-calling.

Simon Magill was standing beside her. He was looking down with a smug look on his face, like he was about to crack a joke. See if you find this funny, buddy. Abby chinned him with a mighty uppercut, a power-packed punch that was on a par with one she'd thrown during an altercation with Michael O'Leary. Taken by complete surprise, Magill flew backwards over a Three-for-Two display of discounted titles, sending bargain books cascading all over the Waterstone's shop floor. Attracted by the initial crash, plus the pitter-patter of sequentially spilling paperbacks, a polo-shirt wearing checkout assistant rushed over to the scene of the crime (in Crime, Thrillers and Mystery, aptly). Another materialized from the Business and Management annex, evidently wondering what the commotion was about.

Abby gave them commotion. She swept the entire Ryanverse on to the floor, everything from *Red October* to *Rainbow Six*, before heading for the door. Like bibliophiles the world over, the Waterstoneans' main concern was the state of their damaged stock and whether markdowns might prove necessary. By that stage, Abby was out of the store and accelerating up Dawson Street towards St Stephen's Green. Magill wouldn't be getting out of there in a hurry, not without paying for the bruised and battered merchandise. He should consider himself lucky they were three for twos.

She grabbed a cab outside the Shelbourne Hotel and, less than five minutes after the fracas, was well on her way to Connolly Station. Bad as things were in Belfast, anything was better than a freshly slit throat and a Dan Brown book cover attached to her chest.

It was only when the cab was crossing Butt Bridge that Abby started having second thoughts. Surely if Magill was going to kill her, he'd have chosen a less conspicuous place. Why hadn't he bumped her off in the Clarence, when he could perhaps have pinned her murder on Dan and thereby destroyed the author's reputation? Even with the most expensive legal team in the world, the subsequent court case would have ruined Brown's career. Or would it?

Unless. Unless. Unless Brown *himself* was the target. Maybe she was being set up for the Clancy coup de grace. She could see the headlines already: Brown Slain By Babe in Bono's Bijou Boarding House. The *All Fall Down* story would doubtless come out. She'd been blackmailing Brown about his plagiarism of Yeats's novel. And when Brown refused to pay up, the bitch whacked him. She'd a history of mental instability, as had her entire family. She'd just lost her job in Belfast, where she'd championed a brand positioning policy based on death. The black rose of Belfast, with murder in mind.

What to do? If she could get to Dan before Magill, perhaps she could spirit him away. Hell, he's not that big. A fireman's lift should do the trick. But of course Bono's there. He'll help. He's a good guy. Unless he too is in on the plot. Impossible. Bono's a saint. He'd never sully his chances of the Nobel Peace Prize. He's a religious nut, though. Opus Dei maybe. And Dan's not exactly the Holy See's go-to guy.

The conspiratorial possibilities were swirling around in her mind, each crazier than the last.

Deep breath. Decision made. Abby redirected the taxi driver to the Clarence, though he wasn't best pleased, since the traffic control system in Dublin city centre is nightmarish on a good day and Dan Brownian on a bad. She paid him off with a tip as big as the Ritz, sprinted past the liveried doorman and shot through the Irish Oak-panelled lobby to the tiniest little lift this side of Lilliput. Two minutes later, she was in the penthouse suite, which was as empty as she'd left it. Abby hurtled up the stairs to the second level, hoping to see Dan sleeping peacefully like before. There was no sign of the ailing author. He wasn't in the en-suite bathroom, nor the upstairs lounge, nor the walk-in cupboard, where she half expected him to topple out, throat horribly slashed. There were no smears, sprays or spatters of blood, much less puddles. Not that she could see, anyway.

On high alert, Abby descended to the lower level and checked everything out. Again, there was no sign of the Danster or any evidence that he'd even been there. What was that? She thought she heard something. Coming from outside. She eased open the balcony doors. The hullaballoo was louder still, strange sinuous sounds that somehow evoked the ancient souks of Marrakesh. Abby couldn't believe her eyes. Bono was sprawled in the rooftop Jacuzzi, under a blood red sky, sipping a Corona. He was wearing the cowboy hat from the *Joshua Tree* tour and singing along to his limited edition U2 iPod, which nestled in a Bose SoundDock with Acoustimass monster speakers.

"New album?" she asked, struggling to avert her eyes from the buck naked philanthropist. The foaming bubbles, fortunately, covered the Irishman's pride in the name of love.

Using the tip of his beer bottle, Bono pushed up the rim of his stetson. "Yeah, Abs. What do you think?" He increased the volume slightly.

The sound of aching, yearning heartbreak rolled and tumbled across the cityscape. It was too incredible for words. "I don't know what to say," Abby said.

He raised his half-empty Corona in acknowledgement. "Come and join me. Get your kecks off. You look a bit flustered. There's only one thing better than seeing a wonderful Dublin winterland and that's seeing a wonderful Dublin winterland from a hot tub with ice-cold beer in hand."

Why not? What was the title of that old song? Oh yes: "I Will Follow". And follow she did. Abby kicked off her barking Louboutins with relief, slipped out of her Lacroix trouser suit and, her modesty preserved by YSL bra and panties, slipped into the Jacuzzi beside a man with a song in his heart and an album to promote.

"Dan?" she asked.

Bono popped a Corona and passed it over to his new best friend.

"Where's Dan?"

"The new album's damn good, if I say so myself. Even Van Morrison at his most magical is no patch on us, Abs."

"Forget Van, where's Dan?"

Bono drained his beer with a sigh of satisfaction, set the empty bottle beside the others on the lip of the bubbling tub and cleared his throat. "He's…" However, the rock star's reply was cut off by an apparition that strode out on to the terrace, fissile with fury.

"What the fuck did you do with Dan?" Magill bellowed at his erstwhile companions. "What the fuck was that all about?" he fumed, glaring at Abby. "I've a good mind to… to… smack your backside."

Bono butted in. "No rumpy-pumpy in the hot tub, children. Not unless I can play too." He looked from one to the other and, after carefully appraising the situation, selected a suitable soundtrack from his iPod playlist. Van Morrison. *Astral Weeks*. "The Way Young Lovers Do". "Cool it, kids," the saintly singer said sagaciously. "Grab a beer, Simon."

"I bloody well won't grab a beer," Magill shouted, unassuaged by the Peace Prize nominee's peace-making moves, pitch perfect though they were. "What did you do with Dan?"

Unfazed by the tantrums of the little people, the superstar shrugged and sipped and said that he'd shipped him someplace safe. The hotel was too public. People would talk. The paps would pick up on it. The penthouse was prey to long-lensed snappers. He'd moved Dan to his house at Killiney, five miles outside town in Rathdown. He'd be safe there. "Ali trained as a nurse, before she gave it all up to look after me. If anyone can get Dan's shit together it's my missus, the Sweetest Thing."

Mortified by his misapprehension of the situation, Magill started mumbling his apologies. Bono waved them off. He knew what it was like to be worried about someone's welfare. Sometimes you just can't make it on your own. Somewhat unsteadily, the rock star rose from the hot tub, covered his crown jewels with the compact cowboy hat – while claiming, unconvincingly, that he really needed a sombrero – and picked up his personalized iPod. Pausing only to check that Simon had his mobile phone number, just in case he wanted to inquire about the Danster's condition, the hairy-arsed rocker padded off towards the penthouse, humming a merry tune: "When Love Comes to Town".

"Before you go, Bono," Magill asked. "Can you tell me where Dan was when he cracked up? Was he in the hotel at the time?"

"Nope," Bono replied. "I'm told he was in the library at Trinity."

"Thanks, man," Magill yelled.

"Peace." The superstar made a V for Victory sign, then disappeared through the double doors with a farewell wave of the cowboy hat. Not a good idea.

The rooftop terrace fell silent, except for the bubbling Jacuzzi and the rumbling traffic noise that floated up from Wellington Quay below.

"So," Simon said.

"So," Abby said.

"So, are you going to tell me why you chinned me or is it your womanly way of keeping men in their place?"

"So, are you going to explain why someone who used to work for Dan Brown would sell his soul to Tom Clancy?"

Magill plonked himself on the wooden slatted seat by the hot tub. He leaned in over the steaming cauldron, where Abby was wallowing like a big beautiful water baby. "I don't actually work for him," he said. "Not yet anyway. I've had a job offer. Well, it's an offer of an offer. I was reliably informed that the author of the Net Force series was recruiting ghost writers. I then discovered that Net Force was one of Tom Clancy's sub-brands. Naturally, I read everything I could about – and by – Tom Clancy and the more I read the more I realized that Dan had stolen his thunder. I was as horrified as you were when the photos came to light. But the more I think about it, the more sense a Tom-attack makes. Creative types are a crazy breed, Abby. They're almost as crazy as PR types, who'd punch you out at the drop of a stetson."

"I'd be inclined to believe you, if it weren't for the convenient coincidence."

"What do you mean?"

"Don't you think it's a bit odd? The fact that you get a job offer from Clancy just as the plot against Dan is reaching a murderous climax?"

"Coincidences are coin of the realm in conspiracy thrillers. Think about the coincidence that took Robert Langdon to the chateau of Sir Leigh Teabing, who just happened to be the bad guy. What are the chances that a Vatican guard would be in position at the head of the disused tunnel from Castel Sant'Angelo and was able to unlock the secret door, thereby letting Langdon and Vittoria Vetra save the day? How likely is it that a nuclear submarine would be in the perfect place beneath the Arctic ice-shelf to pick up three scientists stranded on an enormous iceberg that's just calved from a gigantic glacier?"

"Simon, this isn't a thriller. How many times do I have to tell you?"

"And, how many times do I have to tell you that lolling around in a Jacuzzi doesn't do much for momentum, let alone narrative drive?"

"So you expect *me* to up your thrill quotient? Am I supposed to clamber naked out of this hot tub and cavort around for your adolescent readers' delectation? What do you take me for? The love interest?"

Magill considered his answer for a couple of minutes, downing the Corona in three big slugs. "It's okay, Abby," he said, setting the empty beside the others. "I've got a different thrill in mind, a thrill that involves both of us."

Oh yeah, Abby thought to herself. In your dreams, buster. "And what would that be, Simon?"

"I've worked out what Dan meant by 2–3–5–7-11, bro. I think it'll help us make sense of the cryptic symbols."

"The symbols on the book covers in the chests of Dan's victims?"

"Well, not Dan's victims, but yes."

Abby slapped her svelte thigh ironically. "Is this a thriller, or what?"

Chapter Thirty-Two

The Long Room

The old library was as busy as ever. The crowds, as ever, were there to see the Book of Kells. Encased in its glass sarcophagus, the gilded masterpiece was a triumph of style over content. More than that, it was a triumph of the tourist imagination, since the tiny room where the treasure was housed was so gloomy that next to nothing could be seen of its illuminated glory. In the world of ancient ornamented manuscripts, preservation always trumps presentation. Paying customers don't count.

Murk notwithstanding, the entrance fee was a small price to pay for the delights of the Long Room above. Of all the aesthetic allurements within Trinity College's cerebral stockade – the campanile, the Rubrics, the cobblestone square, the fellows' dining room, the splendidly chandeliered examination hall – none compares with the Long Room itself. A veritable cathedral to biblio-worship, complete with soaring nave and token transept, Trinity's Old Library is one of the seven wonders of the literary world, alongside the long lost Library at Alexandria, the Vatican's super-secret archives, the resplendent reading room at the British Museum and of course Borges's labyrinthine Library of Babel, where every book that ever lived lives on and reproduces by osmosis. Statue-studded, ladder-littered and literally groaning with gigantic leather-bound volumes, Trinity's old library is redolent of Ireland's literary heritage: unsurpassed and unsurpassable.

Any contemporary author would feel humbled in such a place. Sales figures, no matter how mind-boggling, cannot compensate for the humiliation visited upon visitors to the Long Room. Scientists stand on the shoulders of giants – the great forebears whose work new generations add to and build on – whereas artists cower before past masters, who loom over them like bigger than average Brobdingnagians. The fear and trembling of Booker prize-winners or Betty Trask long-listers is as nothing compared to the existential despair that must surely descend on the authors of tendentious technothrillers, the perpetrators of police procedurals and, above all, the battery hens of chick-lit.

It's never pleasant to discover you're a nonentity, and Dan Brown's delicate psyche, already strained by the gnat bites of conspiracy copycats and sick pictures sent by stop-at-nothing rivals, must have been rent asunder in the spectral presence of Oliver Goldsmith, Edmund Burke, Jonathan Swift, Samuel Beckett and the anonymous masters behind the Book of Kells. That was Magill's theory anyway. He expounded it in whispered gobbets as they took the guided tour around Trinity College's glorious gallery of galleys, typescripts and Morocco-bound manuscripts, safely roped off from the awestruck sightseers who circulated like pilgrims at a literary Lourdes.

Abby wasn't so sure. "Why would Dan do that to himself? It seems like a form of mental self-mutilation. Why torture his already tortured psyche?"

"You tell me, Abby. You're supposed to be the expert in guerrilla psychology."

Hmmm. This was far beyond the boundaries of Abby's expertise, book-acquired though it was. Never one to duck a challenge, she hypothesized that it was some kind of authorial oedipal struggle, a thanatic drive of some sort or, failing that, a bit like dogs returning to their own sick. "In a good way, though."

"Yeeeessss. I see what you're getting at. It's a kind of itch that authors have to scratch, a mental scab that they feel compelled to pick, despite the pain it causes. In order to write well, or even write at all, you have to read and read and read. Writers are readers and vice versa. They are, therefore, drawn to places like this even though it's an agonizing experience."

"The Danster should have resisted!" Abby said, more in sorrow than in anger. "Especially given his severely stressed state. But he couldn't help himself. And paid the psychic price."

"That may be part of it," Magill observed, as they paused in front of a display case containing Brian Boru's legendary harp, familiar from countless Guinness ads and coins of the Irish realm. "But I have a simpler explanation."

"Which is?"

"He was looking for a book. A book with the catalogue number 235.711/BRO. He wasn't just telling us his password, or recalling the good old days when he and I used to bandy mathematical sequences about. Nor was he conveying part of a phone number or geographical location or social security number or military serial number, though those possibilities crossed my mind. It was when I walked past the National Library, after being inexplicably punched by someone in Waterstone's, that I realized it was Dewey Decimal."

"Errr, well done," Abby said with amazement. "I wonder what book Dan was after when he had his funny turn."

"That's what we're going to find out. My gut feeling is that he's referring to one of his own, *Angels and Demons*, most likely."

"Why's that?"

"Under Dewey Decimal, numbers between 230 and 240 pertain to theological matters, which are subdivided up into ten major categories of religious concern – angelology, demonology, eschatology, soteriology, mysticism and so on. The BRO is short for Brown."

Understandably, Abby couldn't help but wonder about someone who knew the Dewey Decimal classification off pat. It's the kind of ability that makes train spotters look like raffish men of the world. But beggars can't be choosers. "Do you really think Trinity Library stocks Brown's books? I mean, they're hardly great literature, are they."

"Oh, you'd be surprised what university libraries contain nowadays, everything from rock CDs to TV DVDs to back issues of *Playboy*."

"You speak from personal experience?"

Magill ignored her impertinence, which was a bit rich coming from someone who once worked in an intimate apparel emporium, so called, and less than thirty minutes earlier was cavorting in her underwear on top of the Clarence. "Not in here, obviously. I think we need to look in the working stacks, the everyday library shelves that tourists don't want to know about and earnest undergraduates habituate, when they're not knocking back pints of porter in The Stag's Head, Davy Byrne's or Kehoe's."

"Or indeed all three."

Pausing only to admire Pomodoro's magical sculpture, *Sphere Within a Sphere*, which aptly encapsulated the wheels within wheels of their literary quest, Abby and Simon made a bee-line for the Berkeley library complex. An unsightly 1960s addition to Trinity's elysian campus, the Berkeley is surpassed in its Brutalist barbarism by one building only, the adjacent Douglas Hyde Art Gallery, which is twinned architecturally with the Maginot Line. After talking their way past the bored security guard, who fell for their story of Hustler lecturer, plus glamorous research assistant – albeit the ten euro backhander was more persuasive still – they made their way through the carpeted issue desk area to the Ussher annex, an attractive 2001 addition to the brutish Berkeley.

The Ussher was closed and locked. As term was over and students were few, the librarians were reshelving, stocktaking and generally moving stuff around to mess with the minds of undergraduates. Undeterred, Magill asked to borrow Abby's brooch. With the aid of its sharp clasp, he picked the Ussher lock in double-quick time. He smirked the smirk of a student who paid close attention during safe-breaking class at PWC. Rather than take the lift, which might have signalled their presence to an officious member of staff, they clambered up several flights of stairs to the fourth floor. The stacks-access door was also locked, though it too yielded to Magill's lock-picking prowess.

They slipped inside. One half of the space was filled with closely packed shelving units – unlit, uninviting, uncanny. The other half comprised a communal reading area, which was not only chock-a-block with tables and chairs and postgraduate carrels but also blessed with a wonderful view over Trinity's playing fields, a view that must have distracted more than a few sluggardly students come exam time.

Impressive as it was, the sylvan view wasn't the most dramatic sight that the fourth floor afforded. An enormous airwell separated the browsing and study zones. It plunged all of six stories to the map room in the lower basement of the building. As architectural features go, it was very attractive. As a health and safety issue, the Ussher abyss was another matter entirely. Stressed students at exam time might prefer to hurl themselves into the great seven-storey chute than sit a paper on post-structuralist philosophy or Phillips's painfully prosaic principles of marketing.

Ignoring the view over the snow-speckled playing fields and resisting the vertiginous appeal of peering into the central chasm, Magill led the way to the relevant section. The layout was indicated by numbered labels on the wooden ends of the shelving units. Awakened, like Rip van Winkle from its bookish slumber, the overhead strip lighting hummed unhappily as Simon scanned the collection, looking for 235.711/BRO. Would it be *Angels and Demons* or even *The Da Vinci Code* itself – possibly the illustrated edition, the movie tie-in edition, the large print edition? It was none of them. The book that occupied the requisite location was called *The Mystery of the Cathedrals and Similar Symbological Conundra*. That was interesting enough, if incomprehensible, but it was the name of the author that really took Magill's breath away: Pitcairn Brodie. The BRO stood for Brodie.

"This book is new to me," he said, with undisguised astonishment, "and I thought I knew everything connected with his work. Jeez, I cleared out his office in the Department of Divinity. It took me two weeks." He turned the hefty volume around in his hands. "I've no recollection of seeing this book, neither in typescript nor galley proofs nor author's copies."

Politely, Abby refrained from reminding Magill that she'd helped him de-access Brodie's Edinburgh University office. True, her contribution to the relocation process involved little more than holding the professor's door open and hefting a few book-filled boxes to Magill's long-suffering 2CV, but that was by the by. Instead, she cracked the mysterious volume open and started flicking through it rapidly. Lavishly illustrated, not least with a striking back flap photo of the author in his swaggering Scottish prime, Brodie's book consisted of alphabetized entries on the "unsolved" mysteries of religious and quasi-religious symbology, ranging from the well-known Nazca Lines in Peru, through Mesoamerican temple complexes and the Great Pyramid of Giza to rather less familiar curiosities, such as the labyrinth in Chartres Cathedral, the great cyclic cross of Hendaye and the occult sundial in the grounds of Holyrood House.

"I *know* that one," Abby said excitedly. "The Holyrood sundial was part of the Brodie code we cracked in Edinburgh!" With nary a thought for the sanctity of books, Abby thumbed through the pages rapidly in her haste to get to the Hs. She slowed down as Holyrood hoved into view. However, she never got there. She stopped at the immediately preceding entry on Hendaye, a look of shock and astonishment on her pale, pinched face. She cracked the spine to ensure that the book remained open at the right place – Magill visibly winced at the noise – then passed it over to her companion.

"Crikey," he whispered. There was a colour illustration of the old weathered cross that sat in the centre of a tiny village in the Basque country, on the border between France and Spain. It wasn't the photograph that surprised him, though. It was an accompanying diagram of the four faces of the limestone monument. They were the same set of symbols that were scribbled on the book covers in Brown's macabre photograph album – a sun, a moon, a star and a shield.

Staggered by the unexpected turn of events, they made their way to the reading area for an in-depth study of the text. The tables were piled high with mounds of books for reshelving. Business and management books, mainly. The carpeted floor was also covered with great stalagmites of *Accounting for Non-accountants, Amusing Auditing Anecdotes, Structural Equation Modelling Made Simple* and other assorted wounds on the student body. They cleared a space among the tottering columns and sat side by side reading the Hendaye entry. According to Fulcanelli, the infamous French alchemist – considered by some to be a nom de plume of W. B. Yeats – the curiously carved symbols on the Great Cyclic Cross of Hendaye possess powerful eschatological significance...

"Eschatological?" Abby asked.

"Pertaining to end times," the son of the manse answered.

"As in the Apocalypse?"

"As in the end of the world."

"I don't feel fine."

"Me neither."

Exchanging uncomfortable glances, they continued reading. Believed to be central to Fulcanelli's legendary lost work – *Finis*

Gloria Mundi – the Hendaye cross is an astro-calendrical pointer to the precise date of the impending apocalypse. According to recent calculations by a team of alternative astro-archaeologists, the end is scheduled for 12 January 2009. However, the as yet unbroken Great Cross Code may hold further clues to this intriguing apocalyptic mystery (see Appendix IV).

"12 January 2009?"

"That's next Monday."

"Two days from now."

"Hope your affairs are in order, Abby."

"I'm monogamous by inclination, Mr Magill."

Smiling ruefully, they ploughed on. Aside from his seminal studies on Hendaye, Atlantis (q.v.), the Pyramids (q.v.), the language of the birds and the Emerald Tablet of Hermes Trismegistus, Fulcanelli offers a profoundly original interpretation of the occult symbology of Notre Dame, as regurgitated in the recent bestseller by Dan Brown, *The Da Vinci Code* (q.v.).

"That's it," Abby stage-whispered in a wobbly imitation of a scary movie voice. "We're all going to die!

Click. "Your wish is my command, frilly knickers." Click.

Chapter Thirty-Three

So Not Joe Doe

Magill turned to face his antagonist. Time hadn't improved Wee Joe's look, much less his outlook. The little man was as bald and ugly and aggressive as ever. His false teeth-afflicted palate was as vile as vile could be. He didn't so much look like the cat that got the cream as the sourpuss who'd swallowed carbolic acid by mistake. A sourpuss with a Glock .22 and murder in mind.

Click. "I told ye I'd come back for ye, Gingerbap." Click. "We have a score to settle, so we do." Click. He stroked his skeletal face expressively, reminding Magill of the delicious kisser-kick he'd delivered last time they met.

Unexpected though Wee Joe's arrival was, Magill had long been looking forward to this moment. A boot in the bake did not compensate for the deaths of Pitcairn Brodie and Barton Brady, the savagery of which still assailed him. "You took your time, old man."

Wee Joe licked his lips in anticipation. Click. "Aye, well, the organization had a few personnel problems to sort out after King Billy kauped." Click. "I've been travellin' too, trying to earn an honest crust." Click. "Paris, Rome, Salt Lake City, Sydney and now Dublin." Click. "I've kept body and soul together in them all." Click.

Abby bristled. "So, *you've* been killing Dan's fans?"

Wee Joe doffed his Redsox cap with a self-congratulatory flourish. Click. "Hitman for hire." Click. "No job too small." Click. "Money back guarantee." Click. "Photographs for free." Click. "Torso attachments too." Click. "Code name, Dannyboy." Click. "At your service." Click.

"You pathetic, putrid bastard."

Click. "Shut the fuck up, frillyknickers." Click. "I'll deal with you in a wee minute, after I've taken care of Gingerbap here." Click.

"I see you need a shooter these days," Magill observed. "Slowing down in your old age, Joe? You always were a cowardly cunt. King Billy said so. He told me you only ever killed women and children and people who couldn't defend themselves. He said you were a yellow-bellied son of a bitch."

Even though the jibe was a blatant lie, Wee Joe was too proud of his assassination credentials to ignore it. He placed his pistol on a pile of introductory OB books, reached into the inside pocket of his shapeless tweed jacket – identical to Dan's – and pulled out a pair of bone-handled butcher's knives. Honed to perfection, he couldn't help admiring their extra-keen edges. They glittered obscenely, even in the flat fluorescent light of the library.

Abby seized her moment. She had been edging away from Magill, effectively increasing the viewing arc of the assassin, which might buy a few extra milliseconds when push came to shove. She decided to push for shove by springing towards the madman and bowling him over before he had a chance to attack. But she was too late. Wee Joe's reflexes may not have been as fast as they were in the days when he performed a knife-throwing act in Fossett's circus. However, they were still pretty impressive. The two knives thudded either side of Abby's body, pinning her trench coat, her sweater, her blouse, her very BVDs to a big wooden partition that separated the communal reading area and the semi-private post-graduate carrels. She was all but impaled, mounted like a butterfly on a museum display board. Grunting and groaning, she fluttered desperately to escape. The coat flapped, the body thrashed, the legs kicked, trying to exert some leverage. The mouth emitted a stream of vulgar invective. There was no escape, though.

Distracted by the attack, Wee Joe turned back to deal with Magill. He was nowhere to be seen. Only a forest of management stalagmites faced the diminutive Ulster assassin. Click. "What was that about a cowardly cunt, Gingerbap?" Click. "Who's the cowardly cunt now, you big streak of shite?" Click. "I'm going to cut your balls off and shove them down your fuck-faced throat." Click. As he talked, trying to smoke out his quarry, Wee Joe extracted another knife from the folds of his Harris Tweed, a hunting knife with a wickedly serrated blade. Click. "That's what became of your big brother, wasn't it?" Click. "I heard all about him." Click. "Died with his dick in his mouth." Click. "Come out, come out, wherever you are." Click.

On high alert, Wee Joe advanced steadily into the textbook labyrinth, darting from mounds of research methods wrist-breakers to columns of marketing management doorstoppers, hiding behind the packed and stacked reading tables as necessary, listening intently for the tell-tale sounds of his target.

Magill was listening, too. He'd circled around the Shankill Butcher for hire, moving silently as he'd been taught. Picking up a copy of Kate Phillips's first edition, he hurled it towards a pillar of unread and unreadable Routledge monographs. The asymmetrical assemblage wobbled slightly, then toppled to one side like a landslip sliding into the ocean, a calving iceberg of incomprehensible academese. The crash was followed by the sound of Wee Joe scampering after his stumbling blundering prey. The Glock was within Simon's grasp.

Smiling at the assassin's cries of frustration – which sounded decidedly odd when delivered with a speech defect – Magill stepped out of the forest of *Fundamentals of Finance*. He picked up Wee Joe's automatic from where it lay on the OB obelisk. "You wanted me to come out cuntface. Well, here I am. Are you ready to rumble?"

Wee Joe emerged from a thicket of econometrics classics, covered in dust and cobwebs. He ignored Magill and made for Abby, who was still struggling to escape her confinement while screaming carnal imprecations at the imp. Her time at Some Like It Hot wasn't entirely wasted. She'd somehow wriggled out of the overcoat but was tugging to no avail on the knives which were embedded on either side of her torso. Voluminous outfits may be fashionable but there was a lot to be said for Lycra.

"Step away from the babe, Joe."

The psychopath ignored Magill's warning, as he strode towards Abby with hunting knife in hand and evil intent in mind. Magill didn't hesitate. He released the safety, as instructed on the PWC rifle range, let off a quick burst of automatic fire – all headshots in order to drop the perp before he did any damage – and stared aghast as the gun clicked empty on five separate occasions.

Click. "Ye didn't think I'd leave a magazine in it, did ye?" Click.

Magill wasn't finished. He pulled a heavy HRM tome from the nearest stand of pseudo-scholarship and threw it at the psycho, who was laughing inanely at his success with the old empty-clip tactic. The words of wisdom missed Wee Joe completely and sailed into the airwell beyond. The assassin paused, listened for the sickening thud of the bulky volume six floors beneath, then carried on as before. Abby struggled ever more frantically.

Click. "You can get fined for damaging library property, Gingerbap." Click.

"Face me like a man, you fucker."

Click. "Just wait till I sort out frillyknickers." Click. "Then I'll show ye, ya big ginger glipe." Click.

There was only one thing left for it. "Joe, did anyone ever tell you that you're the spitting image of Benny Hill's sidekick, the ugly little Ulsterman he slapped around the head? Obviously you're a lot uglier, a lot stupider and a lot crazier, but the resemblance is uncanny, all the same."

Clicking like a harpooned dolphin with a speech impediment, Wee Joe whirled round to face Magill. He opened his mouth as if to pour invective on the Englishman. Instead, he removed his slobber-striated dentures with a fiendish flourish. Drool dripped off both sets as he placed them on a convenient David Jobber.

Magill was transfixed by the hideous sight, designed as it was to distract. The psycho was upon him before he knew it, slashing wildly with the serrated blade. Magill leapt to one side, behind a bulwark of branding textbooks. But he was too late. The tip of the knife caught his left cheekbone and carried on cutting to the side of his mouth. Involuntarily, he raised his hand to his burning bloody face, which exposed his unprotected left side. The diabolical dervish slashed and stabbed again. Successfully. Magill felt a red hot poker lance through him. Abby screamed. Despite the pain and the blood loss, Magill grabbed for the weapon. Unsuccessfully. Wee Joe closed in for the kill.

He closed too far. Magill slipped his foot between the ankles of the assailant and twisted as he'd been taught in unarmed combat. Joe tumbled into a pyramid of Michael Porters, which toppled into another, then another, all cascading around the shrieking fiend like an avalanche of competitive advantage. The hunting knife was buried under a mountain of monotony. Wee Joe scrabbled around for a few moments, then abandoned the effort and rose to face his wounded opponent. Magill had height, strength and youth on his side. Monroe was blessed with experience, ruthlessness, psychosis, plus the advantage of smallness and speed. His serial killer credentials were likewise unassailable. He also had a trick up his sleeve. Trouser leg, rather.

"Watch out, Simon," Abby shouted, recalling her encounter with the succubus in Some Like It Hot. "He keeps another knife somewhere."

Despite the blood dripping from his chin, the crimson bloom that was spreading across his T-shirt and the buzzing fuzzies in his ever-lighter head, Magill faced his nemesis without flinching. The killer for hire smiled a gummy grin, his sagging toothless face a picture of infernal delight. His right hand held a glittering switchblade that looked innocuous, but looks can be very deceptive. Click. "I killed all four of them with this, Gingerbap." Click. "It's got your name on it too." Click.

"Are you sure there's enough space for 'Gingerbap'?" Magill asked, taunting his tormentor with the only weapon at his disposal. "Are you sure you know how to spell it?" Magill waited patiently for the lunge that he knew was coming. The murdering madman merely switched the switchblade from hand to hand, akin to a three-card monte dealer. Simon refused to be distracted. He kept his eyes fixed on Wee Joe's wizened face, as Sergeant Crush had hammered into him.

The switchblade was a blur in flight. Fast as it was, Magill was faster. Kate Phillips's 800-page marketing textbook made many students suffer grievously down the years. But Magill had finally found a good use for it. Although the switchblade penetrated deep into the hoary hardback volume, it failed to break through Magill's marketing shield. Magill dropped the tiresome tome and tried to extract Wee Joe's weapon. It was stuck in the textbook like the sword in the stone. He stooped and tugged again. But by that time the psychotic senior citizen had bowled them over. He punched Magill on his wounded side then thumped him again and again in the same place. The agony was almost unbearable, not dissimilar to having one's kidneys devilled internally, then extracted and eaten while still fresh and throbbing. Simon tried to stave his attacker off but the little limpet wouldn't let up.

With a well-practised sawing action, Wee Joe expertly extracted his weapon from its scholarly scabbard. He raised it on high with both hands, yelling maniacally, well-nigh orgasmically, as he prepared to plunge the glittering blade into Magill's unprotected throat. A hand clasped his wrist, staying Simon's execution. A second hand clamped his other wrist. Standing behind him with legs spread on either side, Abby forced the switchblade down, down, down towards the chest of the slobbering assassin. He struggled to hold her off, screeching with the effort. His arms shook and wobbled under the strain. The tip of the blade was millimetres from his breastbone. "This is for Dave Kelley, you fucking Protestant psychopath." Abby shoved with all her might.

However, she spoke too soon and shoved too late. In a last desperate manoeuvre, Wee Joe flung his head back as hard as he could and hit Abby in the tummy with his bony cranium. Winded, she doubled over, only to receive an elbow in the throat for her trouble. Rising, the psycho swung at her with his switchblade. But missed. He slashed again. Abby darted behind a pillar of postmodern marketing primers, which offered little by way of protection, let alone intellectual utility. Joe heaved the benighted books over, shrieking as he shoved. Magill staggered back to his feet, grimacing with the pain. With a deep shuddering breath, he chucked the pierced Phillips at Wee Joe, then made a rush for him, only to slip on the glossy cover of a Consumer Behaviour textbook. It was impossible to tell which one it was, since they're all exactly the same.

Outnumbered, Wee Joe glanced warily from Magill to Maguire. He decided to cut his losses. He turned and made a mad charge for the exit, determined to live and fight and assassinate another day. Magill stared blankly at his saviour.

"What's your problem? Have you never seen a woman in her underwear before? Get after him!"

Struggling to regain his composure – understandable in the circumstances – Magill started after the disappearing dwarf.

Hampered by blood loss and the head start he'd given Wee Joe, Magill was nonetheless equipped with a longer stride and PWC-honed physical conditioning. The push-ups and assault courses and five-mile runs before breakfast were there when he needed them. Arms pumping, Magill pursued the fleeing Shankill Butcher, who had almost reached the door to the stairs. With a desperate dive at the darting form, Magill swiped wildly at his heels, caught one, which caught the other in a copybook touch tackle. Better yet, the falling assassin banged his head against the heavy metal door and was instantly knocked unconscious. The switchblade dropped from his inert fingers.

Exhausted, Magill struggled back to the reading area, where Abby was waiting for him by the airwell. She was still in her underwear and looking pretty darn attractive, he thought. "Better get your coat and stuff, Abby. Better get outta here before a librarian shows up. They might slap a fine on us or remove our reading rights." He felt a presence behind him. It was Wee Joe wielding his switchblade. He had somehow recovered from the knockout blow and picked up the weapon where it had fallen. Magill was still cursing his stupidity as the blade started towards his throat. He was too taken aback to offer any defence, despite all his unarmed combat training. It was like a horror movie made flesh.

Wee Joe's moment of triumph was short lived, however. A brawny arm wrapped itself around his neck and another grabbed his scrawny waist. The astonished assassin was physically picked up, carried to the edge of the six-storey abyss and, with nary a pause for breath, dropped into the crack of doom. The map room broke his fall.

Magill looked around at his deliverance. His features were backlit and impossible to discern. Simon recognized the body shape, though. The tartan trews were a give-away, too. "Pitcairn, is that really you?"

He fainted.

Chapter Thirty-Four

The Da Vinci Coke

It really did hurt when he laughed. So Magill tried not to laugh, which wasn't hard in the circumstances. His side also hurt every time he took a deep breath or moved inadvertently. So he tried to avoid that too, which again wasn't hard in the premier class cabin of EI119, en route to Washington Dulles. His cheek was sore as well, though it looked a lot worse than it was. If anything, the neatly stitched cut gave him the insouciant look of a duelling-scarred cavalry officer. The US Immigration officers might not see it that way, mind.

Magill's physical pain was as nothing compared to the mental anguish he felt every time Pitcairn Brodie's reappearance reappeared in his mind's eye. He thought he'd seen the last of him. He'd found his brutally murdered body, in a roomful of boxes and books. He'd banished the man from his memory, once he fell for the unfounded allegations of paedophilia. But Brodie came back to save him in his hour of greatest need, like King Arthur emerging from Avalon.

Except that it wasn't Pitcairn. It wasn't even Selkirk, Pitcairn's big brother. It was Mickey Finnegan, a plaid-partial U2 security guard, who was keeping a watchful eye on them, as His Bononess had promised. It was Mickey who helped him out of Ussher, ferried him to St Vincent's hospital, where they were well used to patching up private patients, and drove him to Dublin Airport for his flight to Washington DC.

Pitcairn really was dead. Magill felt as if he'd won the National Lottery, only to discover he'd lost the winning ticket. No amount of free champagne and canapés could fill the hollow feeling inside, though they helped with the nagging pain of his flesh wounds. He had another helping. What the hell. Why not?

The helpings didn't help Magill's concentration. Even at his sharpest, however, he'd have struggled with what lay before him. Having "borrowed" Brodie's book from Trinity, he was attempting to crack the Great Cross Code in Appendix IV. It seemed to be a simple substitution cipher, where the alphabet was replaced by numbers, symbols or suitably modified letters, in this particular case a collection of occult sigils, seals, runes and glyphs, strange shapes that most ordinary people would doubtless describe as squiggles. Symbolic substitutions, Magill knew, were some of the most common coding practices. Mary Queen of Scots' Code, which was cracked and precipitated her execution; Rose Greenhow's Cipher, successfully employed by a sultry female spy throughout the American Civil War; the Gold Bug Code, invented by Edgar Allan Poe for an 1843 short story; and the mysterious Dancing Men Cipher, a collection of Lowry-esque stick figures, broken by one Sherlock Holmes, were just some of many symbolic substitution ciphers. Symbol counts usually sufficed to crack simple substitution codes – the most common symbol meant E, the next was T, the one after that A, etc – and even if various modifications, such as homophones or anagrams or semagrams, were made to complicate matters, any reasonably competent cryptographer could crack a symbolic substitution cipher in less time than it took to scarf a canapé or quaff a flute of Krug.

Several canapés and three flutes in, Magill was no further along than before. If anything he had fallen far behind. The first sign of trouble was a symbol that looked like the gyno-glyph beloved by feminists, except that the circle plus cross had an extra pair of horns. Apt, some radical feminists might say, but Magill knew better. He'd seen John Dee's sigil before. Dr John Dee, the foremost sorcerer, cabalist, Rosicrucian and cryptographer of Elizabethan times, was a practitioner of Enochian magic. With the aid of an obsidian scrying plate and a devious Irish seer called Edward Kelley, Dee conversed with angels, recorded the conversations and formulated an extremely complex system of symbolic magic that was extended and elaborated by innumerable infamous adepts, such as those in the Hermetic Order of the Golden Dawn. Enochian magic could be used for good or ill – Dee desired illumination, Kelley wanted gold – but the essential point about the seals, sigils, signs and mind-bending letter squares of his celestial system was that they were apocalyptic. They not only portended but unleashed the apocalypse. Cracking the code could cause the end of the world!

Tudor guerrilla psychology, he surmised with a smile. It hurt. Simon's flesh was unwilling. His spirit was weaker still. High living, high altitude and high ibuprofen count conspired against his ability to crack the Great Cross Code. He opened Brodie's book again. The sigils swam before his eyes. Memories of his previous code-breaking adventure, whilst in the delicious clutches of Ultima Sullivan, drifted back to him. He needed something to take his mind off the challenge, something to relax and distract him, something to let his unconscious mental processes – the creative denizens of the limbic brain – get to work on the symbological conundrum. It was time for an in-flight movie, preferably one without a sibilant psycho-killer. He fumbled around in his luxurious leather seat, searching for the AVOD handset, which was buried in the depths of the armrest. He caught the eye of an adjacent aeronaut, who smiled the smile of an air miles millionaire, someone who had seen it all before and was at home in every aircraft cabin this side of a Sopwith Camel. The smiling stranger set down his half-read novel and gave Magill a brief masterclass on the on-board entertainment system. Half-sozzled, Simon was none the wiser. But rather than embarrass himself any further, he asked about his good neighbour's novel. Was it any good?

The grey-haired stranger turned the cover towards Magill, so that he could see the title; *The Book of Lies* by Brad Meltzer. "It's a piece of shit."

"Why are you reading it then?" Magill never saw the point of persevering with thrillers that failed to thrill. Life was too short. Very short in some instances.

"I'm hoping it'll pick up," he said without much enthusiasm. "It better pick up, because there's five hours of this flight to go and I've seen every in-flight movie I want to see this month."

"Meltzer," Magill continued; "didn't he write *The Book of Fate*?"

The stranger stroked his grey-flecked goatee, deep in thought. "That was a piece of shit, too. The characters weren't so much flat as steamrollered. The plot wasn't thin, it was anorexic. It didn't so much suspend disbelief as lynch it."

Magill was at a loss. "If the last one was bad, why read another by the same author?"

"I'm a sucker for Dan Brown."

"Sorry?"

"I always fall for books whose blurb claims descent from Dan – worthy competitor, better than Brown, the *Da Vinci Code* on speed. You know the kind of thing. Ancient conspiracy. Hidden bloodline. Biblical secrets. Race against time. I've read them all. I've read so many I sometimes forget I've read them already. It was only when I started *Lies* that I remembered how awful *Fate* was. None of them are in the same league as Brown." He looked at the half-read novel disdainfully. "But I'm stuck with it from here to Washington."

Will I or won't I, Magill thought. Why not? What harm could it possibly do?

"I used to work for Dan."

The seasoned aeronaut, who looked cool, calm and collected in his white linen suit – a southern gentleman in all but name – cast aside his Meltzer with alacrity. "You *know* Dan?"

Magill nodded, affecting nonchalance. "Only for the last three years."

Incredibly, the guy actually said "phew", "hot dog", "holy moly" and several other expressions of amazement that are only ever found in clichéd potboilers like *The Book of Lies*. He introduced himself with a handshake, Robert E. Pemberton. He asked about Dan's next book. He asked about the post-*Da Vinci* hiatus. He asked lots of other questions that Magill couldn't answer without spilling the beans about Brown's nervous breakdown.

Before long, they drifted back to their private preoccupations. Pemberton picked up Meltzer and tried again, with a scowl of disapproval. Magill took another stab at Brodie's bewildering appendix, no more successfully than before. Every so often, the aeronaut would interrupt Magill's ruminations to ask a Brown-related question. Have you met Tom Hanks? What's Ron Howard like? Where were the Vatican scenes filmed? When, oh when, will the next book be published? Is it true that Dan sometimes writes under a pseudonym?

Almost tempted to answer, "Yeah, Brad Meltzer," Magill did his best to answer every query, no matter how inane. How Dan managed to stay sane for so long was beyond him. A man could go crazy responding to such stuff day-in day-out, everywhere you go, everyone you meet.

An unruffled demeanour was hard to maintain when Pemberton pitched his big idea, about two hours out from Dulles. He was vice-president of sales promotion for Coca-Cola, the greatest beverage on earth. He had an incredible idea. Do you know the way Dr Pepper promised a free soda to everyone in the United States if Guns N' Roses comeback album was released in 2008? Well, why not do something similar with Dan Brown and Diet Coke? A free can for every single American consumer if Dan unleashes the next novel in 2009. Diet Coke and Dan Brown were a natural fit – hard-working, all-American, hugely successful, equally iconic, controversial on occasion – hell, if Dan'd agree to have Langdon chugging a Diet Coke in the next book, the sky's the limit, sponsorship-wise, going forward.

Magill tried to explain that (a) he no longer worked for Dan; (b) an earlier attempt to place products in Brown's books ended unhappily; and (c) creative artists like the Danster were reluctant to make the necessary compromises that commercialization requires. But there was no stopping the V-P for Sales Promotion. A creative, blue-sky thinker in his own right, Pemberton soon had Langdon leaping from delivery trucks, wrestling with Polar bears and cracking the code of Coke's secret recipe, as well as unravelling universal product codes on the packaging. Magill was mighty relieved when the Airbus A330 landed at Dulles, a few minutes ahead of schedule.

As is Americans' wont, Pemberton passed his business card to Magill while they waited for the unfasten seatbelts signal. He also gave him a couple of complimentary tickets to The World of Coca-Cola, a brand museum "experience" in Atlanta. "Give me a call if you're ever in town."

"Sure thing," Magill replied politely, vaguely embarrassed because he had nothing to repay Pemberton's generosity. He pulled a ballpoint pen from his top pocket. "This belonged to Dan," he lied. "Please accept it with the author's compliments."

The Coke V-P looked genuinely thrilled. Surely a marketer of all people wouldn't fall for such a flagrant ploy. "Wow," he said. "By jiminy," he added. "Ain't that something," he enthused. Clearly, the Meltzers were causing irreparable brain damage.

"That book," he went on, gesturing towards the Brodie tome that had done so much to ruin Magill's journey.

"Yeah, what about it?" Magill replied.

"Has it anything to do with Dan? It's just that I couldn't help noticing it during the flight. I recognized the code you were working on and I was wondering if it plays a part in Brown's new book."

"What do you mean, you recognized the code?"

Adjusting his bootlace tie prior to deplaning, Pemberton raised a sceptical eyebrow, as if to say you don't have to play dumb with me, buddy. "It's the Zodiac code. I've seen the movies. I've read the books. It's a departure for Dan, but if anyone can reinvent the serial killer thriller it's America's greatest writer, right? He's done it before, right? Am I right or am I right, Simon?"

Magill grimaced, as if on the horns of indecision. "You got it, Robert. Damn, you're smart! But, whatever you do, don't tell anybody. It's top secret. Even Dan's publisher doesn't know."

"All right," the Coca-Cola camerlengo exulted, punching the air like he'd won the superbowl. "There's a price for my secrecy, though," he added conspiratorially.

"What's that?"

"Dan Brown and Diet Coke. Know what I'm sayin', Simon. DB/DC."

"Swivel on this, Dr Pepper. Correct?"

"You got it, pal. Give me a call."

"I'll speak with Dan."

They shook hands on the deal and departed, each believing they'd got something worthwhile, a spokesperson who'd add some of that old Brown magic to a bubbly brown beverage, and a key to the code in Pitcairn Brodie's baffling book.

Chapter Thirty-Five

When Will I See You Again?

What is it with men and women's underwear? God help us. Abby was still amazed by the look on Magill's face when she rescued him in her smalls. A word of thanks? No. A thank goodness you're here? As if. A what a magnificent piece of escapology? What a magnificent pair, more like. It was all he could do to stop himself saying cover yourself up, woman, get your clothes on, or my, those goose-pimples look big. It's called cellulite, darling. It's something real women have. Women's limbs aren't like they are in lad's magazines. Grow up!

Still, she shouldn't be too surprised. Something similar happened every week in Some Like It Hot. Not a knife attack, though they weren't exactly unknown. A "male moment". They'd drift into the intimate apparel emporium, blushing and stammering and muttering something about a present for the wife/girlfriend/partner. They didn't know their girlfriend's size. They hadn't a clue about fit. They didn't understand what underwear means to a woman. They were buying the things for themselves, basically. She was often tempted to say, "Want to try them on?" The only thing that stopped her was fear that they might accept. Men professed to hate buying underwear but secretly wanted to try on the scanty panties and prance around the store.

That was Abby's theory anyway. Or was it something she picked up in her guerrilla psychology classes? Sigmund Freud, probably. He looked like someone who wore French knickers under his knickerbockers. What women want, eh? What men want to wear, more like.

Men, they're all the same. All equally useless, clueless, merciless.

Jesus, the look on Wee Joe's face when he thought he had Magill. The delight. The triumph. The madness. The thrill that killing provided. Some men are sick bastards. All men are bastards but some are *sick* bastards. She saw *Psycho* once as a child. It stayed with her for years. Every creak on the stairs at night was a psycho coming to get her. Working on a farm and later in an abattoir inured her to death. It became routine, mechanical, matter-of-fact. She thought she'd got over her fear of Fred West, Peter Sutcliffe, Ian Brady, Ted Bundy, Jeffrey Dahmer and the rest of the serial killer crew. Even the incidents in Some Like It Hot and the Carlton Hotel in Nuremberg hadn't really disturbed her, because she was directly involved, acting on instinct. Spectating was completely different. The sight of Wee Joe, demented grin on his slobbering gob, creeping after Magill, hunting knife in hand – knowing all the time that she was next – would stay with her for ever.

He's dead, Abby. He's dead. He's never coming back. This nightmare will soon be over. No more nightmares. Please.

Unless Clancy hires someone else. Wee Joe was just the murderous monkey. The organ-grinder's still out there. Clancy must be one sick bastard. Writing thrillers clearly wasn't good for authors' mental stability. Just look at Dan. Magill thinks he's in an unfolding story. How mad is that? He didn't predict the appearance of Mickey Finnegan, that's for sure. So much for sodding story structure. He didn't anticipate Wee Joe's homicidal curtain call, a staple of every horror movie known to man. The guy doesn't know semolina from shinola, or whatever the expression was. Shit from saltpetre, was it?

Saltpetre. God, it's been a long time since Dave Kelley explained saltpetre to her. God, the look on *his* face. God, the look on his face when he 'fessed up to Love Pump. God, he was a bastard too. Wonder what he's doing now. He was trouble with a capital T-shirt, the type with tour dates on the back. He even had the gall to confront her once, claiming that she'd got him wrong, that he deserved another chance, that she'd swallowed the lies of his no-good younger brother, without giving him an opportunity to explain.

The nerve of it. Forget him, Abby. Just forget him.

Simon was interested. She could tell. He wasn't her type. Her type only brought trouble. It was gallant of him to send her to

Hendaye, while he went head-to-head with Clancy. What was it with men and this mano-a-mano thing? Must be something to do with the size of their willies. If they only knew what their willies looked like. Put it away, for God's sake. And stop fiddling, while you're at it. Why all the fiddling, for Christ's sake. Leave your crotches alone, boys.

Enough!

Abby struggled to extract herself from the reverie and focus on the task in hand. But the mental image of Wee Joe Monroe kept coming back to her. The Ussher encounter replayed constantly in her mind. When she tried to purge the picture, random thoughts, disconnected thoughts, crazy thoughts frankly, crowded in on her instead, nagging, jostling, insistent. Who psychoanalyses the psychoanalysts? Guerrilla psychologist, heal thyself. Which way to the egress?

She checked the departure board. Another two hours until boarding. She picked up the mysterious marketing monograph. A book about mystic branding by Brodie. It was shelved right next to his *Mystery of the Cathedrals*. Might contain a clue, Magill said, as he flew off on his date with destiny. He had to go alone. He had to confront Clancy in the Ultimate Ordeal. Narrative structure said so.

Yeah, right.

The Secret Language of Brands. Odd title. She'd never heard of it before, even though she studied brands briefly at uni. Branding, it began, was a form of alchemy. It turned the base metal of undifferentiated products into the purest gold of desirable objects. Asda's own-brand bran flakes were indistinguishable from Kellogg's and less than half the price, but Kellogg's was number one in the bran flakes market. Okay, she could do without the lavatorial humour. Primark pencil skirts are made in the same sweatshop as Prada's, yet the price of one is ten times that of the other. True, but most women are wise to that nowadays and shop in Primark accordingly. The Audi TT is a Golf in sleek clothing. If you say so, Pitcairn, but who looks under the bonnet? Beauty was skin deep and the TT was beautiful.

Alchemists, the monograph continued, were regarded as charlatans in their day, little more than cheats and conmen who set out to rob people blind with their fool's gold and false promises of eternal life. The same accusations were made, with good reason, about today's alchemists who go by the names of branding, marketing and management consultants, each with their magic potion, each with their elixir of life, each with wildly exaggerated claims as to the efficacy of their organizational nostrums, strategic febrifuges, post-industrial philtres.

This from a brand whisperer.

Abby read on, with increasing reluctance. Brodie contended that the 4Ps were analogous to the four elements of earth, air, fire and water, marketing plans were modern modes of augury and no more accurate, marketing textbooks were indistinguishable from medieval grimoires, complete with illustrations of pyramids and pentagrams and interlinked circles, and filled with models that are direct descendants of kabbalistic sephirot. Necromantic numerology, moreover, was the norm in eminent marketing research journals. As someone who once sat in Hustler University Library, trying to make sense of unreadable academic articles on retail branding, Abby didn't disagree. But making merry mock was one thing, making a convincing case was another. Brodie's language of the brands left a lot unsaid.

Yawning, Abby wondered whether she should buy a magazine for the flight. There's no way she could keep reading this stuff all the way to Biarritz. Maybe she should write a branding book herself. How hard could it be? She had plenty of requisite experience, which was more than most academics. She'd built up a brand, WeeTube; she'd mismanaged a brand, Belfast's Black Rose; she'd been at the front line of branding in Some Like It Hot (branding irons were one of their biggest S&M sellers). She knew how to do it and, more importantly, how not to do it. Why not a how-not-to book on branding? So not branding. Think of all the great brand disasters she could include – the Edsel, the *Titanic*, the Betamax, the... um... well, there were plenty of them out there. Reverse psychology strikes again. Learn to succeed by studying failure. Bet no one's thought of that before. *Guerrilla Branding*, now there's a title to conjure with.

The monograph sat on her lap. The flight was about to be called. Bin the thing? Better hold on to it, otherwise Magill'll go ballistic. Imagine, a man going ballistic. Hard to picture. Not. Bringing Brodie's book was the lesser of two evils. She flicked through the tome once more. A chapter title caught her eye. Selling Surrealism. What did surrealism have to do with branding?

Everything apparently. Medieval alchemists lived in constant fear that their ideas, methods, secrets would be stolen by unscrupulous competitors. So they wrote their grimoires in riddling language that only they could interpret. This was known as the Language of the Birds. Based upon the ancient idea that man and bird were symbolically intertwined – an idea made manifest in bird gods like Quetzalcoatl, or stories of giant birds like the Roc, or legendary winged men such as Icarus, Mercury and, not least, Angels and Demons – alchemists' writings were the equivalent of birdsong, beautiful, mysterious, powerful, mesmeric, yet meaningful to those in the know.

Fair enough. But where does surrealism fit in? Maybe Brodie was being surreal rather than explaining surreal. Clearly, he was the kind of guy who tried to write wonderfully about wonder but left his readers wondering what he was on about. What bird language was Brodie writing in? Not the Skylark, that's for sure. Raven lunatic, maybe. Hard to swallow, perhaps. She skipped on a few pages. Ah, at last.

Surrealism is popularly associated with unusual visual juxtapositions – lobster telephones, melting watches, fur-lined teacups and so forth. However, surrealism was more of a literary movement than a mode of visual communication. Manifestos, tracts, newspapers, magazines, poems, jokes were more central to surrealism in its day than painting or sculpture. Automatic writing was equally central to the surrealist project. The dream work of Sigmund Freud was also an influence on surrealism. The writings of many modernist artists like James Joyce, Virginia Woolf, Samuel Beckett and W. B. Yeats were shaped to some extent by surrealism, and shaped surrealism in turn. The most powerful literary influence, though, was the hermetic tradition of alchemy and the occult. Hans Arp drew on Jacob Boehme, Joan Miró looked to Ramon Lull, André Breton, the major domo of surrealism, was in thrall to Eliphas Lévi, the foremost French occultist of the nineteenth century and Hugo Ball, the daddy of Dada and a phonetic performance poet, reputedly wished to return to the "innermost alchemy of the word". Max Ernst's alter ego was a peacock-like "bird-superior", Loplop. Many of the surrealists were brilliant self-publicists, Salvador Dalí especially, though the entire movement was publicized incessantly through acts of provocation and controversy that established the template followed by later marketing-savvy artists – Andy Warhol, Damien Hirst, Tracey Emin. So successful was their marketing that Surrealism is the best-known artistic brand after Impressionism, a brand that's part and parcel of the advertiser's repertoire, the Gold Blend cigarettes campaign, most famously.

Okay, okay, okay. But so what?

Surrealism and alchemy come together in Fulcanelli, by far the most influential occultist of the twentieth century. To this day, no one knows who Fulcanelli is or was. In 1926, at the height of surrealism's first flush, he appeared out of nowhere, with the manuscript of a path-breaking book, *The Mystery of the Cathedrals*. Ostensibly about the magical symbolism of France's great cathedrals, which were replete with occult allusions and hidden meanings, the book itself was written in the language of the birds, language that was strikingly similar to the surrealists and their literary avatars like W. B. Yeats.

Fulcanelli effectively reinvented alchemy for the twentieth century. He wrote a second book called *Dwellings of the Philosophers*, then a third book called *Finis Gloria Mundi*, which was so apocalyptically terrifying – a satanic equivalent of the third secret of Fatima – that it was suppressed before publication. Parts of it are believed to be extant, in an appendix on the Great Cross of Hendaye that was briefly appended to *The Mystery* when it was republished in a limited edition after the Second World War. Hendaye was and is a writer's colony. Hendaye was a hide-out for surrealists. Fulcanelli was a surrealist. Funcanelli was a fake, many believe. Others see links between Fulcanelli, the Priory of Sion and Rennes-le-Château, which was where the infamous *Documents Secrets* – a neo-surrealist prank – were discovered in 1975.

Be that as it may, Fulcanelli is a brand, an ambiguous brand, an intriguing brand, an iconoclastic brand, a prototype of

21st-century brands, for which the physical product is offshored to the cheapest Third World sweatshop, while the brand magic, the personality, the image is nurtured by the brand alchemists at headquarters. Fulcanelli is the future.

Time waits for no marketing man.

Or Ryanair passenger.

Chapter Thirty-Six

Ladies Who Punch

Abby eased through customs at Biarritz, picked up a hire car in the compact terminal and less than fifteen minutes later was on her way to Hendaye. The weather was cold and bright. A bracing on-shore breeze – gale, really – blustered in off the Bay of Biscay, where wet-suited surfboarders braved the dancing whitecaps and buzzing water-skis circled like maritime mosquitoes. Abby could feel the wind buffeting her midnight blue Renault Mégane, as the shelter of the belle époque holiday resort fell away and she found herself alone on the coast road, heading south. Dense stands of maritime pine lined the route, planted to prevent the sand dunes advancing ever further inland, like Birnam Wood. The forested ramparts were interspersed with watchtowers in the guise of holiday homes, plus the occasional ruined castle. It wasn't so much the *Côte des Basques* as the *Côte des Bastilles*.

Less than an hour later, Abby reached the northern outskirts of Hendaye Plage, an attractive cluster of chic restaurants, expensive shops and bohemian dwellings that whispered the ineffable words: artists' colony. The oil paintings on sale at the seafront and along the park railings were equally eloquent, as was the outspoken abundance of antique dealers. Abby drove past the marina, then turned inland towards the old town. She found a parking space close to the central square, where a weekly market was in full swing. Tucked in the corner of a tiny courtyard, the Great Cyclic Cross of Hendaye had seen better days. It was weatherbeaten and forlorn, hardly worth looking at, never mind photographing. The Great Cross was a misnomer. The whole thing was an obvious hoax. According to Brodie's book, the surrealists were renowned for their attention-grabbing pranks, such as Marcel Duchamp's infamous fountain (a ceramic urinal signed by the author) and his irreverent addition of moustache and beard to

263

Leonardo's *Mona Lisa*, which he labelled LHOOQ (a phonetic spelling of "she has a hot ass" in French). The surrealist alchemist Fulcanelli was obviously up to something similar with his Great Cyclic Cross, so-called. Clearly, it was a nondescript funerary monument that he elevated to apocalyptic significance, just to see if he could get away with it. What fun.

Dutifully, Abby took a few obligatory photographs, using her iPhone. All four eroded faces of the podium, a couple of snaps of the inscribed saltire on top, and one or two of the entire edifice, fluted column to the fore. She then tracked down the local tourist information bureau, which contained very little of interest on the cross. The counter was overflowing with leaflets about Lourdes, flyers on San Sebastian pilgrimage packages, glossy brochures on the nearby Neolithic caves at Sare, coffee table books devoted to the Ancient Celts, whose standing stones were dotted around the Basque country. There was even a selection of H. G. Wells and Aldous Huxley paperbacks, plus an edition of *The Winding Stair* by W. B. Yeats, all of whom holidayed hereabouts in the 1930s.

Hendaye's spiritual, artistic and occult credentials were incontestable. The home town of Martin Guerre, it had deceptions to boast about too. But the Great Cross, like Churchill's assessment of Russia, was a riddle wrapped in a mystery inside an enigma. Abby reckoned there was nothing inside the enigmatically mysterious riddle. If there had been, the local tourist industry would have exploited the connection to the hilt. If she were the manager of the Hendaye brand – not an impossibility, surely, given her enviable record in black rose city – that's what she would have done. True, the conspiracy theory tourist trade brought more than its fair share of cranks, weirdos and anoraks, but they were harmless obsessives by and large, who had to be fed, watered and sedated. If there was anything to the cross conspiracy, the *vacances* vendors of Hendaye-Ville would have had their trotters in the trough. Managing the tourist trade was like making foie gras. Every morsel of historical information was stuffed into tourists' distended gullets and, unpleasant though this procedure was, the end result was worth a fortune.

Abby repaired to a bistro, L'Amuse Bouche, on the periphery of the stall-filled market square. Torn between *les escargots, moules marinières* and *tête de boeuf*, she ordered *pipérade*, a local delicacy. While waiting for her *plat* to arrive, she tried to translate the only flyer she'd found on the old Hendaye cross. Obviously written by a French surrealist on an absinthe binge, it had something to do with bringing home the bacon. On a whim, she pulled up Wikipedia on her iPhone and entered bacon in the search box. Bacon, she soon discovered, was not only a cured cut of pig meat, but a form of computer spam, an army acronym for airborne communication reconnaissance and a number allocated to actors depending on their degree of separation from Kevin Bacon. Ah, it was also the name of a thirteenth-century empirical philosopher and practising alchemist, Friar Roger Bacon. A celebrated seer, who anticipated the imminent arrival of the Antichrist and the attendant apocalypse, Bacon predicted the invention of lasers, aeroplanes, motor cars, diving suits, poison gas and optical lenses. His geographical writings directly inspired Columbus's voyages, he was the inspiration behind Umberto Eco's *Name of the Rose*, and a woodcut of the great man shows him holding a grimoire, the illustrations on which were similar to those on the Great Cross of Hendaye.

But the cross was supposed to be seventeenth century, wasn't it? Abby returned to the disambiguation page. Francis Bacon caught her eye. Seventeenth century. Check. Alchemist. Check. Apocalyptic. Check. Cryptographer. Check. Lived for a time in south-west France. Check. Moved in influential circles. Check. Intimately associated with the Virginian Plantation in the American colonies. Interesting. Was the intellectual driving force behind both the Rosicrucians and the Freemasons. Very interesting. Was an Ascended Master who discovered the secret of eternal life and assumed many subsequent guises including Count de St Germain, Count Cagliostro and Fulcanelli. Can't keep a good senior citizen down! Wrote the complete works of Shakespeare. What??? Abby re-read the entry. Sir Francis Bacon, statesman, spymaster, politician, pederast, was the author of Shakespeare's entire oeuvre, as numerous cryptic messages in the plays attest.

Well, love a duck. Foie gras filled, or otherwise. Abby shook her head with disbelief. Discovering that Dan Brown had plagiarized W. B. Yeats's potboiler was pretty powerful stuff. But it was much ado about nothing compared with the thought of Bacon rustling up *Romeo and Juliet*, *King Lear*, *Cymbeline*, etc. As you like it? I don't think so. A comedy of errors? Now you're talking. A midsummer's night dream? Try midwinter morn in Hendaye.

Abby finished off her Jurançon, a nice sweet white, settled the bill and left a hefty tip. The lunch had been most enlightening, if undeniably bizarre. She picked up the eclectic collection of flyers and stuffed them in her handbag, prior to sauntering across to the cyclic cross for a closer look. Maybe something would leap out at her.

Something leapt all right.

An overgrown adolescent in leather jacket and jeans strolled past the café. Attractively tousle-haired, he smiled at Abby in that trainee roué way. She smiled back with a still-got-it-babe sparkle. He grabbed her Chloé handbag and sprinted off across the square. The robbery didn't register at first. But when it did, Abby was up and out of her bentwood chair like Marion Jones on EPO. With a head start and youth on his side, the bagnapper was already among the market stalls, darting along the close-packed aisles, shoving grocery bag-carrying browsers out of his way as he ran. One old Frenchman, a war veteran type with a huge handlebar moustache and a nose like a macaw, took a swipe at the miscreant with his walking stick and missed. Abby followed in hot pursuit, shouting what few French phrases she knew. *Arrêtez. Au secours. La plume de ma tante.* It was like something out of the Pink Panther, only for real. A stallholder leapt in front of the sneak thief but he shouldered him aside, back into the display, which collapsed beneath him sending burnished apples, plump pears, golden oranges, luscious lemons, juicy watermelons, succulent grapes and gleaming cherries cascading into the gutter. Temporarily unbalanced, the bag snatcher bounced off another stall, which similarly spilled its load of legumes, artichokes, celeriac and bright red peppers. A third Hendayean did his bit by hurling a big ripe aubergine at the galloping reprobate, only to infuriate the stallholder and an innocent old woman, whom he hit on the back of the head. Mayhem ensued. It was all Abby could do to fight her way through the agitated crowd of Saturday morning shoppers. Dogs were barking, people were shouting, everyone stopped to see what was happening. Fists were shaken for effect.

By the time Abby emerged from the melee, purse snatcher was disappearing into a side-street, picking up speed now that the road was clear. Three years previously, Abby would have given up at this point, panting and purple with exhaustion, but countless hours of circuit training and innumerable hard outings on the River Lagan had given her reserves of stamina that she put to dogged use. He ran along a narrow alleyway. Abby ran after. He skipped down a steep flight of steps, shoving a pram-pushing young mother out of the way. Abby did likewise, pausing only to check that the child was okay. He darted from side-street to side-street, through restaurant-dotted squares, past Renault-peppered passageways, pulling dustbins over en route. Abby kept going. She was completely lost in the warren of Basque country backstreets.

Eventually, they burst on to a riverfront walkway, lined with bars and nightclubs and restaurants, with lots of outdoor seating. He stopped for a breather by a set of decorative railings, hands on knees, panting and heaving, handbag at his feet. The rapscallion looked at her entreatingly, obviously regretting his precipitate action. Regretting, rather, that he'd picked the wrong woman to rob. Abby wasn't in the mood for compromise. She marched up to him menacingly. He jabbered at her, hands up, palms facing outward, realizing what was coming. He reached for the handbag, with a view to throwing it over the railing into the fast-flowing River Bidasosa. Or holding her hostage with the threat. Abby was having none of it. She slipped the rose brooch between her fingers, a substitute knuckleduster, and punched him mightily in the midriff. He doubled over with a woosh of pained exhalation, plus a grunt that betokened broken ribs or jumbled internal organs. She continued with an uppercut that Gentleman Jim Sullivan couldn't have bettered in his most ungentlemanly moment. The miscreant catapulted backwards, where he crashed against the metal railings. They looked just like the taut ropes of a boxing ring. He crumpled to the ground, out for the count. Abby walked over to the fallen delinquent, tempted to toe-poke him into the swirling waters beneath or kick him in the knackers with sufficient force to affect his connubial prospects. She decided not to bother. He wasn't worth it. Wearily, she picked up her Paddington and looked around, wondering where she was and how best to get back to the town square. Her sense of direction was appalling at the best of times, but at the worst of times it went completely haywire.

She looked left and right, trying to work out which way she'd come. A balding, middle-aged man was standing outside one of the nightclubs, the slatted wooden door of which lay ajar. He seemed to be the owner. He was applauding Abby's pugilistic prowess. Bravo, he shouted. Bravo. He invited her in for a celebratory drink, even though the place wasn't open. She could do with a glass of Vichy. Or something stronger. Pernod perhaps. Gratefully, Abby nodded her acceptance, while casting her eye over the premises. It reminded her a little of WeeTube. It felt like home. She glanced up at the fascia. It was called The Great Cross of Hendaye. Better yet, it was an alchemical theme pub. The walls were covered with blown-up black and white images of the old cross and reproductions of surrealist works inspired by the occult artefact. There were prints of infamous alchemists – Agrippa, Paracelsus, Dr Faustus and Francis Bacon himself, all frills and ruffles and how's your father – and photographs of people posing in front of the monument. Was that Salvador Dalí? It looked awfully like him. Which one's Fulcanelli, she wondered. The club owner was a man she needed to talk to. Their chat, though, would have to wait until the band stopped its sound check. Screeches of feedback and hollow mike echo emanated from the tiny stage in the corner of the club. There was a garish flyer pasted up at the side of the dancefloor, announcing that evening's attraction. Pink Torpedo. Abby had never heard of them.

One, two, three, four. The band crashed into its opening number. It sounded vaguely familiar, as did the second and the third, but the sound was so distorted she couldn't make out the words. The lead singer, a long-haired, bushy-bearded guy, slowed things down a little for the next one. The muddy sound finally sorted itself out. Abby sipped her Pernod, its unfamiliar aniseed bite bitter on her taste buds. The anguished opening chords of "Abby It's You" carried across the room. It can't be. It couldn't be. It was.

Dave Kelley was singing their song.

Chapter Thirty-Seven

The Norfolk Folks

Despite the facial laceration, which drew uncharacteristic sympathy from the officer on duty at Dulles, Magill cleared customs and immigration unmolested. Hiring a car, finding a hotel, contacting Tom Clancy and cracking the Zodiac code were his top priorities. The first two were easily done. The third less so, since the instructions he'd received about the Net Force rendezvous were straight out of B-movie central, CIA division, corny script subsection.

Clancy could wait. After checking in at the No Roach Motel, a roadside dive near Alexandria, VA, Magill turned his hand to the Great Cross Code. Instantly dismissing the notion that Brodie was the madman behind the Zodiac murders, Simon soon realized that he was dealing with an antecedent of the Frisco killer's cipher. With the aid of Dan's netbook – which he'd prudently appropriated, given the incriminating photographic evidence it contained – Magill surfed the web for information about the Zodiac bloodbath. As yet unbroken, the serial killer's code was a combination of astrological symbols and the standard English alphabet. The code in Brodie's appendix, by contrast, was entirely composed of astrological symbols, supplemented with Enochian glyphs as homophones. The Great Cross Code was based on a cipher employed by medieval alchemists in their perennial quest to turn base metal into gold and to keep their secret recipes safe from prying rivals. It was a bastardized version of John Dee's original and thus less impenetrable.

Once he'd pinned down the source of inspiration, the Great Cross Code wasn't hard to crack. It took slightly longer than expected – a bag of Planters peanuts from the minibar longer, plus a pair of Mountain Dews – but as cipher text to plain text transitions go, it wasn't unduly onerous.

Unfortunately, the plain text was unenlightening. Brodie's appendix, it appeared, was a spoof, a post-surrealist prank in the style of Fulcanelli. Brodie, the great incorrigible, was playing games with his readers by including a mystery in his book about mysteries. The appendix was actually a collection of the author's thoughts on the Hendaye cross, preparatory notes, presumably, for the section finally published in his handbook. The cross was built as a funerary monument in 1608 and relocated to its present site, beside St Vincent's church, in 1842. The apocalypse it predicted was unusual, though. The anticipated end was neither pestilential nor plague-propelled, as per Biblical portent, but an invisible apocalypse, involving some sort of pan-global vaporization set to take place on 12/01/09 (the digits of which totalled 13).

Unimpressed, Magill gazed outside, across the motel's slush-covered parking lot, towards an unedifying line of fast-food outlets opposite, an unbroken line of carbohydrates that stretched for mile after mile, all the way to Yorktown. If ever an environment bespoke how the west was lost, the strip malls and drive-ins of the Washington-Richmond corridor encapsulated how lean mean American cowboys became lard-arsed American cowards, brought down by the nation's ability to sell anything and consume everything. He loved America, but the American century was over. Like ancient Rome, it had been brought down by bread and circuses and arrogance and hubris. Would vaporization be such a bad thing?

Increasingly morose, Magill read on. The final two pages of the five-page appendix contained information about Hendaye that didn't make the main article. This included details of the complex astronomical calculations behind the doomsday date and Fulcanelli's purported possession of a neutron-bomb type weapon, decades before the Manhattan Project. Best of all was the contention that Elizabethan occultist Francis Bacon was the person behind the Great Cross. One of the carvings on its podium is embossed with his signature code. What's more, an exact copy of the cross exists somewhere in America, on account of Bacon's close association with the Virginia Colony. The copy sits in a churchyard in Virginia's Historical Triangle, where generations of treasure hunters have searched fruitlessly for the legendary Bacon horde, which may contain proof that he wrote Shakespeare's plays, perhaps even a copy of the sequel to *Love's Labour's Lost*, the infamous *Love's Labour's Found*.

Now that, Magill thought to himself, would make an excellent Robert Langdon adventure. It had technology, religion, codes, symbols, an ancient sect, a creepy colonial churchyard, a race against time. All it needed was a few gruesome murders, several disposable characters with alliterative names, a ruthless protagonist determined to right ancient wrongs, ideally with a malformed henchman, and a lithe, green-eyed hottie who falls for Big Bobbie's Harvardian charms.

Enthused, despite the enervation that accompanies long-haul travel, Magill spent a couple of hours surfing and clicking and running stuff down. Bacon's bilateral cipher was a mixture of As and Bs, identical to the four As and two stylized Bs incised on the quartered shield panel of the Great Cyclic Cross. A country bumpkin, Shakespeare couldn't possibly have written the plays that are attributed to him, because they contained arcane information that only well-travelled, high-ranking, Cambridge-educated intellectuals like Bacon possessed in the Bard's day...

Magill woke up in the middle of the night with a terrible taste in his mouth and shooting pains in his side. He'd fallen asleep while surfing. The commandeered netbook gleamed in the darkness beside him. Its animated screensaver, a Vitruvian Man doing callisthenics, had long since kicked in. After washing his face and cleaning his teeth, Magill crawled into bed where he mulled over the mysterious mess he'd gotten himself into. The slaying of Dan's fans he could sort of understand. Creative people were temperamental, bore long grudges and would probably take warped pleasure in pulling off such elaborately staged stunts. Clancy wasn't exactly starving in a garret and procuring hitpersons wouldn't exactly be a problem for someone with his military contacts. That much he could understand. But why the codes on the covers of Dan's books? What did the Great Cross of Hendaye have to do with Clancy's published preoccupations, which tended towards the latest technologies rather than ancient mysteries? Yes, Clancy had invoked nuclear Armageddon in several of his novels; yes, Fulcanelli's presentiment of the atomic bomb and his presumed participation in Operation Paperclip were definitely connected to the Ryanverse; yes, Clancy's latent religious leanings had informed his writings on occasion; yes, he was something of a technological utopian; yes, he had been silent – and possibly seething – during the Dan Brown ascendency; yes, Dan himself was in no doubt about the person responsible. Tom Clancy was Big C. However, it was all a bit implausible, almost as implausible as one of Dan's novels. Or Tom's, come to think of it. Maybe that was the point.

Showered, shaved and still suffering from jet-lag, Magill set off for his meeting with Clancy. The slush-rutted streets and snow-sprinkled countryside did nothing to enhance Virginia's "for Lovers" reputation, though the ramparts of frosted hickory trees along I-64 hinted at how beautiful it could be come fall. Norfolk was nothing to write home about either. It was as flat as its namesake back in Britain and a lot less interesting. Only the enormous naval vessels in the dry docks across the bay gave any indication of the military might that was concentrated in this otherwise nondescript environment. Fort Bragg, Fort Eustis, Fort Monroe and Fort Meade, the legendary Farm where CIA spies learned their undercover trade, were all within spit 'n' polish distance. There were no military personnel in the Waterside, though. There was no one in the Waterside, period. A nautical-themed festival mall that catered mainly for tourists attracted by Virginia's co-called Historical Triangle – Jamestown, Yorktown and Colonial Williamsburg – the Waterside was completely devoid of life, as might be expected on a Monday morning in mid-January. It reminded Magill of one of those killer zombie plague movies, where the entire place is wiped out, apart from one or two doughty survivors who gather in the local mall before the diseased zombies attack. His coffee was diseased, that was for sure, and the glazed donut had been raised from the dead at some point. He was the only person in the entire food court. Surrounded by an archipelago of empty wire-backed chairs and deserted dining tables, he chewed on his zombie donut, shiny with embalming fluid. He waited. No sign of Tom, unless he was posing undercover as a short-order chef in El Cantina. He had a second cup of sludge. Still no sign. The 10.00 a.m. meet time came and went.

Damn and blast.

Magill took the glass-sided elevator – complete with wooden steering wheel, ship ahoy! – up to a high-level walkway that connected to an adjacent parking garage, equally echoingly empty. His emerald green rental, a Subaru sedan, nestled companionless in the corner. He walked to the driver's side then corrected himself with a d'oh. Driver's side is the other side.

Magill never got to the other side.

Chapter Thirty-Eight

Pi Before Phi But Not After e

A black sack was whipped over Simon's head. He was bundled into the back of an SUV. His muffled yells were ignored by the kidnappers, then silenced with the aid of a gun barrel pressed against the Englishman's left temple. The vehicle sped off with a screech of tyres, circling and circling down the garage access ramp like water around a plughole. Magill felt queasy with the pitches and yaws of the super-soft suspension. It was all he could do to keep down the zombie donut, which was on the cusp of yet another disinterment. The SUV hit street level and swerved this way and that, until Magill's ordinarily excellent sense of direction was completely scrambled. Ten minutes later, the 4x4 squealed to a stop. He was shoved outside, where the bitterly cold air caught his chest unawares. He started coughing, which was a strange sensation when hooded. "Gotta give up the baccy, buddy," one of his captors jeered. "It'll be the death of you." Magill could hear a door opening and, with a muscle-bound minder on either side, he was steered along several echoing corridors. His shoes squeaked on the highly polished floor. The voices of his handlers reverberated off a high ceiling, or so it seemed. Several more twists and turns followed, until everything suddenly stopped. He was pressed into a cushioned seat and the constrictive hood was removed. Magill blinked, rubbed his eyes and looked round at his kidnappers, but they were already departing the room.

What a room it was. A magnificent stained-glass window, all tendrils and foliage with glimpses of azure sky and distant mountains, was mounted on the wall opposite. Another, equally resplendent, was positioned directly behind him. A shimmering fire screen rested against the third, whereas the fourth was lined with display units containing brilliantly iridescent vases, bibelots and lampshades. The thickly carpeted floor was dotted with magnificently hand-carved wooden furniture. The stout table in front was obviously part of the same set.

An interrogator sat opposite. He looked awfully young, late 20s or so, about the same age as Magill. "You were supposed to be here on the seventh," he said coldly, without any preliminaries, much less pleasantries.

"I had a family emergency."

"Mr Clancy doesn't take kindly to latecomers. Mr Clancy won't tolerate time-wasters, troublemakers or insubordinates of any stripe." He looked pointedly at Magill's duelling scar. "Got that?"

Reluctantly, Magill nodded his comprehension. It was PWC all over again, except in mufti. "When do I get to meet Mr Clancy?"

"You don't," he said, "not until you sit the entrance examination." A malicious smile crossed his clean-cut features. "Mr Clancy's novels are written by the elite, with pay and conditions to match. We don't take just anyone."

Nor kill just anyone, Magill mused. "Fire away," he said.

"3.141."

Thrown for a second, Magill quickly recovered. He rattled out the digits of pi on demand, continuing from where his interviewer left off. "59265358979323846."

"1.618?"

"Phi's a cool number. 1.6180339887. Do you want me to continue?"

The chisel-chinned jar-head said nothing. Leaning back arrogantly, he tinkled the keyboard of his laptop, pulling up the next item. "At Clancy's I transmit on Toshibas."

Magill almost fell for it. He was so familiar with piphilogical poetry that he could tell a starter for 3.14159 with his eyes closed. With a start, he realized his mistake. It was e not pi. Cunning. "Good try," he said, "but you'll have to do better than that." He rattled off the first twenty digits of e from memory, then paused. "Let me ask you something, Warrant Officer X." The interviewer flicked Magill a disagreeable glance. "Which is the first ten-digit prime in e?"

The NCO tutted dismissively, evidently familiar with the

Googletrap. "7427466391," he said, without missing a beat. The interview then turned to IT issues: Tim Berners-Lee and the birth of the web, cloud computing, denial of service attacks, Web 4.0, public key encryption protocols. All pretty basic stuff. They moved on.

"Who is Bill Clinton?"

Cute. "Bill Clinton is a special FBI agent in Mr Clancy's sixth novel, *The Sum of All Fears*."

"Who is Vladimir Putin?"

Magill winked at his questioner. "Vladimir Putin is the Prime Minister of Russia. If you're referring to Mr Putin's namesake in *The Hunt for Red October*, I think you'll find his forename is Ivan."

The interviewer made no reply. Narratives were next. "How many storytelling templates are there in the western tradition?"

Magill was inclined to ask whether he wanted a precise number or would the nearest integer suffice. But he held his tongue. "One, of course, a monomyth made up of twelve stages from the Call to Adventure via Meeting the Mentor through the Supreme Ordeal to Returning With the Elixir.

The interviewer again said nothing by way of small talk. He turned his laptop over to Magill. "You have ten minutes to sketch out four story scenarios." Without further ado, he got up and left the room.

Smiling to himself, Magill set to work with a spring in his type. Having spent the last two years penning potted plots for the Danster, he had a deep well of ideas to draw upon. KKK, Barnum Brown, Green October and, why not, the Great Cross Code. He was finished in eight minutes flat, then sat back with arms folded waiting for Herbert Hostility to reappear. He had the strangest feeling that someone was watching him. However, there was no sign of video surveillance cameras or similar security devices. He stood up and strolled over to the glassware display. It was exquisite stuff, all Tiffany, though one piece looked out of place. It was warped, buckled and encrusted, almost as if something had gone wrong in the kiln. It was strangely beautiful in its own way. The bent vase, if that's what it was, was the black sheep of the Tiffany family. He knew how it felt.

The tight-lipped interrogator stalked back into the room on

cue. He scanned the scenarios. "None of these are relevant to our organization's needs."

"You asked for four story scenarios. You didn't specify that they should be Net Force scenarios." Magill was merely following orders. He couldn't be faulted, much less defaulted.

"I'm afraid it's a 404, Mr Magill."

"What the hell do you mean, a 404? You asked for four unspecified scenarios in ten. I gave you four in eight. That's following orders 101. Don't 404 me, you fuck."

The interviewer regarded Magill coldly. "Your denial of service has nothing to do with your scenarios... such as they are. There are seven narrative templates in the western tradition, not one, as you appear to imagine. They are Comedy, Tragedy, Rebirth, the Quest, Rags to Riches, Overcoming the Monster and Voyage and Return. We use all seven here. The one storyline story died with Joseph Campbell."

"But Voyage and Return, Rags to Riches and Overcoming the Monster are minor variations on the monomyth. They're quests by another name. Every work of literature involves a quest of some kind, a journey from once upon a time to happily ever after."

"Not around here they don't."

Magill was flabbergasted. He wasn't going to stand for it. He'd travelled all the way from Ireland for this "interview" and he wasn't going to be fobbed off by a frowning functionary.

"And, anyway," the functionary went on, "the Net Force series is being deep-sixed. We are moving over to conspiracy thrillers. That's where the market is nowadays. We have developed a new sub-brand. It concerns a conspiracy-busting SWAT unit called the House of Salomon, adapted from Francis Bacon's *New Atlantis*. We have no further call for mathematicians and IT types. Don't Skype us, we'll email you."

"But the scenarios I gave you are readily adaptable to conspiracy-lit. They're exactly what you're looking for – boy gets grail, boy loses grail, boy gets grail."

Chisel-chin gave the applicant an I-don't-think-so stare.

Right, that's it! "I'm not leaving until I speak with Mr Clancy."

"Mr Clancy is not available."

An irresistible English force confronted an immovable American object. "I know he's behind that stained glass window, watching everything that's going on. Don't bullshit me, you piece of shit."

"I'm afraid I have to ask you to leave, Mr Magill. If you wish," he continued with an unsubtle unspoken allusion to the heavies who'd hijacked Magill earlier, "I can have you escorted off the premises."

"If you wish," Magill said, picking up the hunk of horribly misshapen Tiffany, "I can pitch this, um, pitcher at the presumably priceless window behind you."

The immovable object looked confused, unsettled, outside his comfort zone – his Louis Comfort Tiffany zone. He put a hand to his earpiece, which Magill hadn't noticed up to that point, then promptly snapped shut his laptop, picked it up and walked out without so much as a catch you later. Two minutes passed. The door opened again. A shambling hulk entered the room.

Magill couldn't believe his eyes. "Jack? Jack Clark? Bloody hell!"

Chapter Thirty-Nine

Clancy Pants

Before he knew it, Magill was swept up in an enormous bear hug. Good to see you, man – and several similar expressions of ursine endorsement – emanated from the fatigues-wearing grizzly. The luxurious, Tiffany-garlanded setting was a world away from the Spartan conditions where they last met. But the warmth of the welcome was identical. A full five minutes of back slaps, high fives, handshakes, knuckle-kisses and yo mans followed. Or perhaps it just felt like that.

Magill didn't know where to start. So Clancy started for him. "Some battle buddy you are, Simon. You didn't even recognize that Jack and Clark are the fore- and surnames of my two main literary characters, Jack Ryan and John Clark. And then you have the nerve to apply for a job in my organization, you fuck." He punched him playfully on the shoulder.

Laughing, as the boot camp camaraderie rushed back unbidden, Magill responded in kind. "And there was me thinking you were Mary Higgins Clark in drag. I should have guessed. No woman's that ugly." He hesitated. "Apart from George Eliot, of course. Gertrude Stein was a hard-looking ticket, as well. As for Agatha Christie... Christ, you'd take poison before kissing that coyote."

Much barrack room humour ensued. Clancy apologized for the rough and tumble of the interview process. However, treat-em-mean's the military way and the military way's the way round here. The Clancy factory's only interested in people who won't take no for an answer yet say yes-sir when asked.

"Yes, sir," Magill said.

The commander-in-chief took a seat at the Tiffany table and threw a booted foot on top. Magill did likewise. "Nice place you have here, Tom. Doesn't look too military to me."

Clancy gazed around appreciatively, almost as if he were seeing the set up for the first time. "I used to sell insurance, Simon. I pretty much struck out at school and college. I married young and had a couple of kids to support. So I went into the insurance business to keep body and soul together, all the while dreaming of becoming a writer. I was a good salesman. Damn good. Built the firm up to be the best in the state. I know how to run a business. I know the secret of successful selling. It applies just as much to selling books as it does to selling insurance. Do you know what the secret of success is, buddy?"

Dosed up on zombie donuts, Magill was at a loss. "Luck? Perseverance? Customer focus? Sweating the small stuff?" His mind wandered back to a strangely similar conversation he'd had with the late great marketing guru, Kate Phillips. "Failure?"

"All those things are important," Clancy conceded. "But the real key to opening customers' pocketbooks is monopoly."

As a marketing graduate, B-school lecturer and e-commerce entrepreneur, Magill had come across lots of purported customer keys. Monopoly was not among them. Monopoly was the bad guy, was it not, the bane of western capitalism. "I'm not quite with you, Tom."

Clancy smiled the smile of a boss-man who gets to wax lyrical – uninterrupted and uninterruptable. "The secret is to offer something only you have, something that competitors can't match. Sometimes it's the lowest price. Sometimes it's top-rate service. Sometimes it's instant availability. Sometimes it's fastest delivery. Sometimes it's the best product or the most exclusive product or the prettiest product or the widest range of products. But you must always have a monopoly of some kind or other, something that says you're the go-to guy."

"Ah, you mean a unique selling proposition."

Shaking his bear-like head in mock exasperation, the multimillionaire belittled Magill's business school background and indeed indoctrination. "In many cases, the feature that you use to sell your product or service is not the feature that attracts customers or provides your monopolistic edge. Monopoly, I guess, is another word for branding, though the term branding has been so debased through overuse that most people have lost sight of what a good brand means. It means monopoly. Apple has a monopoly. Disney has a monopoly. Snapple has a monopoly."

"Semantics schmantics," Magill said dismissively. "Did Tiffany make coffee pots at all?" he added, hoping Clancy would take the hint.

He didn't. "You're a word lover, Simon. The beauty of a word like monopoly – unlike brand, which has become meaningless – is that it not only encapsulates what businessmen should aim for but also what they should be wary of. Monopoly is the key to failure, too. Monopolists lose their edge. They get fat and lazy. They think they have a god-given right to succeed. They take customers for granted. They imagine that they don't have to work as hard as before, that the business can run itself, that they can do no wrong. The go-to guy thinks he is the stay-with guy, but go-to can go very quickly. Apple had a monopoly then lost it. Disney had a monopoly then lost it. Snapple had a monopoly then lost it. If he's lucky, the gone-from guy can get his go-to again. But only by getting back to the monopoly that made him."

Magill's head was spinning with go-tos and get-thises. Or was it Go-to 2.0? "I don't see where you're going with this, Tom."

The big man unwrapped himself from the table and chair. He lumbered across to his precious display of iridescent Tiffany glassware, as if trying to decide which one to fondle. He ran a pudgy finger along the curve of a flame-red favrile vase, gently caressing its sinuous torso. "The same thing happens to popular novelists, Simon. We establish a monopoly as the go-to guy for horror, like Stephen King, or fantasy, like J. K. Rowling, or writlit, like John Grisham, or techno-thrillers, like yours truly. Our books become bigger and bigger and bloated and boringly predictable. Our novels get fat and lazy. Literally. We start to believe that anything we write is worth reading. We lose our edge – our monopolistic appeal, if you will – and fall into the worst habits of unappealing monopolists. We repeat ourselves, only at ever- and ever-greater length. It's an inexorable process that I call the Wheel of Retelling. But it applies throughout business life."

"I see," Magill said, recalling a similar conversation he'd had with the late Carlingford O'Connell.

"That's why I turned up at book camp, under cover, with a

nom de guerre. I need to get my mojo back. I haven't published anything since 2003, a toothless book called *Teeth of the Tiger*. I've been keeping busy with the video games business, which is very lucrative if not very rewarding. The choice facing someone like me, Simon, is to sit here counting my millions and feeding my Tiffany habit or show the world that Tom Clancy still rocks. There comes a point where you have to scrape off the barnacles, ring the changes, take hard decisions. That's why we're sixing Net Force and moving over to conspiracies. Remember that lecture at Huntington Library?"

Magill nodded.

Absent-mindedly, the authorpreneur ran a chubby finger along the uneven edge of a classic Tiffany lampshade. A delicate lamp shield – a beautiful, butterfly-shaped glass decoration that dangled under the laburnum lamp, as if drawn by the light – danced from side to side on its filigree chain. "The same thing happened to Tiffany, you know."

"I'm sorry," Magill said, "I'm not too familiar with Tiffany. Out of my price bracket. Until I write my first bestseller."

Clancy threw him the hunk of blackened and distorted glassware that he'd noticed earlier. Magill almost dropped it with the shock, though his wicket-keeping prowess – honed many years earlier on the playing fields of Aylesbury Grammar – stood him in good stead. "That's known as lava glass, Simon. It was inspired by the vitrified vases in Pompeii and Herculaneum. It's extremely rare. Handle with care. That's a million bucks' worth you're holding right there."

The evil sprite within urged Magill to chuck the vessel back whence it came, just to see if Clancy's baseball skills were up to snuff. The guy's a jumped-up insurance agent, after all. It's bound to be fully covered. Sensibly, Magill resisted. "Not Tiffany's finest hour, Tom. It looks like something an amateur potter would throw after an overdose of diazepam." He placed the precious object on the Tiffany table. It looked no better as a centrepiece. But might pass muster as a coffee mug…

Clancy shrugged an each-to-his-own. "Of all the decorative arts," he said, "glass making is closest to writing. It's as old as writing. It's as ubiquitous as writing. It's as mysterious as writing.

It's easily destroyed and can disappear without trace. It comes in multifarious forms, colours, languages and the like – everything from paperweights to picture windows – though there's a basic divide between speciality decorative glass and everyday domestic glass, just like literature with a capital L and trash with a capital T. Most importantly, though, glassmaking remains a craft, a handicraft, a skill that improves with practice, a skill that can be taught and its basic principles passed on, a technique that takes years and years to hone and can be lost if you think about it too much, or if you think you know it all."

"Right."

"Tiffany was a marketing genius, Simon. His products were brilliant but his salesmanship was out of this world. He exhibited at big international trade fairs for the publicity and prizes, he raised his profile by specializing in attention-grabbing church windows, he persuaded museums to add Tiffany to their collections, which he supplied gratis, he barely broke even on splashy, high-profile projects such as Mark Twain's house or the famous Four Seasons panels for Standard Oil. But he made his money on table lamps, decorative vases, favrile inkwells, tiles and trivets, costume jewellery, fire screens like that one over there." He pointed to the exquisite chainmail-effect object that rested against one wall. It was composed of hinged glass plates that stretched between two andiron-like stanchions, which could be moved back and forth in a curtain-ish swish.

"So, he was a bit like today's fashion houses, where the catwalk couture is a loss-leader for the money-spinning scents, cosmetics, accessories, etc."

"Except that Tiffany perfected the idea a century ago. Then he lost touch. Success went to his head. He built an enormous palace close to Cold Spring Harbor, which served as a huge showcase for his art, and hosted more and more elaborate balls, soirees, dinners, levees and the like, all in an attempt to maintain the brand's profile and keep the sales of lampshades ticking over. It was megalomaniacal. It was Icarus. It was asking for trouble and trouble came a-calling. He fell out of fashion in the 1920s, when modernism was all and Art Nouveau was old hat. You couldn't give this stuff away. Only about 10 per cent of Tiffany's favrile survived the glassware holocaust of the 30s, 40s and 50s. It was only in the 60s that Art Nouveau drifted back into fashion and Tiffany's reputation was restored. Success is fickle and fleeting, Simon. Failure is always waiting to pounce. In all walks of life. Writers are especially inclined to forget that and that makes failure all the more likely. In twenty years' time we'll be asking ourselves what on earth possessed us to go Harry Potter crazy or Dan Brown mad."

Clancy's ability to spin a compelling yarn was, if not quite incomparable, certainly on a par with Oscar Wilde's table talk. But his reference to demented Dan was like being punched in the guts by a gloating gorilla. "Dan Brown had help!"

Clancy looked at Magill blankly. "What are you talking about?"

"The madness of Dan Brown. The madness that *you* precipitated."

At a loss for words, Clancy ran a hand over his head with bemusement. "Back up a bit, soldier. What the fuck are you talking about?"

Magill gave him hell. In no uncertain terms, he told him about the murders, the madness, the evidence that pointed to his personal involvement, circumstantial though it was. It was enough to convince Dan, however, and that was enough for Simon. Clancy had the motive, the opportunity, the resources, the necessary connections with paramilitary types.

"The last time I met Dan was at the Blood and Guts Distinguished Lecture in 2004. He was the main speaker. It wasn't long after the publication of *Da Vinci*. Success had gone to his head. He said a few things in the heat of the moment. I let them pass. He started sending me emails, pornographic parodies of my book titles: *The Come of All Queers*, *Red Porn Rising*, *Cocksucker of the Kremlin*, *Sphincter Cell* and suchlike. Must have thought they were funny. It was adolescent. I ignored them. I kinda liked the little guy. If he's in trouble, I'm happy to help."

"So, you're saying that Dan was sending *you* threatening messages, not the other way round."

"Correct. It stopped after the *Da Vinci* frenzy died down. It's cool. I know what it's like to be a struggling author, to get rejected again and again, and then see something take off unexpectedly. That's what happened with *Red October*. I'm glad for the guy. He's obviously lost his nerve over the follow-up. It happens. He's obviously got issues. He's a small guy with small guy issues. Hell, he might be whacking his own fans. Or hiring someone to whack his fans. They can drive you round the bend. Have you thought of that possibility? You've heard of shell shock? Maybe Dan's suffering from sell shock. Writing a follow-up when expectations are high can drive some people crazy."

"And continued success drives some people crazy too," Magill commented drily. "You said so yourself. I mean, what writer in their right mind dresses up in military fatigues, rules over his minions like a fucking five-star general and spends his time lurking behind Tiffany windows and fondling favrile vases? You're Dr Evil in BDU. The Ernst Blofeld of branding."

"Your interview is over, soldier," Clancy said with brook-no-opposition authority. "I'll get the guards to take you back to the garage."

"Don't bother."

"I insist." With a jump-to-it gesture, Clancy signalled towards the wall-mounted Tiffany window. The musclemen appeared on command. Heads shaven, necks non-existent, shirt collar size in triple digits, they didn't look in the mood for discussion, much less debate. Magill knew he only had a couple of seconds before the black hood was back over his head and he was at their mercy. Cognizant that surprise is the single most important military weapon, whether it be hand-to-hand combat or thermo-nuclear exchange, Magill seized his moment. He elbowed one in the face and rabbit-punched the second. Taken aback, both Clancy's grunts doubled over with a grunt. A quick karate kick apiece soon settled their hash. Luckily, they didn't bring any Tiffany treasures down with them, though the fire screen took an unfortunate hit, as one roughneck sprawled ungainly in the intricate netting, like a landed sea bass. Magill snatched up the priceless piece of lava glass and tossed it towards Tom as he closed the door behind him. He could hear it crash as he stalked down the corridor, looking for an exit sign. Baseball's a girl's game, he thought. Only cricketers can catch as catch can.

Chapter Forty

Only in America

"You look as though you had a good time in France."

"Whatever do you mean?" Abby responded, wondering if it was really so obvious.

Magill walked her through the busy Dulles arrivals hall to the parking garage where their emerald rental reposed. "Well, you seem perkier somehow, as if you've had two days of mad passionate sex. Meet a handsome Frenchman, did you, while I've been freezing my butt off in Virginia?"

Abby shot him a look somewhere between oh-grow-up and none-of-your-business. "Must be all the fresh air on the *Côte des Basques*. Or maybe," she added caustically, "it's because of the running around I did in Hendaye." She filled him in on the bagnapping incident, while he did likewise with the Clancy encounter.

After escaping the vehicular vice that is Washington DC, they sallied forth for the Historic Triangle, where the replica cross reputedly reposed. Two hours down the road, they stopped at Fredericksburg, a twee Colonial-era settlement that witnessed some of the bloodiest hand-to-hand fighting during the American Civil War. The battlefield visitors' centre was open, despite the weather, where they watched the video then climbed to the top of the escarpment overlooking the town. From their perch, they could see where the advancing union armies were stopped in their tracks by Longstreet's determined southerners, who stood resolute at the sunken road. It was appropriate somehow, since their quest too had come to a shuddering halt. Clancy, Magill explained, denied all knowledge of the Dan Brown set-up. Far from gloating at his rival's situation, furthermore, he seemed genuinely anxious to help, even though Dan had been sending him obscene emails. The Danster, in his post-*Da Vinci*

Code paranoia, was obviously mistaken about his persecutor, the so-called Big C.

"So you think Dan killed the fans, after all?"

"I'm certain he didn't," Magill said unconvincingly.

"Have you ever heard of Dissociative Identity Disorder?" Abby asked, recalling her guerrilla psychology classes and the gruesome stories of serial killers with multiple personalities – meek and mild one minute, merciless murderers the next, albeit with little or no memory of their momentary blood lust. "Did Dan ever hear voices at all?"

Prior to meeting Clancy, Magill would've dismissed the idea as absurd. The Danster was completely innocent. He knew the guy intimately. But his unpredictable mood swings in recent months and the state he was in in Dublin... well, Simon wasn't so sure any more. He heaved a sigh of defeat, pulled out the Dear John letter he'd been handed in Sydney and passed it over to Abby. "Yeah, he was hearing voices."

A grey squirrel scuttled across the snow-covered ground in front of the old wooden bench where they were sitting. It paused for a second or two then scampered away, leaping like the snow was scalding. Unable to sit still while his companion read in silence, Magill got up and walked along the old line of ramparts. The weather was crisp and cold and silent. Breath pluming in the bitter January air, he tried to draw comfort from the long dead soldiers of both sides who battled bravely in midwinter 1862. He could sense their presence still. Wistfully, he looked out over the battlements. The escarpment afforded a beautiful view of the bejewelled Rappahannock Valley, though the serried ranks of fast-food franchises at the bottom of the slope detracted from the frozen splendour of the scene.

After circling back, he sat down beside her. She was crying. Wiping away an errant tear, Abby returned the letter to Magill. "Dan didn't do it. The man who wrote that beautiful letter wouldn't kill anyone." A few days earlier, Magill would have doubted Abby's diagnosis, since evening classes in guerrilla psychology hardly constitute professional qualifications. But female intuition doesn't require diplomas, much less credentials, and Abby was as intuitive as any woman he'd ever met. She was also saying what he wanted to hear. Abby gave him hope. He gave her a hug.

"What happens now?" she croaked, her voice hoarse in the icy afternoon air.

"Well, narrative theory says that we have two choices, either give up in despair or..."

"Or what?" Abby interrupted. "Better not be 'die a horrible death', thereby denying readers a happy ending."

Magill tightened the belt of his enormous Ulster. "It's a lot worse than death, Abby."

She raised an inquisitive eyebrow, while huddling up for warmth. "Don't tell me it's a fast-food infusion."

"You're getting good at this," he laughed. Arm in arm, they stumbled down the snow-skiffed hill, across the street and into the welcoming warmth of Only in America, a retro recreation of the classic all-American diner. Several refills and four piping-hot donuts later, their existential despair disappeared in a sugar rush of NFL proportions. Magill told her about the Zodiac cipher, the legend that Fulcanelli possessed potentially devastating power of thermo-nuclear proportions and the details of his encounter with Clancy. She recounted the Hendaye trip, Fulcanelli's apparent connection to the surrealist movement and her sense that the whole apocalypse thing was a hoax.

However, another round of donuts prompted ever-wilder speculation on the Spear of Destiny's thermo-nuclear powers, the apocalyptic strain within surrealism, the links between Hendaye Cross and Rennes-le-Château and the outer reaches of Baconianism. In addition to writing the complete works of Shakespeare, overseeing the publication of the famous First Folio and penning the foundation documents of Rosicrucian brotherhood, Bacon had time to reinvent scientific method while working as a senior civil servant, set out the utopian principles that underpinned the virgin queen's Virginian colony and compose large chunks of the King James Bible, when he wasn't gallivanting round the courts of Europe.

"Typical civil servant," Magill moaned, "underworked and overpaid. Bet he retired early and bagged a big, index-linked pension as well."

"Better than that, Simon, he discovered the secret of eternal life and lived on in the form of St Germain, Count Cagliostro, Eliphas Lévi, Fulcanelli and several others."

"Kate Phillips, presumably."

"Huh?"

Reluctantly and with some embarrassment, Magill told Abby about his Kate Phillips encounter, how she intimated that she was immortal, how he believed her at the time and how he still suspected there was something to it, despite his natural scepticism.

"There are more things in heaven and earth than are dreamt of in Bacon's philosophy."

"Well, the witch is dead now."

"You sure about that?"

Simon shrugged. "The obituaries in *Time*, *Newsweek*, *WSJ*, *USA Today* and the *Chicago Tribune* were pretty unanimous."

"Don't believe everything you read in the papers," Abby remarked ruefully.

"I'm not sure what to believe any more." They had reached a dead end. The trail had gone cold, just like their coffee. Only in America's daily routine ebbed and flowed around them – kids playing hooky from the nearby high school, visitor centre attendants on mid-afternoon break, one or two hardy tourists, faces aglow from the cold – as they sat in the red leatherette banquette, talking round and round in ever-wider circles, getting precisely nowhere by a circuitous route.

"What we need is a list!"

"The female solution to everything," Magill moaned, though with no alternative on the Formica table he acquiesced, as most men are inclined to do in the face of females' fetish for inventories. Forget nurturing or empathy or multi-tasking or emotional intelligence, the primal female talent is the tally. A list a day helps them work, rest and play.

With the aid of ample napkins, Abby itemized everything they'd discussed thus far, from the crazy Clancy operation and the symbols on Dan's dead bodies through the details of the impending Hendaye apocalypse to the outer limits of Baconiana, not least the secreted stash of Jacobean gold, silver and assorted textual treasures, such as the long lost plays of Shakespeare.

The alleged links to the Spear of Destiny, the Holy Grail, the surrealist movement, the founding of America, the Freemasons, the Rosicrucians were also added to the list, which ran to four napkins in total. "Okay, the next step is to develop a tree diagram, that'll help us see the links between the elements. Dan's at the centre…"

Magill rolled his eyes. "You forgot something," he said with more than a little exasperation.

"Oh yes?" The smile of encouragement said it all. How dare you criticize my list-making capability! "What's that, Simon?"

"It's something I mentioned earlier," he complained, in a voice that wasn't conducive to the companionable pursuit of enlightenment. "Bacon's House of Salomon. The secret society from *New Atlantis*. Clancy's thinking of using that name in a new range of conspiracy thrillers now that Net Force is deep-sixed. You forgot that."

Magill's ungallant remarks were met with strategic incomprehension. "I assume you're referring to the House of Solomon."

"No," he said in a prickly pernickety tone that revealed his former occupation as an academic, as well as an earlier unhappy encounter with a Solomon-related organization. "I'm referring to the House of Salomon with an 'a', as per the French ski manufacturer, as per Francis Bacon's *New Atlantis*, as per Clancy's new serial. I did speak with the man, Abby."

"Yes, but have you actually read *The New Atlantis*?"

"I've read about it," he countered defensively. "Enough to know that the inhabitants' secret research facility was called the House of Salomon."

"Well," she counter-countered, "if you take the trouble to download the document from Project Gutenberg, as I did, you'll see that Bacon's House was based around the teachings of King Solomon. Salomon was an attempt to render Atlantean speech phonetically. It's Solomon, Simon. Not that it matters," she added, having out-quibbled the quibbler and turning back to more important matters in hand. Namely, the list…

Magill stayed her hand. He grabbed her wrist excitedly, his face flushed with the euphoric aftermath of an "aha" moment, the divine spark of creativity that comes unbidden, usually when least expected, rarely when commanded or required. "It might just matter. It might just matter a very great deal."

"How come?" Abby asked, getting swept up by Magill's effusive attitude.

"Dan's abandoned book was called *The Solomon Key*! The obvious connection between key and house – the Key to the House – must mean something, mustn't it?"

"Whatever you say." Abby was hoping for more than a linguistic connection, made under the dubious influence of excess sugar ingestion and a serious caffeine overdose. "Is Francis Bacon in the book? Does the House of Solomon feature prominently? What is the key to the Dan Brown mystery?"

Taken aback by the blizzard of questions, Magill almost burst into laughter. "I've absolutely no idea."

It was Abby's turn to roll her eyes. "You've no idea," she echoed.

Speaking rapidly, Magill explained that he'd never actually read the book. Dan wrote it before he started work for the great man. He refused to talk about it. *The Solomon Key* was a taboo subject, off limits, a mistake, a creative failure on the Danster's part. It was the reason he got the job, for goodness' sake. The guy needed new scenarios in the wake of the *Key* debacle. Something different. Something to re-boot the Langdon franchise.

"So you know nothing. That's just great. Call yourself a PA?"

"Well," Magill blustered, struggling to regain lost ground. "I naturally assumed it had something to do with Solomon's Temple in Jerusalem and the well-established fact that the Knights Templar discovered a great secret there, the source of their immense wealth and power and influence and, ultimately, their downfall in 1307."

"Forgive me, Simon," Abby said with asperity, "But surely that stuff was included in *The Da Vinci Code*. The Templars' discovery was that Mary Magdalene bore Jesus's children and that the holy bloodline was alive and well and disporting itself in the south of France. Dan would hardly include the same stuff in his next book, would he?"

"That's never stopped John Grisham or Stephen King or Dick Francis or Barbara Taylor Bradford. Why would the Danster be any different?"

Underwhelmed, Abby stared out of Only in America's picture window. The blue sky had disappeared, taking the sun with it. The snow started to fall. Unlike the thin and watery snowflakes in Belfast, these were big fat fluffy American snowflakes that fell with aplomb, assurance, razzamatazz. Even the snow is better in America, though typical of them to squander the world's snowflake resources for their own selfish purposes.

"Someone once told me," Magill said plaintively, thinking back to a half-remembered conversation in Belfast, "that *The Solomon Key* had something to do with the Freemasons. The Founding Fathers are in there too, as far as I know. There's also something about the geography of Washington DC. And buried treasure, I think. Maybe. I'm not sure."

With a spare-me sigh, Abby turned away from snowflake showtime. There's no business like snow business but she had other matters in mind. "So here we are in the commuter belt of Washington DC, where the Founding Fathers of the United States first settled, where a famous proto-Freemason called Francis Bacon may have buried priceless treasure and where his utopian vision is being re-written as we speak. You don't think there's a connection?"

"There's only one way to find out, Abby."

"What's that, Simon?"

"Dan's netbook is in the car. *The Solomon Key* is on it. I noticed the folder when we were in Dublin. Let's read the thing and see what's what."

"I think we need more coffee, Simon."

"Donuts would be nice."

Chapter Forty-One

The Solomon Key

In a vain attempt to avoid the supersized snowflakes, Magill sprinted across the road to the visitors' centre parking lot. After fifteen minutes, Abby started to get concerned about him. It was a five-minute dash, max, even allowing for the weather. Although she wasn't the panicky type – quite the opposite, if anything – a vague sense of unease crept over her. Magill's account of the Clancy operation sounded very suspicious. Meet in a car park, hood over the head, secret lair filled with Tiffany trinkets. If not quite Austin Powers, it was definitely Cubby Broccoli. Creative types are an odd lot, she'd found. Men are an odd lot generally, come to think of it. All that obsession with status and achievement and anorakish arcana couldn't possibly be healthy, let alone conducive to mental stability. But Clancy's set up seemed to be a couple of production lines short of a manufacturing plant.

Anxiety mounting, Abby started to ease out of the sticky banquette in order to follow him back to the parking facility. When a snowman walked into the diner. Far from adhering to the snowperson stereotype – chubby, cheerful, coal-buttoned, carrot-nosed – this particular snowperson was tall and thin and coping badly with anger management issues. Magill shook himself. An avalanche descended from the upper slopes of his enormous Ulster overcoat and accumulated at his size fourteen feet. His face was a picture. Hellboy freezes over. Abby tried not to laugh as she eased back into her naugahyde nook. He stomped between the tables, shedding snowballs along the way, then sat down with a seriously salty oath. "I was stopped for jaywalking."

Abby couldn't keep her face straight. The look on his smacker. "It's not funny."

The more infuriated he got, the funnier it became. A cop spotted him. Titter. Started to book him. Snort. Explained he was a tourist. Guffaw. Tried a bribe like the movies. Roar. The officer finally let him go with a $150 on-the-spot fine. Cash or credit, she inquired, helpless. Didn't it occur to him that there'd be cops around a donut-dealing shop, getting their daily dozen intake. He was watching the wrong movies.

"Tell me about it."

"Still, at least he didn't cuff you and take you back to the cells where a 300lb child molester eyes up your buff booty while you wait your turn for a phone call."

"You're supposed to be on my side," he said, smiling at last.

"Who ya gonna call?" she chanted, "Codebusters!"

The lightness of their mood rapidly evaporated as they speed-read *The Solomon Key*, Dan Brown's famously unfinished fifth novel. Far from being a rough draft, a mish-mash of missing chapters full of gaps to be filled with up-to-date facts and figures, it was complete in every detail – acknowledgements, author's note, page numbers, the lot. It was the literary equivalent of the *Flying Dutchman*, a novel that was good to go, but presumably pulled at the last minute for some unfathomable reason. Legal action, possibly? Another plagiarism suit? Something more suspicious?

They huddled beside each other on the retro banquette, staring at the tiny eight-inch screen, constantly adjusting their speed reading to each other's tempo. As with every Dan Brown, it was tremendously exciting, page-turning stuff. They couldn't stop reading even if they'd wanted to. Unlike *The Da Vinci Code*, which was a chase narrative – the French cops pursue Langdon and Sophie – and unlike *Angels and Demons*, which was a quest narrative – get the Hassassin before the bomb goes off – *The Solomon Key* was a combination of both. Langdon was hunting a killer while he was hunted by the same. All the Dan Brown devices were in place: a prologue featuring a spectacularly gruesome murder; a late night phone call to Robert "the dolphin" Langdon in Cambridge, MA; a series of cryptic clues and baffling symbology and unsettling ciphers and ever more brutal murders; a hot-bodied helper called Harriet Callaghan – not classically beautiful but lithe, long-legged, red-headed, green-eyed and extra, extra clever – who worked as an analyst for the FBI; and an apocalyptic conspiracy involving an ancient millennial cult within a cult that planned to release a deadly toxin in Washington DC during the presidential inauguration ceremony.

That wasn't what caused the mood to deflate, though. On the contrary, it was Brown's best book yet, a brilliant combination of erudition and excitement. Dan's characters, often derided as not so much flat as flatulent, were much more believable than before. The chase sequences were particularly thrilling, especially a creepy nocturnal scene in the George Washington Masonic National Monument, an extravagantly esoteric temple to the first president in Alexandria, Virginia. Better still, Brown's infamous propensity to stop the action in order to deliver heroic doses of arcane knowledge was kept under control. The author's research was delivered in luscious little dollops, judiciously introduced by a cast of unforgettable characters, not least Cuthbert Pike, an obese 33-degree Scottish Rite Freemason with an encyclopaedic knowledge of occult lore, and the brilliant Brigham Oldman, the stuttering l-l-l-leader of a team of LDS hitmen whose clean-cut good looks, perfectly tailored black suits and disarmingly affable grin-to-win demeanours disguised brutally efficient killing machines, akin to theological Terminators. The climactic scene, where Professor Robert Langdon and "Dirty Harriet" Callaghan pursue Brigham Oldman up all 897 steps of the Washington Monument – that mainly Masonic tribute to a mainly Masonic president – was so spellbindingly cinematic in its intensity that a third Tom Hanks Oscar was not an impossibility, notwithstanding Hollywood's reluctance to award action movies the ultimate accolade.

The cause of Abby and Magill's concern was the killing spree. The cryptic killings that Langdon was called on to solve involved a roster of prominent Freemasons, all of whom had their throats ritualistically slit. But only after strange sigils were carved into their chests. The sigils pointed to Hendaye Cross, which pointed to Francis Bacon, which pointed to the Rosicrucians and the Founding Fathers and the hidden codes in Shakespeare, which pointed to William Friedman, America's foremost cryptologist of the twentieth century, the man who cracked the Imperial Japanese Purple Code, the man whose warnings about Pearl Harbor were ignored, the man who spearheaded America's contribution to the Enigma Code breakthrough, the man who founded the NSA in 1952, which burgeoned into the biggest surveillance operation on earth and, not least, the man who published a landmark book debunking the Francis-Bacon-is-Shakespeare hypothesis at the height of the Cold War.

The Solomon Key, in effect, was being enacted for real. With Abby and Simon as active participants! Their enactment of the novel was inverted, perverted and parodic in certain respects, but it was an enactment all the same. The systematic killing of Dan's fans, a community of like-minded conspiracy lovers – a freemasonry of fandom, as it were – exactly paralleled the brutally slaughtered brethren in Brown's book. The throat slitting and ritualistically carved sigils in Dan's work of fiction had been replicated, with a post-mortem book-cover twist, in Paris, Rome, Salt Lake City and Sydney. The cross of Hendaye, the Baconian codes, the Shakespearean connection, the apocalyptic countdown, the Big C Cuthbert Pike character, were precisely what they too had encountered in their amateurish quest to comprehend the mystery of Dan Brown's breakdown.

The mystery was solved. What author wouldn't crack under the strain of their writing coming to life? When those writings were unpublished, moreover, it was a miracle he'd held it together for so long. Why didn't Dan tell the cops? Fear of adverse publicity perhaps or, more likely, having the killings pinned on him by publicity-hungry police officers.

"God Almighty," Magill whispered, when they finally closed the file they'd opened two hours earlier. The snowstorm had stopped. Daylight was rapidly draining into evening. Darkness wasn't far off, even though it was only 4.00 p.m.

"The devil, more like," Abby retorted. "Why would anyone want to recreate Dan's novel? How did they get hold of it? You said the thing was unpublished."

"He's got a lot of enemies, Abby. The Catholic Church for starters. Citroën for seconds. Jealous rivals for thirds. If the book's ready to roll, that means publishing people may have seen it and read it – agent, editor, fact checker and so forth."

"But why would anyone at Doubleday want to do Dan

down? Jobs depend on their star author's continued success. A big brand-name book is a bonanza, is it not? They'd be slitting their own throats."

"Not a good analogy," Magill observed. "Sometimes blood is thicker than water," he went on, impervious to his own figurative faux pas. "The book trade is riddled with freemasons and similar fraternal types. The old boy network is alive and well and meddling in manuscripts. Maybe the Masons are getting their retaliation in first. Or even the LDS. The Mormons don't like washing their dirty linen in public and having it washed in public by someone as high profile as Dan Brown would not go down well in Temple Square. I've been to Salt Lake City. I know what they're like. The levers of power in this country are firmly in the hands of the LDS. The best business schools, for example, are full of them."

"Seems a bit extreme, though. It seems to me that they'd benefit from the publicity. Opus Dei's enrolment increased after *The Da Vinci Code*. The Albino society garnered its best publicity for years. The Catholic Church was invigorated by the *Da Vinci* debate. No doubt Illuminati membership will soar in the aftermath of this summer's movie adaptation. Freemasonry will be exactly the same. Mormonism too."

"The old guerrilla psychology gambit, eh Abby?"

She flicked open her hands in an anything's possible gesture. They sat in silence, surrounded by the remains of an afternoon's comfort eating. Outside, the streetlights' amber glow gave the newly deposited snow a jaundiced, sickly tinge. It looked like Abby and Simon felt.

"There is, of course, another ugly possibility," Magill ventured.

Abby raised her eyebrows expectantly.

He closed the file, exited the folder, switched off the netbook and waited for the shutting down sequence to subside with its signature tinkle. "The NSA. They don't exactly cover themselves in glory in *The Solomon Key*. Dan didn't exactly endear himself to the NSA in *Digital Fortress*. Dumb though they are, the National Security Agency has got some pretty powerful surveillance tools on tap. Maybe they've been keeping a beady eye on Dan's drafts."

"Maybe," Abby conceded, rubbing her aching neck.

"Maybe," Magill concurred, yawning inelegantly. "All we know for certain is that someone had access to *The Solomon Key* and that they used it as a recipe for a real-world killing spree."

"So what's our next move?"

"Well, I guess we could raid Doubleday's offices in New York or try to do a deal with Dan's agent."

"Agents and Dealers," Abby quipped.

Magill ignored her flippant remark. "Or…," he mused. "Or… or… we could follow the recipe too. If the killer's using the novel as a template, perhaps we can do likewise to catch him."

"I'm no Harriet Callaghan, Simon."

"Oh, I don't know," he smiled, a twinkle in his eye.

"And you're no Robert Langdon!"

The twinkle faded. "I don't wear a tweed jacket and sport a mullet, if that's what you mean."

Abby took in Magill's voluminous Ulster and bright ginger buzz-cut. She refrained from comment.

"I do own a Mickey Mouse watch, mind you."

"Where to next?" Abby asked.

"First stop Colonial Williamsburg."

"Bruton churchyard, I take it."

"Where else?"

Despite the invaluable information she'd gathered in Hendaye, Abby was unaware that an exact replica of the Great Cross had been sent to Virginia in the late nineteenth century, as an Aquitaine equivalent of the Statue of Liberty. Just as a copy of Liberty sat on the Ile de la Cité, so too a duplicate of the occult monument rested in Colonial Williamsburg, marking the point where Bacon's secret manuscripts were buried. According to *The Solomon Key*, that is. When Abby queried the reliability of Dan's research, Magill huffed and puffed and finally admitted that the Danster may have made one or two factual errors in the past, before his books went mega and were subject to detailed line-by-line scrutiny. But that was no longer the case. If Dan claimed that an apocalyptic obelisk lurked in Bruton Church graveyard, you can be darned sure that the thing's still there.

"What about the toxin?" Abby asked. The toxin in the novel was interred in the churchyard. Far from containing a cache of

Shakespearean manuscripts, the Bacon burial site was the resting place of a deadly bacillus – analogous to avian flu – that Bacon had distilled by alchemical experiment in order to bring about the apocalypse he earnestly yearned for. The untimely death of Bacon, famously attributed to an accident with a frozen chicken, was actually caused by a vicious mutation of the flu virus that devastates the world at regular intervals, most notably 1603, 1776, 1857 and 1918. Bacon not only perfected the experimental method, he precipitated the Great Plague.

"I guess we'll find out when we get there."

"Perhaps we should stop on the way for a couple of gas masks."

"A shovel or two wouldn't go amiss."

She fluttered her eyelashes. "I think one'll suffice, don't you Simon?"

"Okay, Abby, if you prefer a pickaxe, that's cool."

"Pickaxes R Us is probably closed by now."

"This is America, Abby. They've probably got nuclear-powered pickaxes on offer in Wal-Mart."

"Is that nuclear or nucular, as per George Bush's malapropism?"

"Tomato. Tomato."

"Let's call the whole thing off?"

"It's too late for that, Dirty Harriet Callaghan."

"You really know how to make a punk's day, Professor Langdon."

Chapter Forty-Two

Bacon's Bacillus

Annoyingly, it took them thirty minutes to find their way to I-95, heading south. They were held up, not by the heavy snowfall, which was cleared off the main roads with efficient dispatch, but by the blizzard-blanketed signposts, which were completely indecipherable. Rand McNally wasn't much help either, since its urban street treatment was insufficiently detailed for navigational purposes. Still, at least they stumbled upon a Dollar Tree, one of the new breed of deep discount stores that are springing up throughout the States in the wake of the recession. Dollar Tree made Sam's Club look like Saks Fifth Avenue.

They bought a couple of one-piece contamination suits for ¢99 apiece. The full-face gas masks also set them back the best part of a dollar. The shovel was slightly dearer at $2.50 and the pickaxe was positively outrageous at three bucks even. Unsurprisingly, Abby expressed doubts as to the degree of protection a ¢99 contamination suit might afford its wearer in the face of a deadly 400-year-old bacillus. As a former marketing lecturer, Magill confidently assured her that it was no different from a Cerruti contamination suit. They were probably made on the same production line.

As an ex-entrepreneur who knew a thing or about cutting corners, Abby wasn't so sure.

In a fit of extravagance, Magill threw a fifty cent satnav into their shopping cart. With a couple of date-expired Snickers, an everlasting torch and an Indian blanket – just in case they got caught in a snowdrift – the bill for the expedition came to twelve dollars and fifty cents, plus tax. "This is so not a Dan Brown book," Magill murmured as they queued at the only cash register in operation. "Hey, who needs CERN or nuclear submarines or supersonic aircraft or priceless works of art or super-duper supercomputers? We got a fifty cent satnav to guide us."

"Yippee."

The satnav was a compass with a sucker. The illustration on the box was misleading, to put it mildly. But Abby and Magill didn't have time to complain at the unmanned customer service counter. Ever the improviser, Magill stuck the compass on the dash and provided the running satnav commentary. "At the next junction, turn left." He soon got bored with that. So he resorted to different languages – guttural German, emphatic Japanese, rapid Italian, phonetic French – none of which he actually spoke. He threw in the requisite hand gestures for free.

"What did you think of Dan's novel?" she asked in desperation, since anything was better than Magill's Inspector Clouseau.

The multi-linguist adjusted the heater, which was going full blast. "Excellent. Really excellent. I can't understand why he didn't publish it back in 2004 or 2005. I can only assume that the plagiarism suits held things up, and then the intimidation started."

"I was thinking more of the narrative side, Simon. You know, the story arc that you keep banging on about. Is Dan's arc seaworthy?"

"You tell me," Magill sighed. "I'm biased where the Danster's concerned. The book's written for the average reader. Not that you're in any way average, Abby," he added hastily.

"Well," Abby said, snuggling into the driver's seat for what little comfort it afforded, "I thought the Shakespeare angle was really neat. If you're trying to follow Leonardo da Vinci, it has to be with an artist of similar calibre. Switching from visual art to works of literature was also a savvy inversion. I had no idea about the supposed codes in Shakespeare's plays."

"The scenes in the National Archives were riveting."

Abby agreed. "I really liked the masculinity material as well. The idea of the destructive power of the perennial masculine was very convincing, a great complement to the eternal feminine's nurturance that featured in *Da Vinci*. I mean, just look at what's happened since Dan wrote the book. If Iraq and Afghanistan aren't copybook demonstrations of the perennial masculine, I don't know what is."

"I wasn't so sure about that bit," Magill sniffed. "All that stuff about the Spear of Destiny. That it's not a physical object, as such, but the Bacon bacillus, a bioweapon of mass destruction. It was too reminiscent of his take on the Holy Grail, only in reverse."

"Yeah, I'm with you on that."

"Also, that business about tremendous success and eventual misfortune befalling the spear's owners, on account of the miasmic bacillus, didn't quite ring true."

"That's odd," Abby said, "because that bit's based on the truth." Sensing Magill's scepticism, she recounted her own close encounter with the spear and revealed that it was rumoured to be in Dan Brown's possession. She added that its ownership not only explained the Danster's towering literary achievement in *The Solomon Key*, which was infinitely superior to *Da Vinci*, but also why he had failed to release the novel, because the spear gnaws away at the possessor's psyche, bringing calamity, misery, anguish, pain. "The spear exists, Simon. I've seen its reliquary. The bacillus stuff is poetic licence, though. I think…"

They drove in silence for fifteen minutes. Only the intrusive tyre noise broke the eldritch hush. The pine trees that crowded either side of the I-64 were half-coated in wind-driven drifts. They looked like giant upturned icicles, the fossilized jaw bone of an Ice Age titan. The Ice Age in the emerald Subaru thawed before long. As the possessor of the Holy Grail, Magill could hardly quibble over the Spear of Destiny's existence. Instead, he launched into a long, learned discussion of US government agencies and successive presidents' vain attempts to get them to co-operate, George Bush's USIC being the latest in a long line. Its logo was a spear – spooky! – a neat narrative link missed by the Danster.

Waiting for the tide of geekspeak to recede, Abby concentrated on her driving. Colonial Williamsburg, twenty miles. Eighteen. Fifteen. When the lapsed anorak finally wound down, she wrapped things up. "The best twist, for me, was that bit about the CIA and how they suppressed Friedman's real findings to further the cultural Cold War. Faced with Russian cultural giants like Tolstoy, Pushkin and Dostoyevsky, the west couldn't possibly acknowledge that Shakespeare was a sham, a front for

Francis Bacon, the infamous pederast-cum-conman who finished up in the Tower of London. It would be like admitting that Paul Revere was a double agent, in cahoots with Benedict Arnold. So they blackmailed Friedman and he altered the evidence that backed Bacon's case."

"Yeah, that was a great twist," Magill acknowledged. "Don't know if it's true but it works brilliantly in the book. That scene in the Folger Library, where the First Folio saves Langdon from the knife-wielding Mormon assassin, was sheer genius."

The chit-chat about Brown's aborted blockbuster continued until the satnav announced, in incomprehensible Romanian, that Colonial Williamsburg was nearby. Thanks to the Danster's potted exposition, both knew that the Virginia colony began with a mystery (the first settlers in Roanoke disappeared without trace), continued with controversy (the Jamestown settlement of 1607 descended into semi-civil war) and only stabilized in 1697 when Williamsburg became the state capital of Virginia. It too fell into disrepair when the capital moved to Richmond in 1780. The renaissance began during the Great Depression. A heritage-loving cleric, the Reverend Dr Goodwin, persuaded the Rockefeller Foundation to fund a massive restoration project, which was nothing if not controversial but brought the buildings, the settlement, the entire Historical Triangle back to life. Much criticized for its Disneyfication of the past – resting actors dress in period costume, spouting authentic homilies to tour-bus deposited dragoons of digital camera-equipped visitors, plus the occasional world leader – Colonial Williamsburg remains one of the biggest tourist attractions in the state and a pioneer of museum merchandizing, whereby specially selected items from the collection are reproduced under licence and sold in up-scale retail stores. Most brand-name museums in the United States have followed where Colonial Williamsburg led.

After parking their rental just off Franklin, Abby and Magill trudged through the snow-covered streets of the living history museum. There was no sign of life. The feeble gaseous glow from ye olde streetlamps, coupled with the milky mid-winter moonlight, cast eerie shadows along the tree-lined thoroughfares. They clumped past the silent Raleigh Tavern and skirted the creepy Courthouse, heading in the general direction of Bruton churchyard. The combination of fresh snow over icy sidewalks made progress slow and difficult. They were further hampered by the unwieldy pickaxe and shovel, which Magill threw over one shoulder, and the contamination suits and gasmasks, which Abby carried in a plastic bag. Every so often, a huge deposit of snow would drop from the branches above, landing on Duke of Gloucester Street with a dull woomph. Equally unsettling was the clanking of the pick and shovel, which touched and tinkled as Magill slithered along, trying to keep his feet and maintain his balance. The gently chiming digging implements bespoke ghoulies and ghosties and great grimpen goblins rattling their chains. Not the kind of thing Abby wanted to hear when about to break into a graveyard and excavate the toxic remains of Francis Bacon's bubonic bequest.

The triple-decker tower of Bruton Church, home to the oldest Episcopal congregation in America, loomed ahead of them in the moonlight. Snow-topped and surrounded by a stark trellis of leafless trees, it looked like something out of an M. Night Shyamalan-inspired snow globe. Unabashed, they mounted the three granite steps outside the main entrance in the west transept and tried the door. It opened with a blood-chilling groan. They tiptoed inside. The inky blackness enveloped them. A brief blip with their everlasting $1 torch picked out the pulpit (donated by Theodore Roosevelt), the pews (where once sat George Washington, Thomas Jefferson, James Monroe and more) and the phosphorescent glow of the Jamestown font (which harked back to the church's establishment, if not the actual building, in the mid-seventeenth century). As Brown cogently explained in *The Solomon Key*, Bruton Church has been rebuilt more times than the temple on the Dome of the Rock.

Ignoring the hand of history, the resurrection man and woman plonked themselves down on a pew and struggled into their slinky one-piece contamination suits. Magill's was too small. The bottoms stopped mid-calf and the sleeves gave out halfway between elbow and wrist. If the Bacon bacillus crept up his inside leg, Simon'd be in serious trouble. At least his gasmask was snug, though the condensation that misted the goggles made them all but ineffective.

Abby wasn't one to talk, let alone laugh, since she insisted on wearing her trusty Aquascutum over her protective clothing. Given the chill, this was understandable and, from a fashionista's perspective, it was the only acceptable alternative. The Dollar Tree own brand had to be kept hidden at all times, if a modicum of street-cred were to be maintained. The sartorial outcome was less *CSI Miami* than *Miami Vice*. And even less like the Centre for Disease Control, Atlanta.

They exited the church, their plastic-sheathed legs swishing as they walked. An owl hooted in one of the full-grown elms dotted around the cemetery. The milky moon shed sufficient light to pick their way between the broken headstones, the weathered statuary, the tumbledown funerary furniture. However, even with the aid of their Dollar Tree torch, it was difficult to distinguish between the grave markers, especially as fresh snow had adhered to one side of many stelae, making ready identification impossible.

"See any you recognize, Abby?"

Setting down the shovel, she stared around the necropolis, hoping to catch a glimpse of the Hendaye cross-alike. *The Solomon Key* said it was a mini-replica of the real thing. Nothing caught her eye. Shouldering the shovel once again – just like the good old bad old days on the family farm – she made for the encircling stone wall. "Dan said it was close to the edge, didn't he? Let's work our way round till we find it." Sensible though that suggestion was, the lack of a perimeter footpath made the going heavy to horrid. They kept tripping over snow-covered ledgers and funerary urns, which triggered many a sacrilegious swearword. The gasmasks didn't help either. Every so often, they'd stop at a passing obelisk then brush the snow away to better see the inscription. Without success. They had almost circumnavigated the cemetery when the Hendaye Cross copy finally loomed large, half-hidden behind a massive yew tree. They parted the branches to get a good look at the memorial, dislodging a snowdrift for their trouble.

"Are you sure this is it?" Magill whispered.

"Well, I can't be certain in these goggles. I think so."

He gave the torch a touch. The yew screened them sufficiently from the road to risk an extended burst of illumination. The illumination never came. The everlasting torch had lit its last. You get what you pay for. The same principle applies to pick-axes. When Magill took a swing at the ground cover beneath the occult tribute to Francis Bacon, the implement buckled under the impact. Frozen, the adamantine ground refused to yield its subterranean secrets. Not to a Dollar Tree pickaxe, which was not only unfit for purpose but a threat to life and limb, because the head went one way and the shaft shot off another. "Goddam it," he shouted.

A cocked trigger clicked behind them. "I won't have any of that language in my churchyard," a quiet voice admonished. "Now raise your hands and turn around slowly."

Abby and Magill did as they were bid. A startling sight greeted them, though the lack of adequate illumination made it seem more startling than it was. A British redcoat, complete with tricorn hat, knee-button breeches, criss-cross webbing belts and big buckled riding boots, stood to one side of the yew, musket in hand. The business end of the barrel pointed at the centre of Magill's chest. More startling still was the fact that it was a female redcoat in full regalia. She looked as though she wasn't taking any prisoners.

Magill glanced down at the Ferguson single-shot breech-loader. Historically accurate, though few were in service during the American War of Independence, it was unreliable in cold weather and, with only one round at her disposal, the redcoat could be rushed with a good chance of success. He weighed up his options.

"I've a pistol in my pocket," she added, sensing her captive's calculations.

"Am I glad to see you," Abby interjected. "This man accosted me in the parking lot and forced me to wear this plastic outfit... presumably for perverted purposes... which I'm quite looking forward to..."

"Button it," the redcoat snapped. "Any more lip and this trigger slips. Step away from the shovel. Now let's all make our way back into town, where we'll have a little chat before I call the cops."

Chapter Forty-Three

Better Late Than Neveu

Arms aloft in surrender, Magill and Maguire were steered out of Bruton churchyard, with much slipping and sliding and stumbling. They got no sympathy from their captor. She shoved the musket in Abby's back from time to time, prodding her forward, fouling her mood. Magill tried to catch his companion's eye, with a view to intimating restraint. But their gasmasks weren't built for interpersonal communication. They were hard enough to breathe through.

The prisoners were prodded past the church, through the gate, down the steps and along the street to Rainbow's End, a kitsch recreation of an old-time goldsmiths. Without a word of explanation, they were herded into its steel-barred strongroom, a surrogate cell. Their gaoler rested her rifle against the whitewashed side wall and placed her pistol on the hickory counter. She pulled up a walnut Windsor chair and sat herself down, knees spread, tricorn doffed. Plain of face, pious of expression, pasty of complexion, plumpish of physique, pudding bowl of hairdo, she was the kind of woman that tamed the wilderness and won the west. Single-handed. "Unauthorized disinterment is a felony, as well as a sin. Why were you digging up the Oakeshott plot? Explain yourselves."

Pedantically, Magill was preparing to point out that they hadn't actually broken ground. Broken the pickaxe, yes, but the hallowed ground, no. Any half-decent attorney would get them off the grave-robbing rap. They weren't trespassing either, since Colonial Williamsburg isn't private property, strictly speaking. People can come and go as they please at any time of day or night. So open the cell and we'll be on our way with no hard feelings.

He never had the chance. Abby was already on the case.

"Oakeshott?" she said, ripping off the gasmask with a relieved shake of the head. "The Oakeshott plot? We were looking for Bacon."

Their captor stared at them distastefully. She ran a hand through her dull brown hair, tucking flyaway strands behind elephantine ears. "You're lookin' for Bacon, are you?"

"Yes, ma'am," Magill said in a conciliatory tone, while pressing his gasmask to his chest in a gesture of deference. "We discovered that a cache of documents belonging to Sir Francis Bacon is buried beneath a copy of the Great Cyclic Cross. We obviously mistook the Oakeshott plot for the Bacon burial site. In the snow…"

The redcoat rose from her seat, straightened her tunic and tightened her white silk cravat. "At your service, sir."

Baffled by the bizarre remark, Magill didn't know what to say.

"Reverend Dr Delia Bacon, at your service."

"Any relation?" he asked.

She smiled regretfully. She wasn't a descendant. Nor was her great, great aunt, also a Delia Bacon, who first put forward the idea that Bacon wrote Shakespeare and was driven mad by the hostility of the Stratford orthodoxy, those who believe an illiterate money-lender-cum-marketing man from the boondocks of Britain actually penned the works of art that surpass just about everything in western culture, the paintings of Leonardo included.

The reverend doctor was given free rhetorical rein and she waxed extra lyrical about her ancestor, who was a pioneer feminist at a time when women were seen and not heard, who talked many leading men of letters round to the Bacon-is-Shakespeare theory, Nathaniel Hawthorne and Mark Twain among them, and who somehow persuaded the Mayor of Stratford-upon-Avon to let her excavate Shakespeare's supposed tomb, which started a fashion for disinterring Bacon's buried horde, wherever it may be. One Doctor Owen spent fifteen years in the vicinity of Chepstow Castle, damming the River Wye and digging by the light of the silvery moon. One Calvin Hoffman opened the tomb of Christopher Marlowe in Chislehurst, Kent, only to find nothing but sand. Bruton Church entered the Bacon stakes in the 1950s, when the wife of Manley Hall, a celebrity mystic, got it into her head that the Elizabethan nobleman made a deposit in the land of the free, his model for *New Atlantis*. She petitioned J. Edgar Hoover, a prominent thirty-three degree Freemason, twisted the Rockefellers' arms until they surrendered, organized a seismographic survey of the graveyard, made several unsuccessful excavations and would have continued doing so until the entire cemetery was turned over. When Bruton church put a stop to her Baconian shenanigans, she claimed that there was a conspiracy against her. This was led by the CIA, the FBI, the NSA and President Truman himself, who was another high-ranking Freemason and therefore determined to do her down. "You're not the first," Dr Bacon concluded with a sigh.

"I see," Magill said. "Dan contends that there really was a conspiracy to do her down. The Hendaye chapter of the *Mystery of the Cathedrals* was appended to the second edition in 1957. The Friedmans' book on the Bacon code was published in 1957. It was also the year of Sputnik and America's realization that it was losing the Cold War."

The barrage of information passed over Reverend Dr Bacon's head. Only one word connected. "Dan?" she inquired. "Is that Dan, as in Dan Brown?"

With an ingratiating grin, Magill conceded that it was and acknowledged his connection to the great man, hoping that the stardust of literary celebrity would work its magic on the holder of the Colonial Williamsburg key, goldsmiths division. Sadly, he miscalculated.

"A few years ago, there was a rumour that Bruton Church would feature in Brown's next book, on account of the Francis Bacon connection. Nothing came of it. But the threat was sufficient for us to sell the cyclic cross."

"You sold it?" Abby groaned.

"But it would have been a money-spinner of the first order," Magill added, echoing his companion's disappointment. "Think of the extra visitors you would have had in the wake of publication. Brown's been a bonanza for Paris and Rome."

"It would've put Williamsburg on the map," Abby weighed in.

An unimpressed expression crossed the good reverend's unprepossessing countenance, as she fiddled with her wayward hair once more. "Williamsburg's already on the map. It has been since 1699."

"We didn't mean it like that," Magill insisted, shooting Abby an admonitory look.

"I know," Bacon replied. "Visitor numbers have been falling lately and Williamsburg could do with a boost. But it didn't seem like that five years ago, when the economy was soaring and visitor numbers were rising, especially during our tercentenary celebrations. We weighed up the pros and cons of a Brown windfall and concluded it was incompatible with the Colonial Williamsburg brand, with the authenticity of our customer offer."

Abby was staggered by the management-speak, doubtless regurgitated straight from an "experiential marketing" consultancy report. "But Williamsburg isn't authentic," she said. "It's anything but authentic. It pretends to be authentic. However, it's no more authentic than Disneyland. I can't believe you bought into that authentic branding BS."

Magill kicked her ankle surreptitiously. For God's sake, Abby, we're trying to get out of here.

Surprisingly, his partner's outburst didn't antagonize their gaoler. Like Abby, she too had learned bitter lessons about branding. "Yes, well, we made our bed. Look at it this way, if the Cross were still in situ, the Dan Brown multitudes would be excavating the place willy-nilly, without permission." Bacon looked at the pair of them pointedly. "And with a surname like mine, my life wouldn't be worth living. Can you imagine?"

They saw her point. Dr Bacon dilated on the downturn, the struggle to keep visitor numbers up during a recession, the redoubled emphasis on living history, hence her outfit. She was on her way home from rehearsing Valley Forge: The Rematch, when she spotted the activity in the cemetery. Nice outfit, her captives chimed, trying to nudge her towards an unselfish act of fraternal forgiveness. But Bacon knew the thin edge of a wedge when she saw one and, at the risk of mixing her metaphors, was determined to nip it in the bud. Prosecute the first two grave-robbers and the Brownian multitudes will receive a don't-mess-with-Bruton signal. Abby tried to convince her that such a policy would have the opposite effect. The principles of reverse psychology applied, because the publicity that attended their arrest would trigger a tidal wave of curious sensation seekers, treasure hunters and suchlike.

Reverend Bacon was resolute. She'd've called the cops already if it weren't for the fact that cellphones are prohibited on parade. "The price of authenticity, eh?" Abby observed with ever-mounting asperity.

Struggling to keep their interrogation on an amiable footing – since sweet talk always trumped cheap shots when persuasion was the objective – Magill placed a restraining hand on the arm of Abby's contamination suit. "Let me handle this," he whispered, while covering his comments with a cough. "Who did you sell the replica to?"

"Ah," Bacon smiled, "that was the one smart move we made. We sold it to Busch Gardens. It's just down the road. Our hope is – was, rather – that Williamsburg would benefit from proximity. The bulk of the Brown brigade go to Busch, then some come over to us. Everyone's a winner. They're better geared up for Dan diggers than we are."

"Busch Gardens," Magill said disingenuously, because he'd spotted a signpost on the road to Williamsburg. "What's that?"

Amazed by the Englishman's ignorance – albeit his plummy accent belied his Irish connections – the Reverend Dr Bacon explained that Busch Gardens was a theme park in the grounds of Anheuser Busch's nearby brewery. Once part of the Williamsburg estate, the land was sold to the Budweiser people in the late 1960s and the theme park opened in 1975. An exaggerated version of the Irish theme pubs that pollute downtown shopping districts worldwide, Busch Gardens was based around a bunch of national themes. There's an English area, a French district, a German zone, an Italian region, a Scottish tract and an Irish quarter. All the national ingredients, basically, that were part of America's melting pot. Each of the zones was full of appropriately themed restaurants, rides, shops and shows.

"Sounds like Stereotypes Central," Abby said sarcastically, unable to resist contributing her two-penny-worth.

Fortunately, the Reverend Bacon agreed with her remark, though she was obviously prepared to sup with the devil when the brewer's price was right. "Yes, they've received some negative publicity about that. Hence the Dan Brown project."

"*What?*"

"Well, I've been reliably informed – though this is only hearsay, I must stress – that Busch Gardens is planning to broaden its appeal and deflect some of the criticism by developing a Dan Brown theme to link in with the publication of his book featuring the Founding Fathers. When we sold them the monument we assumed it was for the French Village, a little bit of authenticity in an otherwise ersatz experience. Our cross is a replica of course," she added, with a look that forestalled any Abby interruption. "But it's still one hundred years older than anything else in Busch."

"Anyway," Magill said, encouraging her to continue with the story.

"Anyway, it turned out that the cross was part of a much bigger project. It was cooked up, apparently, by some management consultancy in Las Vegas. The plan was to pre-empt the Harry Potter theme park in Orlando. There was some kind of treasure hunt, plus the usual restaurants and rides."

Almost as soon as she had spoken, Magill could see the amazing possibilities. "You mean like an *Angels and Demons* helicopter plunge, a *Digital Fortress* centrifuge, a *Deception Point* shark attack, a speed-of-light ride in the CERN collider, a loop-the-Louvre roller-coaster?"

"I don't know the details. I'm not an expert on the books," Bacon said, with a superior I-don't-read-such-trash tone. However, she seemed pretty well informed for an agnostic. "I think they were planning to brew a special Dan Brown beer, similar to Sam Adams. Langdon Lite, was it?"

"Makes sense." Magill nodded. "There's plenty of scope for themed beverages – Bob's Brew, Sophie's Spritzer, Beaujolais Neveu, Hassassin Hooch."

"I suppose so," she said noncommittally, then noted with an "oh well" shrug that it wasn't to be. The plans fell into abeyance. The book never came out, to her knowledge. They were the first

318

people to have come around asking about the cross. Was publication imminent?

Diplomatically, Magill assured her that *The Solomon Key* had been indefinitely delayed. She seemed disappointed. The visitor shortfall was obviously preying on her mind; even the inauthentic spin-off from Busch Gardens would be welcome at this stage of the economic cycle. Magill hinted that publication *could* be accelerated, but only if they were released from captivity. Bacon wasn't falling for that one.

"It's a shame you can't make it up there tonight," she said. "They're having a big party to celebrate the end of George Bush's reign of terror. You'll be partying in Colonial Williamsburg cop shop, my friends." She stood up. The interview was over. "Do you have a cellphone I can borrow?"

Abby snorted with disbelief. "Sorry," she lied, "I left it in the rental."

"What about you?"

"Never carry such ghastly things," he fibbed, in an exaggerated English accent.

"You can body search me, if you wish," Abby suggested, with a wink. "I love a girl in uniform. Just let me slip out of this, um, little one-piece plastic number. Or would you rather I kept it on? You can wear the gasmask, if that's your thing. Oh baby. Oh baby."

Magill couldn't believe what he was hearing, though he liked it a lot. The come-on worked its magic, however, because the Reverend Dr Bacon promptly fled the scene, saying she'd be back in ten minutes."

"Quick." Magill snapped his fingers. "Your brooch."

Unzipping her one-piece, Abby unpinned the black rose brooch from her lapel. With a wiggle and a twist and a grimace and a click – extra-quick lock-picking tricks he'd practised at PWC – Magill prised open the surrogate cell door.

"What about the weapons?" Abby asked, pointing to the musket and pistol, which rested where Bacon had left them, in her haste.

"Let's bring them," he said, pocketing the pistol and grabbing the tricorn hat as a souvenir. "Let's leave our contamination suits behind. Fair exchange and all that."

319

"Hey, maybe they'll turn them into a tourist attraction. The Great Escape."

"You reckon?"

"Nah, not authentic enough. Ye Olde Escape might work, though."

"Bacon Breakout's better, Abby."

"Harriett Callaghan and Robert Langdon ride again."

"They do indeed. You can't keep good fictional characters down"

Chapter Forty-Four

What You Will

They scudded though the silent streets like the flickering shadows of a faltering hurricane lamp. For a famous living history museum, Williamsburg was fortuitously devoid of life. Ears cocked for a cop car siren, which never came, they made it back to Franklin Street without incident.

"Where to?" Abby intoned, as she settled back behind the steering wheel.

Holding his painful side, which felt like a six times stitch, Magill was having trouble talking. "Busch Gardens," he finally gasped, gritting his teeth.

"Won't the cops be waiting for us?"

"We'll be less conspicuous in a crowd than on the highway. Mind you, something tells me that they won't be throwing up too many roadblocks. Not on a Monday night. Not when the football's on. Not during the playoffs. Would you drop everything on a freezing cold night, on the word of a woman dressed as a redcoat who'd seen ghosts in the churchyard?"

Slamming the Subaru into gear, Abby sped off, searching for a sign to Busch Gardens. "She looked pretty persuasive to me. Our contamination suits are still in the store."

Magill swore silently. "Yeah, we should have chucked them in a dumpster. If we're lucky, they'll call in forensics, which should hold them up for a while. No point crying over spilled bacillus."

Incongruously, Abby burst out laughing. "I'm not sure the suits would've helped much if we'd unearthed Bacon's botulism. The sight of you with your long legs sticking out…"

"I thought I looked quite natty, actually."

"Nutty, maybe."

The theme park was less than five miles away. It was easy to find. The floodlights were so bright that there was no call for their satnav. They headed for the sodium glow. The route was lined with come-ye-all billboards, announcing the evening's event. Evidently, it was a celebration of the end of George W.'s woeful presidency, plus a pre-inauguration party, which went by the snappy name: The Busch Bush Putsch. The parking lot was full, despite the televized football.

With Barack in prospect, the mood in Busch Gardens was euphoric. The main entrance was lined with the flags of the nations evoked within. But with an additional Obama twist – Scotland (Yes We Cannie), Italy (Yes We Cannelloni), Ireland (Yes We Beercan), France (Yes We Can-Can), Germany (Yes We Can Make You Talk, Schweinehund) and England (Yes We Can't).

"National stereotypes are alive and well and living in Williamsburg," Abby groaned, while paying $59.95 for the privilege of enduring them at close quarters. "I think I can guess what the Irish sector contains: a grisly mix of Blarney stones and River-dancers and lepping leprechauns and Irish stew sellers."

"Got it in one," Magill confirmed, scanning the guests' guide book. "Don't knock it, though. It's effective branding. Marketers trade in stereotypes, though we call them segments. Stereotyping is an innate human trait, hardwired into the mammalian cerebellum. You must have covered that in your evolutionary psychology lecture. The knack is to use stereotyping to best commercial advantage, not put up a futile fight about pernicious misperceptions."

"I see the English district has a red telephone box, a replica of Big Ben, a couple of camp Pearly Queens, a bunch of Beefeaters with B.O. and a troupe of Morris dancers from Much Binding in the Marsh."

"Bastards!"

"Or is that much effing and blinding in the marsh?" she went on, twisting the knife. "Hey, Simon, I wonder if jellied eels are on special offer tonight, along with warm beer and pork scratchings. Or would you prefer clotted cream tea with crumpets, old bean?"

Manfully ignoring her jibes, Magill scrutinized a giant map of the park, conveniently situated by the main entrance. He tried to work out the quickest route to the French *pays*. "This way," he said, cutting left through the Italian section, a piazza- and pizzeria-peppered celebration of Leonardo da Vinci's manifold inventions. These, apparently, included the Flying Machine Ride and the swooshing, swinging Battering Ram, a hair-raising reminder of the great man's contributions to theme park science. Despite the cold, the gelato vendors were doing good business. The well-muffled crowds flowed downhill in family groups, pausing to watch the heroic few who braved the Roman Rapids Watersplash. Heroes of another kind filled the spans of a high-level footbridge across the River Rhine, a touching memorial to the war dead in Iraq and Afghanistan.

The ear-shattering howl, when it came, was completely unexpected. Feeling twitchy already – due to the presence of uniformed security guards among the merry milling crowds – Abby lepped like a leprechauness when the cold night air was cleft by a scream of doom. The Big Bad Wolf, Busch Gardens' signature loop-the-loop roller-coaster, complete with a Stuka-like siren, rushed out of the undergrowth through the snow-dappled pines and pirouetted among the bare-naked treetops, to the unalloyed enthusiasm of applauding onlookers on the bridge. Magill wasn't among them. A bookish boy at heart, stomach-churning roller-coasters weren't his idea of fun.

Forgoing the speed-of-fright ride, they hurried through the German sector to the French village beyond. But found their way blocked by beaming, beer-swilling burghers in front of Das Festhaus, where free samples of Anheuser-Busch's best brews were being served as a salute to Obama's new broom.

Abby pointed out a poster on the periphery of the festive crowd. *Twelfth Lite*, it proclaimed. For one night only! Shakespeare like you've never seen before! Starting in the Globe Theatre at 8.00 p.m. "I didn't see a Globe Theatre in the English quarter, did you?"

"Must have been obscured by all that London fog," Magill riposted. "A real pea-souper, my loverly," he added in his best Dick Van Dyke.

The Curse of Der Kastle, a demonic dark ride in a mutant mock-up of mad Ludwig's Neuschwanstein – with added gothic gargoyles – loomed through the klieg lights ahead. It had started snowing again, the big backlit flakes falling like black balls of bacillus. Their breath plumed as they eased past the long Der Kastle line. It was full of foot stompers and arm flappers, trying to keep out the cold while waiting for the chills within. Before long, they were in the foothills of the Bavarian Alps, where Busch Gardens' horror-of-horrors, an upside-down roller-coaster themed around a ski lift, offered to take guests on a trip that, in panic attack terms, was second only to the north face of the Eiger.

"You know," Magill observed, "I can see why Busch and Brown were working together. Dan's stories are a perfect fit for this place. There's the Leonardo da Vinci element, the Bavarian Illuminati would feel right at home, the French village is bound to be a replica of Rennes-le-Château and there's a Best Bacon theatre in the English sector, hidden under that blanket of fog. The target market makes sense too. All the current attractions are aimed at kids and teenagers. There's nothing for their parents, except fast food and cheesy shows. A Dan Brown treasure hunt, taking in the whole park, might be a real money-spinner. Don't you think?"

"Yeah," Abby agreed, her teeth chattering, "And weather like this is perfect for *Deception Point*. That's the one in the North Pole, isn't it?"

"I can see it now," he said with a shudder, "a calving iceberg ride, one of those ones that drops like a stone."

Climbing rapidly uphill towards the Aquitaine village, they passed through an area devoted to logging and lumberjacks. French Canada, Magill noted. The crowds were much sparser in this part of the park, in keeping presumably with the untamed wilderness theme. Or perhaps it was the lack of knock-em-dead rides. The French hamlet was equally deserted, though the raucous sounds leaking from its Moulin Rougesque nightclub suggested that a suitably bowdlerized show was in progress. They walked up and down the cobbled streets in a futile search for the copycat cross. The only item of civic statuary was a fili-greed fountain, which had frozen into phantasmagorical ice sculpture, a *coup de théâtre* of twisted, tortured thermoplasticity that somehow captured the spirit of post-structuralist French philosophy. Or perhaps the free Bavarian beer was stronger than Magill realized.

They searched again, taking in the nooks and crannies and

service area side-streets. The Hendaye cross was either in storage, awaiting the publication of *The Solomon Key*, or was being put to good use in the Da Vinci's Italian Garden of Inventions, which was full of statues and stelae. They hadn't looked too closely on the first pass, distracted as they were by a raucous shoot-the-chutes dark ride, The Fall of Pompeii. "Dammit," Magill muttered, "Hidden in plain sight. I should have realized."

"What's that noise?" Abby asked, placing an arm across his chest. They stopped and listened.

"It's only Big Bad Wolf," Magill assured her.

"No, Simon, Big Bad Wolf's behind us. That noise is straight ahead." They unfolded the guidebook and stood under a cast-iron street lamp, while they worked out where they were on the map. Jack Hanna's Wild Reserve and something called Pet Shenanigans lay directly in front, just beyond a pick-up/set-down point for the elevated sky-ride.

"Jesus. It's a wolf-pack enclosure, with a bunch of bald eagles for good measure. If the cross is in there, it can stay there, because I won't be going in to check it out."

"Don't be daft, Simon. They're bound to be well-fed wolves and the eagles' talons are sure to be clipped. I'll go in, if you want."

"Let's try Leonardo's statue garden first." As the oh-la-la extravaganza was still on-going in the Royale Palace Theatre, the line at the sky-ride station was quite short. The view from the gondolas was spectacular by night. The snow-draped trees, bushes and flowerbeds, the ice-locked River Rhine, the whizzing, whirling, spiralling, corkscrewing roller-coasters, all brightly illuminated, the swaying, shouting, sing-along, half-cut crowds of Obama lovers congregating in Festhaus Platz, where an oompah-oompah band was going at it hammer and tongs, were visible from their elevated perch. It was a truly amazing sight.

Their sky-ride was a waste of time, however. The Italian garden was stuffed with statues. Roman columns and carved pediments filled every available vista. There was even a mock-up of the Sforza Horse, Leonardo's legendary equestrian statue that failed to come to fruition. But here was nothing that looked like the Great Cyclic Cross of Hendaye.

"The wolf-pack it is, then."

"Don't be such a wuss, Simon. I'll do the needful. Wild animals are nothing to be afraid of. It could be a lot worse than wolves."

"There are evil eagles too," Magill cautioned.

Abby couldn't help herself. While he was distracted by the sight of the Sforza Horse, which was mounted by an armoured knight with fiercely pointed lance, she ran her fingers up his back and sank a pretend set of talons into his unprotected neck. He leapt even higher than the leprechauness had done earlier. "Never fear, Simon. I'll sort the eagles out as well." She flapped her wings and eek, eek, eeked as they wandered back towards the skylon, attracting amused looks from merry passers-by. *Twelfth Lite* was about to start. Excited crowds were milling around outside the Globe Theatre, a huge structure immediately adjacent to the main entrance, easy to overlook in the hustle and bustle.

Magill read the attraction synopsis in his guidebook. Busch Gardens' Globe Theatre was twice as big as the original, thus bizarrely counterbalancing their one-third size Big Ben. "Maybe we should check out the show," he said. "Francis Bacon wrote Shakespeare, after all. *The Solomon Key* is built on a Francis Bacon foundation. The wolves can wait, Abby. It'll be quieter later on. They might be asleep."

"If Shakespeare doesn't send us to sleep first," she said beneath her breath.

Abby needn't have worried. The production was incredible. Although the programme went to great lengths to explain the potted plot of *Twelfth Night*, and although it was at pains to explain the symbolic significance of Twelfth Night, a traditional time of carnivalesque inversion, where kings become commoners and commoners kings, and although it played fast and loose with Shakespeare/Bacon's original, the elaborate explanation was unnecessary. The play's meaning was self-evident. It was set in a semi-mystical land, The White House, where a bumbling king and scheming courtiers got caught up in a series of unfortunate events that sowed the seeds of confusion, involved unconscionable acts of torture and threatened the very stability of the state. However, it turned out all right in the end when Viola/

Condoleezza, a statuesque African-American, was shown to be Sebastian/Obama too. The allegory wasn't exactly subtle, but it was just what the doctor ordered.

Better yet, the company's adaptation of the source material didn't stop at George W. Bush baiting. Channelling Sir Toby Belch through Oliver Hardy, Malvolio through W. C. Fields, Orsinio through Charlie Chaplin, Olivia through Marilyn Monroe and, best of all, Viola/Sebastian via Mae West was pretty close to genius. Every line was milked for double-entendres, single entendres and bare-faced cheek. Those that weren't milked were replaced with product placements for Anheuser Busch: If Budweiser be the food of love, sip on. I am a great eater of beef but I prefer a brewski. Many a good Bud prevents a bad marriage. My purpose is, indeed, a horse of the Clydesdale colour. I'll be revenged on the whole six-pack of you.

All in all, the production was little short of brilliant. The show-stopper, however, came in Act 2, Scene 1, when Olivia met Viola in the Rose Garden of the White House. The Washington Monument was clearly visible in the background. Except that it wasn't the Washington Monument. It was the cross of Hendaye, with a false cap to make it look more obelisk-ish. Abby excitedly nudged her co-conspirator. "I see it, I see it," he said, before being ssshhhed into silence by the rapt audience, which was a bit rich since most of them chomped popcorn throughout and the groundlings of Shakespeare's day weren't exactly tongue-tied when it came to passing judgement on performances. "Shame about the wolf-pack," he whispered with a smile.

"Now is the woodcock near the gin."

Sssssshhhhhhh.

Chapter Forty-Five

Pump It Up

The performance ended to tumultuous applause. Curtain calls, bouquets of flowers, thank-you-thank-you-thank-you speeches from the stage, toasts to the incoming president and raspberries for the outgoing, went on for much longer than was strictly necessary. By the end, the audience was applauding itself for its perspicacity, presence of mind and the fact that it had chosen to attend something worthwhile rather than veg out on the couch in front of the football.

The evening wasn't over, however. A firework display was scheduled for midnight, a firework display that was apocalyptic in its intensity, or promised to be. As the crowds gathered in Parliament Square, waiting for the pyrotechnics to begin, Abby and Magill slipped down the side of the Globe Theatre to the stage door. The clasp of Abby's brooch proved its worth once again, as Magill picked his way into the vast wooden structure. A steep flight of steps wound upwards through the gloom. The lights were off but their passage was eased by voices ahead. Post-performance euphoria was still coursing through the players. The whoops and huzzas and who's-the-daddies echoed down the stairwell. They crept past the communal dressing room, all mirrors and bulbs and clinking glasses and smells of greasepaint and sweat, to the backstage area. Props were scattered hither and yon – the Oval Office desk, among them – but the Hendaye Cross was nowhere to be seen.

"Must be beneath the stage," Magill murmured. "On a hydraulic platform of some kind."

Abby pointed. "No, there it is over there." An obelisk-like structure could just be discerned in the dark. A midden of ropes and pulleys and lighting rigs and scenery flats lay in front of them. They stepped gingerly through the *Twelfth Lite* tip, trying to be as quiet as possible. "It's about half-size, by my reckoning," Abby said, running her hands across the smooth limestone surface. "Though it's a lot less heavily weathered than the original."

"What about the secret compartment?"

Abby felt for the eye inside the crescent moon on one face of the podium, while Magill positioned himself in front of the grimacing sun symbol. He placed his thumbs in the eye sockets, as per Dan Brown's thriller. "Okay," she said, "push on my say-so. Three, two, one. Push."

In the novel, Robert Langdon and Harriet Callaghan accessed a secret compartment, which contained an ancient coded scroll. When decoded, it provided clues to the whereabouts of Bacon's treasure trove. However, the real replica had no such hideaway. They pushed and pressed several times and felt carefully for the slightest evidence of a hollow cleft.

"He must have made that bit up," Magill sighed.

Abby swore. "So much for his Author's Note! What was it again? References to all works of art, tombs, tunnels and architecture are entirely factual."

"Well, in fairness to the guy, the replica cross *does* exist and therefore it's entirely factual. He's just embellished it a bit."

"A bit."

Magill stepped back and looked up and down the apocalyptic object. "Is this an exact replica, Abby? Can you see any differences between this one and the original? They might be important."

"Hold on," she said, pulling an iPhone from her coat pocket. She flicked through the images at speed, skimming past her grisly copies of the murder victim snaps. Then stopped dead. "I've just noticed something."

"So there is a difference. Excellent."

"No, Simon. It's not that. The photos of Dan's fans. The jpegs had tags on them. Cruel labels that mocked the dead. Can you remember what they were?"

Like a flash of theatrical lightning, illumination suddenly arrived. "Of course," Magill groaned, annoyed by his obtuseness. "Come up and kill me sometime. On the whole, I'd rather slay in Philadelphia. Here's another fine mess you've got me into. We've been following the clues in Dan's book, Abby. Instead of our own trail of evidence. Let's go."

"Hope we're not too late."

Convinced that they'd bypassed the culprits in their haste to see the Cross of Hendaye, they hurried back to the dressing rooms, clattering and banging and stumbling over hotchpotch props. They never got there. Charlie Chaplin stood at the end of the passageway, blocking the path. Still in silent-movie character, he said nothing. He didn't need to. His Ruger Redhawk did all the talking. He waved the revolver towards the stairwell. Abby and her companion took the hint and did as they were bid.

"Ah, Mr Magill, Ms Maguire, we meet at last." For a curmudgeon, W. C. Fields looked awfully pleased with himself. "Sit yourselves down and make yourselves uncomfortable." Shoved from behind by the Little Tramp, they took a seat at the read-through table in the centre of the dressing room. Mae West, Marilyn Monroe and Oliver Hardy looked over as one, appraising the newcomers. The scene was decidedly surreal, albeit apt in the circumstances.

In any other circumstances, Magill would've been delighted to make Marilyn Monroe's acquaintance. Despite the look of confusion on her face, she was exquisite. Even more so when she removed her wig to reveal a shock of striking auburn hair. "I'm Assumpta," she said, shaking Simon's hand. "Assumpta Lynch." Magill felt a tingle of electricity run through his fingers. He was smitten. But not for long, as Monroe and Hardy were ushered out by the more senior cast members, with much mwahing and air kissing and catch you later at O'Houlihan's. We have business to attend to.

The atmosphere was much less jovial without Oliver and Marilyn. The flat-panel monitors flickered into life, as Chaplin brought up the crime scene photographs that had driven Dan to the brink of madness. They looked even more gruesome on the big screen, a slide show of serial killer slaughter.

Magill was lost for words. "Who? Why? How do you know our names?"

"Haven't you worked it out yet?" Fields said gruffly. "We're the NSA."

"The National Security Agency?" Abby inferred. "You did all this just because Dan Brown held your organization up to a little bit of ridicule?"

With brazen aplomb, Mae West pulled a cheroot from one frilly garter and a Zippo lighter from the other. Arching her eyebrows at Abby – like what you see, sister? – she lit up with a flourish. "We're not the National Security Agency. We're New Serendipity Associates." Abby was none the wiser.

"Barton Brady's old outfit?" Magill asked.

"Precisely," Fields drawled, "formerly the finest management consultants west of the Pecos. A company effectively killed off by you and your friends in P4, the secret marketing society headed by Dan Brown. The pair of you also deep-sixed our colleague Yasmin Buonarroti. Without our front man and our driving force, we were left in the lurch."

Magill tried to protest his innocence. But Fields wasn't one to be interrupted in full flow.

"Chang and Eng here are creative geniuses," the misanthrope went on, with a smile at his colleagues, "and I'm pretty good at collecting debts," he sniffed, then blew gently on his knuckles before rubbing them against his lapel. "But without Barton and Yasmin we had nowhere to go. And when we were offered the chance to exact our revenge on the people who'd got us into this mess, we seized it with all six hands."

Magill couldn't believe what he was hearing. "Barton Brady was my friend," he shouted. "I had nothing to do with his death. He was killed by Wee Joe… Dannyboy… or whatever his code name was. Brady was killed by the very man you hired to do your wet work!" Furious, he pointed at the corpse-filled screens, as if that would prove his point. Fields remained impassive. He extracted a Smith and Wesson 1006 from his jacket pocket and placed it in front of him on the dressing room table. "Dan Brown is not part of P4," Magill continued, in as calm a voice as he could manage. "Yasmin Buonarroti shot *herself*. We had nothing to do with it."

West exhaled. A fug of smelly cheroot smoke filled the smoking-prohibited dressing room. "That's not what Big C said to us."

"And when Big C says something," Chaplin carried on, "its accuracy goes without saying."

Taken aback by the latest twist, Abby joined Magill in a fug of disbelief. "Tom Clancy? You're part of the Clancy Corps? Clancy denied all knowledge of the murders. Didn't he, Simon? Clancy said he was being set up too. Isn't that right?"

"Clancy isn't the Big C," Fields guffawed. "He was just a patsy, a hate figure for Brown to focus on and obsess about. We sent Clancy's abusive emails to Brown and Brown's to Clancy. If Dan believed that a jealous rival was behind the vendetta, he'd never put two and two together to work out who really bore him a grudge and was determined to settle the score."

"I was quite pleased with that touch," Chaplin boasted. "Though Mr Rosencreutz here was the brains behind it all," he added deferentially. Fields/Rosencreutz nodded in modest acknowledgement.

"Well," Magill said, "if Tom Clancy isn't the Big C, who is? Who are you taking your orders from?"

West drew and drawled. "Big C's not a he." She paused for effect, as any actor would. "Nor even a she," she added, cognizant of the tension-ramping power of a lull in the proceedings. "It's an it."

"An it?" Abby echoed.

Determined to get his oar in, Charlie Chaplin duly delivered the punchline. "CIA, of course. The Big C is the CIA. We work for the CIA. Everyone in this place works for the CIA. The Farm is just up the road. Spies are actors, basically. They pretend for a living. Busch Gardens is a training facility, as is Colonial Williamsburg. The Rockefeller Foundation has been a CIA front for decades. This land was sold to Anheuser Busch by the Rockefellers. It's been a real money-spinner for The Company, as we call it. NSA is CIA, once removed."

"Only the CIA," Fields acknowledged, "has the resources to mount an operation like this. The fact that we exact retribution on the people who ruined Serendipity Associates is a bonus, really."

A terrier, Abby wouldn't let go. "But why does the CIA work though you and what does the CIA have against Dan Brown?"

Mae West shook her head, astonished at the ignorance of the younger generation. "The CIA always works through front organizations. Guatemala, Iran, Vietnam, Ecuador – wherever the CIA operates, you'll find a front. They provide the plausible deniability that the Company demands. The CIA was set up by Yalies and, to this very day, is dominated by the East Coast elite. Barton Brady was a Yale man, a member of Scroll & Key no less. All his connections, all his successes, we now realize, were down to the Scroll & Key network, plus of course his training in the liberal arts. The CIA is full of liberal arts types, as is the British Secret Service. Why do you think so many spooks write novels? Ian Fleming, John le Carré, Somerset Maugham, Grahame Greene, Compton MacKenzie, Cord Meyer, E. Howard Hunt. The CIA is a hive of poet-spies, the last refuge of the western liberal tradition. The CIA is the Ivy League writ large. The CIA was behind Serendipity Associates from the outset, though we only learned about the connection after the passing of Brady and Buonarroti. And when they made us an offer we couldn't refuse."

"You used to be snow white and then you drifted," Abby observed with distaste.

"I used to be coal dust, sister," the statuesque African-American replied cattily.

Magill cut them off. "You still haven't told us what the CIA has against Dan Brown."

Casually checking MySpace while the others declaimed, Chaplin chimed in. "You mean, apart from his diabolical novels and unspeakable prose, plus the fact that he eliminated one of the Company's key commercial assets. I'd've thought that was reason enough."

"Dan had nothing to do with the death of Barton Brady! Any semi-competent investigation would've revealed that fact. There are a lot worse writers out there than Dan, if it's the state of the western canon they're worried about."

Fields stroked his chin thoughtfully, as if trying to tot up the extent of Dan Brown's literary shortcomings. "You appear to have forgotten that *The Solomon Key* makes mock of the CIA and there are scattered critiques throughout his body of work."

"Driving him mad," Abby interrupted, "seems like a harsh penalty."

With a resigned sigh, Fields picked up his Smith and Wesson

and pointed it towards Simon Magill and his nagging sidekick. "Don't fuck with the Farm. Let that be a lesson to you."

"Thank you for that," Magill said. "Can we go now?"

West stubbed out her cheroot, then flicked a do-it-now glance at her co-star. "Fraid not," she said. "We can't have you spilling your guts about us."

"So we're spilling *your* guts," Chaplin chipped in with a smirk.

"Let Abby go," Magill said gallantly. "She's nothing to do with this. She has no connection to the Danster. I dragged her into my mystery, against her better judgement."

Shrugging regretfully, Fields screwed a silencer on to his weapon. "She's here, isn't she? Dan's fans got whacked because they were in the wrong place at the wrong time. Ms Maguire is no different." He cocked his Smith and Wesson and took aim at Abby's forehead. As if on cue, the fireworks display started outside, booming, banging and crackling with cascading menace. He looked at the silencer as if minded to remove it, now that another source of gunshot suppression was available.

"Not so fast, fucker."

Fields's jaw dropped. His eyes popped. He looked as though he'd seen Banquo's Ghost. In a way he had, though it was closer to Hamlet's worst nightmare. Dan Brown and Tom Clancy stood at the doorway, packing pump-action shotguns, with menace aforethought.

"Place your piece on the table and move away from the weapon." Dan chambered a round and shouldered his Winchester M12. He was locked, loaded and ready to let fly. Fields raised his arms and with a display of submission prepared to set his silenced shooter on the table. He did so, to everyone's relief, since a fire-fight at such close quarters would be a bloodbath worthy of the Bard himself.

They sighed too soon. Fields upended the read-through table with an almighty crash. An acknowledged sharpshooter, Clancy loosed a couple of rounds. The heavy mahogany table took the hit and shattered in an eruption of splinters. When the gunsmoke dispersed, Fields was nowhere to be seen. A back door lay ajar. Without further ado, Magill ran after him.

Chapter Forty-Six

Top of the Globe, Ma

Arms pumping, legs driving, Magill hurtled up the narrow stair-case, as it curled ever higher around the circumference of the supersized Globe Theatre. He could hear Fields galloping ahead of him, his leaden footfalls reverberating throughout the wooden structure. The noise suddenly stopped and, fearful of an ambush at the top of the stairwell, he slowed down, inching round the uppermost bend. A trapdoor to the roof lay open. Magill clam-bered up the little ladder and poked his head above the parapet, expecting to fend off a surprise attack. There was no sign of an assailant. Only a dark blur, picking its way around the outer edge of the theatre on a flat and decidedly uninviting wooden walkway. To the left lay an 80-foot drop into Parliament Square beneath, with impalement on Big Ben a very real possibility. To the right, the sloping inner roof of the theatre angled away steeply towards an open air-well in the middle, akin to the Eliza-bethan original. The plunge to the stage was less than 50 feet but more than enough to make a mess on the apron.

As the fireworks exploded overhead, casting occasional flashes of illumination on the nerve-jangling scene, Magill was faced with a choice. He could either inch his way round the perimeter, hoping to avoid an impromptu plunge, or make a dash for the fleeing thespian, who was already at the far side of the hexagonal edifice, searching for another stairwell to safety. Alternatively, he could go back the way he came.

After PWC, there was no decision to make. Fortune favours the brave. Magill ran as fast as he could, skidded on an icy patch but somehow kept his balance, albeit not without a glimpse of the fate that awaited. Fifteen more strides and he was on him, since Fields was of the safety-first persuasion. Magill's momen-tum was its own downfall, however. Fields flung back an elbow just as Magill was about to grab hold. It caught him full in the face and, before he realized what was happening, he was tumbling down the angled roof of the theatre, bouncing towards the pit in the middle.

As he shot over the edge, Magill threw out an arm and managed to grab the guttering that protected the groundlings from rainwater run-off. The gutter came away in his hand, section after section, like the poppers on a full-metal bodice. The racket was ear shattering, but Magill somehow held on as his momentum carried him to a cast-iron drainpipe. He grabbed hold and, with the briefest of glances at the orchestra pit beneath, scurried up the downpipe as the dislodged guttering hit the stage with a heart-stopping crash. He hoisted himself back over the lip and scampered across the tiled roof, which clattered and shattered beneath him. Fields was tugging frantically at a trapdoor, the equal and opposite access route to the one they'd come through. It wouldn't budge.

Magill was closing in on him as he angled across the precarious rooftop. Fields looked round, then made a decision. He took a couple of deep breaths and started running along the perimeter walkway, getting faster and faster and faster. He launched himself off the roof with a mighty leap and grabbed at a passing Skytrain gondola. He missed. But, miraculously, caught hold of a decorative metal runner attached to the bottom of the bright yellow pod. Such was his momentum that the entire capsule swung alarmingly upwards, as if it were a giant trapeze. The stressed ride groaned alarmingly, though few onlookers seemed to notice as the booming fireworks display continued unabated on the far side of the building.

The next pod was coming into view. Magill eyed it carefully, trying to assess its speed and tracking. Mind made up, he charged down the rickety wooden runway, huge Ulster overcoat flapping behind him. He looked like Batman. He hurled himself into space. He missed the runner. He'd jumped too soon. He crashed on top of the gondola. If it weren't for a frantic grab at the umbilical arm that attached the car to the cable, he'd have overshot his objective completely and plunged head first into a red telephone box. As it was, he clung desperately to the stanchion, legs flailing over the edge, scrabbling for purchase on the pod's domed canopy.

Eventually, he staggered to his feet. The gondola swayed beneath him, whining for all it was worth. As it inched over the all-but deserted theme park – everyone, it seemed, had crowded into the English/Scottish/Irish zone for a hilltop view of the fireworks display – Magill could just make out a burly figure beneath the cabin ahead. Fields appeared to be holding on quite comfortably, refusing to take the risk of clambering into the cabin, waiting for a suitable spot to drop to safety. That spot might be some way away. The ground fell steeply towards the River Rhine, which was frozen solid. Magill tried not to think what would happen if anyone crashed through that.

Once again, the pursuer had a choice. Either to wait it out, watch for a falling figure then follow suit. Or make something happen by shaking his prey from its perch. Fields's gondola was about 30 feet ahead. Magill knew from his workouts on the PWC assault course that he could manage hand-over-hand along a 30-foot cable, though there was a world of difference between daytime exercises on a bone dry rope in southern California, where the worst case scenario was a 12-foot fall into a muddy pond, and a night-time sortie along an oily cable in freezing Virginia, where the worst case scenario was a 50-foot fall on to a cobbled re-creation of an Aquitaine village square.

In for a penny. Magill knew that movement was paramount when arm over arm was attempted. Momentum was all. Hesitation meant death. He launched himself down the cable, which throbbed under his hands. He hadn't anticipated the vibration from the drive mechanism, which threatened to shake him off. He kept going as quickly as he could, trying to keep some swing in his hips as he worked his way rapidly along, hand over hand, breathing steady as she goes. He overreached at one point. His hand slipped. He was holding on for bare life, one-handed, legs thrashing wildly as the Skylon passed over the Clydesdale stables. He prayed the bald eagles were tucked away for the night.

With a sudden twist of the torso, Magill managed to wrap his free hand around the cable once again, then continued his progress, trying to regain the impetus that was lost. He was within 8 feet of the cable car when it suddenly bounced as Fields let go. He had no idea whether his quarry had relinquished his grip through choice, on account of a possible soft landing, or whether holding on with hands growing colder and colder finally proved too much. He didn't have time to reflect on the conundrum, because the bounce shook him loose. Magill plummeted down, his overcoat flapping above his head like a parachute that hadn't opened properly.

The ground he hit wasn't solid, thankfully. But it was moving. He'd landed on the cowcatcher of Runaway Train, a high-speed roller-coaster which hurtled unchecked down a precipitous polypropylene mountainside, through passes, along tunnels, via ravines. Groggily, he raised his head and looked towards the caboose. Fields was in a carriage at the far end, looking equally dazed and confused. Magill clambered past the replica engine and on to the lead wagon just as the roller-coaster click-clacked to the top of its chain. It paused dramatically at the apex of the first drop, then tore downwards, twisting, turning, thundering like there was no tomorrow.

Magill ignored the tumult as he worked his way back towards the thespian, wagon by wagon. He had no idea of what lay behind him, as the runaway train surged and swayed and swung up on its side at very steep angles. Praying that there wasn't a loop the loop or even an Immelmann turn – since every other ride in the park seemed to contain one or two – he managed to get to within a few carriages of Fields. The look of glee on the grumpy comedian's face was a warning and he ducked down as fast as he could, narrowly avoiding the low-roofed entrance to a tunnel, which would have decapitated him otherwise.

When he raised his head again there was no sign of his quarry. It was too late, however, as the train barrelled into its final tight turn and dropped into a watersplash beneath. Magill glanced upwards, back the way he came. The climax of the firework display lit up the sky with an almighty crash. A shadowy figure was working his way down the railroad track, just above the penultimate bend, heading for an enormous support pillar with a maintenance platform and a ladder down the outside.

Magill jumped off the back of the caboose. One foot plunged

into the freezing water, but the other got purchase on the railway track, which ascended steeply to the gantry above. He sprinted up the track, from sleeper to sleeper. It was like running upstairs, only with no risers and an ever-steeper fall if a foot should slip. Running upstairs is a lot faster than picking one's way downstairs and Magill closed rapidly on Fields, though the curmudgeon got to the platform before him. Simon looked up at his target ahead, only to see him take aim with his Smith and Wesson. How the hell did he get hold of that, Magill swore, as he flung himself to the trackbed, what little there was. Two shots rang out, both missing wildly. No silencer. Must be a different weapon. He could hear Fields breathing heavily, as he steadied himself for a third pop. Tired. Exhausted. Can't hold the gun steady. Magill's training kicked in. He dashed for the derrick, dodging from one side of the track to the other, thereby denying his target a straight shot. The inky darkness in the aftermath of the fireworks display also helped, albeit the squelching of his left boot, sodden from the watersplash, was a bit of a giveaway. A shell winged him in the right shoulder, but by then Magill was upon him. Head down, he wrapped his arms around the big man's waist and slammed him back against the protective steel railings around the minuscule maintenance platform. Fields pounded on his back with the butt of his weapon, attempting to break Magill's hold. Such was the thickness of his Ulster overcoat that the pummelling had little effect. Magill heaved with all his might, trying to hurl the sonofa over the side. But despite his size and weight and the impact of Magill's charge, the metal railings held firm, though the weapon fell from his grasp. It clattered on to the platform. Magill dropped to grab hold of it but Fields kicked out at the revolver. It slithered over the lip, glittering in the moonlight as it tumbled into the Nature Reserve beneath.

With Magill at his feet, Fields stamped on the Englishman's back. Then stomped again. And again. Magill seized his assailant's standing ankle and pulled. Fields crashed to the floor of the platform, which groaned and shook ominously. Magill punched him in the face, then grabbed the lapels of his topcoat and bashed the back of his head against the steelwork. He got a knee in the crotch for his trouble, followed by a ferocious wallop on his wounded shoulder. The pain was excruciating. His injured side was killing him too. Fields seized his advantage. He pinned Magill down, using his not inconsiderable bulk to keep him in check, then placed one knee on each arm, holding him steady for the *coup de grâce*.

But Magill had been trained for this kind of situation. As instructed in unarmed combat, he kicked out with both legs as hard as he could, while raising his hips and thrusting simultaneously. It worked. Fields was not only thrown off but almost over the edge of the platform. Magill planted the sole of his boot on the bruiser's sizable butt and shoved with all his might. He shot off the derrick with a despairing yell.

Still shaking, Magill got feebly to his feet. He looked over the edge with relief. There was no sign of a broken body in the snow-blanketed wasteland below. A hairy hand grabbed his ankle and yanked. Fields had been hanging under the platform, as he'd done earlier on the gondola. Magill had relaxed too soon. He cursed himself bitterly as he dropped at high speed towards the rock-strewn terrain, 50 feet beneath the Runaway Train track.

Chapter Forty-Seven

Dantánamo Bay

"Do I know you?" Dan Brown said, pointing his Winchester at Abby.

"I'll discuss it," she retorted, "when you stop waving your willy at me."

Hesitantly, he lowered his shotgun and looked querulously at his captive. "I've seen you before somewhere."

"Let's just keep our hands up, shall we?" Clancy announced, "while we work out what's what. You two," he commanded West and Chaplin, "up against the wall, arms spread, legs apart." This was an obvious opportunity for a whiplash one-liner straight from the movie star's sassy repertoire of gold-digger zingers. But Mae West kept quiet, obviously taken aback by the sudden explosion of high velocity violence and the equally sudden disappearance of NSA's major domo. The clomping of Fields and his pursuer reverberated throughout the immemorial wooden O, double-sized in every loving detail.

Charlie Chaplin stayed silent, too.

"And why don't you lower your voice, Mr Clancy. You're not in the military now. Put down your popgun then we can talk." Abby folded her arms defiantly, though she'd be the first to admit that the prim pose looked odd, when surrounded by the bullet-ridden wreckage of a mahogany table, plus one or two smouldering flat-screen monitors that got caught up in the firestorm. The dressing room looked more like *Good Morning Vietnam* than *Goodbye to Berlin.*

Clancy ignored her. He highfived the Danster. "Didn't I tell you packin' heat is more fun than a barrelful of monkey-wrenches? We should do this more often, Dan my man."

The author of *Angels and Demons* didn't look quite so excited as his companion. On the contrary, he looked as though he'd

343

really rather be in the Widener Library at Harvard, perusing ancient manuscripts, cracking cryptic codes and wrestling with symbological mysteries. Dan's mucho-macho technothriller days were a distant memory. Or so it seemed to Abby. He came across as a fundamentally decent guy who got lucky and still hadn't quite come to terms with his good fortune. "You're looking a lot better than you did in Dublin," she said, smiling sweetly at the former invalid.

"Ah, of course, Dublin. That's where I've seen you before. Those beautiful Irish features are a dead give-away," he added chivalrously.

"Bono's been taking good care of you then?"

"Well, Ali really. She's a wonderful nurse. A real Florence Nightingale. The Mother Teresa of rock 'n' roll."

Abby laughed. "You'll be asking why she gave it all up to marry a multi-millionaire. Bono was too busy saving the world, I take it?"

Clancy took umbrage at Abby's disrespectful remark. He ticked her off for taking Bono's name in vain. If it weren't for Irishmen like him, the world would be a lot worse off, overrun with pinkos, terrorists and Taliban fellow travellers. Abu Ghraib was too good for them. Guantánamo Bay's fine by him. Obama's a wuss who'll set the country back decades. Where's Ronnie Reagan when you need him. Now, Ronnie was a proper Irishman...

The Danster rolled his eyes. He didn't need to say anything. Convalescing beggars can't be choosers.

"How did you get here so quickly, Dan?"

The recuperating writer didn't have a chance to answer. Clancy leapt in, evidently energized by the earlier exchange of fire. "Well, little lady," he said, "as a long-time admirer of Dan's writing, I know Langdon likes nothing more than taking trips on supersonic aircraft, the faster the better. So I called in a few favours. I've still got some clout in military circles." He clapped Dan on the shoulder. "The F-22 twin-seater Raptor's some baby. Bet you're glad to be home, pal."

"Glad to be home in one piece, Tom."

Roaring with laughter, the fatigues-wearing bear wrapped a

big arm round his little friend's shoulder. "Yeah, well, the Raptor ride isn't the smoothest. But by God that baby kicks butt. Make sure you mention it in your next novel. One hundred per cent American technology. Yes, sir. Best on the motherfuckin' planet."

"The R&D overspend," Dan whispered to Abby, "almost beggars belief. The X-Mantra, its high-spec variant was abandoned because of budget overruns and congressional pork barrelling."

Abby had nothing to add, since the nuances of boys' toys were of no interest to her. The secrets of Coco Chanel's atelier she could handle, or even Balenciaga's theories of bias-cut evening dresses, but once muzzle velocities and thrust vectors and heads-up displays worked their way into the conversation, she worked her way out. She watched as Clancy frisked Chaplin and West, no doubt regretting he'd left his water-board at home. She could see that Dan was drawn to the surviving computer monitors, where the unspeakable snaps of his victims were still on display. She could also see the colour draining from his face, as the horror hit home once more. "Dan," she murmured, "Dan."

He turned to her, ashen.

"It's okay, Dan. We worked out what happened. These people were acting on CIA orders. They had access to your *Solomon Key* manuscript. They hired a hitman to kill people according to your fictional specifications. They tracked your movements. They were trying to tip you over the edge, same as they did to Castro back in the 1960s. They wanted you to confess to something you hadn't done and thereby destroy your reputation."

"Why didn't they just kill me," Brown croaked, overcome by emotion. "I'd rather they killed me than murder innocent people, people who just happened to like what I've written."

Brusquely, Mae West put him right. "Because death would only have increased your popularity. Death's a canny move in the cultural industries. Heath Ledger's gonna win an Oscar for his overacting in *Batman Returns*. And why? Because he's dead. The careers of James Dean, Jean Harlow, Janis Joplin, John Keats, Mozart and many more got a boost when they died prematurely. Your passing was no good to us. We set out to kill your reputation instead."

345

"But how..." Brown continued, struggling to maintain a modicum of composure. "But how did you get hold of my manuscript? No one's seen *The Solomon Key*. Not Simon. Not my wife. Not my editor. Nobody. Nobody. Nobody, I tell you."

Dan was getting hysterical. A relapse was imminent. His furlough from Fort Madness was coming to an end.

Livid, Clancy looked as though he was about to pistol-whip Mae West, for having the temerity to tip his new best friend back over the edge. But his gentlemanly instincts, vestigial though they were in the aftermath of an adrenaline-surge shoot-out, carried the day. He wrapped an ursine arm around his literary mini-me and steered him into an undamaged chair, which he picked up and positioned with one hand. Clancy hunkered down in front of the stricken author. "It's Stargate, Dan."

Abby didn't know what he was babbling about, nor did Brown by the look on his face. "Stargate?" he echoed hollowly.

Practically perspiring for-your-eyes-only insider information, Clancy launched into a lengthy explanation. "I don't know if you've read my multi-million selling debut novel, *The Hunt for Red October*, but it was about a Typhoon-class Russian submarine. Our knowledge of the Typhoon class owes everything to Stargate. Stargate also helped pinpoint Russian TV22 spyplanes that crashed in the depths of the African jungle. It located hostages in Lebanon and Iran. It helped with the hunt for Carlos the Jackal. It identified a misfiring nuclear missile in an underground Chinese bunker. It even spotted our own Stealth bombers when they were being developed in top, top secret. Stargate was awesome – is awesome, I should say – and it's based right down the road from here in Fort Meade, the Farm."

Abby was none the wiser. Dan didn't look enlightened either. Even Chaplin and West were lost. Abby could see them exchanging bemused expressions.

"Stargate," Clancy continued, "is a branch of psyops that focuses on paranormal activity – telepathy, clairvoyance, precognition, psychokinesis. The initial aim was to control the human mind from afar and likewise watch what people were doing, at a distance. Remote viewing that was called. Remote viewers helped find MIA prisoners being held in Vietnam. They successfully predicted an Iranian rocket attack on the USS *Starke*. They located General William Dozier when he was kidnapped by the Italian Red Brigade. Reading someone's hard disk drive is child's play to a remote viewer. Hell, they could probably move the files around and purge your desktop trashcan, if they put their minds to it."

Try as she might, and notwithstanding her training in guerrilla psychology, Abby couldn't keep her scepticism in check. She didn't exactly say tell us another one, Tom, much less pull the other leg, it's got bells and whistles on it. But she may as well have done.

Clancy sensed her mood and raised his hands in apologetic surrender. "Yeah, I know. I know. Stargate sounds completely crazy. Officially the operation was closed down in 1995, not because it was unsuccessful – if anything it was too successful – but because of the giggle factor. Joe Public simply wouldn't accept it. Stargate was beyond the bounds of scientific possibility, even though it produced very real results. The Company was concerned that remote viewing might give the wrong impression – namely, that the CIA was filled with kooks, crazies and crackpots, which of course it was. MK Ultra, the LSD debacle and the attempts to kill Castro with poisoned cigars were rock solid proof of that. Ironically, Stargate was one of the CIA's most benign programmes. Nobody died. No governments were overthrown. No assassination operations were mounted. No dirty deals were done with dictators or criminals or drug traffickers or arms dealers or rogue regimes, who consider democracy a dirty word."

As Clancy was obviously winding himself up to the sort of distended dilation only found in Dan Brown novels, Abby prudently intervened. "Stargate was killed off for PR purposes. Is that what you're saying?"

"Pretty much," Clancy replied curtly, clearly annoyed that he couldn't go on and on and on. The doyen of 900-page blockbusters, as well as a raconteur first class, Tom Clancy wasn't used to being cut off when on a rhetorical roll. Grumpily, he scrutinized his Winchester M12, checking that a shell was in the breech, that the safety catch was on and that he was ready to rumble if need be. Hell, if a remote viewer had turned up unbidden, he'd've been blown away on the spot.

Abby threw him a bone. "But you reckon Stargate's still going, even though the programme was halted in the mid-1990s. It certainly seems suited for today's virtual world, where remote viewing via the World Wide Web seems second nature."

"Why don't you ask them?" Clancy groused, gesturing towards the captives, who still stood uncomfortably splayed against the dressing room wall.

"Okay, I'll do that. Tell us about Stargate, guys."

"Only if we stop this interrogation charade." Chaplin took his hands off the wall and straightened up.

Abby stared expectantly at Clancy. He assented, albeit with reluctance. The prisoners took a seat. West perched in front of a makeup mirror, checking her pancake. Chaplin sat in a swivel chair by the monitors, rubbing his aching wrists and flexing his leaden legs. "I don't know anything about Stargate," the Chinese-American confessed. "We were told it was an unprotected data pen. Dan delivered a speech at some book camp in California and picked up a little Trojan for his trouble. His laptop's been under scrutiny ever since. It was done before our time. We just followed orders. We're the monkeys here, not the organ grinder."

"Who's the organ grinder?" Dan asked with surprising vehemence.

"We already told you," West answered curtly. "The CIA. The Company. The likely lads at Langley."

Rebooted by the prisoners' prevarication, Clancy cut through the crap. "Who's your contact? Every operative has a contact, every field agent a handler. Who's your handler?"

Chaplin exhaled slowly. "We can't tell you that. It's more than our life's worth."

"We'll goddamn see about that," Clancy bellowed, whipping a monstrous .44 Magnum out of his hip-slung holster and cocking the elephantine weapon with a blood-curdling click. "Speak now, Charlie, or I'll forever hold my piece against your forehead. Forever being the next five seconds. Five… four… three…"

Chapter Forty-Eight

Da Vinci Cored

If, as legend has it, life passes in front of you as death approaches, then Simon Magill must have led a very sheltered life. As he plunged earthwards from the platform, while his assailant clambered down the access ladder and thus to safety, the Englishman thought about Dan Brown. Not the great man himself, though Magill had been enormously fortunate in that regard. Being mentored by a literary giant is a privilege extended to very few budding writers. True, it ended badly in Sydney, but Simon had benefited enormously from the experience.

Magill, rather, was filled with memories of Dan Brown's second book, *Angels and Demons*. In chapter seven of Robert Langdon's first outing, the Harvard symbologist sees CERN's Free Fall Tube, a vertical wind tunnel whose powerful updraughts keep people afloat as if weightless. A form of stress relief for CERN's overworked scientists, the Free Fall Tube provides Langdon with a vital piece of information that saves his life later on. He is told that something as small as one square yard of drag can slow a falling body by 20 per cent. When he plummets from a fleeing helicopter at the story's climax, Langdon is saved by a sheet of tarpaulin, which arrests his three-mile fall into the rushing River Tiber. Phew!

Trusting that the Danster's research was legit – an heroic assumption, admittedly – Magill held open his heavy Ulster overcoat as he fell. He spread his arms like a flasher and gripped for grim death as the wind whipped past. The bottom half of his coat flapped uselessly but the bit above the belt slowed him fractionally.

It was the snowdrift that saved his life, though. Arms and legs outspread, he whoomped into a deep drift, close to the edge of the Wild Reserve, beneath a dark stand of pine trees which had deposited their snow loads in a sizable accumulation. Like a huge pillow, the powdery snow broke his fall. The hole he carved for himself was not unlike those in Hanna-Barbera cartoons, where the spread-eagled shape of the falling object is sculpted into the surface of the ground cover, be it mud or concrete. Unlike Roadrunner or Wily Coyote or Tom the Cat, however, Magill did not emerge from his self-shaped grave seeing stars or with birds twittering round his discombobulated cranium. He lay groaning at the bottom of the pit, knowing that he'd been very lucky to escape with body intact and limbs unbroken.

Coughing and spluttering and spitting up blood, Simon turned over with difficulty. He stared up at the night sky. The snow had stopped. The moon was out. The stars were bright. Two yellow eyes looked down at him. They were joined by a second pair, then a third, then a fourth. The Wild Reserve's wolf-pack wasn't going to pass up on a suppertime snack. The alpha male pack leader stuck his shaggy head over the edge of the snow pit and bared his fangs with a snarl. The beta males and females followed suit. Magill could smell their feral breath, which plumed into the pit like a dry ice machine. Moved to comment on the room service offering – Reserve service, rather – one sizable female howled her approval. Two or three others joined in, ululating lupine thanks for what they were about to receive.

The pack leader was preparing to leap into the pit. His heavy winter coat bristled along the haunches. The jaws were wide, the fangs stripped for action. Desperately, Magill reached into his voluminous overcoat pocket, which still held the pistol that he'd misappropriated in Williamsburg. It was only an old-fashioned flintlock, loaded with dummy ammunition, but the bang might be enough to frighten them off. He cocked the hammer back with his thumb, taking aim at a point between the ghastly glowing eyes of the alpha male. Trusting that the gunmaker had done his job properly, Magill pulled the trigger.

He hadn't anticipated the flash, which erupted as the flint connected with the lock. The gunshot was much louder than he'd imagined, moreover. Magill's ears were still ringing in the aftermath of his one-man volley, though he could just about hear the wolves yelping as they disappeared into the trees. He scrambled frantically to get out of the pit but the snow was soft and yielding and provided little by the way of a foothold. He rammed his toes into the sidewall, as if he were wearing crampons, and managed to heave his torso above the trench, only to find himself staring into the snarling face of the pack leader, back for a second attack on his snack. Terrified by the sight, Magill tumbled back into his snow-lined grave, where he crouched down, weighing his options. The wolf's grey head appeared above the edge of the pit, its hot saliva dripping on to the main course below.

Okay, Magill thought, trying to remain calm, as the pack's eyes started to reappear overhead, like malevolent moons, galaxies and andromedae. The overcoat will afford some protection, he thought. The boots too. If he could make a dash for the wooden fence at the edge of the reserve, approximately thirty yards distant across uneven ground, he might get away with a mild savaging. The key was not to be pulled down by the pack leader. He tightened his overcoat, preparatory to going over the top. The belt! The belt buckle! With a yank, he pulled the belt out of its loop-secured groove and grabbed hold of the end. He lashed out at the pack leader. The metal buckle caught the creature in the eye, which exploded on impact. The wounded animal turned away, wailing and whimpering, and was instantly set upon by ancillary pack members. Magill seized the moment. He hoisted himself out of the trench, sloughed through the snowdrift and, once he reached solid ground, ran as fast as his legs would carry him in the direction of the perimeter fence. The wolf-pack was in a bloodlust frenzy several yards away, as they snapped and bit and tore at each other in a roiling ball of fur and fangs. Magill was halfway to the split-log palisade when one of the pack animals broke away from the howling horde and sprinted towards the fleeing first course. It was joined by one or two others, then the entire pack, which streamed towards Magill like huskies pulling an invisible sled.

The fence was about 18 feet high. Escape seemed impossible. However, Magill knew from his assault course experience at PWC that if sufficient speed is built up, a foot planted high up on the wall would provide sufficient lift and leverage to reach the top. Then, his upper body strength would be enough to surmount any barricade. Fortunately, the ground dipped towards the fence, which increased Magill's arm-pumping, leg-pounding impetus. Unfortunately, no matter how fast a man can run, a wolf runs faster. The replacement pack leader caught the hem of his flapping Ulster and dragged with all its strength, using its rear haunches as a brake. Stumbling slightly, Magill lanced his arms behind him, thus allowing the coat to be torn off more easily. He happily sacrificed his overcoat to the Busch Gardens beasts, who ripped the heavy fabric asunder in lieu of its wearer.

Freed from the constraints of his covering, Magill sprinted into the fence, planting one foot firmly on a split pine log and leaping for the top. He grabbed it with both hands and started hauling himself up, legs scrabbling for purchase, as the pack gathered below him. Honed by punishing push-ups – courtesy of Drill Sergeant Crush – Magill's upper body strength was sufficient to hold his weight. However, his right shoulder had been winged by Fields and it buckled under the strain. Magill found himself hanging by a single arm, crooked over the parapet. His legs had slipped in the slump and dangled invitingly above the pack, which leapt and snarled and snapped at his heels. His left arm held firm, fortuitously, and with a mighty asymmetric heave, he threw a foot around the topmost edge and worked himself up on to the wooden palisade.

Panting, gasping, sweating profusely despite the cold, he looked around, trying to catch his breath, while the wolf pack bayed in protest. Fields was standing on the walkway, one hundred yards distant, watching the bestial spectacle he'd initiated. The bastard. He noticed that Magill had noticed him and turned to flee, hurrying towards the Irish section and Scotland the Brave beyond.

Magill had a choice. He could tiptoe along the top of the fence back to the walkway, trusting that he wouldn't topple into the wolf pit, whose ravenous denizens would doubtless track him all the way. Or he could drop into the next field, trusting that it didn't contain mountain lions, grizzly bears, Sasquatch, or worse. Bald eagles can't be that bad, can they?

He dropped into the field.

The ground rose steeply in the general direction of The Loch

Ness Monster, a carnivorous roller-coaster with interlocking loops, which sat at the top of the hill overlooking the river valley. Magill loped easily over the surprisingly snow-less and rock-free meadow, aiming to head Fields off at Flodden Field, Glencoe Pass, Krankie Pankie or whatever the Hibernian hamlet was called. As he ran, he thought he could hear puffing and panting behind him. He dismissed it as an echo of his own exertions, but upped the pace all the same. The huffing and puffing continued, getting ever louder as the slope flattened out near the crest. It was an animal of some kind. A big animal. A very big animal. At best a bison, at worst the Loch Ness Monster itself, heading back to its sett after a nocturnal paddle in the Rhine and a frolic with nymphomaniacal *Rheintöchter*.

Running flat out, Magill had almost reached the chain-link fence when he was nudged in the middle of the back. He went sprawling against a five-bar gate, which clanged like a barnyard fire alarm. He looked over his wounded shoulder. A massive creature loomed above him, snorting. It was a Clydesdale, one of Budweiser's gigantic heavy horses that had been part of the company's promotional repertoire since the 1930s, when a team of dray horses clomped into Washington DC to celebrate the repeal of Prohibition and a new dawn for Anheuser Busch.

The carthorse nuzzled his chest, snuffling and truffling for a carrot or apple. Magill was clean out of snacks, albeit he'd nearly been one five minutes beforehand. Although it was years since he'd ridden – since childhood, in fact, when he wanted to become a jockey before pubertal growth spurts kicked in – Magill mounted his steed as to the manor born. Grasping the mighty mane with one hand, he bent over to open the paddock gate and clip-clopped out on to the theme park's main drag. From his elevated perch, he could see Fields cutting through the dispersing crowds in Parliament Square towards Escape from Pompeii, a dark ride that provided ample opportunity to hide out till the coast cleared.

That was not going to happen.

With a Hi-ho Silver, Magill dug his heels into the flanks of the Clydesdale. It reared alarmingly – its rider only just clinging on, arms wrapped around its huge hocks – then set off at an impressive clip. Not quite a gallop but more than a canter and more than enough for Magill who bounced and bobbed on the animal's bare back, hoping against hope that he'd survive the inevitable fall.

Akin to riding a bike, equestrian skills are never forgotten. Magill quickly found the horse's rhythm and urged him on as their distant target closed in on Pompeii. The thunderous ringing of hooves on asphalt soon drew an awestruck crowd, as the reluctantly departing guests turned back to the theme park to witness an unscheduled addition to the evening's entertainment. They whooped and yelled and shouted way to go. Unanticipated the encore may have been but it was welcome for all that. Magill momentarily wished he still had his overcoat, tricorn hat and flintlock pistol. He always fancied being a highwayman. He decided to make do with hunting down the Fields fox.

The horse and rider were rapidly gaining on the thick-set thespian. They were going to beat him to the entrance! At the last second, their prey swerved off into the trees, cutting across rutted flowerbeds and ploughing through boxwood hedges, slashing with his arms to hack a temporary path. Magill desperately steered his steed to the right, but it was hard to control. The Clydesdale slipped on a patch of ice, its hooves clittering and clattering like an eight-legged tap-dancer. Sans saddle, Simon was thrown off. However, he managed to hang on to its flowing mane with one hand – the one attached to his good arm – and, despite the tearing of the thorn bushes, as the horse ripped into the hedgerows, he scrambled back on board and even remembered to duck as the drooping snow-draped branches of deciduous trees barred his path.

Fields was running across Da Vinci's Garden of Inventions. He paused beside a phony Bellini statue, staring back at his relentless pursuer. Magill urged his charger on. The NSA man started running again, looking frantically over his shoulder instead of concentrating on the obstacles ahead. He stumbled over a column plinth, fell face-first into a fountain and emerged dripping from the dunking, gasping with the cold and the exertion. Magill hauled back on his mighty mount's mighty mane, the equine equivalent of an emergency stop. The Clydesdale reared to its full height above Fields's head. He put his arms up to protect himself. The huge hooves crashed in front of him. The ground trembled beneath. The carthorse rose again, neighing for all it was worth. Whinnying for victory.

"Who was your handler?" Magill shouted, as his stallion reared and bucked once more.

The captive cupped a hand round his ear in an I-can't-hear-you gesture.

"Who was your CIA contact? I want a name. Who's the rogue operative behind all this?"

Fields looked up at the pale rider. He opened his arms in a dramatic show of daren't-do-it resignation. He turned and started running again. Only to be hampered by his sodden doublet and hose. He'd never get away. Nor did he. Once again, he failed to look where he was going and was hit amidships by the Battering Ram, an oversized swing that swept to and fro across the Italianate piazza. He was catapulted 20, perhaps 30, feet over a rose bed and on to Leonardo's great equestrian statue, with its lance-bearing rider. Fields was impaled upon the sharp marble spear, where he wriggled like a skewered piglet – squealing, squirming, shuddering, struggling unsuccessfully to say something.

Despite his revulsion, Magill cantered up to the statue.

"Fu-Fu-Fu-"

"Yeah, fuck you too, Fields."

"Fu-Fu-Fu-"

Magill bent over to catch his foe's deathbed confession. It was hard to comprehend. Then realization slowly dawned. "Oh. My. Sweet. Jesus."

Chapter Forty-Nine

Whose Company?

"The thing I don't understand is why the CIA's preying on Dan." Abby wasn't directing the remark at anyone in particular. She was making conversation to keep Clancy calm, to call off his countdown. "Surely the CIA's focus is on foreign affairs. Shouldn't it be out catching Islamic terrorists, or spying on renegade Russian scientists or helping James Bond save the world? A best-selling, true-blue American author shouldn't be on the CIA's radar, much less be its target."

Even though the room was full of CIA employees, CIA boosters and CIA victims, no one wanted to answer Abby's question. She'd opened a can of worms that the Director of the CIA couldn't untangle, let alone wrangle.

Holstering his Magnum with considerable reluctance, Clancy gave it a go. "I've been writing about the CIA for years, ma'am. Jack Ryan, my hero, is a CIA analyst and occasional field agent, who rises through the ranks, eventually heads the company and then makes the leap to President of the United States. I thought I knew everything there was to know about the Agency. But even I have been baffled by what's happened since 9/11. Ever since the fall of the Berlin Wall, basically, the organization has lost its reason for being and it's been casting around for something to do. As an institution, it was designed to deal with a big obvious enemy, a mirror image of itself, the KGB. It can't cope with tiny autonomous cells of resistance, such as al-Qaeda. You'd think it'd've learned something from its involvement in Northern Ireland, but no. It hadn't a clue 9/11 was coming. Well, it had lots of clues, but no one paid any attention to them. What's worse, when George W. Bush wanted to kick Middle-Eastern butt, the agency told him what he wanted to hear in order to keep their budget intact. The CIA's an enormous bureaucracy. It needs to invent enemies, threats, challenges, to keep resources rolling in. It got involved in all sorts of underhand scams – the narcotics trade, counterfeit goods, property deals, industrial espionage – to keep itself afloat."

Limited though her experience was in Belfast City Council, Abby could well imagine what would happen when the bureaucratic mindset went critical, postal, walkabout.

Clancy was stalking around the dressing room by this stage, lambasting the company's many and varied shortcomings. If not quite a raging bull, he was undoubtedly a bear with a sore head. "It's no longer the Central Intelligence Agency, ma'am, but the Calamitous Intelligence Agency. When the CIA was established in 1947, many feared that it would abuse its unaccountability and become a kind of shadow government. Staffed by elitist Yalies who thought they knew best, the agency assassinated and tortured and schemed with abandon and fomented revolutions when it felt like it. It worked on the principle that the enemies of communism were America's allies – the Mujahedeen in Afghanistan, for example. We supplied weapons to the very people we're now fighting. American grunts are dying every day because of the CIA's shortsightedness. The CIA isn't so much a shadow government as a rogue state within the United States. The homeland security threat, so-called, has enabled them to further extend their influence internally. Despite its charter, the company never confined itself to international waters. It worked on the rationale that foreign spies operated in America and were therefore the company's responsibility. These days, the company has tabs on every US citizen but hasn't got a fucking clue about terrorists in Tehran."

"I still don't see what this has to do with Dan."

Clancy kicked a collaterally damaged computer monitor in frustration. It fizzed and crackled and sparked. He glared at West and Chaplin. "Do you two wanna take it from here?" They sat impassively refusing to add to their refusal to talk.

"You're doing pretty good, Tom," the Danster said appreciatively. "I know it can't be easy for you, given the great selling job you've done on the agency down the years."

"Thanks, buddy," Clancy responded, patting his pal on

the shoulder. "But I guess it's all about selling nowadays. The company, like any big commercial organization, is obsessed with its image, its press, its PR. The attacks of investigative journalists they can handle, usually with a bit of bribery or blackmail or a blank refusal to comment on classified matters, though as they define what's top secret, it's a great way of getting off the hook. However, when a novelist of Dan Brown's stature decides to take on the CIA, they get very, very worried. Fiction has much more impact than dry facts. Just look what Dan did to Opus Dei and the Catholic Church. The bloodline theory was out there for decades, but the so-called factual books didn't have a fraction of Dan's impact. So, when the CIA got wind of his interest, they had to blow him away. The asswipes used me as a patsy, what's more, after all I've done for them. Guess they were pissed when I ended the Jack Ryan series and stopped writing nice things about Langley. Hell, it was an artistic decision – Ryan was president, he had nowhere else to go. But I guess the company didn't see it like that. They thought I was deserting them in their hour of need when a Tom Clancy clone was launching a full-frontal assault. Two birds with one stone, I suppose."

"Forgive me, guys," Abby interjected, "but you'd think the CIA would welcome thrillers set in Langley's hallowed halls. Surely all the James Bond stuff and the Ludlum stuff reinforce the CIA's aura of invincibility."

"In the good old days, maybe. Not any more. Not after the agency's very public failings in Iraq. It said Saddam had WMDs: he didn't. It said Iraqi soldiers would surrender without firing a shot: they didn't. It said the Fedayeen wouldn't fight: they did. It said Osama bin Laden was in cahoots with Saddam: he wasn't. An Opus Dei-style exposé from the author of *The Da Vinci Code* could be the literary straw that breaks the company's back. Books have always been very important to the CIA. The agency's founders were literary types, remember. During the Cold War, the agency had a front organization called the Committee for Cultural Freedom, which supplied enormous sums of money to underwrite western literary culture through magazines, conferences, grants and book deals for authors who said the right things about American cultural values. The Cold War was as much a cultural confrontation as a military stand-off. The funds were funnelled through all sorts of front organizations, most notably the Ford, Rockefeller and Carnegie foundations. Books have always been a big deal at the agency. Langley is literary. They loved me. I owed my success to President Reagan, who was a company man through and through."

"Don't be so modest, Tom," Brown said. "You owe your success to storytelling talent. You're the best in the thriller business."

Shrek-alike Clancy's chunky features crumpled into a semblance of a smile. "Thanks, pal. I wish it were true. But we both know there are a lot better writers out there. We got the breaks."

"The world looks very different when you become a brand."

"That it does, buddy. But you gotta separate yourself from your persona. Otherwise you end up becoming your brand. The image eats you up." Ruefully, Clancy looked down at his camo gear, his holster and ammo belt, his pump action shotgun, his laced-up kick-ass army boots. "I used to sell insurance."

"I used to be a teacher," Dan said, "until I wrote a book about the NSA."

"Yeah, but you were unimportant then, a nobody. At most, they'd have intercepted your emails and tapped your phone. Now that you're a superstar with the Pope's scalp under your belt, the intelligence community can't afford to ignore you."

"Does the Pope have a scalp?" Dan said with a feeble smile.

"Dunno," Clancy retorted, clapping his bear-like hand on the Danster's thigh. "But he sure as hell shits in the woods."

"The funny thing is, *The Solomon Key* didn't contain that much about the CIA."

"Yeah," Clancy drawled, "But it's all a matter of timing. Ten years ago, they'd have laughed it off. Not after Iraq. Not after Afghanistan. Not after North Korea, which they know fuck all about."

"I'm just relieved it's over."

"You think?" Clancy cocked his head, listening intently, fatigues fatigue forgotten. "What's that noise? Do you hear something? Someone's coming. Quick, grab your weapon."

Chapter Fifty

It's Too Late to Stop Now

Mighty relieved, Clancy lowered his Magnum when Magill barged in, sweaty, dishevelled, coatless, shot in the shoulder. "What the hell happened to you?"

Magill didn't reply. He clumped straight across to Dan and gave him a big brotherly hug and said how great it was to see him, looking fit and well and something like his old self. Overcome with emotion, Simon struggled to explain that they'd solved the mystery of the Solomon Key killings, that Big C was the CIA, that the nightmare was over, that Fields finally got the point and wouldn't be sticking around. But Dan was having none of the glib James Bond quips. True gentleman that he was, he apologized for his unconscionable behaviour in Sydney, Salt Lake City and elsewhere.

"I've got a first aid kit," Clancy said, "if you want me to have a look at that shoulder." He pulled open a pouch attached to the side of his belt, extracted a field dressing and started unwrapping it.

"Later." Magill picked up Clancy's pump-action shotgun, checked that a shell was in the breech and released the safety catch. He marched up to Mae West and planted the barrel in the middle of her forehead.

"If you want to know who our contact is," she drawled, underwhelmed by the he-man tactics, "you may as well shoot. It's a cleaner way to go that what's in store if we sing."

"I'm not interested in your handler, right now."

"If you want to know why Dan was singled out, it's because of a cryptic clue he included on the cover of *The Da Vinci Code*, which alluded to the Kryptos sculpture at Langley. That set the alarm bells ringing and triggered an executive decision, which is agency terminology for a black op. Once black ops get a green light they keep going till they're in the red, if you catch my drift."

Disgusted, Magill shoved the barrel even harder into her forehead. "That's good to know. I'm sure Dan's delighted to discover your demented rationale. But I'm not interested in Langley's logic right now."

"If that pump-action pecker of yours leaves a mark on my expensively Botoxed brow, buster, I'll bite your John Thomas off. What do you want, dickhead?"

"What is the Fulcanelli code?"

West chortled. "The fuckin helly code? You Brits crack me up with your crazy accents and even crazier cuss words."

Magill looked from West to Chaplin. The anxiety etched on the Little Tramp's face was palpable. They made an odd couple, one Chinese-American, the other Nigerian-American, one tall, one tiny, one talkative, the other taciturn. But they were a couple for all that. Magill swung the M12 round to the moustachioed midget. There was a circular dent in West's forehead, a Winchester bindi. "Fields's last words were that the Fulcanelli code was about to go critical. The final countdown had begun. What was he talking about, Charlie? What's the Fulcanelli code?"

Omertà intact, Chaplin said nothing. He twitched his little toothbrush moustache in that so-what manner. He twirled his bowler hat, just like he did in those deeply unfunny movies. He also glanced anxiously across to his celebrity partner. She nodded her approval. "Tell him," West said, with a sigh of resignation. "It's too late to stop now, anyhow."

"The Fulcanelli Code," Chaplin confessed, "is a piece of computer software, a virus, a very lethal virus based on the surrealist alchemist's apocalyptic weapon, coupled with the end of the world scenario in *The Solomon Key*. I was thinking of calling it The Marketing Code but Fulcanelli's got a better ring to it. It's designed to wipe out the hard disk drives of every single marketing professor. All their research, all their data, all their pdfs, all their files, figures, formulae, fuck-a-duck PowerPoint presentations. Their entire life's work, in short, will be wiped, thanks to an infected attachment that every one of them will open. It's foolproof, if I say so myself. It went out at midnight. Marketing professors the world over are about to crash and burn. Marketing apocalypse is nigh."

"But what have business schools ever done to you?" Abby asked naively. "Marketing academics are harmless enough. They're pretty incompetent but unusually innocent, in my experience."

Tom Clancy cleared his throat. It sounded like a corncrake with chronic catarrh. "I think I can answer that one," he rasped. "When I said that the CIA was bookish and that the Ford Foundation was one of many fronts for the company, I should have mentioned that the Ford Foundation was behind the rebooting of business schools at the height of the Cold War. The Cold War wasn't just fought on a cultural front, it was fought on an intellectual front too. Before Ford, American business schools regarded management as an art, a body of sector-specific knowledge that was slowly acquired through experience, savvy, common sense, craftsmanship and the passing along of accumulated received wisdom. Much like glassmaking, in fact."

"The Tiffany doctrine," Magill said.

Clancy nodded. "However, the CIA, via its Ford Foundation front, reckoned that craftsmanship was insufficient in an age of satellites, A-bombs, cybernetics, think tanks and suchlike. So management was reinvented as a technoscientific academic discipline, driven by facts, figures, quantitative methods and controlled experiments. The aim was to develop a body of theory that was universally applicable, to turn management into a hard science on a par with chemistry, biology or physics. B-school courses were altered to that end. Faculty with an experimental, number-crunching mindset were hired. Financial resources were poured into places like Harvard and Stanford and Carnegie Institute of Technology, which acted as standard-bearers for the rest. Rising stars, like Professor Kate Phillips, were spotted, groomed and trained up as Ford Foundation fellows and urged to write the textbooks that spread the good word, as defined by the CIA. The ultimate objective was to beat the Russkies through better marketing management."

"And they succeeded." As a former business school scholar, Magill was speaking from personal experience.

"In a sense," Clancy conceded. "They succeeded insofar as every B-school fell in line, and as the management science mindset still prevails. Indeed, it's so engrained that B-schools have forgotten they're a CIA front. But the problem, as with so many of the CIA's grand schemes and hare-brained theories – such as the domino principle – was that their analysis was plain wrong. The B-school revolution they instigated was based on a false premise. Hell, I used to sell insurance. I was an ace insurance salesman. And selling insurance has got damn all to do with the bullshit they teach in business schools. I, for one, will shed no tears if marketing thought, so called, is obliterated."

Bemused, Abby interrupted Clancy's nuke-em management monologue. "But why would the CIA want to obliterate B-school research?"

"Because the chickens have come home to roost. The MBA mindset has infected generations of managers. Management science is the norm not the exception. It's the only show in teacher town. The Enrons, the RBSes, the Bear Stearns of this world, were led by MBAs. Today's economic cataclysm is a direct consequence of what CEOs were taught at B-school. The schools will deny it, but the CIA knows where the bodies are buried. They know they're ultimately responsible, that the trail leads back to them, that not only has the company failed in its formal duty as a collector of intelligence, but it has undermined the very foundations of America's powerbase. Our unsurpassable ability to sell stuff."

"I see," Magill sighed.

"Wiping out academic marketing is obviously a CIA smoke-screen, an attempt to divert attention from the true perpetrator, though I suspect that there's an element of shutting the stable door after the horse has bolted. Management science was a mistake. The company's trying to wipe the slate clean. They're starting with marketing because marketing academics will believe anything." Clancy glared at Chaplin, whose toothbrush moustache twitched nervously. "Am I right?"

The Little Tramp nodded.

"So you're just going to let this happen?" Abby was astounded. "I'm no fan of academic research. I studied marketing for years and its theories were no use to me when I set up my own business. But, you know, academic research doesn't do any harm. Nobody reads it. Nobody believes it."

"No loss, then," Clancy announced, while slapping a field dressing on Magill's flesh wound, despite the Englishman's protestations.

"On the contrary," Abby countered, drawing on her knowledge of guerrilla psychology, "It *is* a loss. Marketing practitioners need someone to blame, a whipping boy, a fall guy. Moaning about useless academic research gives them something to bitch about. When things go wrong – as they always do in business life – managers need a scapegoat of some kind. Otherwise they'd be forced to admit that they themselves are at fault. If academics actually produced meaningful, valuable, universally valid and applicable research findings, then practitioners would be at fault for failing to implement the ideas properly. They'd have no other excuse. Managers and academics need each other, basically. They're locked in a kind of S&M co-dependency. You can't have one without the other. They have a symbiotic relationship. If the B-school is obliterated, management will implode too. The CIA's attempt to wipe the slate clean is yet another of the company's ill-considered schemes. They've got to be stopped!"

Magill concurred, convinced by Abby's case, which was delivered with her usual irrepressible passion. "I'm signing up for that guerrilla psychology class as soon as I get home."

"Nah," she laughed, "they'd never enrol the likes of you."

"And anyway," Brown said, "you're coming home with me, Simon. I need a dogs-body."

"Since you put it like that, Dan, I can hardly refuse."

"Well okay, let's call it a business manager, a go-to guy. No more Langdon scenarios, though."

"None?"

The Danster looked at Magill. Magill looked at the Danster. Their unbreakable brotherly bond, first forged at the Bellagio and stress-tested to destruction, was renewed, rewound, recommenced, reconsecrated.

Energized, Magill settled himself down in front of the one remaining computer monitor. "So, how does the Fulcanelli virus do its dirty work, Mr Chaplin?"

"You're too late. I already told you."

Stroking the keyboard like Liberace performing the *Moonlight Sonata*, albeit without the simper, Magill felt in total control of his instrument. "Let me worry about that, Charlie. Now, how does it work?"

"Well, the email purports to come from Harvard Business School Press. They're planning to posthumously publish the late Kate Phillips's final article and they want to check that it's okay to cite the recipient's work. If they peruse the attached file just to make sure that Phillips got the details of their research right, then Harvard can proceed with publication."

"Christ," Magill groaned. "Every marketing academic in the world will open that attachment. Citation is the crack cocaine of scholarship."

With a smug, self-satisfied smile, Chaplin chuckled. "Yeah, and the best bit is that the article's about viral marketing."

"A viral marketing virus?" Abby gasped.

"Correct," Chaplin crowed. "Fulcanelli was a surrealist prankster, remember. The emails went out at the stroke of midnight. By 9.00 a.m. tomorrow, every hard disk in the country will be wiped.

"Marketing's doomed," Abby whispered.

With a heavy sigh of defeat, Magill stopped tinkling his keyboard. "I fear you're right."

Chapter Fifty-One

Return to Sender

"Are you sure you're up for this?"

"Don't worry about me."

"Because I can do it myself, if it's too much for you."

"After rescuing the marketing world, Simon, this holds no fear for me."

He stopped the car. "I think you'll find that I saved the day."

Abby smiled across at him. She knew he was winding her up in the familiar Irish manner – yanking her chain, as Americans like to call it – but she played along anyway. "Okay, Simon, you pressed the return key that sent out our email. However, I composed the message. Thank heaven for my in-depth knowledge of reverse psychology."

"Reverse psychology had nothing to do with it. It was straight-ahead psychology, if you ask me."

"I prefer to think of it as reverse reverse psychology."

Laughing, Magill looked around, trying to get his bearings. The woods were thick in the valley bottom, though at least the worst of the snow had melted. It was two days after their tour of duty in Busch Gardens and the portents were good. All the evidence suggested that the world's marketing academics had indeed opened their email first and purged the Phillips citation invitation, as instructed. True, the Antipodean academic community was pretty much wiped out, due to time zone differences between Williamsburg and Wollongong, which meant that many were at their machines when Chaplin's diseased message arrived. They'd already opened it and watched their data disappear in a puff of digital smoke before the Magill/Maguire email popped into their in-box, like the last-gasp arrival of Seventh cavalrymen in creaky cowboy movies. However, as the Antipodes have never contributed anything of note to academic marketing endeavour, the loss of their research was no big deal.

It was Abby who calculated that there was an academic urge more powerful than citation. An actual publication in a posthumous anthology edited by Harvard's late great Ted Levitt was an offer that no scholar would refuse. In the academic scheme of things, publication always trumped citation. Forced to choose between a career-enhancing publication and an ego-flattering citation, the former unfailingly won hands down. Most marketing faculty would sell their aged mothers into bondage in return for a half-decent publication.

In fairness, it was Magill who came up with the title of Levitt's phantom anthology. Abby wanted *The Monster Book of Marketing Masterpieces*, but Magill insisted that *The Customer Key* was more intriguing. Although Abby had learned, from her close encounters with Dr Dave Kelley, that publications were the coin of the academic realm, the key to health, wealth and an endowed personal chair, Magill had actually been a marketing lecturer and was thus more attuned to the nuances of educators' motivation. *The Monster Book of Marketing Masterpieces* was just too crude. It would have worked perfectly among the bottom-feeding consultancy fraternity, but scholarly cogitations occupy a higher plane.

Whoever was responsible for the email that saved marketing civilization, Simon was solely responsible for uncovering Big C. Although he had repaired to O'Houlihan's Tavern with a view to chatting up Assumpta Lynch, aka Marilyn Monroe, and although Abby had thoughtfully informed him that Marilyn was way, way out of his league, Magill's Bud-bonding with Ms Monroe and Mr Hardy was highly productive. Intrigued by the secretive behaviour of their co-stars in the comedy collective, they'd decided to track down the shadowy figure behind W. C. Fields, the person who really called the shots. They discovered that Big C wasn't a person but a place. That place was called Langley, the Langley floor of the Cultra Communications Centre. The official headquarters of MI6 in Northern Ireland, Cultra Communications Centre was also home to the smallest CIA station in the western world. Hence its ironic designation: Big C.

Having extracted this priceless nugget of information from Marilyn and Oliver, who were keen to help when parts in the next Dan Brown/Tom Clancy movie adaptations were dangled in front of them, Abby and Magill were on their way to confront Big C's commander-in-chief.

After confirming once more that Abby was able to cope with what lay ahead – not that he doubted her resolve – Magill slipped the car into gear and drove on. Shrouded in conifers and studded with satellite dishes, the red-brick, three-storey building nestled in a little glade, fast-flowing stream on one side, grid-locked car park on the other. They stole a disabled space close to the main entrance – Magill's injuries were still hurting – and made their way through the atrium to reception. Five minutes early for their appointment, the terrible twosome were invited to tarry in an uncomfortable seating area, behind a screen of oversized indoor plants: ferns, ficus, pampas grass and the biggest parlour palm Magill had ever seen. Unable to observe the comings and goings at Cultra Communications Centre – oh, those spies and their secrecy! – they quaffed much-needed cups of Nespresso, as recommended by gorgeous George Clooney. While the caffeine did little to dispel the jetlag, induced by a transatlantic overnighter on Continental Airlines Supercramped Class, it nonetheless fortified them for the unpleasant task ahead.

A flunky arrived with security passes and directed them to the lifts. Abby pressed the button for Langley on the first floor, while noting that the top floor was called Vauxhall Cross and the basement, Lubyanka. Spooks have a sense of humour, evidently. Their host was sitting in a glass-sided conference room, adjacent to the lifts. Back to the door, his feet were crossed on the gleaming table. He drew deeply on a cigarette, while staring out the picture windows towards the sylvan glade, seemingly deep in thought. He roused himself on their knock and, pausing only to close the venetian blinds for privacy, ushered them in to his smoky lair.

"Good to see you, Simon," he said with an endearingly amiable chuckle. "You're looking well. You've filled out. America's been good to you."

"America's been good to you too, I gather."

369

"Aye," he chortled, patting his protuberant belly. "Those KFC family buckets are hard to beat."

"They'll be the death of you, Ian."

Dr Kane's porcine features retained their affable expression, even as his piggy eyes implied otherwise. "I thought that's what *you* were here for."

"I'm not here to take you out, Ian," Magill said, secure in his PWC-inculcated knowledge of the death grip. "I just want to know why you persecuted the Danster in the way that you did."

"And I want to know," Abby interjected, "what a CIA officer's doing teaching guerrilla psychology at the OU."

Stubbing out his cigarette, Kane coughed and wheezed in his trademark manner. "Questions, questions, questions," he gasped, before breaking into a cough like a consumptive caribou. "Okay, here's the deal. I first met Dan Brown back in 2001, when he spent some time at St Stephen's Retreat, after the disastrous failure of his last-chance book, *Deception Point*. I met him through Father Mannion, who was my main contact within the IRA."

"Father Mannion was an informer?"

Ian Kane's fleshy face flushed with remembered pleasure. "Let's just say we had an arrangement. I ensured that immigration didn't bother him on his trips to the States. He had a thing about Hollywood celebrities and the bath-houses of San Francisco, if you catch my drift. In return, he kept me posted on the IRA's business activities. I'd no interest in the political or military stuff, so he never really felt he was giving away anything important. It was a nice arrangement. Anyway, he introduced me to Dan Brown. We hit it off. Started talking about storytelling. I mentioned my plan to write a management thriller – a religious conspiracy page-turner, with a business twist – then, lo and behold, he publishes *Da Vinci* two years later. I told you all about this, Simon, when you started work at the University of Hustler. Have you forgotten so soon?"

"Yes, but you didn't tell me you were plotting revenge."

"Oh," Kane said airily, "I was plotting revenge long before I met you, Simon. The *Solomon Key* re-enactment was my third attempt to get even. Much as I wanted to kill the guy, or have him whacked, I knew that dying young would only increase the bastard's sales figures. So I set out to ruin his reputation. First, with a fake manuscript by W. B. Yeats, which Dan was supposed to have plagiarized."

"You wrote *All Fall Down*?"

"Well, I am a storyteller, Miss Maguire. And when I heard your outburst at the St Stephen's conference, I realized you were the perfect transmission vehicle."

"You were in the audience that day?"

"Oh yes. I got a call from Peregrine Faulkner. Received a message, rather. So I leaned on Father Mannion and he loaned you the Yeats thriller."

"Did you write the poem, as well?"

"No, no. That was Pitcairn Brodie's handiwork, the interfering fool. His blundering around ruined my Citroën operation."

"You sent the threatening emails to Citroën?"

"Yes. And, as I calculated, they concluded Dan Brown was the culprit. I hoped they'd publicize his cynical self-publicizing activities and bring the bastard down. Then Brodie stuck his oar in. He paid the price, however."

"So you killed Pitcairn," Magill groaned, distraught.

Defiantly, Dr Kane shook his head. His flapping dewlaps looked as though they were going to take flight. "Not personally. P4 sanctioned that one, though as a high-ranking member of that august organization, I did have some input into the decision. Let's just say that he paid the price for pissing on my parade. I thought the Citroën chevrons in the eyes were a neat touch."

"But... but...," Magill stammered. "You assured me that they were the Freemasons' compass and square."

"I'm a storyteller, Simon. Telling convincing stories is what I do. I too am a graduate of the Patton Writing College. That's where I was recruited by the CIA. That's how I heard about Dan's guest lecture. That's how I got access to his pendrive, his computer files, his diary, his draft manuscript. That's when I came up with a plot to impale him on his own plot. The fact that you were working for him, Simon, made it all the sweeter."

Magill was at a loss. "Me... what... how... where do I come into it?"

"You were the man who shopped me to Hustler University,

who told them I'd ordered the assassination of King Billy, the institution's principal benefactor. You're the person who lost me my lecturing job. You're the man who forced me into teaching evening classes in guerrilla psychology at a second-rate academic institution."

Angrily, Magill denied the accusation. He'd had no contact with Hustler University since he quit. Maybe it was May Day who spilled the beans about Kane's extra-curricular activities. Had he thought of that? Or did he naively believe that she really cared for him, as Magill too once foolishly concluded.

Abby had no idea what they were talking about, though she could see that Magill's cruel jibe had forced Kane to reassess his reading of the situation. "I enjoyed your classes," she said lamely. "They taught me a lot."

Smiling at his erstwhile student, Kane continued in confessional mode. "You wouldn't've enjoyed them so much if you'd known I was behind the WeeWii suit that brought your business down. Or would have done if it hadn't gone up in flames," he added with a smirk. "Pity about that."

"What?!" Abby yelled. "But why? Because of my connection to Brodie?"

"Nothing so trivial," he sniffed. "Because you stymied the Company's investment in Carrickfergus. The Commercial Intelligence Agency had invested a lot of its hard-earned cash in that particular property development. We don't take kindly to people who fuck with our portfolio."

Abby couldn't believe the business-is-business mindset of the guy. "There are some things I still don't get."

"Such as?"

"Why did the CIA employ *you*?"

"I'm the ideal agent, Abby. The antithesis of the traditional clean-cut, finely honed, lean and mean image. Try to remember what you learned in your guerrilla psychology classes," he added good-naturedly. "What's more, whereas the FBI has always been dominated by Irish Catholics, the CIA is an Anglo-Saxon Protestant organization. It's basically sympathetic towards Ulster Protestant paramilitarism and because of my connections to that particular group, coupled with my IRA contacts, I was perfectly positioned from the company's perspective. My lecturing post at HBS, which enabled me to keep tabs on the business community, also helped. I was the perfect guy for their B-school take-down operation. My training in esoteric philosophy came in handy with the alchemical angle, as well."

"MIT," Magill moaned. "Midlothian Institute of Theosophy."

Kane placed a finger by his eyebrow and saluted. "However, by far the most important factor was that I told them what they wanted to hear."

Abby nodded. "Storytelling, I presume."

"I'm likeable too," he went on. "Likeability is a very important personality trait, especially in business. Likeability is hard to lick, let me tell you."

"What did you have against Clancy?" Magill demanded. "You sent threatening messages to him as well, purportedly from Dan."

Kane bristled. "I have nothing against Clancy. I met him once at St Stephen's. The guy's a natural raconteur, a great storyteller. However, he does tend to perpetuate an unrealistic image of the agency, an image of superspies that reality can't match. The very image that led Abby to infer that I wasn't company material. The CIA has taken a terrible battering in recent years, primarily because the Clancy-propagated image raised expectations so high that no matter how good our company's product is, it's not good enough for the customer in the White House. Our reputation, accordingly, has suffered unfairly and I thought it only fair that Clancy should suffer too."

"Even though he's written dozens of books extolling the agency's technothrilling virtues."

"*Especially* because he's written books singing our praises. Silence is golden, Simon, particularly where spooks are concerned. Clancy's been pretty quiet of late. Haven't you noticed? I thought you were an aspiring literary type, with your finger on the publishing pulse."

The cynicism of the espionage community beggared belief. Here was a man who not only set out to destroy someone's career in his misplaced desire for revenge – sheer jealousy, rather, since his book was nothing like *Da Vinci* – but also thought nothing of arranging the murder of entirely innocent people who happened to get in the way or whose death might help further his petty plots against entirely innocent literary celebrities. Although he was warned never to use the death grip, there were certain occasions when the just-say-no philosophy of self-defence had to be set aside. If anyone deserved to die, it was Dr Ian Kane.

"I guess," Abby spat at the flaccid operative, "you used your irresistible likeability to recruit New Serendipity Associates. Or were they psychopaths too?"

Kane chuckled contentedly. "Well, they were certainly odd. They took to the celebrity lookalike scam like proverbial ducks to water. But, actually, they came to me in the aftermath of Barton Brady's slaying. I used to write a blog – a management storytelling sideline, basically – under the nom de post Rhetorical Butler. GoneWithTheWindows dotcom, it was called. They were at a loose end after Brady and Buonarroti passed on and they suggested we join forces against Hank Wittgenstein, a metaphor-selling management consultant outta Reno, who was undercutting Serendipity Associates. But I had a better idea, one that exploited their dramaturgical flair. Everyone's a showperson in Vegas, right? It also threw a bit of work Wee Joe's way. He was at a loose end after King Billy was whacked and he's the kind of person that's best kept busy."

Balling his fists with fury, Magill had heard enough. Live and let live be damned. Kane was going down. With nary a thought for the operative's lurking bodyguards – there was a lot of body to guard, mind – Magill made the first move. However, he was too late. Abby had beaten him to the punch. Literally. Smiling sweetly at her pudgy part-time teacher, she felled Dr Kane with a mid-Ulster uppercut, then grabbed him by the throat. Chins, actually. She prised his jowly jaws open, popped her black rose brooch into his mighty malodorous maw and clamped his mouth shut with one hand. She used the other to pinch his nose between forefinger and thumb, forcing him to swallow. Kane thrashed and twisted and kicked his stumpy little legs, like a small boy throwing a tantrum. But Abby held him in an abattoir-honed grip. Years of wrestling with frightened farm animals, who somehow sensed that death was imminent, had taught her how to hold wrigglers down with efficient dispatch. "Swallowing sharp objects can kill if you're not careful," she announced grimly, staring impassively into Kane's petrified piglet peepers. "It's a very painful death, I gather."

Struggling and heaving for all he was worth, Kane's ordinarily florid physiognomy flowed from pink to scarlet to purple to indigo. He literally bust a gut trying to prevent his gut busting. With a mighty muffled moan, he arced upwards like a bloated bucking bison, then suddenly expired, shuddering. Heart attack? Terminal indigestion? Toxic trapped wind? Who cared? Who could tell? Let the coroner sort it out.

Like the Good Samaritans they purported to be, Abby and Magill called for assistance and in the paramedical pandemonium that followed – all oxygen masks and CPR and defibrillation paddles and mouth-to-mouth resuscitation attempts – they slipped out of Langley and made their way to the CCC car park. Magill was heading back to the International Airport, another transatlantic flight in prospect. Abby asked to be dropped off at D'Anger Castle, Carrickfergus, where she had a date with destiny, a.k.a. Dave Kelley.

"What's next for you, Abby?" Magill asked, as they clambered into their hire car, a souped-up Mini Cooper.

"I was thinking of going into the treasure hunting business. I noticed that the Hendaye crosses differed slightly and that might be a clue to the Bacon hoard. Dave's had enough of the music business and he's had a thing about graveyards since he was a teenage goth. We're goth to go."

"Sounds like fun. Keep me posted."

"Will do," she smiled. "What about you, Simon?"

Magill blushed the blush of a Gingerbap, which far surpassed the beam from any Dollar Tree torch. "I'm thinking of asking Marilyn Monroe for a date."

Abby nodded her approval and, for once, said nothing untoward. "Lucky girl."

"The Danster wants me back. He doesn't really need me now that he's back on song. But if I sit at his feet for a few more years and keep practising, I might have a novel in me. Actually, I was thinking of writing this up."

"This?"

"Our adventures, Abby. They'd make a good thriller, don't you think? This is how I see them…"

Abby placed a finger on Simon's lips, shook her head with a smile and kissed him gently.

"I knew it!" Magill gasped, when she released her grip. "The storytelling template is never wrong. The climactic kiss. They head off into the sunset, hand-in-hand. Happily ever after, here we come."

"Sorry, Simon," Abby sighed. "The kiss is just to let you know that, although I love you like a brother, if the character you base on me is anything less than an absolute hottie – slim, svelte, sexy – I'll hunt you down like a dog."

"But you are a hottie," Magill murmured.

"Designer labels would be nice, too. Lots of them."

"But you look fantastic in that outfit. Versace, isn't it?"

Flicking back her silken mane of thick black hair, while grinning gloriously with her gleaming pearl-white teeth, the best-dressed, most beautiful woman in Ireland, Abby "Armani" Maguire, embraced him one last time. "That's my boy."

Chapter Fifty-Two

Stairlift to Heaven

21 February 2009

"Na, na, na, na, na, na, na, na, naaaah."

The crowd responded in kind. "Na, na, na, na, na, na, na, na, naaaah."

"I can't hear you, Sydney," the lead singer teased. "Let's try that one again. Na, na, na, na, na, na, na, na, naaaaah."

"Na, na, na, na, na, na, na, na, naaaaah," the 3,000-strong crowd roared back with gusto, most wondering with a titter if they'd met their heroes' expectations.

The lead singer shook his head, golden ringlets still miraculously intact, with pretend disapproval. Boy, he'd missed these call and response moments. There's nothing quite like it. On stage, it's the greatest feeling in the world. Better than sex. Better even than a groupie sandwich. And the lead singer should know.

"I still can't hear you," he yelled. "Gimme all you got, cobbers." The band members shared a there-he-goes-again moment, since the singer did this at every gig, only changing the city name and the blokeish salutations. Do they still say "cobbers" in Sydney? Still, it was unsurpassingly, spine-tinglingly thrilling for them too. Just like the good times bad times of many years before.

"Na, na, na, na, na, na, na, na, naaaaaaaaaaaaaaaaaahhhh-hhhhhh," the lead singer intoned, challenging the audience to match his legendary lung power. They giggled in anticipation. Sensed from the stage, a gigantic collective giggle is the most exquisite, life-affirming vibe on the planet. Only the first hit of H stands comparison and where that habit leads sure ain't life-affirming, as their lead guitarist could testify. It's a miracle he's still alive and, even more of a miracle, has lost none of his fret-board dexterity.

377

"Na, na, na, na, na, na, na, na, naaaaaaaaaaaaaaaahhhhhhh-hhhh," the crowd responded, matching the singer's every nuance. The Sydney Opera House had never heard anything quite like it. One of the most iconic buildings in the world hosting one of the world's most iconic rock bands. Just as the building was once mired in controversy and ego-clashes and elephantine overspend, so too Led Zeppelin was once mired in controversy (their supposed pact with the devil in particular), ego-clashes (the lead singer and guitarist had "musical differences", as they say) and elephantine overspend (specially liveried private jets, suitcases stuffed with money and coke, demolition derbies in hotels worldwide).

Forty years on from their simultaneous birth, the band and the venue had grown old together: cherished, canonized, crumbling and, well, coasting on their reputations.

But the middle-aged crowd weren't here to hear the latest sounds or see a cutting-edge light show. They were here to relive their youth, when they were lithe and beautiful, almost as lithe and beautiful as the greatest rock band of all time. The three creaking geezers on stage, plus the son of their long-dead drummer, represented the hottest ticket in town. And their tiny warm-up gig in the hoity-toity Opera House, prior to the stadium shows at ANZ in the Homebush Bay suburbs, was the hottest ticket in Australia's star-crossed history, bigger even than the opening ceremony of the 2000 Olympics.

"Nobody's fault but mine," Robert Plant bellowed, a golden god again, geriatrics forgotten. The band kicked in, Jimmy Page and John Paul Jones in blistering symphony. He repeated the line, rocking to the rhythm, microphone stand in hand. Then repeated it again. A volcanic fill from the drummer dropped immaculately into place. The late great Bonzo Bonham could never be bettered but, by God, his son gave him a run for his money. The band thundered on, as one. Just like the good old days, only better.

The number crashed to its conclusion. The Australians went ape. There are certain gigs that stand out in the memory – Earls Court '75, Albert Hall '70 – but Sydney Opera House 2009 was right up there with the best of them. They'd be talking about this one for years to come. In all likelihood, they were burning bootlegs already.

"What's next?" the lead vocalist mouthed to his brothers in arms, having forgotten the set list in the intoxication of the moment. Sydney Opera House was partially modelled on stepped Mayan temples, where sacrificial ceremonies were held and shamanistic visions of apocalyptic tomorrows were received by the peyote-addled priesthood. Never was an echo more apt.

Robert Plant got his answer with the opening chords of Jimmy Page's showcase, "Dazed and Confused". As he unsheathed his talismanic violin bow, to the delight of the enraptured audience, the uncrowned king of cock-rock felt the good vibes disappearing and a darker atmosphere descend. Just like the bad old days. Percy Plant, as puerile music journalists insisted on christening him, had little love lost for "Dazed and Confused", even though he'd performed it a thousand times or more. There was something about that song, something scary, something unholy, something that somehow tapped into the black magic that Jimmy Page dabbled in way back when. More than dabbled. The guy was channelling Aleister Crowley at one stage. He bought the "Great Beast's" spooky Scottish mansion, Boleskine House. He acquired the evil magician's ceremonial robes. He opened an esoteric bookshop and republished Crowley's malignant manuscripts. He etched the wizard's infamous watchwords – do what thou wilt is the whole of the law – on the run-off of the band's third album. He included a picture of the necromancer on the cover of one long player and others boasted allusions to the Tarot, human sacrifice, crop circles and baleful black obelisks. He even insisted that they adopt a personalized rune for the fourth album, which may have been deeply meaningful and powerfully symbolic but it antagonized the record company no end.

Mind you, Plant mused, as he stalked to the side of the stage for a surreptitious ciggie while Page strutted his stuff, the album sold pretty well...

"Dazed and Confused" wasn't the most up-tempo of numbers. It was a set-killer, frankly, a throwback to the over-indulgence that plagued the band in its pre-punk pomp and was so far out of vogue nowadays that it made loon pants and long hair look fashionable. Plant checked his grizzled but still golden mane in a back-stage mirror, grateful for the respite that their lumpen standard afforded. He peeped around the amp to check on Page's progress. A spectral pyramid of laser beams rotated around the lead guitarist, as he pointed the violin bow at the upper circle of the Opera House. Some old-timers in the topmost tier shouted their approval, though most of the audience were content to have a nap before the climax of the set, "Stairway to Heaven".

The revolving lasers were speeding up now, a sure sign that Page's solo showcase was ending. Plant took a couple of deep breaths and nodded across to Jonesy, who was slipping on his Fender fretless bass, while Jason eased behind his late father's blood and thunder drum-kit. Bounding on stage for the final verse and chorus and climactic crash of power chords, the goateed vocalist led the applause for his musical familiar's solo. Something unusual caught his eye, however. The still-spinning lasers were describing an unusual pattern on the stage floor. A quirk of the Opera House, perhaps? No, no, it was quite deliberate, it was part of Page's act, something that hadn't been discussed beforehand, much less agreed upon. The circling lasers were describing a pentagram. A fucking pentagram, for fuck's sake. What the fuck is that fucker calling forth now? He just can't leave it a-fucking-lone.

Plant sashayed across to his partner. He slapped him on the shoulder, for the benefit of the admiring crowd, which was rising for a standing ovation. Get over yourselves, you koala-fucking bastards. Robert leaned into his unnaturally invigorated compatriot, ostensibly whispering words of admiration into his shell-like, the one without the hearing aid. "I saw what you were doing, you bastard. We agreed that there'd be none of… that stuff. Have you lost your fucking mind? Again? At your age. Grow fucking up. Or I'm quitting."

Jimmy Page smiled and said nothing. He raised his hands and milked the applause, then punched out the chords that carried the song to its conclusion.

"Ladies and gentlemen, the one and only James Patrick Page, axeman extraordinaire, fret-dancer deluxe, fingerpicker first class."

The crowd erupted.

"Sydney, you're the best," Robert announced, as the tumult fell away. "The best of the best." He said that every night, of course, though this time he almost meant it. "We are truly humbled. We feel... well... transported on an... um... Stairway to Heaven." With that artful segue, the greatest rock band of all time started playing the greatest rock anthem ever recorded.

But something wasn't right. A rogue laser from the preceding song was still operational and skittering across the stage, jumping back and forth. What was it with the lighting people? This didn't happen in rehearsal. Arses would be kicked later, since the show must go on. The red dot paused on Page's upper torso. He looked over to the lead vocalist in confusion. The laser moved again and stopped at the giant gong behind Bonham's riser. The pencil-thin beam wobbled and jerked as if someone was yanking the lighting rig back and forth.

Then the penny dropped. Australian dollar, rather. Some joker had got hold of a cheap laser pointer and, tired of troubling airline pilots as they come in to land, they'd sneaked it into the Opera House. The godforsaken things had a range of 1,500 yards or so. There'd be hell to pay for this. The problem with artsy-fartsy auditoria is that they don't take security seriously enough. Festival organizers frisk fans as a matter of course but opera houses waved everyone in. They could be carrying anything, for Christ's sake. He'd have to stop the bloody show. Nothing looks worse than special pleading from the stage, especially when it's allegedly Olympian rock gods doing the hand-wringing.

Although Robert called a halt with reluctance, if he hadn't stopped the band no one would have heard the first rifle shot. The second and third shots would probably have gone unnoticed too, though the horrified howl from the audience ensured that the fourth and fifth were drowned in the uproar. No one was hit, thankfully, though the explosive shattering of the circular sound baffles above the stage and their cascading crash on to the apron and amplifiers precipitated wholesale panic. The audience dashed en masse for the exits just as the band dashed en masse for the dressing rooms, effectively screened by black-suited security personnel, one of whom drew a hand gun and started firing wildly into the upper tiers. The screaming redoubled, the stampede for the exits accelerated.

There are many serious design problems with the Sydney Opera House, not least the fact that the conch-shell exterior and dog-hutch interior are completely mismatched. However, the biggest problem with the building is its constricted stairways with an extremely steep rake. Many concert-goers stumbled and fell as they tried to get out of the hall. Many more trampled over the fallen as they elbowed their way to the doors. For old-timers, long past the first flush of youth, they showed an impressive ability to run for their lives.

Ironically, the fallen were the lucky ones, despite being trampled underfoot. The access staircases outside the auditorium are even narrower and steeper than the internal aisles. They were an accident waiting to happen and in the panic-stricken emergency evacuation, the inevitable accident happened. The human logjam on the Block A stairwell was such that when one anxious concert-goer – a burly businessman from Bondi – tripped and fell forward, the resultant domino effect and consequent crush led to the untimely deaths of three Led Zeppelin lovers. Another leaped over the banisters to avoid the corporeal cascade, only to plunge 30 feet on to the concourse below. His fall was broken by a family group from Manley, two of whom joined the Bondi businessman in the celestial surfers' paradise. They played "In My Time of Dying" at the funeral.

Chapter Fifty-Three

A Rose By Any Other Name

Da da da daaaa. Da da da daaaa. Da da da da, de da de da. Da da da da, de da de da.

Dan Brown picked out Beethoven's Fifth on the mighty Mulholland Organ, feeling the power of the chords surge through fingers, feet and floor. He then segued into "Angels & Demons", one of the songs from his sadly neglected second album, and finished up with a free-form improvisation on "Stairway to Heaven".

Simon Magill knew better than to ask Dan directly about the Sydney scenario, not least because of an earlier promise to desist from potted plots. Instead, he told his mentor about the history of the Ulster Hall, the Victorian auditorium in the centre of Belfast, where they were passing the time, shooting the breeze, checking things out. He informed him that the very first live performance of "Stairway to Heaven" took place in the city's famous old venue. Likewise with "Black Dog", "Rock and Roll", and most of the other songs from Zeppelin's sublime fourth album. The concert hall also showcased some of the greatest hard rockin' bands in history, from Thin Lizzy and Def Leppard to AC/DC and U2.

The Danster looked around appreciatively. The city council-owned auditorium was entirely empty, just the two of them seated at the prodigious pipe organ behind the stage. Abby Maguire had called in a favour at City Hall – the Health and Safety Officer owed her, apparently – and Hard Rock, or whatever his name was, arranged special access passes for the pair of them.

"Let me ask you a question, Dan."

The best-selling author arched his aching back, still stiff from one super-duper supersonic flight too many. "Sure. Sure. Fire away."

"Who buys your books? Who's your ideal customer? What's your target market?"

"That's three questions, Simon," Brown groaned with a getting-old grimace. "However, the answer to all three is the same. Everyone. My books are bought by everyone, regardless of creed or colour or market segment. They might buy them for different reasons – priests and cardinals because they hate me, art historians because they hate me even more, jealous authors because they hate me most of all. But my readership's pretty catholic. With a small 'c'," he added self-consciously.

Magill massaged the author's knotted neck. In a manly manner, naturally. "No, Dan, you're wrong. In my capacity as your go-to guy, I've studied the market for Dan Brown blockbusters. Your prototypical customer – that is the people who actually buy your books and recommend them to others – is a middle-aged, middle manager, who picks one up in an airport bookstore and reads it while jetting to the next sales meeting. Notwithstanding your association with the Eternal Feminine, most of your readers are male and although they like to think of themselves as post-chauvinistic, they don't like it much when their boss is a woman. It's no accident that your two least successful novels had female protagonists."

"Unsuccessful, as in several million copies sold apiece?" Dan said drily, rolling his shoulders with a moan of relief.

Sensibly, Magill gave ground. "In relative terms, though, you've got to agree that *Digital* and *Deception* didn't do quite as well as *Da Vinci*'s 60 million and *Angels*' 25. According to my calculations, male, middle-aged middle managers are the rock upon which the Brown brand is built and that's the rockin' rock you must appeal to. Male, middle-aged middle managers love rock 'n' roll music and they *really* love Led Zeppelin, who were at their peak when they were spotty adolescents. Research shows that the music boys listen to in their teenage years stays with them for ever. That's why hanging a thriller on the Led Zeppelin reunion tour has real Langdon potential, in my humble opinion. You used to be in the music business, Dan, so you know it inside out. You know the pressures of live performance, Dan, so you can draw upon your own painful experiences. The occult material is meat and drink for Robert Langdon. Just think of all the symbols and runes he could decode. Aleister Crowley was a member of the Golden Dawn, which was descended from the Rosicrucians. We're talking conspiracy theory central, Dan! Secret societies within secret societies, Dan, complete with schisms, splinter groups and more symbology than you could shake a cloven hoof at. Pacts with the devil, Dan! Spooky houses in Scotland, Dan! Coded messages on vinyl albums, Dan! What more do you want, Dan? There's even scope for a hidden treasure subplot since millions went astray, as they say, when Zeppelin were in full financial flight. What do you reckon, Dan?"

Simon's enthusiasm was infectious. But not infectious enough. With a weary sigh, Dan shook his head slowly, sadly, sensitively. As a former schoolteacher, he knew how to let keen pupils down with their excitement intact. He praised parts of Magill's treatment, especially the setting, but pointed out that including living people was a non-starter. Real people like Robert Plant or Jimmy Page could sue and, with their very deep pockets, probably would sue.

Unsurprisingly, Magill was a tad taken aback. This from a man who was famous for naming fictional characters after real people, mostly former colleagues from Exeter College. This from the man whose books made abusive remarks about Bill Gates, Madonna and Elton John, among others, to say nothing of real-world organizations like NASA, the NSA, Opus Dei and, for heaven's sake, both the Papacy and the Presidency. This from a man who obviously based Kohler – the marketing-minded head of CERN – on a world-famous marketing guru called Kotler. This from the man who, in Sir Leigh Teabing, anagrammed the name of an eminent alternative historian.

Unable to continue biting his tongue, Magill politely interrupted Brown's avuncular debrief. "But, Dan, you are legally entitled to include real people in novels, public figures in particular, and if the treatment is parodic then you're on pretty safe ground. The Elton John ruling clearly…"

"Simon," Dan said, in a voice that hinted at hard-earned lessons, "I have parodied people in the past and ended up in court. I've no desire to repeat the experience."

"Do you really think that Robert Plant or Jimmy Page would go to court? Can you imagine what would come out under cross-examination? There's no way they'd sue you. I mean, would *you* sue if someone parodied *you* in a book?"

Thrown by the very ludicrousness of the suggestion, the mega-selling author was momentarily lost for words. "Well, now that you mention it, probably not. One two-day cross-examination was quite enough. Not unless they said I was a serial killer, or somesuch."

Magill's own hard-earned lessons told him it was time to back off, and back off he did. "Tell you what," he said, changing the subject, "why don't you release *The Solomon Key* instead? I took the liberty of reading the manuscript while you were indisposed and it's an absolute corker, by far the best thing you've ever written, far better even than *The Da Vinci Code*. You've gotta get it out there, Dan. It's time to stop casting around for a new story, when there's a barnstormer on your netbook, ready to roll."

Half-expecting a severe dressing down – how-dare-you-read-my-files-without-permission – Magill metaphorically covered his head with his hands. However, the figurative protection helmet proved unnecessary.

"Do you remember our conversation in Rome, when you pitched the Ku Klux Klan plan?"

"Yes, of course I do, Dan. You were right, it was a silly suggestion. I'm truly sorry about that."

Brown dismissed Magill's apologies with a wave. "You said that it fit the formula."

"Erm, so I did. But in a good way, Dan. In a good way."

The superstar shot Simon a sceptical look and, turning back to the keyboard, tinkled out Fleetwood Mac's Tell me lies, tell me sweet little lies. "Yeah, well, I was thinking about releasing *The Solomon Key*. But I now realize that it is hopelessly formulaic."

"What on earth do you mean, Dan?"

"You know what I mean, Simon – the grisly murder in the first chapter, the evil antagonist who's gruesomely malformed, the will-they-won't-they race against time, the codes and ana-grams and mathematical sequences, the unresolved sexual tension between Robert and his feisty female companion, the scene where someone falls from a very great height…"

"You mean like Chartrukian's plunge into the computer pit in *Digital Fortress*, the Hassassin's downfall from Castel Sant'Angelo in *Angels and Demons*, Rachel, Mike and Corky's giant leap off the calving polar icecap in *Deception Point*, the bar of soap in *Da Vinci*, which jumped on to a speeding truck outside the Louvre and, dare I say it, the cramped stairwell incident in my Sydney suggestion?"

"That's exactly what I mean."

Unthinkingly, Magill blundered on, before he could properly stop himself. "Yes, and don't forget your formulaic fixation with sweat and urine and nausea and vaginal symbolism and sex acts between senior citizens and Sir Leigh Teabing's todger sticking out on stage…"

"I think you'll find that it was hanging out, Simon."

Magill roared with laughter. Dan laughed too, despite the insinuations. "Anyway," he said, when they'd finished snorting and sniggering like schoolboys, "*The Solomon Key* is formulaic and it's staying where it is."

Decision made, Dan turned to other matters. He was very taken with Belfast. The city had really come on since his last visit. The place had energy, zip, get-up-and-go. Shame about the branding campaign. Bibbity Bobbitty Belfast was in full swing and Belinda, the Belfast bunny, was everywhere. The mutant lovechild of Jessica and Bugs, her floppy-eared, fluffy-tailed features were plastered on TV ads, radio jingles, dedicated websites, cinema commercials, 48-sheet posters on prime shopping streets and the side of every single bus and train, Enterprise Express included. As a city council property, the Ulster Hall was also bedecked with bunnies. The place looked like Watership Down during rutting season.

Magill recounted the story of the Belfast branding campaign and how Abby's black rose idea was nipped in the bud. Ever partial to a bit of rose symbolism, Dan drank it in like an athlete chugging Gatorade after the Alice Springs Triathlon. A germ of an idea was obviously forming. At least that was something, Simon thought. He tried again.

"So, you're definitely not releasing *The Solomon Key*?"

Dan shook his head resolutely and turned away, discussion over.

When he turned back, Simon had something for him. He held up the beautiful bright blue locket that had worked its mesmeric magic in Dublin. It twisted and turned and glittered and gleamed. Having succumbed once before, Dan couldn't resist its hypnotic spell. He was open to suggestion and the Englishman duly suggested that he do the decent thing by his fans: unleash *The Solomon Key*. Manifestly a man of immense mental fortitude – he needed to be to cope with the *Da Vinci Code* furore – the Danster resisted Simon's Svengalian suasions. Evidently, the memories attached to the manuscript were too painful, too deep. It was only when Magill suggested that he rename the novel that the world-renowned author was persuaded to relent. Thinking of Abby's adventures, Dan wanted *The Last Symbol*. Thinking of Abby's adventures, Simon preferred *The Lost Logo*. They compromised, though it would always be *The Solomon Key* to them both.

"There's another thing, Dan."

"What's that, master?" the author mumbled in a mechanistic monotone.

"The Spear of Destiny. Do you have it?"

"I do."

"Give it to me."

"Your wish is my command." Slowly, as if in stop-motion, Dan eased a hand into the inside pocket of his trademark tweed jacket and withdrew a very old, very discoloured spearhead, about the size of a pocket comb. For an immemorial religious artefact, it was unprepossessing to the point of nondescript. Magill took the malign object, a strangely seductive source of initial good fortune and ultimate bad luck. He knew just the person it was perfect for. Colonel Cyrus C. Clamber, the chief recruiting officer for the CIA's sick puppy platoon, the even bigger C behind the Big C. Big C's C-in-C, in fact.

Or maybe he should just chuck it into the mud and slime of Belfast's Clarendon Dock, where it could settle for evermore beside the ill-fated Victorian submarine, *King Billy-Goat*.

The Danster sighed with a mixture of regret and relief, as his "precious" was finally removed from his possession.

Magill clicked his fingers. Brown looked around, dazed and confused. "There's something I've been meaning to ask you, Dan."

"What's that?"

"How did you and Tom know that we were in the Globe Theatre? That was one hell of a lucky guess."

"Luck had nothing to do with it, Simon. Tom's henchmen slipped a tracking device into your pocket when they picked you up."

"What, like the incident with Robert Langdon in *The Da Vinci Code*? Are you telling me that Clancy stole your idea? The nerve of it!"

"Yeah, well, I owed him."

"So you're quits?"

The Danster nodded while noodling on the keyboard.

Magill gazed around the newly refurbished auditorium, where the ghosts of past performers still stood on stage, all remembering the magical alchemical moment when singers and spectators, actors and audiences, politicians and people, marketers and market are as one. "Do you know what's next for us, Dan?"

"What's next for us?" Brown shook his head. "You hum it, I'll play it."

Author's Note

For this, the final volume of my "management thriller trilogy", I've made a few modifications to my working methods. When writing *The Marketing Code* and *Agents and Dealers*, I went to great lengths to ensure that the places mentioned in the novels were "as described". The original climax of *TMC*, for example, was set on top of the Eiffel Tower at the Paris Hotel-Casino in Las Vegas. But when I visited the location I discovered that the viewing platform is really, really tiny and thus couldn't have accommodated the action sequence I'd devised. So I rewrote the ending to take "reality" into account.

I've been less scrupulous this time around. When dealing with locations, I've tweaked reality, as necessary. Busch Gardens theme park really does exist, as do many of the rides I describe. However, the Runaway Train is an invention, as is the Sforza Horse statue. Likewise, it is impossible to leap on to the skyride from the roof of the Globe Theatre. In other words, I've followed the Hollywood movie model, where reality is adjusted to suit the story, rather than the conspiracy thriller model, where geographical reality is pretty much sacrosanct.

My inventions aren't confined to places, of course. All of the characters are entirely fictional, even the "real" ones. Especially the real ones! The people who populate Belfast City Hall are equally imaginary. I have no doubt that some of the City Council posts described herein – Health & Safety Officer, etc. – actually exist in reality but I have had no contact with the individuals concerned, nor do I know who they are. The city council cast list is entirely a figment of my imagination. The location is exactly as described, mind! The city branding exercise lies somewhere in between, insofar as the city has recently been "rebranded", though I personally played no part in the proceedings, nor did I have access to any of the consultancy reports that (presumably) contributed to the process. I made all that up. FYI, the city council's new logo is a heart-shaped letter B. Hey, don't knock it…

This mix of reality and fantasy has been adhered to throughout. The Clarence Hotel in Dublin is pretty much as described – the marketing manager, Column Fleming, very kindly gave me a full guided tour and answered all my inane questions – as is the Ussher extension to Trinity Library. The enormous air-well in the latter really is quite disturbing and the wonderful view across the playing fields must be rather distracting for students come exam time. The Patton Writing College, by contrast, is totally fictional, though there is a pine-screened space close to UCI's sports facility that *could* accommodate such a facility, if one existed. The Newport Bay Ecological Preserve is as striking as I endeavour to describe in chapters nineteen and twenty-three, albeit there are no piranhas thereabouts (to my knowledge). If you are ever in Pasadena, the Huntington Museum-cum-Library is well worth a visit. The same is true of Fredericksberg, but don't go looking for Only in America, much less No Roach Motel. You'll have trouble finding Rainbow's End goldsmiths in Colonial Williamsburg, moreover. Tom Clancy's Tiffany-stuffed lair actually exists, oddly enough, though it goes by the name of the Chrysler Museum of Art! Spanky's nightclub, likewise, is alive and kickin' in Salt Lake City, or it was when I last visited the place some years ago.

Anyway, I think you get the general picture. Rather than belabour my point, let me just direct you toward further sources of information. As an academic, I feel obliged to cite my sources and, as some of you may be interested in digging a little deeper, the least I can do is indicate where the textual treasures are buried. Dan Brown's books have been debunked time and again. There is a mini industry in Brown debunking, to be honest, and much of it is pretty distasteful (inasmuch as the "attack Dan" authors shamelessly bite the hand that feeds them). An amusing exception is David A. Shugarts. His fact-by-fact deconstructions of *The Da Vinci Code* and *Angels and Demons* are great fun and well worth reading (contained in Dan Burstein's *Secrets of the Code* and *Secrets of Angels & Demons* respectively). Shugarts has also written a primer for Dan's unpublished novel, *The Solomon Key*. It's called *Secrets of the Widow's Son: The Mysteries Surrounding the Sequel to* The Da Vinci Code (Sterling Publishing: New York,

2005). Greg Taylor covers similar ground in *Da Vinci in America: Unlocking the Secrets of Dan Brown's* The Solomon Key (Daily Grail Publishing: Brisbane, 2004).

The sylvan beauties of South Belfast, recounted in chapters one through sixteen, are detailed in Norman Weatherall and George Templeton *South Belfast: History and Guide* (Nonsuch Publishing: Dublin, 2008). Other useful sources are Jonathan Bardon's classic volume, *Belfast* (Blackstaff Press: Belfast, 1982); J. C. Beckett and R. E. Glasscock, *Belfast: Origin and Growth of an Industrial City* (BBC: London, 1967); C. E. B. Brett, *Buildings of Belfast 1700–1914* (Friar's Bush Press: Belfast, 1985); J. C. Beckett et al, *Belfast: The Making of the City* (Appletree Press: Belfast, 1983); and G. McIntosh, *Belfast City Hall: One Hundred Years* (Blackstaff Press: Belfast, 2006).

Believe it or not, the KKK material in Chapter Two is entirely true. The riot in South Bend, Indiana, took place pretty much as described (see T. Tucker, *Notre Dame versus The Klan*, Loyola Press: Chicago, 2004). All the stuff about anti-Catholicism is equally kosher, so to speak. The gruesomely fascinating history of the Klan is painstakingly described in D. M. Chalmers, *Hooded Americanism* (Duke University Press: Durham, 1987) and W. C. Wade, *The Fiery Cross* (Oxford University Press: New York, 1987). If you're looking for a snappy summary, however, check out the chapter in L. Moore, *Anything Goes: A Biography of the Roaring Twenties* (Atlantic Books: London, 2008).

Simon Magill's scenario about the *Fenian Ram* (Chapter Six) is of course a figment of my imagination, since the Harland & Woolf shipyard built luxury liners, not submarines. However, *Clan-na-Gael* did indeed work with John Holland on a so-called "salt-water enterprise" and the organization's attempts to assassinate Queen Victoria are well documented: see C. Campbell, *Fenian Fire* (HarperCollins: London, 2003); R. K. Morris, *John P. Holland: Inventor of the Modern Submarine* (University of South Carolina Press: Columbia, 1998); and T. Golway, *Irish Rebel: John Devoy and America's Fight for Ireland's Freedom* (St Martin's Press: New York, 1998).

I won't go into the critiques of Mormonism (Chapter Eight), since they have been done to death. The idea of the secret document was prompted by Simon Worrall's fascinating book about Mark Hoffman, who forged many LDS documents before embarking on a bizarre killing spree (*The Poet and the Murderer: A True Story of Verse, Violence and the Art of Forgery*, Fourth Estate: London, 2002). No less fascinating is the story of wartime deception that features in the discussion of Abby's Guerrilla Psychology course (Chapter Nine). The source here is N. Rankin, *Churchill's Wizards: The British Genius for Deception 1914–1945* (Faber & Faber: London, 2008).

Barnum Brown, the dinosaur detective in Simon Magill's Sydney scenario, is once again a real person. If ever anyone was ripe for a biography, it's surely the remarkable man who discovered the T-rex. His wife, Lilian Brown, wrote a light-hearted account of the great man's excavations in India – its tone is vaguely reminiscent of Durrell's *My Family and Other Animals* – and Brown's journals from an 1895 bone hunting expedition have also been published (see L. Brown, *I Married a Dinosaur*, Harrap: London, 1951; and M. F. Kohl, *A Triceratops Hunt in Pioneer Wyoming*, High Plains Press: Glendo, 2004). But the man himself remains a cipher, sadly. The "Bone Wars" between Cope and Marsh are brilliantly described by Bill Bryson in *A Short History of Nearly Everything* (Doubleday: London, 2003).

The chapters set in PWC are of course entirely fictitious, but I was greatly helped by a little handbook that lets army recruits know what they're in for. Written by Don Herbert, it's called *Sixty-Three Days and a Wake-Up: Your Survival Guide to United States Army Basic Combat Training* (iUniverse Inc: New York, 2007). General George S. Patton has more biographies than you could shake a swagger stick at. There's even a self-help book based on his barnstorming bon mots (P. B. Williamson, *General Patton's Principles for Life and Leadership*, MSC Inc: Tucson, 1988). The business-is-war metaphor has also been repeatedly beaten into submission. It was very popular around the time of the Iraq invasion (see, for example, K. Allard, *Business as War: Battling for Competitive Advantage*, Wiley: New York, 2004). The history of bookburning is covered by F. Baez, *A Universal History of the Destruction of Books* (Atlas & Co: New York, 2008). Meanwhile, Magill's conversation about *Trilby* owes much to a fantastic book by D. Pick (*Svengali's Web: The Alien Enchanter in Modern Culture*, Yale University Press: New Haven, 2000).

Tom Clancy and the Ryanverse have generated a substantial secondary literature (to say nothing of the four blockbuster Hollywood movies, plus one in production). I found the following of use: W. Terdoslavich, *The Jack Ryan Agenda: Policy and Politics in the Novels of Tom Clancy* (Tom Doherty Associates: New York, 2005); R. Baiocco, *Readings on Tom Clancy* (Greenhaven Press: San Diego, 2004); and M. H. Greenberg, *The Tom Clancy Companion* (Fontana: London, 2005). Incidentally, the USS *Charlotte*, a (real-world) nuclear submarine that Tom Clancy "sinks" in *Debt of Honor*, is miraculously restored to full working order in Dan Brown's *Deception Point*!

Of all the places that are mentioned in *TLL*, the one most worth visiting is The Long Room library at Trinity College. Its history is summarized by P. Fox, *Trinity College Library Dublin* (Trinity College Dublin Press: Dublin, 2003). On the lure of beautiful libraries generally, see R. Manguel, *The Library at Night* (Yale University Press: New Haven, 2008) and the glossy coffee table book by C. Höfer (*Libraries*, Thames & Hudson: London, 2005).

Turning to Abby and Simon's flights from Dublin, there are several noteworthy sources of information. The Hendaye Cross mystery is thoroughly recounted by alternative archaeologists Jay Weidener and Vincent Bridges (*The Mysteries of the Great Cross of Hendaye: Alchemy and the End of Time*, Destiny Books: Rochester, 2003); the Fulcanelli phenomenon has exercised many commentators, most notably G. Dubois (*Fulcanelli and the Alchemical Revival*, Destiny Books, Rochester, 2006); the debt owed by Surrealists to the mystery literature in general and alchemists in particular is mentioned in most histories of the movement (e.g. D. Hopkins, *Dada and Surrealism*, Oxford University Press: Oxford, 2004); Enochian magic is a very intricate mode of occult practice, affiliated to angelology (see D. Tyson, *Enochian Magic for Beginners: The Original System of Angel Magic*, Llewellyn Publications: Woodbury, 2005); the literature on codes and ciphers has exploded in the wake of *Da Vinci*, though the ultimate source remains F. B. Wrixon, *Codes, Ciphers, Secrets and Cryptic Communication* (Black Dog & Leventhal: New York, 1998); and, as for the Bacon-is-Shakespeare controversy, look no further than John Michell's seminal volume, *Who Wrote Shakespeare?* (Thames & Hudson: London, 1996). Presumably, you don't need me to tell you that the "number of plots" discussion in Chapter Thirty-Eight is heavily indebted to Christopher Booker's outstanding book, *The Seven Basic Plots: Why We Tell Stories* (Continuum: London, 2004).

Much has been written about Louis Comfort Tiffany and rightly so. I visited the Metropolitan Museum of Art as part of the research for this project and the Tiffany display therein is well worth a look (the furniture, curiously enough, is particularly striking). The most cogent account of his working – and marketing – methods is contained in a little volume about creativity by Paul Johnson (*Creators: From Chaucer to Walt Disney*, Phoenix: London, 2006). As the title indicates, the book isn't solely devoted to Tiffany, but it's excellent on the glass/writing/craftsmanship issue that Clancy refers to in Chapter Thirty-Nine.

Clancy also puts forward a model of hubris-nemesis, and nowhere is it more pertinent than in the case of the CIA. Accounts of the decline and fall of that particular organization almost defy belief. My discussion, from Chapter Forty-Five onwards, is not exaggerated in any significant way. The CIA really was started by Yalies and considered itself to be the last great hope of the western liberal arts tradition. The cultural cold war did transpire pretty much as described. The Ford Foundation was among its many fronts. Stargate was only one of countless left-field projects initiated by the company's psyops people. For further details, check out T. Weiner, *Legacy of Ashes: The History of the CIA* (Penguin: London, 2007); M. Farren, *CIA: Secrets of "The Company"* (Chrysalis Books: London, 2003); H. Wilford, *The Mighty Wurlitzer: How the CIA Played America* (Harvard University Press: Cambridge, 2008); F. S. Saunders, *Who Paid the Piper? The CIA and the Cultural Cold War* (Granta: London, 2000); J. Ronson, *The Men Who Stare at Goats* (Picador: London, 2005); and S. Coll, *Ghost Wars: The Secret History of the CIA, Afghanistan and Bin Laden, From the Soviet Invasion to September 10, 2001* (Penguin: London, 2004).

Actually, now that I think about it, there is another once

illustrious institution whose standing has fallen even further than the CIA's. I'm referring to the business school. But let's not go there…

Let's move on to happier things. As this is the final part of my management thriller trilogy, I'd like to thank Pom Somkabcharti and Martin Liu, my truly fantastic publishers, for supporting this decidedly unorthodox adventure. I'd also like to say a big thank you to Alun Richards, Mia Hammar and Mark Tadajewski for reading a draft version of *TLL*. My wonderful wife, Linda, and delightful daughters, Madison, Holly and Sophie, were never less than grateful when I disappeared upstairs to write another chapter. Dan Brown too has been supportive, if only in absentia. He hasn't sued me. Yet. Good luck with your new book, Dan, and with all the Langdon novels to come.

Stephen Brown
July 2009

Also by Stephen Brown

"I read *The Marketing Code* from beginning to end in one sitting. I had to know how it turned out. It shows great imagination, clever plotting, and a Rabelaisian scale of outrage and wit."
– Philip Kotler

"A marketing text written as a novel … You cannot fail to be amused, entertained and engrossed by this gem of a book."
– *Marketer* magazine

"Pitch perfect."
– *Harvard Business Review*

SOMETIMES YOU HAVE TO KILL TO MAKE A KILLING

Death stalks the streets of Edinburgh as marketing lecturer Simon Magill receives a gruesome message about a mysterious website. He is plunged into a marketing maelstrom that sweeps from the glitz of Las Vegas to the grime of West Belfast, taking in the Freemasons, the Knights Templar, the conspiracies surrounding the sinking of the *Titanic* and, not least, the insidious marketing campaign behind Dan Brown's blockbuster novel, *The Da Vinci Code*.

As Simon Magill struggles to make sense of the riddle, he uncovers a startling truth about the irredeemably commercial character of the Holy Grail. Racing against time, he discovers that there is, and always has been, a cabal at the heart of Western capitalism – a secret society that possesses the key to business success. Based at a prominent American business school, this clandestine organization has been systematically misleading the marketing community for millennia. As Magill soon discovers, it will stop at nothing to prevent its jealously guarded secret being revealed…

ISBN 978-1-905736-82-9 / £7.99 Paperback

Also by Stephen Brown

"Packed with wit, wisecracks and wickedness, Brown's tongue-in-cheek thriller throws light on the hidden mysteries of marketing in this unforgettable and unputdownable page-turner."
– John Ling, The Chartered Institute of Marketing

"Laced with Irish eloquence and wit, unflaggingly reflexive and polymorphously perverse, this brandfest of a book does not disappoint."
– John F. Sherry, Jr, University of Notre Dame

LOVE OF CUSTOMERS IS THE ROOT OF ALL EVIL

A feisty final-year student at the University of Hustler, Abby Maguire is on punitive work placement. While struggling to dress the shop window of Some Like It Hot, a saucy lingerie boutique, she is attacked by two lapsed paramilitaries, who destroy the store and almost destroy Abby. With the aid of her placement tutor, Dave Kelley, Abby escapes the psychopathic enforcers only to plunge into a noisome netherworld of arms dealers, money launderers, secret agents, neo-Nazis, paedophile priests, literary forgers and, most horrifying of all, freelance management consultants.

An action-packed prequel to *The Marketing Code*, *Agents and Dealers* races from Edinburgh to Nuremberg via Belfast and Dublin. Spine-chilling and side-splitting by turns, it reveals the whereabouts of the legendary Spear of Destiny, uncovers the equally legendary encounter between Adolf Hitler and W. B. Yeats, exposes a ruthless secret society at the heart of Ireland's unstoppable Tiger economy and unmasks the blood-soaked background to Dan Brown's bestselling books, *Angels and Demons* and *The Da Vinci Code*.

ISBN 978-0-462-09916-3/£9.99 Paperback

Also by Stephen Brown

Nearly every business book promises to purvey the secrets of success. They come in a multitude of forms: neatly wrapped up in a nifty concept like "creative destruction" or "the balanced scorecard"; summarized in a smattering of snappy slogans such as "stick to your knitting" or "big hairy audacious goals"; or scattered in a scrabblefest of three-letter acronyms like CRM or CSR. No matter which, you can be sure you will be getting some variation on that elusive magic formula that is guaranteed (isn't it?) to help you run your business better.

Yet the *real* secret of success is something that your average how-to book doesn't dare mention. Whisper the word: failure. Yes, failure. In fact, most success stories in business have a back story of botches, blunders, cock-ups, and catastrophes. Far from ignoring them, we should be dragging them out into the limelight. For it is the ability to learn from failure, to refuse to be beaten, to fail, fail, and fail again that separates the high-fliers from the no-hopers.

Fail Better! celebrates flops, fumbles, and fiascos of every flavour and salutes those who triumphed when they should have tanked. Through the chequered histories of 25 self-made contrarians from Madonna to Rupert Murdoch, it shows that playing things by the MBA marketing manual is no match for stubbornness, single-mindedness, and serendipity.

If you fail to read *Fail Better!*, you are sure to fail miserably. If you choose to read it, you will at least fail with a smile on your face. Or, who knows, you might just learn a thing or two from this motley crew of mavericks who scorned the well-trodden paths to fame and fortune yet scored spectacular successes all the same.

ISBN 978-0-462-09904-0/£12.99 Hardback